CHRIST-CENTERED

Exposition

Series Dedication

Dedicated to Adrian Rogers and John Piper. They have taught us to love the gospel of Jesus Christ, to preach the Bible as the inerrant Word of God, to pastor the Church for which our Savior died, and to have a passion to see all nations gladly worship the Lamb.

—David Platt, Tony Merida, and Danny Akin
March 2013

Acknowledgments

This commentary is the fruit of God's grace in the lives of many brothers and sisters. I am especially grateful to God for David Burnette's diligent and wise editing and for Cory Varden's consistent and gracious service. I am ever grateful to God for Heather as well as Caleb, Joshua, Mara Ruth, and Isaiah; I am blessed beyond measure with the family He has entrusted to me. And I am deeply grateful to God for The Church at Brook Hills, a faith family who eagerly opened their Bibles every week not only to hear but also to obey the voice of God in Matthew for the glory of God among the nations.

—David Platt

NT / COMMENTARY

AUTHOR **David Platt**

SERIES EDITORS **David Platt, Daniel L. Akin, and Tony Merida**

CHRIST-CENTERED

Exposition

EXALTING JESUS IN

MATTHEW

HOLMAN
REFERENCE

NASHVILLE, TENNESSEE

TABLE OF CONTENTS

SERIES INTRODUCTION

Augustine said, "Where Scripture speaks, God speaks." The editors of the Christ-Centered Exposition Commentary series believe that where God speaks, the pastor must speak. God speaks through His written Word. We must speak from that Word. We believe the Bible is God breathed, authoritative, inerrant, sufficient, understandable, necessary, and timeless. We also affirm that the Bible is a Christ-centered book; that is, it contains a unified story of redemptive history of which Jesus is the hero. Because of this Christ-centered trajectory that runs from Genesis 1 through Revelation 22, we believe the Bible has a corresponding global-missions thrust. From beginning to end, we see God's mission as one of making worshipers of Christ from every tribe and tongue worked out through this redemptive drama in Scripture. To that end we must preach the Word.

In addition to these distinct convictions, the Christ-Centered Exposition Commentary series has some distinguishing characteristics. First, this series seeks to display exegetical accuracy. What the Bible says is what we want to say. While not every volume in the series will be a verse-by-verse commentary, we nevertheless desire to handle the text carefully and explain it rightly. Those who teach and preach bear the heavy responsibility of saying what God has said in His Word and declaring what God has done in Christ. We desire to handle God's Word faithfully, knowing that we must give an account for how we have fulfilled this holy calling (Jas 3:1).

Second, the Christ-Centered Exposition Commentary series has pastors in view. While we hope others will read this series, such as parents, teachers, small-group leaders, and student ministers, we desire to provide a commentary busy pastors will use for weekly preparation of biblically faithful and gospel-saturated sermons. This series is not academic in nature. Our aim is to present a readable and pastoral style of commentaries. We believe this aim will serve the church of the Lord Jesus Christ.

Third, we want the Christ-Centered Exposition Commentary series to be known for the inclusion of helpful illustrations and theologically driven applications. Many commentaries offer no help in illustrations, and few offer any kind of help in application. Often those that do offer illustrative material and application unfortunately give little serious attention to the text. While giving ourselves primarily to explanation, we also hope to serve readers by providing inspiring and illuminating illustrations coupled with timely and timeless application.

Finally, as the name suggests, the editors seek to exalt Jesus from every book of the Bible. In saying this, we are not commending wild allegory or fanciful typology. We certainly believe we must be constrained to the meaning intended by the divine Author Himself, the Holy Spirit of God. However, we also believe the Bible has a messianic focus, and our hope is that the individual authors will exalt Christ from particular texts. Luke 24:25-27, 44-47; and John 5:39, 46 inform both our hermeneutics and our homiletics. Not every author will do this the same way or have the same degree of Christ-centered emphasis. That is fine with us. We believe faithful exposition that is Christ centered is not monolithic. We do believe, however, that we must read the whole Bible as Christian Scripture. Therefore, our aim is both to honor the historical particularity of each biblical passage and to highlight its intrinsic connection to the Redeemer.

The editors are indebted to the contributors of each volume. The reader will detect a unique style from each writer, and we celebrate these unique gifts and traits. While distinctive in approach, the authors share a common characteristic in that they are pastoral theologians. They love the church, and they regularly preach and teach God's Word to God's people. Further, many of these contributors are younger voices. We think these new, fresh voices can serve the church well, especially among a rising generation that has the task of proclaiming the Word of Christ and the Christ of the Word to the lost world.

We hope and pray this series will serve the body of Christ well in these ways until our Savior returns in glory. If it does, we will have succeeded in our assignment.

David Platt
Daniel L. Akin
Tony Merida
Series Editors
February 2013

Matthew

The Gospel of the Kingdom

MATTHEW 1:1-17

Main Idea: The Gospel of Matthew is an account of the life, death, and resurrection of Jesus Christ, the Messiah and King predicted by the Old Testament.

I. **The Gospel of the Kingdom**
   A. The book of Matthew is a Gospel (an account of good news).
   B. The book of Matthew is one of four Gospels.
      1. John: Jesus is the Son of God.
      2. Luke: Jesus is the Son of Man.
      3. Mark: Jesus is the Suffering Servant.
      4. Matthew: Jesus is the Sovereign King.
II. **Introduction of the King**
   A. He is the Savior.
   B. He is the Messiah.
   C. He is the son of David.
   D. He is the son of Abraham.
III. **Overview of the Kingdom**
   A. Gospel: The message of the kingdom
   B. Disciples: The citizens of the kingdom
   C. Discipleship: The demands of the kingdom
   D. Church: The outpost of the kingdom
   E. Mission: The spread of the kingdom
   F. Demons: The enemies of the kingdom
   G. Hope: The coming of the kingdom
IV. **Salvation through the King**
   A. God saves only by His sovereign grace.
   B. God saves ultimately for His global purpose.
V. **The Bottom Line**
   A. Like the leaders, will you completely reject Jesus?
   B. Like the crowds, will you casually observe Jesus?
   C. Like the disciples, will you unconditionally follow Jesus?

The book of Matthew is a Gospel, an account of good news. That point may sound obvious, but we can't overlook it as we consider this first book of the New Testament. "Gospel" literally means "good news," and Matthew's purpose in this book is to write an account of the good news of Jesus Christ—how Jesus came, what Jesus did, what Jesus said, and what Jesus accomplished in His death and resurrection. These truths are intended to change our lives and the entire world.

In order for us to rightly interpret Matthew's Gospel, we need to understand what it is and what it is not. First, as we consider this Gospel, we need to remember that **it is not a congregational letter**. Matthew is not like 1 Timothy, a letter written by Paul sent to Timothy and the church at Ephesus. This Gospel is not primarily addressing a certain congregation in a certain situation; rather, it is presenting Jesus Christ—who He is and what He has done—to all people. Second, as you read through Matthew you will also notice that **it is not a comprehensive biography**. Matthew was not trying to include every minute detail of Jesus' life. There are many things that have been left out. Matthew chose various stories and abbreviated teachings from Jesus' life in order to accomplish a specific purpose. This Gospel includes what it does because the author wants to say something specific about the person and work of Jesus Christ.

Finally, concerning the purpose of Matthew's Gospel, we see that **it is not a chronological history**. Obviously, time plays a role in Matthew's arrangement, since he begins with Jesus' birth and ends with Jesus' death and resurrection. However, within this broad framework, Matthew has intentionally arranged his material around specific emphases. In particular, Matthew organizes his Gospel around five distinct teaching sections, and in between sections he tells us different stories, or narrative accounts. After the first four chapters of narrative in Matthew, we come upon the first teaching section in chapters 5–7, a section we know as the Sermon on the Mount. Immediately following Jesus' teaching in the Sermon on the Mount, Matthew says, "When Jesus had finished this sermon . . ." (7:28). We might think of these summary statements to be the "seams" stitching together the major teaching sections. Consider the following five seams:

1. **7:28-29** — "When Jesus had finished this sermon . . ."
2. **11:1** — "When Jesus had finished giving orders to His 12 disciples . . ."
3. **13:53** — "When Jesus had finished these parables . . ."

4. **19:1** — "When Jesus had finished this instruction . . ."
5. **26:1** — "When Jesus had finished saying all this . . ."

Matthew's structure is not accidental. It is intentional—even beautiful. After each of the five key teaching sections, he gives us one of these summary statements. By this organization, Matthew gives us a beautiful portrait of Jesus' words and deeds. In considering this structure, we need to remember the main point of this Gospel, namely, to give us an account of the life, teaching, death, and resurrection of Jesus Christ. Next we'll consider Matthew's portrait of Jesus in relation to the other Gospels.

The book of Matthew is one of four Gospels. Each Gospel writer gives us an account of Jesus' life, death, and resurrection. Now there are certainly similarities among all four Gospels, but each one uses different stories at different times and in different ways in order to emphasize different truths about Jesus. It's as if the good news about Christ is a multicolored diamond that you can look at from a variety of different angles, with each angle giving you a unique and glorious glimpse of the Lord Jesus. Still, at the end of the day, it's the same diamond. While Matthew, Mark, Luke, and John are composed by different writers and written with different emphases, each Gospel is written under the inspiration of the Holy Spirit (2 Tim 3:16).

The following is admittedly an oversimplification, but it may help us to see some of the different emphases of the four Gospels. These emphases are even evident in the way that the Gospels begin:

- **John: Jesus is the Son of God**. Instead of including a genealogy like Matthew, John begins by saying, "In the beginning was the Word, and the Word was with God, and the Word was God" (1:1). John is showing us Jesus' divinity from the start. He even gives us a purpose statement toward the close of the book: "But these [signs] are written so that you may believe Jesus is the Messiah, the Son of God, and by believing you may have life in His name" (20:31).
- **Luke: Jesus is the Son of Man**. Jesus' significance for all humanity is emphasized from the very beginning of Luke's Gospel. His genealogy in chapter 3, for instance, is framed differently from Matthew's. **In ascending order, Luke traces the physical lineage of Jesus to Adam**, whereas Matthew begins with Abraham and moves forward to Jesus.

- **Mark: Jesus is the Suffering Servant**. Mark doesn't give us a genealogy. Instead, from the very start, there is a clear emphasis on Jesus coming, not to be served, but to "serve, and to give His life—a ransom for many" (10:45). Mark also highlights the suffering that will come to all who follow Jesus.
- **Matthew: Jesus is the Sovereign King**. From the very beginning, Matthew makes clear that Jesus is the King, coming from the line of King David (1:1), and He is the Messiah, the promised One from the line of Abraham (1:1). **In descending order, Matthew traces the legal lineage of Jesus from Abraham**. Matthew shows us that Jesus came not simply from Adam, but more specifically from the line of the kings in Israel. He is the promised King!

A few more points regarding Matthew's genealogy may be helpful. First, he is not giving us a comprehensive genealogy, that is, not every descendant in the family tree is included in this list. This genealogy is specifically arranged in groups of 14, as Matthew himself tells us in 1:17: "So all the generations from Abraham to David were 14 generations; and from David until the exile to Babylon, 14 generations; and from the exile to Babylon until the Messiah, 14 generations." Matthew has arranged his genealogy this way for a reason that goes all the way back to the Hebrew name for King David. The Hebrews recognized something called *gematria*, a system of assigning numerical values to certain words based on the corresponding letters of the Hebrew alphabet. When you add up the numerical values of the Hebrew consonants in David's name, you get a total of 14 (Blomberg, *Matthew*, 53). In addition, David's name is the fourteenth in Matthew's list (Blomberg, 53)! Clearly, Matthew intended to connect Jesus to King David.

Once we see some of these pieces put together, it should be clear that Matthew's genealogy should not be skipped over in order to get to the "good stuff." These opening verses help clue us in to the purpose of Matthew's Gospel.

Introduction of the King
MATTHEW 1:1-17

As we consider Matthew's genealogy in verses 1-17, it may be helpful to highlight several significant names along the way. This list is saturated with Old Testament history. Consider the following: David (1), the first name mentioned, is the king whose line God promised to establish for all time (2 Sam 7). Abraham (v. 1) was the one through whom God's promised blessing would come to the whole world (Gen 12:1-3; 15:1-6). Isaac (v. 2), Abraham's son, was a miracle-baby born to a mom named Sarah, who was shocked to find out that she would have a child. This supernatural birth would set the stage for Mary (v. 16), who was also pretty shocked (though for different reasons) to find out that she was going to have a child. Tamar is the first woman mentioned (v. 3). According to Genesis 38, Tamar was Judah's daughter-in-law, and it was sinful incest that led to the birth of the twins mentioned in verse 3, Perez and Zerah. The second woman mentioned is Rahab (v. 5), a prostitute who was spared when the people of God came into the promised land (Josh 2). Ruth is the third woman mentioned (v. 5). She was a Moabite (Ruth 1:4), a people known for their sexual immorality, and who at one time were forbidden to come into the assembly of God's people. These 14 generations leading up to King David make up the first of three sets of 14 generations.

In the second set of 14, we see the fourth woman mentioned (she is not explicitly named here)—Bathsheba, the wife of Uriah (v. 6). Bathsheba was brought into David's kingly line through adultery and murder (2 Sam 11). Then, picking up with Solomon, Matthew lists the kings in Israel leading up to the exile (vv. 7-11). A few of these kings honored the Lord, but most of them were evil, leading the people of God into sin and idolatry. This eventually led to the destruction of Jerusalem and the exile to Babylon (Jer 52). Thus ends the second group of 14 generations, which, again, would have sparked images and conjured up emotions and stories in the minds of Jewish readers who knew their Old Testament.

In the third set of 14 generations, in verses 12-16, Matthew traces Jesus' genealogy from the deportation to Babylon to the birth of Jesus Christ.

All in all, this is one crooked family tree! Yet, this was the family tree through which the incarnate Son of God stepped onto the pages of human history. So why is this genealogy important? Why was it significant for Matthew to begin his Gospel in this way, both for the original hearers and for us today?

First, consider the original audience. Most of Matthew's readers were either Jewish people who had put their faith in Jesus as the Messiah, or they were Jewish people who were contemplating trusting in Jesus. Either way, this thoroughly Jewish genealogy would have been massively significant. Mark, by contrast, likely had a predominantly Gentile audience in mind, so it wasn't as critical for his original hearers to understand the Jewish lineage leading to Christ. But for Jewish men and women who were considering trusting in Christ as the Messiah, or for those Jews who had already trusted in Christ as the Messiah and were as a result losing their families, their possessions, and their own physical safety, this genealogy was extremely significant.

In his introduction of Jesus as the King, Matthew points out that **He is the Savior**. Verse 1 begins, "The historical record of Jesus Christ." The name "Jesus" is the Greek form of the name "Joshua" or "*Yeshua*," which means "Yahweh saves," or "The Lord is salvation." This theme fits with the angel's instructions to Joseph later in the chapter: "She [Mary] will give birth to a son, and you are to name Him Jesus, because *He will save His people from their sins*" (v. 21; emphasis added). Recall from the Old Testament that Joshua was the leader appointed by God to take His people into the promised land; now, Jesus is the leader appointed by God to take sinful people into eternal life.

After looking at the name "Jesus," we turn to the title "Christ." By applying this title to Jesus, Matthew is telling us that **He is the Messiah**. It is important to keep in mind that "Christ" is not Jesus' last name. No, "Christ" literally means "Messiah" or "Anointed One." Throughout the Old Testament there were promises of a coming anointed one, a Messiah, who would powerfully deliver God's people. Here Matthew says of Jesus, "This is He, the One we've waited for!"

Next, continuing in verse 1, we learn of Jesus' royal identity: **He is the son of David**. When we think about the son of David, we're reminded of David's desire to build the temple of the Lord in 2 Samuel 7. Here is God's response:

> When your time comes and you rest with your fathers, I will raise up after you your descendant, who will come from your body, and I will establish his kingdom. He will build a house for My name, and I will establish the throne of his kingdom forever. (2 Sam 7:12-13)

The Lord informed David that he, David, would not be the one to build the temple, but that his son Solomon would. God made a covenant with David in the context of this discussion and promised him two primary things. First, David was promised that **a continual seed will endure to the end** (2 Sam 7:13). This was a promise that God would bless Solomon, David's son. However, we know that the promise extends beyond Solomon, because God was not just referring to the next generation—the throne of this kingdom would be established "forever" (v. 13). That word "forever" is repeated over and over in 2 Samuel 7 (vv. 16, 24, 25, 26, and 29). God was telling David that his seed, his family, would endure forever. As readers in the twenty-first century, we should be struck by the fact that a promise given in 2 Samuel 7 is still active today. This promise is literally shaping eternity.

The second thing God promised to David was that **an honored son will reign on the throne**. This promise had an immediate reference to Solomon; however, God promised that the throne would be established *forever*. "Your house and kingdom will endure before Me forever" (2 Sam 7:16). The Old Testament had been pointing to a continual seed that would endure and an honored son from the seed of David who would reign on the throne. This is precisely what the prophets spoke of.

Isaiah 9:6-7:

> *For a child will be born for us,*
> *a son will be given to us,*
> *and the government will be on His shoulders.*
> *He will be named*
> *Wonderful Counselor, Mighty God,*
> *Eternal Father, Prince of Peace.*
> *The dominion will be vast,*
> *and its prosperity will never end.*
> *He will reign on the throne of David*
> *and over his kingdom,*
> *to establish and sustain it*
> *with justice and righteousness from now on and forever.*
> *The zeal of the Lord of Hosts will accomplish this.*

Isaiah 11:1-3a,10:

> *Then a shoot will grow from the stump of Jesse,*
> *and a branch from his roots will bear fruit.*
> *The Spirit of the Lord will rest on Him—*
> *a Spirit of wisdom and understanding,*
> *a Spirit of counsel and strength,*
> *a Spirit of knowledge and of the fear of the Lord.*
> *His delight will be in the fear of the Lord*

. . .

On that day the root of Jesse
will stand as a banner for the peoples.
The nations will seek Him,
and His resting place will be glorious.

Jeremiah 23:5-6:

"The days are coming"—this is the LORD's declaration—
"when I will raise up a Righteous Branch of David.
He will reign wisely as king
and administer justice and righteousness in the land.
In His days Judah will be saved,
and Israel will dwell securely.
This is what He will be named:
Yahweh Our Righteousness."

Ezekiel 37:24-25:

My servant David will be king over them, and there will be one
shepherd for all of them. They will follow My ordinances, and keep My
statutes and obey them.

They will live in the land that I gave to My servant Jacob, where
your fathers lived. They will live in it forever with their children and
grandchildren, and My servant David will be their prince forever.

In each of these passages there is an assumption that God's promise is continuing. For instance, in the final passage—Ezekiel 37—the people are in exile, having been ripped away from their home city, Jerusalem. The temple has been destroyed and the people are wondering, "Have God's promises failed?" And while King David was dead at this point, Ezekiel still speaks of David being king. The prophet is picking up on God's promise that through the line of David, God's kingdom would be established forever. The covenant would be an everlasting covenant (Ezek 37:26). To a people who for generations had longed for a Messiah from the line of David, Matthew is not just giving a list of names in this genealogy; he's announcing the arrival of the King.

After telling us that Jesus is the Son of David, Matthew then tells us that **He is the son of Abraham** (v. 1). Once again we're thrust back into the Old Testament, all the way back to Genesis 12. Here is God's word to Abraham:

Go out from your land,
your relatives,
and your father's house
to the land that I will show you.
I will make you into a great nation,
I will bless you,
I will make your name great,
and you will be a blessing.
I will bless those who bless you,
I will curse those who treat you with contempt,
and all the peoples on earth
will be blessed through you. (Gen 12:1-3)

Based on this passage, we see the following:

- **God will form a covenant people.** God would make Israel into a "great nation."
- **God will give them a promised inheritance on earth.** This inheritance would become known as the promised land.
- **God will use them to accomplish a global purpose.** Abraham and those who come from him will be a blessing to all the families of the earth.

God's promise to Abraham is reiterated in chapter 15 and then again in chapter 17. In 17:5-6 God says, "Your name will no longer be Abram, but your name will be Abraham, for I will make you the father of many nations. I will make you extremely fruitful and will make nations and kings come from you." Through Abraham's line God says that **He will send a King**. Then in verses 15-16 of the same chapter, God says of Sarah, Abraham's wife, "I will bless her; indeed, I will give you a son by her. I will bless her, and she will produce nations; *kings* of peoples will come from her" (emphasis added). Speaking of Abraham's line again in these verses, God says that **God's kingdom will one day expand to all people groups**. This truth is reiterated later, in Genesis 49:10, where Jacob prophesies, "The scepter will not depart from Judah or the staff from between his feet until He whose right it is comes and the obedience of the peoples belongs to Him." Again, God is promising a royal line.

God works out His promise to Abraham in Israel's history and ultimately through His Son, Jesus Christ. Nothing in history is accidental.

Every detail in the Old Testament, even from the very beginning (Gen 3:15), was pointing to a King who would come. History revolves around a King who would come—a King who now *has* come! Jesus Christ, the son of David, the son of Abraham, is the center of it all.

You are not at the center of history. I am not at the center of history. Our generation is not at the center of history. The United States of America is not at the center of history. Billions of people have come and billions have gone; empires have come and empires have gone; countries, nations, kings, queens, presidents, dictators, and rulers have all come and gone. At the center of it all stands one person: Jesus the Christ. This is the bold claim of Matthew's Gospel. And if this Jesus is the King of all history, then it follows that He should be the King of your life. When you realize His rule and submit to His reign, it changes everything about how you live. Everything.

Overview of the Kingdom

In light of what we've seen above from Matthew's opening words and the promises of the Old Testament, God's kingdom figures prominently in this first Gospel. Consider how a number of concepts fit within this kingdom framework:

- **Gospel: The message of the kingdom.** The central message in the mouth of Jesus is clear: "Repent, because the kingdom of heaven has come near!" (Matt 4:17).
- **Disciples: The citizens of the kingdom.** In Matthew 5–7, which we refer to as The Sermon on the Mount, Jesus begins by telling us what kingdom citizens are like.
- **Discipleship: The demands of the kingdom.** Following this King is costly, for He says in Matthew 10, "Anyone finding his life will lose it, and anyone losing his life because of Me will find it" (v. 39).
- **Church: The outpost of the kingdom.** Matthew is the only Gospel writer who actually uses the word for church—*ekklesia*. We're going to see that Jesus has designed His people under His rule to be a demonstration, a living picture, of the kingdom of God at work. Do you want to see what people look like who live under the rule and reign of King Jesus? Look at the church, Matthew says.

- **Mission: The spread of the kingdom.** The church proclaims the gospel of the kingdom, and not even the gates of hell will be able to stop it (Matt 16:18).
- **Demons: The enemies of the kingdom.** The Gospel of Matthew makes very clear that the Devil and all his minions are absolutely opposed to this King and everyone and everything in His kingdom, including you and me. But, Satan's power is limited and his doom is assured.
- **Hope: The coming of the kingdom.** In the Gospel of Matthew we get a dual picture of the coming of God's kingdom.
  - On the one hand, **the kingdom is a present reality**. The great announcement in the book of Matthew is that **the King is here!** Jesus Christ has broken into a dark and hurting world, bringing healing and forgiveness. He binds up the brokenhearted, He gives rest to the weary, He gives sight to the blind, and He gives life to the dead.
  - On the other hand, Matthew will also show us that **the kingdom is a future realization**. Jesus dies on the cross, rises from the grave, and before departing from His disciples, He promises to return. **The King is coming back**. At His first coming, Jesus came as a crying baby. At His second coming, Jesus will come as the crowned King.

Salvation through the King

We've seen already that Matthew's genealogy is so much more than a list of names or simply a historical record for first-century Jewish readers. It presents Jesus Christ as the climactic fulfillment of God's promises of a coming King and His kingdom. Also included in this genealogy is a picture of how God saves. Matthew tells us at least two things in this opening section about the nature of God's salvation.

First, **God saves only by His sovereign grace**. The list of names in verses 1-17 is full of evil kings and sinful men and women, a description that includes Abraham and David as well. Abraham was a polygamist patriarch who lied about his wife twice. David was an adulterous murderer. And the list goes on and on. It's amazing to think that the great, great, great, great, great grandparents of Jesus hated God and were leading other people to hate Him too. Clearly, then, **Jesus**

came not because of Israel's righteousness, but in spite of Israel's sinfulness. Throughout Scripture we **see the sinful responsibility of man.** Evil kings and evil men lived their lives in rebellion against God, and they were responsible for their sin. Nevertheless, God was working in and through these people. In the midst of man's sinfulness, we also **see the supreme will of God.** At no point were any of the men and women mentioned in this genealogy outside of the sovereign control of God. Yes, *they* were choosing to disobey God, and *they* were responsible for that. At the same time, God was ordaining all of this to bring about the birth of His Son.

In addition to the men mentioned earlier, the list of sinful women on Matthew's list is equally stunning. The message is clear: **Jesus came for (and through) the morally outcast.** Tamar was guilty of incest (Gen 38). Rahab was a prostitute (Josh 2). Ruth spent a rather shady night at Boaz's feet (Ruth 3), but more importantly she was a Moabitess, a people known for their sexual immorality. Finally, the wife of Uriah is mentioned (Matthew doesn't actually record her name—Bathsheba), even though she committed adultery with David. So we have adultery, sexual immorality, prostitution, and incest; you'd think Matthew would have chosen some different women to include here! You may also have recognized the last woman on this list—Mary, the mother of Jesus. As an unwed, pregnant woman, she was surrounded by rumors of sexual scandal (1:18-25). This is a surprising way to introduce the Savior of the world.

So why is this theme of sexual immorality so prominent in this genealogy, and why are *these* people included in the line that leads *to* Christ? For the same reason *your* name is included in the line that leads *from* Christ—solely because of the sovereign grace of God. Praise be to God that He delights in saving sinful, immoral outcasts! This theme of sovereign grace even applies to Matthew, the author of this Gospel. Matthew was a tax collector, a Jew who made his living by cheating other Jewish people. When Jesus called Matthew to follow Him, the only people Matthew knew to invite to his house for a party were moral reprobates (9:10-13)! Matthew knew he was the least likely person to be writing this Gospel, which is fitting for a book that announces good news. God saves not based on any merit in us, but totally on sovereign mercy in Him. If He didn't save like that, we would all be damned.

Not only did He come for (and through) the morally outcast, but also **Jesus came for (and through) the ethnically diverse.** These women—Tamar, Rahab, Bathsheba, and Ruth—were all Gentile women. Bathsheba may have been an Israelite, yet Matthew calls her "Uriah's wife," for Uriah was a Hittite (2 Sam 11:3). This ethnically diverse genealogy leads to the second aspect of God's salvation in this genealogy: **God saves ultimately for His global purpose.** Recall the promise to Abraham in Genesis 12:3, that "all the peoples on earth will be blessed through you." God's promise to His people is for the sake of all peoples. This universal plan will reappear throughout Matthew's Gospel, and at the center of this plan is none other than Jesus Christ Himself.

Matthew shows us repeatedly that **Jesus fulfills God's promise to bless His chosen people.** This helps explain why his Gospel is loaded with Old Testament references. Jesus came to bring salvation to the people of Israel, a point Matthew makes clear (15:24). But that wasn't all: Just as God promised to bless His chosen people Israel for the sake of *all* peoples, so **Jesus accomplishes God's purpose to bless all peoples.** Jesus would pour His life into twelve Jewish disciples, and then He would tell them, "Go, therefore, and make disciples of all nations" (28:19). The end will not come, Jesus says, until the "good news of the kingdom" is "proclaimed in all the world as a testimony to all nations" (24:14).

Matthew's Gospel teaches us that an emphasis on missions is not just a made-up program that man has come up with; it's all over the Bible. Missions have been the purpose of God from the very beginning of history, with His saving acts culminating in the person and work of Christ. Now all followers of Christ are on a global mission to make this King known among all nations, to spread the gospel of this kingdom at home and among every people group on the planet.

At the end of the day, how does God save us? Solely by His sovereign grace. Why does God save us? Ultimately for His global purpose. This is at the heart of Matthew's genealogy. The question then becomes how we will respond.

The Bottom Line

As we move forward in the book of Matthew, we are going to see three distinct groups of people: (1) The religious leaders who deny Jesus, (2) the crowds of people who follow Jesus as long as He gives them what they want and attracts their interest (but who ultimately and eternally walk away), and (3) the very small group of disciples who are going to follow Jesus, learn from Him, and eventually lose their lives for Him. As you read Matthew's Gospel, you must decide which group you are in.

Like the leaders, will you completely reject Jesus? We are going to see attacks on Jesus' character and attacks on Jesus' claims throughout this book by people who pridefully choose to deny that Jesus is King.

Like the crowds, will you casually observe Jesus? This is the place where many church attenders, probably even many church members, find themselves today. Content to observe Jesus, to give Him token allegiance, they add Him as a part of their life. These are people who do good things and are actively involved in the church in different ways. They are, in some way or another, associated with Jesus. And one day they will say, "Lord, Lord, didn't we prophesy in Your name, drive out demons in Your name, and do many miracles in Your name?" (7:22). And Jesus will say to them, "I never knew you! Depart from Me, you lawbreakers!" (7:23).

Like the disciples, will you unconditionally follow Jesus? In a day when nominal Christianity and lazy discipleship are rampant in America and in many places around the world, will you rise up and say to Jesus, "You are King, and because You are King, there are no conditions on my obedience to You. I will follow You wherever You lead me, I will give You whatever You ask of me. I will abandon all I have and all I am because You are King and You are worthy of nothing less"? This is the heart of what it means to be a disciple of Jesus the Christ.

How will you respond?

Reflect and Discuss

1. What is Matthew's overall purpose in writing this Gospel?
2. How is it possible for the four Gospel writers to each have a purpose in mind yet write accurate historical accounts?
3. How is Matthew's Gospel different from a New Testament letter?
4. Which person in the genealogy do you most resonate with, and why?
5. What is the significance of the term "Christ"?
6. What did the Old Testament prophets promise the Jewish "Messiah" would be, and how is He also good news for the Gentiles?
7. How did morally outcast people figure in to Jesus' coming?
8. In what way does this Gospel have a global purpose?
9. Explain how the kingdom has arrived *and* is yet to arrive.
10. How should true disciples respond to Jesus as a result of Matthew's Gospel?

Our Mysterious and Majestic King

MATTHEW 1:18-25

Main Idea: Jesus Christ is fully God and fully human, and He has come to save His people from their sins.

I. **How Jesus Came**
   A. To a virgin mother
   B. To an adoptive father
   C. Amidst a fallen world
II. **Who Jesus Is**
   A. As the Son of man, Jesus is fully human.
   B. As the Son of God, Jesus is fully divine.
   C. The Incarnation is the most extraordinary miracle in the whole Bible.
   D. The Incarnation is the most profound mystery in the whole universe.
III. **What Jesus Confirms**
   A. God is the Creator and Re-Creator of all things.
   B. God is always faithful to His Word.
   C. God is transcendent over us, yet He is present with us.

In the latter half of Matthew 1 we encounter the most extraordinary miracle in the whole Bible, and the most remarkable mystery in the whole universe. This miraculous mystery is described in eight simple verses. Referring to this miracle, J. I. Packer said, "It is here, in the thing that happened at the first Christmas, that the profoundest and most unfathomable depths of the Christian revelation lie" (Packer, "For Your Sakes He Became Poor," 69). Our souls ought to be captivated with fascinating glory in the midst of a familiar story.

Personally, this is a story that I have a new perspective on, because Matthew 1:18-25 is really a story of adoption.[1] A short time ago, my wife and I returned from China with our new daughter. I am mesmerized by

---

[1] To be clear, when using the analogy of Jesus' adoption, we are only referring to His relationship to Joseph. Jesus was not adopted by God, but has eternally existed as the Son of God, the Second Person of the Trinity.

this little girl, and it's such a fascinating dynamic. Biologically, it's obvious that I'm not her father; yet, she is my daughter, and I love her and am smitten by her as a daddy. After spending a month in China filling out paperwork and writing her first name next to my last name, I've been reminded that this little girl is now fully a part of our family. As I consider Matthew's account of Jesus' birth, I'm struck in a fresh way that Joseph was in very similar shoes—Jesus was not his biological son.

How Jesus Came
MATTHEW 1:18-25

Several aspects of this passage call for some explanation. Matthew begins by talking about the "birth of Jesus *Christ*" (18; emphasis added). Remember that "Christ" is not Jesus' last name; rather, it means "the Messiah," the Anointed One. The word "engaged" in verse 18, which the ESV translates as "betrothed," is also important to consider, since an engagement was much more binding in the first century than it is in the twenty-first century. Once you were engaged, you were legally bound, so to call off an engagement would be equivalent to divorce. After the engagement, the only thing left to do was for the woman to go to the man's home to physically consummate the marriage and for them to live together (Blomberg, *Matthew*, 57). This would happen approximately a year after the engagement began. So when Matthew says that she was pregnant "before they came together" (v. 18), he is saying that Mary was with child before she and Joseph consummated their marriage physically.

Also of note is the comment in verse 18 that Mary was pregnant "by the Holy Spirit." Matthew is clueing us in to something supernatural that was going on, though Mary and Joseph would not find out this "by the Holy Spirit" part until a little later. Put yourself in this young couple's shoes: Mary, having never had a physical relationship with a man, finds out that she's pregnant. Imagine the thoughts and emotions, the confusion and the worry, that would be going through your mind. Or consider Joseph: as a husband, you've yet to bring your wife into your home to consummate the marriage, and you find out that she is pregnant! There is only one possible explanation in your mind—she has clearly been with another man.

What would you do if you discovered that the woman you love, the one you've chosen to marry, was pregnant right before you took her into your home? Verse 19 gives us a glimpse into Joseph's thought here: "So her husband Joseph, being a righteous man, and not wanting to disgrace her publicly, decided to divorce her secretly." Joseph had a couple of options at this point. He could either go public and shame Mary, or he could quietly divorce her. In righteous compassion, he resolved to do the latter.

Notice that Joseph is addressed by the angel as "son of David," which reminds us that Joseph is in the line of King David. The angel gives Joseph the shocking news that "what has been conceived in her is by the Holy Spirit" (v. 20) The virgin birth may be familiar to us, but such a reality was absolutely unheard of for Joseph. Then the angel tells Joseph that Mary will "give birth to a son" (v. 21), a son whom Joseph had no part in bringing about, and that this son would be named "Jesus" because He would "save His people from their sins" (v. 21). So, Joseph was told to adopt this boy as his son, and the legal name by which He would be called—Jesus—means "Yahweh (the Lord) saves." Now that's an announcement! Matthew then says in verse 22,

> Now all this took place to fulfill what was spoken by the Lord through the prophet:
> See, the virgin will become pregnant
> and give birth to a son,
> and they will name Him Immanuel,
> which is translated "God is with us."

We don't know exactly what Joseph felt at this point, but I imagine he was puzzled. Nevertheless, Matthew gives us a great picture of Joseph's obedience in verses 24-25: "When Joseph got up from sleeping, he did as the Lord's angel had commanded him. He married her but did not know her intimately until she gave birth to a son. And he named Him Jesus." Joseph obeyed without questioning God or laying down conditions. He didn't ask for another night's sleep to see if anything changed; he simply obeyed. And when it says that he "did not know her intimately" in verse 25, Scripture is telling us that Joseph did not have physical relations with Mary. Matthew ends the chapter by telling us that Joseph called the child "Jesus," just as the angel had said. This is how the King of creation came into the world.

Based on what we've seen so far, we can say several things about how Jesus came. First, He was born **to a virgin mother**. This is an absolutely shocking pair of words—a "virgin mother" is naturally impossible, which points us to the supernatural aspect of Jesus' birth. **Physically, Jesus is Mary's son**, for even in the genealogy, where we read over and over that one individual fathered another, verse 16 identifies Joseph as Mary's husband and Mary as the one "who gave birth to Jesus who is called the Messiah." The text is careful not to call Joseph the father of Jesus. Instead, it points out that Jesus was biologically the son of Mary.

The fact that Matthew never explicitly refers to Joseph as Jesus' father reminds us that Jesus was born **to an adoptive father**. After being named and taken into the family by Joseph, **legally, Jesus is Joseph's son**. And being Joseph's son means that this adoption ties Jesus to the line of David as a royal son. Finally, in terms of how Jesus came, Matthew tells us that all of these things happened **amidst a fallen world**. Jesus came to a world of sin in need of salvation, which is why it is crucial to see that **ultimately, Jesus is God's Son**. The problem of sin needed a divine solution.

Part of the purpose of the virgin birth of Jesus is to show us that salvation does not come from man, but from God. Salvation is wholly the work of a supernatural God, not the work of natural man. There is nothing we can do to save ourselves from our sins, which is evident even in the way in which Jesus entered the world. This baby born in Bethlehem was and is the center of all history.

Who Jesus Is

The story of the virgin birth in Matthew 1 forms the foundation for everything we know about who Jesus is. This truth is foundational for why we worship Him, why we follow Him, and why we proclaim Him to the nations. With so much at stake in this one doctrine, we need to think carefully about how we understand this baby born in Bethlehem. The truth here is multifaceted.

As the Son of man, **Jesus is fully human**. He was born of a woman, so just like any other child, He came as a crying, cooing, bed-wetting baby boy. Don't let yourself picture Jesus apart from His true humanity. It was a holy night, but it wasn't silent. After all, whoever heard of a child coming out of the womb and staying quiet? After sleepless nights of putting my own children to sleep, I can only imagine trying to put a baby down when the cows keep mooing and the donkeys keep braying. Jesus wasn't born with a glowing halo around His head and a smile on His face; He was born like us.

As one who is fully human, **Jesus possesses the full range of human characteristics**. He is like us **physically** in that He possesses a human body, and as Matthew will later show us, this body grew tired at points (8:24). That's right, the Sovereign of the universe took on the human limitation of being dependent on sleep! Not only did Jesus grow weary, but He also became hungry (4:2). This was a baby that needed to be fed and nursed and nurtured. He had a body just like ours.

Jesus was also fully human **mentally**. He possessed a human mind that Luke says, "increased in wisdom" (2:52). He learned in the same way that other children do. Sometimes we get the idea that Jesus came out of the womb using words like "kingdom," "righteousness," "substitution," and "propitiation," but that's not the case. Jesus had to learn to say the first-century Jewish equivalent of "Ma-ma" and "Da-da." He possessed a human mind.

Jesus was also like us **emotionally**. In Matthew's Gospel we see the full range of human emotions: for example, Jesus' soul was troubled and overwhelmed, such that He wept with loud cries and tears (26:36-39). It also seems reasonable to conclude from Scripture that Jesus laughed and smiled; He was not boring.

Finally, after seeing that Jesus was like us physically, mentally, and emotionally, Matthew also says that He was like us **outwardly**. Or, to put it another way, Jesus' humanity was plain for all to see. For example, when Jesus taught in the synagogue in His own hometown, the people were amazed, saying,

> How did this wisdom and these miracles come to Him? Isn't this the carpenter's son? Isn't His mother called Mary, and His brothers James, Joseph, Simon, and Judas? And His sisters, aren't they all with us? So where does He get all these things? (13:54-56)

The people who were closest to Jesus for much of His life—His own brothers and the people in His own hometown—recognized Him as merely a man, just like everyone else. He was fully human (Grudem, *Systematic Theology*, 534–35).

So why is this important? Why emphasize Jesus' humanity? We must affirm Jesus' full humanity, because it means that **Jesus is fully able to identify with us**. He is not *un*like us, trying to do something for us. No, Jesus is truly representative of us. Follower of Christ, you have a Savior who is familiar with your struggles—physically, mentally, and emotionally. He is familiar with your sorrow. He is familiar with your suffering

(Heb 2:18). This is why it's comforting to affirm that Jesus was born of a woman, as the Son of Man.

As we affirm Jesus' humanity, in the very same breath we must acknowledge that **as the Son of God, Jesus is fully divine.** Just as Jesus possesses the full range of human characteristics, so **Jesus possesses the full range of divine characteristics.** Consider all that Matthew shows us. First, Jesus has **power over disease.** He is able to cleanse lepers, give sight to the blind, and cause the lame to walk, all by simply speaking healing into reality. At strategic points, Matthew talks about how Jesus went about healing every disease and every affliction among the people (4:23-24; 9:35). He graciously exercises His power over the whole range of human infirmities.

Second, Jesus' divinity is on display as He shows His **command over nature.** In Matthew 8 Jesus rebukes the storm and it immediately calms down, to which the disciples respond, "What kind of man is this?—even the winds and the sea obey Him!" (8:27). Only God possesses this kind of power over nature.

Third, Jesus has **authority over sin.** That is, He is able to forgive sins, something Matthew tells us explicitly in Jesus' healing of the paralytic (9:1-6).

The fourth way in which Matthew points to Jesus' deity is in His **control over death.** Jesus not only brings others to life (9:23-25), but He even raises Himself from the dead (John 10:17-18). These claims may sound extravagant, yet this is precisely the portrait Matthew gives us of Jesus. He is fully able to identify with us, and as God, **Jesus is fully able to identify with God.**

When you put these truths concerning Jesus' nature together, you begin to realize that **the incarnation, the doctrine of Jesus' full humanity and full deity, is the most extraordinary miracle in the whole Bible.** And if this miracle is true, then everything else in this Gospel account makes total sense. After all, is it strange to see Jesus walking on the water if He's the God who created the very water He's walking on? Is it strange to see Him feeding 5,000 people with five loaves and two fish if He's the One who created their stomachs? Furthermore, if what Scripture says is true, is it even strange to see Jesus rise from the dead? No, not if He's God. The strange thing, the real miracle, is that Jesus died in the first place. The doctrine of the incarnation and Christ's identity as fully human and fully divine is the fundamental point where Muslims, Jews, Jehovah's Witnesses, and countless others disagree with Christianity. It is the ultimate stumbling block. Furthermore, if we're honest, this important doctrine contains some mystery even for those who hold firmly to the biblical witness. So how do we even begin to understand it?

There are some things we must keep in mind if we are to uphold the truth of the incarnation. **Clearly Jesus' human nature and divine nature are different**, that is, they are to be distinguished in certain ways. One of the heresies that had to be rejected in the early centuries of the church's life was the idea that the human nature of Christ was absorbed into His divine nature, with the result that a third nature was formed, a nature that was neither God nor man. Such a view undermines Jesus' role as our mediator (Grudem, *Systematic Theology*, 556).[2] Consider how Scripture holds together the separate truths of Christ's human and divine natures:

- He was born a baby and He sustains the universe.
- He was 30 years old and He exists eternally.
- He was tired and omnipotent.
- He died and He conquered death.
- He has returned to heaven and He is present with us.

While we have to maintain a distinction between His natures, we must affirm that **Jesus' human nature and divine nature are unified**. He is one person, so we don't have to specify in every instance whether Jesus performed a certain action in His divine nature, or whether it was His human nature that did it. The Gospel writers don't say that Jesus was "born in His human nature" or that "in His human nature he died." No, He acts as a unified person, even if His two natures contributed in different ways. Scripture simply says, "*Jesus* was born" or "*Jesus* died." One theologian gives the following analogy to illustrate this point: If I were to write a letter, though my toes had nothing to do with the writing process, I would still say, "I wrote the letter," not "My fingers wrote the letter, but my toes had nothing to do with it." I simply say that I wrote the letter, and the meaning is understood (Grudem, *Systematic Theology*, 562). Similarly, everything that is done by Jesus is unified in such a way that we don't need to distinguish between His two natures when we speak

---

[2] This ancient heresy is known as monophysitism, or Eutychianism after its founder Eutyches (AD 378-454), the leader of a monastery at Constantinople.

of Him.[3] It does not matter whether His divine or His human nature is specifically in view, because they are always working in perfect unity.

The Incarnation is the most profound mystery in the whole universe. This mystery is encapsulated in what Matthew writes about the virgin birth of Jesus. There are, after all, other ways Jesus could have come into the world. On the one hand, if He had come without any human parent, then it would have been hard for us to imagine or believe that He could really identify with us. On the other hand, if He had come through two human parents—a biological mother and a biological father—then it would be hard to imagine how He could be fully God since His origin would have been exactly the same as ours. But God, in His perfect wisdom and creative sovereignty, ordained a virgin birth to be the avenue through which Christ would come into the world (Grudem, *Systematic Theology*, 530).

What Jesus Confirms

In light of everything we've seen so far in Matthew 1, there are three clear takeaways. First, **God is the Creator and Re-Creator of all things**. Interestingly enough, the word Matthew uses for "birth" in verse 18 is transliterated "genesis," which means origin—the origin of Jesus Christ. The imagery, then, in the first book of the New Testament takes us all the way back to the first book of the Old Testament, for **in Genesis, the Spirit brings life to men**. Scripture opens with the Spirit giving life to all of creation: "In the beginning God created the heavens and the earth. Now the earth was formless and empty, darkness covered the surface of the watery depths, *and the Spirit of God was hovering over the surface of the waters*" (Gen 1:1-2; emphasis added). Then the Lord breathes life into Adam, the first man (Gen 2:7). Now **in Matthew, the Spirit gives life to the Messiah**. There were pagan stories of mythological gods who physically procreated with mortal humans, but there is nothing of that kind in this text (Carson, *Matthew*, 74). This is a picture of the Spirit breathing life into the Messiah in Matthew 1, just as He did for man in Genesis.[4]

---

[3] Many of the points concerning Jesus' incarnation and the relationship between His human and divine natures are taken from Grudem, *Systematic Theology*, 556–63.

[4] Later in Matt 19:28, Jesus speaks of the new creation using the term *palingenesia*, a term that speaks to the "cosmic renewal of God's creation." Osborne, *Matthew*, 721.

You may recall that **in Genesis, God promises a seed from a woman.** Specifically, He promises to raise up a seed, a singular offspring, who would crush the head of Satan, the serpent (Gen 3:15). Now **in Matthew, God delivers that seed through a woman.** The parallels between Matthew and Genesis can be drawn out further: **in Genesis, a man is born who would succumb to sin.** The first man, Adam, initially lived in unhindered communion with his Creator before rebelling against God and falling into sin. Paul tells us in Romans 5 that from Adam's one sin condemnation came to all men (vv. 12-21). We have all inherited a sinful nature from Adam, and we have all succumbed to sin. But with Jesus the story is different.

In the virgin birth, Jesus did not inherit a sinful nature, nor did He inherit the guilt that all other humans inherit from Adam. However, we shouldn't conclude from this that Mary was perfectly sinless, as the Roman Catholic Church has historically taught. Scripture nowhere teaches this; instead, Jesus' birth was a partial interruption in the line that came from Adam. A new Adam has come on the scene, a man who would not succumb to sin. In contrast to the first Adam, **in Matthew, a man is born who would save from sin.** The God who creates in Genesis 1 is re-creating and redeeming in Matthew 1. He is making a way, through the virgin birth of Christ, for humanity to be rescued from sin and reconciled to God. Just consider how glorious it is that God is the Creator and Re-Creator of all things:

- He takes the hurts in our lives, and He turns them into joy.
- He takes the suffering in our lives, and He turns them into satisfaction.
- He takes the rebellion in our lives, and He clothes us in His righteousness.
- He takes the sin in our lives, and He brings salvation.

In addition to being the Creator and Re-Creator of all things, Matthew 1:22 tells us that **God is always faithful to His Word.** What has been promised will be fulfilled. As Matthew quotes Isaiah 7:14 and the prophecy of the virgin birth, he says, "Now all this took place to fulfill what was spoken by the Lord through the prophet." This is the first of ten times that Matthew uses this kind of phrase to speak of Jesus' fulfillment of Old Testament prophecy and expectations (1:22; 2:15, 17, 23; 4:14; 8:17; 12:17; 13:35; 21:4; 27:9). Matthew makes clear throughout this book that when God makes a promise in His Word, He fulfills it in the world.

We can be certain that God is faithful to His Word, but **what we don't know** for sure is how to understand the fulfillment of Isaiah 7:14. **Is Isaiah 7:14 a prophecy with a single or double fulfillment?** The prophet says, "Therefore, the Lord Himself will give you a sign: The virgin will conceive, have a son, and name him Immanuel." This prophecy was given at a significant point in Israel's history, approximately seven hundred years before Jesus' birth in Matthew 1. King Ahaz, who was mentioned earlier in the genealogy (Matt 1:9), was a wicked king facing threats from foreign nations, and instead of seeking the Lord for help, he sought the help of the Assyrian king. Isaiah brought news to Ahaz that God would deliver His people, but Ahaz refused to listen. This is the context of Isaiah's promise; despite the people's rebellion, God would give a sign as a guarantee that the people of God and the line of David would be preserved, not destroyed.

The question is whether or not that sign—the virgin giving birth—was in any way fulfilled around the time of Isaiah's prophecy. Some scholars believe that this sign was partially fulfilled by a virgin who got married, had relations, got pregnant, and gave birth in the seventh century BC, but then the sign was ultimately fulfilled in the birth of Christ hundreds of years later. Other scholars believe this sign was only fulfilled in the birth of Christ. In the end, it's difficult to determine whether this prophecy has a single or a double fulfillment; nevertheless, there are some things we *do* know.

What we do know is that **Isaiah 7:14 is a prophecy with certain fulfillment in Christ**. The God we worship made a promise through the prophet Isaiah that was fulfilled seven hundred years later in the virgin birth of Christ, and based on that picture, we can be sure that this same God will also prove Himself faithful to us today. So when God says, "I will never leave you or forsake you" (Heb 13:5; Josh 1:5), that is a guarantee. When He says that He is your "refuge and strength, a helper who is always found in times of trouble" (Ps 46:1), you can bank on it. And when He says that "not even death or life, angels or rulers, things present or things to come, hostile powers, height or depth, or any other created thing will have the power to separate us from the love of God in Christ Jesus our Lord" (Rom 8:38-39), you can be confident in His sustaining power. And when God says that there is coming a day when "He will wipe away every tear from their eyes. Death will no longer exist; grief, crying, and pain will exist no longer, because the previous things have passed away" (Rev 21:4), that too is a guarantee. God is always faithful to His Word.

Finally, Matthew 1:18-25 teaches that although God is transcendent over us, He is present with us. That is, in His glory, God is far above us, but in His grace, He is near to us. He is "Immanuel," which means "God is with us" (v. 23). Stop and consider who this is who promises to be with you: this is the God who spoke the world into being, the God who rules over all creation—every star in the sky, every mountain peak, every grain of sand, the sun and the moon, all the oceans and all the deserts of the earth—the God whom myriads of angels continually worship and sing praise to, the God whose glory is beyond our imagination and whose holiness is beyond our comprehension. *This* God is with you.

I once had an opportunity to bear witness to the incarnation while sitting across the table from a group of Muslim men in the Middle East during Ramadan, the Muslim holy month. We were finishing a meal late one night (they had just broken their fast), and they asked me to share with them what I believe about God. Knowing that Muslims believe Jesus was a good man, but certainly not God in the flesh (such a claim is blasphemous in Islam), I began to share about who Jesus is. I told them that when I decided to ask my wife to marry me, I did not send someone else to do it for me; I went myself. Why? Because in matters of love, One must go Himself. That's a picture of the incarnation.

This astounding truth of Christianity—the reality that God became flesh (John 1:14)—may be incomprehensible to many, but to those who believe it is irresistible. There is an infinitely great God, mighty in power, who out of His love for us has not simply sent a messenger to tell us about His love. Even better, He has come Himself. And what He came to do is the greatest news in the whole world:

- He came to heal the sick (Matt 4:23-25; 8:14-17).
- He came to feed the hungry (14:13-21 and 15:32-39).
- He came to bless the poor (specifically the poor in spirit; 5:1-12).
- He came to bind the brokenhearted (6:25-34 and 11:28-30).
- He came to deliver the demon-possessed (8:28-34).

As we reflect on these and other blessings of Christ' s ministry, we must remember that **ultimately, He came to rescue the lost** (1:21). Jesus came to a sin-stained world to endure the penalty of sin and to stand in the place of sinners. He came to die on a cross, to give His body, to shed His blood—all so that you and I could be rescued from our sin and reconciled to God. That's the good news of the incarnation. That's why Jesus came.

Reflect and Discuss

1. How does a denial of Jesus' virgin birth affect the gospel message?
2. What details of Jesus' earthly ministry demonstrate His full humanity?
3. List several characteristics of Jesus' ministry that display His divinity.
4. Explain how Jesus' divine and human natures are different, yet unified.
5. Why is it insufficient to say that Jesus was only a great moral example for us?
6. How did Jesus' birth fulfill the promise of Genesis 3:15?
7. How is Jesus contrasted with Adam?
8. How did Jesus fulfill Isaiah 7:14?
9. How would you explain to an unbeliever that Jesus is both God and man?
10. How should Matthew 1:21 shape the way you read the rest of this Gospel?

The Magi and the Messiah

MATTHEW 2:1-12

Main Idea: Like the magi, we ought to respond to Jesus with extravagant praise, for all nations will come to this King.

I. **The Magicians**
   A. What we don't know
   B. What we do know
II. **The Constellations**
   A. Numbers: A star
   B. Isaiah: The light
III. **The Opposition**
   A. A world leader intimidated by Jesus
   B. Religious leaders indifferent to Jesus
IV. **The Quotation**
   A. The place a king was born
   B. An insignificant village
   C. The King is a shepherd.
V. **The Deception**
   A. Herod pretended kindness.
   B. Herod intended killing.
VI. **The Introduction**
   A. Exceeding gladness!
   B. Extravagant gifts
      1. Gold, emphasizing Jesus' royalty
      2. Frankincense, emphasizing Jesus' deity
      3. Myrrh, emphasizing Jesus' humanity
VII. **The Conclusion**

Matthew 2:1-12 is another reminder that our traditional picture of the Christmas story is in need of some tweaking. Two well-known Christmas carols have already been debunked in Matthew 1: the night of Jesus' birth was not a silent one, and with all due respect to those who sing "Away in a Manger," it is highly unlikely that a baby would not cry while cattle are lowing. In Matthew 2:1-12 we're going to debunk another favorite Christmas carol as we consider the magi who came from the east to visit Jesus (vv. 1-2). If you've ever sung "We Three Kings," this passage may cause you to rethink these familiar lyrics.

The point of highlighting some of our mistaken Christmas notions is not to take the joy out of this holiday; rather, we need our false notions of these events and our watered-down versions of their significance to be obliterated by the Word of God. When we understand what Scripture says, singing is indeed a fitting reaction to the birth of Jesus. In fact, worship, praise, surrender, and the sacrificial offering of our lives are the only proper responses to the coming of our Savior. We get a glimpse of this kind of worship-filled response as we consider the magi in the first part of Matthew 2. In these verses we learn about the global purpose of God in all of history and the ultimate purpose of God for our lives.

The Magicians
MATTHEW 2:1

In verse 1 we are introduced to the magi *(magoi),* translated as "wise men." There's a bit of mystery surrounding these guys. They weren't just wise men in general; they were known to be astrologers—students of the stars. So don't think of David Copperfield-like magicians when you think of these magi, though their name is where we get our words "magic" and "magician." There are some things we do know and some things we don't know from Scripture about these mysterious men.

First, we'll look at **what we don't know.** Though most believers traditionally picture three wise men at the manger scene, Scripture doesn't tell us **their number.** The idea of three wise men probably comes from the fact that these men bring three gifts later in the passage (v. 11). There could be 10 or 30 of them—we simply don't know. So the idea behind "We Three Kings," though well-intentioned, is conjecture. In fact, we're not even told that they were kings. Another thing we *don't* know about these magi is **their names.** Tradition tells us that their names were Melkon (later Melchior), Balthasar, and Gasper (Carson, *Matthew,* 85). According to some reports, one was Ethiopian, one was Indian, and one was Greek. It has also been claimed that they were all baptized by Thomas, and a bishop in the twelfth century even claimed to have found their skulls. You can believe what you wish, but none of this is mentioned in Scripture.

What is most important about these magi is **what we do know**. First, we know **their setting: the east**. Obviously that's a pretty general geographic area, and there are a variety of possibilities as to their specific origin (Babylon, Persia, Egypt, and the Arabian desert have all been mentioned). The only thing we know for sure is that they were from the east, which helps us debunk one last Christmas carol—"The First Noel." We may sing, "They looked up and saw a star, shining in the east, beyond them far," but Matthew 2 says that these wise men were *from* the east (v. 1), not that the star was shining in the east.[5] The wise men actually needed to go west in order to find Jesus.

Another thing we know about the wise men is their **prominence: high-ranking officials with power and influence**. When we picture these men, we shouldn't think of them as an isolated star-gazing club. These men were well-respected, with roles in both religion and politics in their own land (Blomberg, *Matthew*, 62). They almost certainly had a high position, wherever they came from. Their position is evident in the wealth they brought with them, and they probably didn't travel alone. We learn about men like this in the book of Daniel, and it's likely that these men were influenced by Jewish teachings. Now, through their study of the stars, they were drawn by a star on a journey to worship the One born King of the Jews.

The Constellations
MATTHEW 2:2

In verse 2 the wise men ask, "Where is He who has been born King of the Jews? For we saw His star in the east and have come to worship Him." This reference to a "star" has an Old Testament background in the story of Balak and Balaam in Numbers 22. The book of Numbers recounts the journey of God's people from Mount Sinai to the edge of the promised land, and as they journeyed they grew in power and might. This scared Balak, the king of Moab, so he called for Balaam, a magician—a seer. Balaam had been summoned from the eastern mountains to curse the house of Jacob and the people of Israel (Num 22:6), but as the story continues, God makes clear to Balaam that he is not to curse

---

[5] The phrase "we saw His star in the east" is likely not the best translation in verse 2. The translation "we saw His star when it rose" is probably more accurate (ESV; NIV). Carson, *Matthew*, 89.

the Israelites but to bless them (Num 22:22-35). Balaam obeyed God
and blessed Israel three times. Balaam's final oracle begins in Numbers
24:16-17:

> *The oracle of one who hears the sayings of God*
> *and has knowledge from the Most High,*
> *who sees a vision from the Almighty,*
> *who falls into a trance with his eyes uncovered:*
> *I see him, but not now;*
> *I perceive him, but not near.*
> *A star will come from Jacob,*
> *and a scepter will arise from Israel.*

The last two lines tell of a scepter that will arise from God's people,
referring to one who rules, and a star that will come. This prophesied
King associated with a star is one who will, as the passage continues,
deliver the people of God from their enemies (24:17-19). See, then,
the Old Testament promise in **Numbers: A man from the east prophesying a star and a King among the Jews**. Balaam's prophecy was widely
regarded as a Messianic prophecy, a picture of the coming Anointed
One (Carson, *Matthew*, 86). It's no coincidence, therefore, that we read
of the following fulfillment in **Matthew: Magi from the east following a
star to the King of the Jews**. That which God had foretold is now coming
to pass in the birth of Jesus Christ.

The prophecy of a star—a light—to whom the nations would
respond is not only found in Numbers. Toward the end of the book of
Isaiah, the prophet tells of coming glory for God's people:

> *Arise, shine, for your light has come,*
> *and the glory of the LORD shines over you.*
> *For look, darkness covers the earth,*
> *and total darkness the peoples;*
> *but the LORD will shine over you,*
> *and His glory will appear over you.*
> *Nations will come to your light,*
> *and kings to the brightness of your radiance.*
> *Raise your eyes and look around:*
> *they all gather and come to you;*
> *your sons will come from far away,*
> *and your daughters will be carried on the hip.*

Then you will see and be radiant,
and your heart will tremble and rejoice,
because the riches of the sea will become yours
and the wealth of the nations will come to you.
Caravans of camels will cover your land—
young camels of Midian and Ephah—
all of them will come from Sheba.
They will carry gold and frankincense
and proclaim the praises of the Lord. (Isa 60:1-6)

Once again, we have the promise in **Isaiah: Nations will come to the light of God's people**. These nations would bring riches and gifts for worship. Then we read the following in **Matthew: Nations are drawn to the light over God's Son**. Consider how striking it is that in Matthew's Gospel, a book aimed specifically at a Jewish audience, the first people we see worshiping Jesus are magi from the nations! This is clearly a picture of God drawing those nations to the Jewish Messiah. This promised Messiah is not merely the King of the Jews; He is King of all peoples.

The wise men journeyed from the east to the west, estimated by some scholars as a journey of hundreds or even a thousand miles, in order to find the star. Their natural stopping place was Jerusalem, the capital city of the Jewish people. They were certain that this was where the child would be, but as they began asking around about this One born King of the Jews, all they got were blank stares. No one knew whom these men were talking about, which set the stage for their encounter with King Herod.

The Opposition
MATTHEW 2:3-4

When King Herod was notified of the arrival of the wise men and their reason for coming, the opposition to Jesus officially began. Verse 3 says, "When King Herod heard this, he was deeply disturbed, and all Jerusalem with him." We have in King Herod **a world leader intimidated by Jesus**. Some background on Herod will help us understand his concern even better. Herod had been given control of Judea by the Romans in approximately 40 BC, and he was considered the "king of the Jews." He was a vicious, bloodthirsty tyrant. Whenever he suspected anyone of plotting to take over his rule, he would have them killed. He even went so far as to murder wives and sons at various times when he didn't trust them! So when Herod hears that officials with power and influence have journeyed to Jerusalem to find a baby born "King of the Jews," Matthew says that he is "disturbed," which is really quite an understatement. The word for "disturbed" literally means "in turmoil" or even "terrified" (Blomberg, *Matthew*, 63). Herod is threatened by the announcement of One who would supposedly usurp his reign. Many other people in Jerusalem, including religious leaders, are troubled as well (v. 3).

Next we read in verse 4 that Herod called together the chief priests and scribes, the second group that opposed Jesus. Matthew writes, "So he [Herod] assembled all the chief priests and scribes of the people and asked them where the Messiah would be born." In this case we see **religious leaders indifferent to Jesus**. Interestingly, Matthew references these chief priests and scribes more than anyone else in the New Testament, so we will see them again as the narrative unfolds. Here is a quick breakdown of these religious leaders and what they represent:

- **Chief priests: Representing Jewish worship**. Despite God's purposes in appointing priests, these religious leaders had essentially become a group of corrupt, religiously oriented politicians at the time of Jesus birth.
- **Scribes: Representing Jewish law**. The scribes were basically lawyers who knew, taught, and interpreted the Jewish law (both Old Testament law and the traditions that had developed around this law), which is frightening given the way we see them opposed to Jesus throughout His ministry.

The spiritual state of the priests and the scribes is a sobering reminder that mere knowledge of the Scriptures is not enough. You can know the text well yet still miss the point. May God keep us from this kind of deceptive rebellion in our own lives and in our own churches.

When Herod inquired of these Jewish religious leaders as to where the Messiah was to be born, they quoted from the Old Testament, revealing that He would be born in Bethlehem. What is startling is that these men who knew of the Messiah's birthplace did absolutely nothing about it. Again, it is a dangerous thing to know the Word and fail to respond. These religious leaders were indifferent to Jesus, and this indifference and apathy soon developed into outright opposition.

Eventually, this outright opposition would lead them to have Jesus killed. The next time the "the King of the Jews" label is ascribed to Jesus in Matthew's Gospel is when He is beaten and mocked before his crucifixion (27:11, 29, 37; see also 27:42 where Jesus is derisively called the "King of Israel").

The Quotation
MATTHEW 2:6

The prophecy cited by the religious leaders was a quotation from the Old Testament prophet Micah. Matthew basically paraphrases this quotation, adding a couple of things for interpretive reasons. He wanted to emphasize certain aspects of Micah's prophecy that help us understand the significance of what was happening with the coming of Jesus in Matthew 2. Compare the citations below:

Micah 5:2:	Matthew 2:6:
Bethlehem Ephrathah,	*And you, Bethlehem, in the land of*
you are small among the clans of	*Judah,*
Judah;	*are by no means least among the*
One will come from you	*leaders of Judah:*
to be ruler over Israel for Me.	*because out of you will come a*
His origin is from antiquity,	*leader*
from eternity.	*who will shepherd My people Israel.*

Instead of saying "Bethlehem Ephrathah," Matthew says, "Bethlehem, in the land of Judah." You may recall from chapter 1 how intentional Matthew has been, not just about telling a story, but more specifically about weaving through this story the theme of Jesus' lineage in the line of Judah (1:2) and the line of David (1:1, 6). By mentioning Judah in his citation of Micah, Matthew is referencing Jesus' kingly line. He's reminding readers that **the place where King David was born becomes the point where King Jesus is born.** Bethlehem, a town in the land of Judea (another name for Judah), was known as the place where King David was born and raised. And since Matthew is constantly tying Jesus to David, it becomes clearer why he mentions Judea three times in chapter 2 (vv. 1, 5, 6). Only a member of the tribe of Judah could qualify for the throne of David.

A second change Matthew makes to the quotation of Micah 5:2 occurs in verse 6. Speaking of Bethlehem, Matthew says that it is "by no means least among the leaders of Judah." Christ's birth means that **a relatively insignificant village becomes an extremely important city** in God's plan. Bethlehem, a small village five or six miles south of Jerusalem, is hugely important in the context of redemptive history. Matthew says a "leader" will come from Bethlehem—another clear paraphrase of Micah 5:2—before adding, "who will shepherd my people Israel" (v. 6). This language of shepherding is important, and it too stems from the Old Testament.

In 2 Samuel 5:2 the Lord had said to David, "You will shepherd My people Israel and be ruler over Israel." This picture of King David and the Davidic line as a shepherding line would continue throughout the Old Testament (Ezek 34:11-24; see also Isa 40:11 and Jer 31:10).There of course were kings who failed over and over again in shepherding Israel, including David himself. However, all of this was pointing to the fact that one day a good shepherd, the perfect shepherd, would come, and He would, as King, lead God's people back to their God. This is precisely what we see in the person of Jesus (Matt 9:36; John 10:1-18). Matthew shows us that **the One who reigns as the King will rule as a shepherd**.

The Deception
MATTHEW 2:7-9

In verses 7-8, it becomes apparent that Herod is scheming:

> *Then Herod secretly summoned the wise men and asked them the exact time the star appeared. He sent them to Bethlehem and said, "Go and search carefully for the child. When you find Him, report back to me so that I too can go and worship Him."*

As we'll find out later, this is a bold-faced lie. King Herod had no intention of worshiping anyone else as "king of the Jews." He wanted Jesus dead, no matter what it took.

Herod pretended kindness, and it seems that the wise men, at least at this point, believed this to be his true intention. In reality, **Herod intended killing**. He was plotting to murder Jesus, so he sent the wise men away on a five- to six-mile journey to Bethlehem. Matthew tells us what happened next in verse 9: "After hearing the king, they went on their way. And there it was—the star they had seen in the east! It led them until it came and stopped above the place where the child was."

This is actually the first time that we see the star move, and it literally—supernaturally—led the wise men to Bethlehem.

The Introduction

MATTHEW 2:10-12

Like the pillar of cloud by day and fire by night that led the people of God through the wilderness in the Old Testament (Exod 13:21), the star led the wise men to the place where Jesus was. They must have been ecstatic, for Matthew says in verse 10, "When they saw the star, they were overjoyed beyond measure." Seeing the child Jesus was the culmination of their journey. This encounter likely took place long after the night of Jesus' birth. Verse 11 tells us that Joseph, Mary, and Jesus had settled into a house by this time. Soon after this Herod would calculate that this child had to be somewhat less than two years old (v. 16), based on what he had heard from the wise men (v. 7). So Jesus was certainly months old, if not over a year old, by the time the wise men arrived. It looks as if our nativity sets that have the wise men bowing with the shepherds at the manger need some adjusting! Those shepherds were long gone, and months, maybe many months, had passed before the wise men ever showed up.

Regardless of when the wise men showed up, we know they were filled with **exceeding gladness**. Overjoyed, they responded in the only appropriate way: "Entering the house, they saw the child with Mary His mother, and falling to their knees, they worshiped Him" (v. 11a). These eminent men from the east, nobles of nations, are bowing down and worshiping a baby! You only bow down when you are in the presence of one far superior to you, as if to say, "I am low, and you are high." That's exactly what the wise men were saying. It's no wonder they obeyed the angel's warning not to return to Herod with Jesus' location (v. 12).

Next, these wise men offered **extravagant gifts**. Verse 11b says, "Then they opened their treasures and presented Him with gifts: gold, frankincense, and myrrh." It was customary, particularly in the ancient East, to bring gifts when approaching a superior. Some commentators say that these gifts don't represent any particular type of symbolism, but rather they are collectively a picture of an extravagant, costly offering before this baby born King of the Jews. At the same time, when you look in history, and even in Scripture, there are ideas associated with these gifts. While it's not universally agreed on as to what is symbolized by each of these gifts, it's definitely possible that in the design of God they had special significance. These are *possible* connections (see John MacArthur, *Matthew 1–7*; and William Hendriksen, *Exposition of the Gospel According to Matthew*):

Gold, emphasizing Jesus' royalty: Throughout Scripture, whether these wise men realized it or not, gold is associated with royalty—kings, queens, and princes. For example, when we see Solomon's wealth described in 1 Kings 10, gold is mentioned no less than ten times in seven verses. This association of gold with royalty is found elsewhere in the Old Testament (Pss 45:9, 13; 72:15; 2 Kgs 5:5), and it fits one of the main thrusts of Matthew's Gospel, namely, to show Jesus' kingship. Matthew made clear that Jesus deserves royal honor in chapter 1, and now Jesus is receiving it in chapter 2.

Frankincense, emphasizing Jesus' deity: Frankincense was used in the Old Testament not only for royal processions, but also in various offerings to God. It was stored in the chamber of the sanctuary (Neh 13:5). When it is used in the Old Testament, frankincense usually refers to something related to the worship or service of God (Exod 30:34; Lev 2:1).

Myrrh, emphasizing Jesus' humanity: Myrrh was basically a perfume with many different purposes.[6] Whereas frankincense would be associated with the worship of God, myrrh is more associated with the anointing of man. This is quite fascinating, particularly in light of other appearances of myrrh in the Gospels. **Jesus was presented myrrh as a King in a cradle.** However, in Mark 15:23 when Jesus was being hoisted onto the cross, Mark tells us that they offered Him "wine mixed with myrrh." So not only was Jesus presented with myrrh as a King in a cradle, **He would be offered myrrh as a King on a cross**. John 19:38-42 tells us that Nicodemus and Joseph of Arimathea used myrrh to prepare Jesus' body for burial in the tomb.

In this gift of myrrh, given soon after Jesus' birth, we have a foretaste of His impending death. He came for one reason—Jesus was born to die. He came to take the payment and penalty for our sins on Himself. And this shouldn't be a surprise, for Matthew has already told us through the angel's announcement that Jesus came to "save His people from

---

[6] In addition to being used as a perfume, myrrh could also be used in combination with wine as an anesthetic, or as a spice used to prepare bodies for burial.

their sins" (1:21). See, then, in Jesus' birth the significance of His death on your behalf. God loved the world so much that He sent His Son to live a life of perfect obedience, a life we couldn't live, and then to die the death we deserved to die. Jesus then rose from the grave in victory over sin and death, so that whoever believes in Him will never perish, but have eternal life (John 3:16). Bethlehem is a key part of this gospel message. Like the wise men, let us put aside our pretense and our pride, and let's worship this King.

The Conclusion

Matthew 2 gives us a powerful and, in many senses, prophetic picture of joyful, reverent worship. This text has the potential to change everything about how you think about your life, your job, your family, and the entire world around you. These twelve verses teach us that **the global purpose of God is the glad praise of Christ among the peoples of the world.** Consider how God accomplishes His purpose in this particular text. In order to lead the wise men, **He directs nature.** Speaking of the star shining in the sky, John Piper says that God "wields the universe to make his Son known and worshiped" (Piper, "We Have Come to Worship Him"). How amazing to think that God arranges the sky to announce His Son! He exercises His authority as the Sovereign over the universe to make clear that the King has been born, and that He is worthy of our worship. God uses the stars to shout the supremacy of Jesus Christ.

God not only directs nature to announce the glory of His Son, but also **He draws nations** for this purpose. Matthew's aim is to show us that Jesus is born King of the Jews, but he goes beyond that as well. Jesus has come, right in line with the promise to Abraham in Genesis 12:1-3, to bless God's people *for the sake of all peoples.* So don't be like the Jewish lawyers who had their noses in the Scriptures but who missed the main point of the text. Instead, see what the astrologers saw—the promised King. God was and is drawing the nations to Himself. But how is God doing all of this? How is He directing nature and drawing nations to Himself?

First, He sends the Christ. That's what we've seen so far in Matthew 1–2, and it's what we celebrate at Christmas. The invitation at **the beginning of Matthew is clear: Come and see the King!** God invites the magi and He invites you to see His Son and to **joyfully offer your life as a worshiper.** The people of God should, regardless of their personality, smile and sing and lift their hands. They should get excited, for the King has come! Worship involves joyful, affectionate, uninhibited praise. Like these powerful, influential men in Matthew 2, we should be over-whelmed, bowing down in homage and humble worship. We give to Christ the extravagant offering of our lives, everything we have and everything we are. We lay it down before Jesus, and we do it joyfully. He is the King, and as we see His royalty, His deity, and His humanity, we're compelled to shout and sing about His great worth.

After God sends the Christ, **then, He sends the church.** Much of what Matthew is setting up in these opening chapters will find resolu-tion toward the end of the Gospel. At the beginning of Matthew the message to the nations is clearly to come and see the King. And at the end of Matthew, Jesus tells His disciples to **go and spread the kingdom to the nations!** More specifically, "Go . . . and make disciples of all nations" (28:19). Joyfully offer your life as a worshiper, and then **passionately spend your life as a witness.**

The God who two thousand years ago sovereignly arranged the stars in the sky, the God who sovereignly directed these magi to the Messiah, is the God who has sovereignly arranged your life and every detail in it—your family, your job, your school, your background, and your relation-ships. This God wants to use your life to make the glad praise of Christ known among people everywhere. Whether you're leading coworkers to joyfully worship Christ or you're a student leading other students on your campus to be glad in Him, God wants to use you. Every believer has the responsibility and the privilege of spreading the gospel to the ends of the earth.

Live for this purpose. Die for this purpose. Give your life and your possessions and your plans and your dreams for the cosmic, global pur-pose of God—the glad praise of Christ among all the peoples of the world. Let the nations be glad and sing for joy (Ps 67:4).

Reflect and Discuss

1. How does accurate knowledge of the details of the nativity scene help you to worship?
2. What's the difference between magi and modern day magicians?
3. How should our response to Jesus look like the magi's response?
4. What was the significance of the "scepter" (Num 24:17) and the "light" (Isa 60:1-3) in the prophecies about the Messiah?

5. Describe the reaction of the religious leaders to Jesus' birth. How does this reaction serve as a warning?
6. Why was Bethlehem a significant location for Jesus' birth?
7. Why would Matthew specifically refer to Judah in his quotation of Micah 5:2?
8. How does Matthew point to Jesus' kingship in this passage?
9. How is it clear that the star was not merely a natural phenomenon?
10. How does this passage speak to God's desire to reach the nations with the message of Jesus?

Christmas Pleasure amidst Worldly Pain

MATTHEW 2:13-23

Main Idea: Jesus fulfills the Old Testament by inaugurating a new exodus, ending the mournful exile, and loving His fiercest enemies.

Three Reasons for Christmas Rejoicing

I. **Jesus Inaugurates the New Exodus**
    A. God saved His people by bringing miraculous deliverance from Egypt.
    B. God saves His people by bringing the Messianic Deliverer from Egypt.
II. **Jesus Ends the Mournful Exile**
    A. There is hope in the midst of hurt.
    B. There is life in the midst of death.
III. **Jesus Loves His Fiercest Enemies**
    A. In our minds and in our hearts, we have all rejected Him.
    B. By His grace and for His glory, He has redeemed us.

Matthew 2:13-23 reminds us that the Christmas story many of us are so familiar with actually relates to biblical stories that go back hundreds of years prior to Christ's coming. God's work throughout the Old Testament had everything to do with this baby born in Bethlehem, and if we listen closely to what Matthew is telling us, we just might find an altogether fresh perspective on Christmas. There may be more reason to rejoice than we ever knew.

A brief summary of these events may be helpful to set the context. Our passage begins after Jesus was born and after the wise men had visited Him some time later. When the wise men left they were warned in a dream not to return to King Herod, so they traveled home a different way (2:12). At the same time, Joseph had a dream in which God told him to take his family to Egypt, because Herod wanted to kill Jesus (v. 13). So in the middle of the night, Joseph took his wife and his Son, and they traveled about 75–100 miles to Egypt (v. 14). And you thought your Christmas travels were rough!

Meanwhile, when King Herod heard nothing from the wise men, he decided he had only one option for destroying this child born King of the Jews. He had all the male children two years old and younger put to death (v. 16). It is estimated that the population of Bethlehem at that time was less than a thousand people, so there were likely somewhere between ten and twenty families that lost a son that day in a tragedy that surely shook the entire town to the core. Not long after that Herod died, and Joseph had another dream in which God told him to take his family back to the land of Israel (vv. 19-20). But Herod's son Archelaus, another ruthless ruler, was now reigning over Judea, making it unsafe to go back there. So Joseph, warned yet again in a dream, took his family back to the place where he and Mary had once lived in Galilee—to Nazareth (vv. 21-23).

So how do these things relate to Christmas, and what do they have to teach us today?

Three Reasons for Christmas Rejoicing
MATTHEW 2:13-23

In Matthew 2:13-23 we see three reasons for Christmas rejoicing, and these reasons literally go back three thousand years. Matthew quotes from the Old Testament three different times, and each time he says that the words of the prophets were fulfilled (2:15, 18, 23). Consider the first quotation in Matthew 2:15: "He [Joseph] stayed there until Herod's death, so that what was spoken by the Lord through the prophet might be fulfilled: Out of Egypt I called My Son." Matthew is actually quoting from Hosea 11:1, and in that particular context Hosea is talking about God's deliverance of His people from slavery in Egypt. This Old Testament context is important for understanding Matthew's point.

In Exodus God used ten miraculous plagues to deliver Israel (Exod 7–10). The first nine plagues—water-to-blood, frogs, gnats, flies, livestock, boils, hail, locusts, and darkness—all led to the tenth and final plague, what we know as the Passover, when the Lord struck down all the firstborn in the land of Egypt (Exod 12:29). However, for His people, God prescribed a way to escape this plague of death. The Israelites were to put the blood of an unblemished lamb on their doorposts and on their lintels (Exod 12:7), for when the Lord saw this blood He would withhold judgment from that household. The Passover was a picture of God's gracious deliverance. This deliverance then climaxed in Exodus

14 when God fully and finally saved His people from the hands of the Egyptians at the Red Sea.

In light of this background, when Jesus and His family flee to Egypt and then later return from Egypt, Matthew helps us see that **Jesus inaugurates the new exodus**. The flight to Egypt for Jesus and His family was about much more than simply running away from Herod; this was about painting a picture, so don't miss the parallels:

- **The mercy of God in the Old Testament: He saved His people by bringing miraculous deliverance from Egypt.** God's people recounted the exodus events every year, telling them over and over to their children. God mercifully delivered His people, and this deliverance became a picture of what was to come in the New Testament.

- **The mercy of God in the New Testament: He saves His people by bringing the Messianic Deliverer from Egypt.** Matthew 2:15 speaks of a new deliverance, a new exodus. Recall that Matthew 1:21 says that Jesus will "save His people from their sins." Just as God delivered His people from the Egyptians in the Old Testament, so now He was delivering His people from sin in the New Testament. Just as Israel was God's son, brought out of Egypt (Exod 4:22; Hos 11:1), so now Jesus as God's Son was brought out of Egypt.

Matthew's quotation of Hosea 11:1 in verse 15 sets the stage for the second quote from an Old Testament prophet in verses 17-18: "Then what was spoken through Jeremiah the prophet was fulfilled: A voice was heard in Ramah, weeping, and great mourning, Rachel weeping for her children; and she refused to be consoled, because they were no more." This quotation occurs right after Herod kills all of the infant boys in Bethlehem, and it's taken from Jeremiah 31:15. The prophet is talking about the time when the people of God were taken into exile. The Babylonians came and attacked Jerusalem, razing people's homes and destroying the entire city, and then they took all the people to Ramah, a place just north of Jerusalem. At Ramah the people were put into caravans and scattered apart from one another. This was a scene of unimaginable anguish.

Consider your reaction if you were taken to a place where you were separated from your family and your friends with the prospect that you might not ever see them again. Imagine the weeping and crying—the loud lamentation—that would take place in a scene like that as families were torn apart. This is the kind of scene that Matthew refers to when he describes the weeping and crying over children who had died in Bethlehem. But there's a deeper significance here as well, for the prophet Jeremiah says right after this in verses 16-17,

> *This is what the LORD says:*
> *Keep your voice from weeping*
> *and your eyes from tears,*
> *for the reward for your work will come—*
> *this is the LORD's declaration—*
> *and your children will return from the enemy's land.*
> *There is hope for your future—*
> *this is the LORD's declaration—*
> *and your children will return to their own territory.*

Jeremiah tells the people that God has not forgotten them, and that He will initiate a new relationship, a new covenant with them (31:31-34). God was going to unite His people together around that covenant.

So when Matthew quotes from Jeremiah, it's as if he's saying amidst the bitter tragedy of Bethlehem, "Yes, the pain is real, but there is hope for your future, and that hope is here. Jesus has come!" **Jesus ends the mournful exile**. Notice the contrast in Matthew 2. On the one hand, there is horrible news—children dying and mothers mourning and weeping. On the other hand, **there is hope in the midst of hurt. There is life in the midst of death**. And what is that hope? Where is this life? Matthew tells us: A new King is born—a King who will conquer death, a King who will heal our hurts, a new King who will reconcile us to God.

Along with the coming of a new King, **a new covenant is beginning**. Matthew quotes from Jeremiah 31, the same chapter where we are promised that God will enter into a new covenant with us through Christ, so that all God's people will know and love and worship God. Jesus brings hope in the midst of hurt and life in the midst of death.

After showing us that Jesus inaugurates the new exodus and ends the mournful exile, Matthew now shows us that **Jesus loves His fiercest enemies**. In verse 23 we read, "Then he went and settled in a town called Nazareth to fulfill what was spoken through the prophets, that He will be called a Nazarene." If you have trouble tracking down that Old Testament reference, it's because Matthew is not quoting from any particular prophet. In fact, none of the prophets ever say precisely, "He will be called a Nazarene." For that matter, the prophets never even talk about Nazareth as a place at all. So why does Matthew say this?

We learn throughout the rest of Matthew's Gospel and the other Gospels that Nazareth was not a very well-respected place. It was at the bottom of the socio-economic scale, to say the least. Recall from John's Gospel that when Nathanael heard that Jesus was from Nazareth, he responded by saying, "Can anything good come out of Nazareth?" (John 1:46). Nazarenes were scorned, derided, and generally despised. It is this idea of scorn that is all over the prophets, maybe most famously in Isaiah 53, where the prophet says of Jesus, "He was despised and rejected by men . . . and we didn't value Him" (53:3). This seems to be what Matthew is getting at—the King who has come is going to be rejected by the world. He will be a Nazarene. He will be scorned. But this is actually good news in the end, as we will see.

This final quotation in verse 23 brings chapter 2 to a fitting conclusion. The King of the universe has come to save sinners, and from the start He is defied and derided by the very sinners He came to save. Whether it's Herod, the chief priests, or the scribes, they are all setting themselves up against Jesus as His enemies. The reality is, we do the same thing.

In most of the stories we love, even biblical stories, you have a good guy and a bad guy, and of course, we love to identify ourselves with the good guy. Think about these pairs: Goliath and David, Cain and Abel, Pharaoh and Moses, Delilah and Sampson, Esau and Jacob. Likewise in Matthew 2 we've got good guys and bad guys. The good guys are the wise men, Joseph, and Mary; the bad guys, King Herod and the Jewish religious leaders. Whom do you identify with more? If we're honest, at the core of who we are we probably identify most with King Herod. Instead of bowing in full surrender before the King, we're afraid of how Jesus is going to invade our kingdom, our lives, our plans, and our desires. The reality is that **in our minds and in our hearts, we have all rejected Him**. This is the core of what it means to be a sinner, and this is precisely whom Jesus came to save.

The story of Matthew 2 and the story of Christmas are not simply about what happened two thousand years ago in the time of the New Testament, or three thousand years ago in the time of the Old Testament. This story is also about you and me. We're all enslaved to sin, in need of an exodus, in need of deliverance. And we are familiar with pain and hurt in this sinful world. We know suffering in our own lives and we see suffering all around us, and we long for an end to mourning. Yet, in our sin, we are enemies of the Savior. But He, Jesus, has come to inaugurate a new exodus, to make our deliverance from sin possible. He has come to end our mournful exile, to bring hope in the midst of hurt and life in the midst of death as a new King with a new covenant that unites us to God. And none of this is based on our work for Him, but on His work for us. And He has come to love us in all our sinful rebellion, though in our minds and in our hearts we have all rejected Him. **By His grace and for His glory, He has redeemed us.**

Christ has come. He has given His life for us, He has shed His blood as a perfect sacrifice, and He has risen from the grave to bring eternal life to all who believe in Him. This is the gospel that brings Christmas pleasure in the midst of worldly pain.

Reflect and Discuss

1. How does Jesus fulfill Hosea 11:1?
2. How was God's providence evident in Jesus' flight to and return from Egypt?
3. What are the parallels between the exodus story and salvation in Christ?
4. What does it mean that Jesus ends the mournful exile?
5. Can you sometimes identify with any of the reasons King Herod feared and hated Jesus?
6. How is Matthew 1:23 a fulfillment passage if the Old Testament doesn't mention Nazareth?
7. How would you respond if someone said that Matthew is simply pulling Old Testament quotations out of context?
8. How does this passage as a whole make you rethink Jesus' relationship to the Old Testament?
9. What does the supernatural nature of God's acts of deliverance say about our sin?
10. How does this passage flesh out Jesus' claim in John 5:39 that (Old Testament) Scripture speaks of Him?

Repentance and Resolutions

MATTHEW 3:1-17

Main Idea: Entering the kingdom of heaven requires repenting of sin and trusting in the Son whom God has sent for sinners.

I. **The Ministry of John the Baptist: Prepare the Way**
   A. The man
      1. Prophesying boldly
      2. Living simply
      3. Baptizing openly
      4. Serving humbly
   B. The message
      1. Repent . . .
      2. . . . for the kingdom of heaven has come near.
   C. The method
      1. The baptism of Jews
         a. Renounce your dependence on self.
         b. Rely on the mercy of God.
      2. The baptism of Jesus
         a. The Son obeys.
         b. The Spirit anoints.
         c. The Father speaks.
II. **The Ministry of the Church Today: Tell the World**
   A. Repent and be baptized.
   B. Resolve to proclaim this gospel.

New Year's Day is a time for resolutions. We look back at the previous year to see what went well, and we look forward to the coming year and think about what might go differently. Of course, not everyone keeps these resolutions; simply compare the crowd at the gym at the beginning of January with the crowd in mid-February. Nevertheless, the desire for change can be a really good thing, even a necessary one. Matthew 3 talks about a change that needs to take place in the life of every individual, even if it's not on their resolution list.

John the Baptist came on the scene in Matthew 3 and introduced an entirely new day in redemptive history. As a part of this new day, he called people to start over in their lives. Matthew 3 also gives us a glimpse into the inauguration—the first day, so to speak—of Jesus' ministry on earth. Around 30 years pass between Matthew 2:23 and Matthew 3:1, so we miss almost all of Jesus' early childhood, His teen years, and His twenties. Matthew hones in on that which is critical for us to hear and believe.

The Ministry of John the Baptist: Prepare the Way
MATTHEW 3:1-17

In order to understand Matthew 3 and the beginning of Jesus' public ministry, we need to remember the context, including how the Old Testament ended. Just a few pages before Matthew's Gospel, in the last two verses of the Old Testament, the prophet Malachi predicted the following:

> *Remember the instruction of Moses My servant, the statutes and ordinances I commanded him at Horeb for all Israel. Look, I am going to send you Elijah the prophet before the great and awesome Day of the LORD comes. And he will turn the hearts of fathers to their children and the hearts of children to their fathers. Otherwise, I will come and strike the land with a curse.* (Mal 4:5-6)

God announced through Malachi that He would send Elijah the prophet to announce the fearsome Day of the Lord. This Elijah would turn people back to one another, but he would also bring a decree of destruction. After this prediction there were four hundred years of silence, and then John the Baptist came on the scene. John is a figure who is in many ways parallel to Elijah—a prophet calling the people back to God after a long drought. Consider Jesus' description of John the Baptist in Matthew 11:7-15:

> *What did you go out into the wilderness to see? A reed swaying in the wind? What then did you go out to see? A man dressed in soft clothes? Look, those who wear soft clothes are in kings' palaces. But what did you go out to see? A prophet? Yes, I tell you, and far more than a prophet. This is the one it is written about:*
> > *Look, I am sending My messenger ahead of You;*
> > *he will prepare Your way before You.*

I assure you: Among those born of women no one greater than John the Baptist has appeared, but the least in the kingdom of heaven is greater than he. From the days of John the Baptist until now, the kingdom of heaven has been suffering violence, and the violent have been seizing it by force. For all the prophets and the Law prophesied until John; if you're willing to accept it, he is the Elijah who is to come. Anyone who has ears should listen!

The Man

Jesus makes clear in these verses that Malachi was not prophesying a literal reappearance of Elijah, but rather the coming of a prophet just like Elijah who would prepare the way of the Lord. Matthew 3 tells us at least four things about the man John the Baptist. First, he would come **prophesying boldly**. Matthew quotes from Isaiah 40:3, where Isaiah told of a prophet who would come crying in the wilderness, "Prepare the way of the LORD in the wilderness." The imagery here in ancient times is of a herald who would come before a king, announcing the king's coming and making sure the road on which the king would travel was smooth and ready. John's first words in verse 2 speak to this preparation ministry: "Repent, because the kingdom of heaven has come near!" Clearly, this was no ordinary king.

Second, not only is John prophesying boldly, but he is also **living simply**. John was in the wilderness with a garment of camel's hair with a leather belt. This is how 2 Kings 1:8 describes Elijah, as a "hairy man with a leather belt around his waist." Matthew also tells us that John ate locusts and wild honey (3:4), so there was nothing elaborate or attractive about him at all.

Third, John was **baptizing openly**, which is where he gets the name "John the Baptist" or "John the Baptizer." From the beginning of the New Testament, the picture we have of baptism is of immersion in water. John was, after all, in a river that people came down into to be baptized. This word "baptize" literally means "to plunge" or "to dip" (BDAG, 164–65). So the prophet could even be called "John the Dipper."

Fourth, John came **serving humbly**. The prophet knew his role. Later, in verse 11, he says of Jesus the Messiah, "I am not worthy to remove His sandals." John didn't feel worthy to do one of the lowliest, most servile tasks imaginable in relation to his Lord. We hear John's heart most clearly summarized in John 3:30, where he says, "He must increase, but I must decrease." John the Baptist knew that his place in human history was not to point people to himself, but to prepare people for the King.

The Message

After considering the man, now we turn to the message. In order to prepare people for the King, John came preaching, "**Repent**, because the kingdom of heaven has come near!" (3:2) But what does it mean biblically to repent? In the Greek, this word "repent" *(metanoeo)* was sometimes used to describe a change of one's mind, but the biblical idea of repentance, the kind of repentance John was calling for here, involves much more than simply a change of thoughts. Biblically, **repentance involves confession (admission of sin)**. We read in verse 6 that people were coming out to the wilderness to be baptized by John, and they were confessing their sins. Throughout Scripture, God calls His people to take responsibility for their sins by confessing them. Simple recognition or admission of sin is useless.

In several different places in Scripture we read about people who merely acknowledged their sin but went no further. In Exodus 9:27 Pharaoh acknowledged his sin against the Lord before Moses and Aaron; in Joshua 7:20 Achan admitted his sin to Joshua; in 1 Samuel 15:24 an insincere Saul confessed to Samuel his sin of keeping back what the Lord had commanded him to destroy. The examples of Pharaoh, Achan, and Saul teach us that there's more to repentance than confession. Beyond mere confession, **repentance involves contrition (sorrow over sin)**. There must be a deep realization in your heart that you have sinned against God. It's the kind of sorrow we see in Psalm 51 as David, in contrite brokenness, cries out to God, saying, "Against You— You alone—I have sinned" (v. 4). This is not merely sorrow over getting caught, the kind of worldly sorrow Paul speaks about that is nothing more than selfish regret; rather, godly sorrow is deep realization that you have offended God, and this leads to godly repentance (2 Cor 7:10).

Biblical repentance means more than simply feeling bad about sin. Later in Matthew, we'll see the rich young ruler who walked away from Jesus was sorrowful but not repentant (19:16-22), for he didn't want to part with his possessions. And later we read that Judas was sorrowful for betraying Jesus, but he wasn't repentant (27:3-10). These examples lead us to a third aspect of biblical repentance: **Repentance involves a conversion (turn from sin)**. That's what this word "repent" means: to "be converted" (BDAG, 640). So yes, we must recognize our sin and be sorrowful for it, but we must also renounce it, or turn from it. We must do what Elijah commanded the people to do in 1 Kings 18 when he was surrounded by the prophets of Baal: "If Yahweh is God, follow Him. But if Baal, follow him" (v. 21). Next we learn why this kind of repentance is so urgent.

We must repent, John the Baptist tells us, **for the kingdom of heaven has come near**. This is the first of 32 times in the book of Matthew that we will see this phrase "kingdom of heaven." The other Gospel writers typically use the phrase "kingdom of God," which basically has the same meaning. The kingdom of heaven is the rule and reign of God, and it was breaking into the world in a new way in the ministry of Jesus.

With the arrival of this kingdom, two realities are crystal clear, one of which is this: **salvation is here**. When we put together the truths of the coming of the kingdom in Matthew 3:2 and the naming of Jesus in Matthew 1:21 ("He will save His people from their sins"), it's evident that God's salvation has come in the person of Jesus Christ. This is why God graciously warns us through John the Baptist to confess our sins—because the One who has come to save us from our sins is here. The proclamation that the kingdom of heaven is at hand is a great word of encouragement, but there is also a strong warning in these words, too, a warning that's reiterated throughout chapter 3.

The arrival of the kingdom means salvation is here, but it also means that **damnation is near**. This sobering reality becomes clear in verse 12, but even at the outset of John's announcement, the good news of God's kingdom was terrible news for all who refused to repent. The day of the coming of the Lord, prophesied throughout the Old Testament, was a day of blessing *and* judgment (Joel 2:1-2; Amos 5:18-20; Zeph 1:14-16). This is why John's message of repentance comes with such urgency.

The Method

We've seen the man and the message, and now finally we turn to the method of John the Baptist. The picture of baptism that we see in Matthew 3 is particularly instructive here, both **the baptism of Jews** and of Jesus. Baptism was not common in Old Testament history leading up to the time of John the Baptist. In fact, the only people who were baptized were Gentiles who decided to become followers of Yahweh. Baptism was a way of saying, "I am an outsider, renouncing my former ways, and embracing faith in the one true God, the God of Israel." Therefore, it is astonishing that people from Jerusalem and

Judea—*Jewish* people—came to be baptized. They were admitting that their Jewishness did not guarantee them a right standing before God. They realized that they needed to personally confess their sins and profess faith in God. Here, for the first time in Scripture, we begin to see the significance of baptism.

To be baptized is to **renounce your dependence on self** and to acknowledge that there is nothing inherent in you that can save you before God, including **your family heritage**. Ethnicity was extremely important to Jews, many of whom believed that simply being an Israelite meant that they were right before God. This kind of belief helps explain why John sternly confronts the Pharisees and Sadducees in verses 7-10. These two groups of Jewish leaders were on different pages in a number of ways, but they were on the same page in one central way: they both believed that their Jewish heritage made them right before God. However, when these groups came out to John's baptism, John referred to them as a "brood of vipers!" (v. 7), literally the offspring of snakes. He warns them in verse 9 not to presume that their status before God was safe simply because they could trace their lineage to Abraham. A refusal to repent will result in judgment, regardless of one's ethnicity. And this judgment is near, for John tells these religious leaders that "the ax is ready to strike the root of the trees!" (v. 10).

We continue to need to be reminded that our family heritage cannot save us. With all due respect to brothers and sisters from traditions where infant baptism is practiced, many of whom are close friends of mine, the New Testament picture of baptism indicates that Jesus is opposed to the idea that one is born into God's family by physical birth. It is dangerous and potentially damning for people to believe that because they were born into a Christian family, and maybe even baptized into a Christian family, their status before God is secure. This kind of thinking is rampant around the world, where "Christian" is a family or social identification. However, in Scripture baptism is not a sign that you have been born into a covenant family; instead, it's a sign indicating that regardless of what family you've been born into, you must personally repent, confess your sins, and put your faith in the Lord.[7]

---

[7] John's baptism looks forward to Christian baptism, though it is not identical with the baptism spoken of in the Great Commission (Matt 28:19) and throughout the rest of the New Testament following Jesus' death, resurrection, ascension, and the giving of the Spirit at Pentecost (Acts 2).

In baptism you not only renounce your family heritage; you renounce **your personal righteousness**. The Pharisees, in particular, were known for their extensive study and attentive keeping of the law. They based their lives on Jewish laws and traditions, working to attain righteousness before God. Yet, as we've already seen, baptism is an admission that you are not righteous and you need to renounce your sinful ways.

Baptism also means renouncing **your worldly success**. This applies especially to the Sadducees, who were known as rich landowners and beneficiaries of profits at the temple. They lived for present reward in this world, but baptism is a confession that we are living for future reward in the world to come.

Baptism is such a common symbol for many in the church today that if we're not careful, we'll miss some of the imagery here. This is a picture of death. Dipping (immersion) symbolizes a decisive, even violent, turn from yourself and your way of life, including any dependence on your heritage, your righteousness, or your success. Baptism indicates that you are going to **rely on the mercy of God**. It is a confession, a profession, that there's nothing you can do to save yourself from your sins; you need the Lord to do that. That's the good news John brought in verse 11: "I baptize you with water for repentance, but the One who is coming after me is more powerful than I. I am not worthy to remove His sandals. He Himself will baptize you with the Holy Spirit and fire." Baptism is a foretaste of a greater reality to come.

The good news, John says, is that **the Savior King is coming**. The One who will save you from your sins is coming, and He will baptize you with "the Holy Spirit and fire" (v. 11). This verse is potentially confusing on a couple of different levels, so a brief explanation may be helpful. First, when John talks about Jesus coming to baptize with the Holy Spirit, he isn't saying that water baptism won't be important once Jesus comes on the scene. We know that because Jesus tells His disciples at the end of Matthew's Gospel to go and baptize people in all nations (28:19), and that's exactly what we see the followers of Jesus doing in Acts (2:41; 8:12). Baptism with water would be an outward symbol of an inward reality, the inward reality of the baptism of the Spirit.

A second clarification may also be helpful here related to this baptism with the Spirit. The baptism of the Spirit is not a special baptism for a few select Christians that some associate with speaking in tongues; rather, baptism with the Spirit is a way of referring to Jesus' transforming work of putting His Spirit in us and changing our hearts from the

inside out. This baptism with the Spirit happens at the point of our salvation. John says that **Jesus will transform your hearts**. The Old Testament
prophesied about this new work of God, for Jeremiah tells us that God's
law would be written on the hearts of His people as a part of a new covenant (31:33). Ezekiel likewise speaks about God giving His people a
"new heart" and a "new spirit" (36:26), while Joel speaks of a day when
God would pour out His Spirit on all His people (2:28-29). Jesus will
transform your heart, John says, and **He will purify your lives**. That's
what it means when it says that Jesus will baptize with "fire" (Matt 3:11).
There's a debate about whether fire here refers to purification or the
judgment that Christ brings. In Acts 2:3 we see the Spirit coming on the
church in tongues of fire, so at least at that point purification is in view.
At other times in Scripture, fire is a picture of purification, refining, and
cleansing (Num 31:23; Zech 13:9; Mal 3:2-3).[8]

The coming of the Savior King wasn't all John announced. He also
warned people that **the Righteous Judge is close**. In verse 12 He said
of Jesus, "His winnowing shovel is in His hand, and He will clear His
threshing floor and gather His wheat into the barn. But the chaff He
will burn up with fire that never goes out." This imagery of winnowing
may not be familiar to us, but it refers to the process of separating *grain*,
the seeds, from *chaff*, the hulls that cover the seeds. A farmer would take
a winnowing shovel, toss both the grain and the chaff together into the
air, and the grain, which was heavier, would fall to the ground, while the
chaff would blow to the side. The farmer would then keep the grain,
and he'd sweep all the chaff together and throw it into a fire. This winnowing process is a vivid picture of the judgment of God. Jesus' ministry
means not only that God's salvation is near, but also that **His wrath is
imminent**.

When Jesus refers to the "fire that never goes out" (v. 12), He is
making clear that **His judgment is eternal**. This may sound severe,
but we must keep in mind that God is righteous, and He is wholly set
against sin. Some might think of John as the first "hellfire and damnation" preacher, but don't forget that John was also the first to preach
grace, mercy, and rescue in Jesus Christ. He announced to the people
that though they were condemned in their sin, destined to receive the
imminent wrath of God, there was a way out. The Savior King had come.

---

[8] In Matthew 3:12 Jesus speaks of fire in the context of God's judgment.

After Matthew describes John and his message in verses 1-12, the scene switches to Jesus' appearance in the wilderness in verses 13-17. We've moved from the baptism of the Jews to **the baptism of Jesus**, the very Son of God. We can actually see all three members of the Trinity involved in this baptism. First, **the Son obeys**, which requires some explanation given what we've already seen thus far about the meaning of baptism. Jesus had no need to renounce Himself and no sin to repent of; so why does He need to be baptized? That's exactly what John wondered, but Jesus responds in verse 15, "Allow it for now, because this is the way for us to fulfill all righteousness." There are many different opinions about what Jesus means here, but it seems that Jesus' baptism is the convergence of a variety of factors. We'll consider three of these factors.

First, Jesus' baptism is **an identification with sinners**. Jesus came, according to Isaiah 53:12, to be "counted among the rebels," and ultimately this has to do with their sin, though Jesus Himself had no sin (Heb 4:15). We identify with Jesus when we are baptized, being united to Him in His life, death, and resurrection, so it makes sense that baptism is in a very real sense His identification with us. **He who had no sin took His place among those who had no righteousness.** This is the essence of what Jesus came to do (see 2 Cor 5:21).

In addition to identifying *with* us, Jesus also sets an example *for* us. His baptism is **an example for saints**. Jesus models obedience for His followers by being baptized, which is an obedience that He will eventually command His followers to submit to (Matt 28:20). Jesus is validating here the central importance of baptism. **He begins His ministry by showing what would be central in our mission.** Baptism is not something that man has made up; it's something that God has commanded, something He has called every follower of Christ to do, and something He has told us to do in all nations (28:19). Jesus sets the stage for this at the beginning of His public ministry.

Finally, baptism is not only an identification with sinners and an example for saints, but it is also **a picture of salvation**. Baptism pictures death and resurrection to new life, such that here at the beginning of Jesus' ministry, we get a picture of the climax of this ministry. That is, **His immersion portrays His future death and resurrection.** And now, every person who trusts in Christ for salvation is baptized, immersed in water, as a picture of our dying to sin and to ourselves and rising to new life in Christ.

Having seen, then, that the Son obeys in baptism, we see next that
the Spirit anoints: "The heavens suddenly opened for Him, and He saw
the Spirit of God descending like a dove and coming down on Him"
(v. 16). Keep in mind, this was not the Spirit coming on Jesus for the
first time, as if the Spirit had never been on Him before; the Holy Spirit
was on Jesus even before He was born (Matt 1:18, 20). The picture in
Matthew 3 is a public display of exactly what Isaiah prophesied—that
the Spirit of the Lord would anoint the Messiah "to bring good news to
the poor . . . to heal the brokenhearted, to proclaim liberty to the captives and freedom to the prisoners" (Isa 61:1). So while the Spirit was
present with Jesus prior to Matthew 3, Jesus was set apart in a unique way
by the Spirit for His public ministry at His baptism.

The Son obeys, the Spirit anoints, and in verse 17 **the Father speaks**.
In this verse we get an unobstructed glimpse into the perspective of
the Father and the Son—what a scene! God says, "This is My beloved
Son. I take delight in Him!" This is a clear allusion to at least two passages. In Psalm 2 the Lord says, "You are My Son; today I have become
Your Father. Ask of Me, and I will make the nations Your inheritance
and the ends of the earth Your possession. You will break them with
a rod of iron" (vv. 7-9). Notice the word "Son" in both Psalm 2:7 and
Matthew 3:17. **Jesus is God's beloved Son**, gloriously crowned here as
the promised King from God. Similarly, in Isaiah 42:1, the introduction
to the Servants Songs in Isaiah, God says through the prophet, "This
is My Servant; I strengthen Him, this is My Chosen One; I delight in
Him." The word "delight" in that last phrase reflects the same idea in
Matthew 3:17, as the Father expresses His delight for the Son. Isaiah
prophesies that this Servant would be "pierced because of our transgressions, crushed because of our iniquities" (Isa 53:5). **Jesus is our
Suffering Servant**.

The Ministry of the Church Today: Tell the World

In many ways the ministry of John the Baptist was unique, but there are
also many ways in which the church's ministry today is similar to John's.
At least two ways in which we should imitate John's ministry are worth
highlighting.

First, we must tell people to **repent and be baptized**. This initial message of John's was repeated verbatim by Jesus in 4:17: "Repent, because
the kingdom of heaven has come near." Clearly, the message of John the
Baptist and of Jesus is the message of the Bible to every single person in

the world today. You must **turn from your sin**, which means renouncing dependence on yourself, your family heritage, your personal righteousness, and your worldly accomplishments. All of these things will burn up when it matters most, at the day of judgment.

Repentance is not simply turning from your sin; you must also **trust in the Son**. The beloved Son of God came to save you from your sin. As you trust in Him, you **rest in His righteousness**. Matthew 3:17 says that Jesus is God's beloved Son in whom He is well pleased, so unite your life to Jesus by faith. Then, when the Father looks on you, He will see His Son and be pleased in you. It is amazing to think that we are right before God, not by trusting in anything we have done, but simply by trusting in Christ, by resting in His righteousness. And as you rest in His righteousness, **bear the fruit of faith in Him**. This was John the Baptist's message to the Pharisees and Sadducees: "Therefore produce fruit consistent with repentance" (3:8). But what does it mean to bear the fruit of faith?

First, as a Christian, you should be baptized. I am always shocked to see how many followers of Christ have never been baptized. If that's you, don't wait another minute, because you are living in disobedience to Jesus Christ. And you're missing out on the joy of identification with the Christ, the King who died and rose from the grave for you. Though other kinds of public professions of faith have become common— raising hands, walking aisles, taking stands—baptism is *the* biblical, visible, public picture of saving identification with Christ.

Second, for those followers of Christ who have been baptized, live your lives as the overflow of faith in Him. The essence of following Christ, as initially displayed in baptism, is death to self and to every effort to improve yourself by obeying God in your own strength and resolve. Don't look to yourself; trust in Christ. Then ask Him to work in you so that you might trust Him more with every aspect of your life—your marriage, your family, your schedule, and your possessions. Ask Him to do things in and through you that you could never do on your own. That's what it means to bear "fruit consistent with repentance" (3:8).

After repenting and being baptized, the second overall application we can take from John's example is that we must **resolve to proclaim this gospel**. John's purpose on the pages of human history was to prepare the way for the coming of Christ. Everything he did was for that purpose. Obviously, we don't prepare the way for Christ's coming; instead, we tell the world that **God's Son has come**. We don't say, "He's coming," but "He's come!" This is good news: Jesus, the King, has come to save us from our sins. But there's bad news too. Just as John the Baptist warned of impending judgment, we must do the same. We must tell people that **God's judgment is coming**—imminent wrath and eternal punishment. You may think, "I can't tell somebody *that*," but in reality, there's nothing more unloving than *not* telling people that. Proclaim the good news to friends, coworkers, and everyone else you meet. Tell them about the Savior who has come.

Reflect and Discuss

1. Why is it significant that John's first command had to do with repentance?
2. What is the difference between regretful confession and true repentance?
3. How are some church attenders similar to the Jews who counted on family heritage for salvation?
4. How would you counsel someone who professes Christ but shows no marks of repentance?
5. How did the arrival of the kingdom point to the nearness of both salvation and damnation?
6. How would you explain to a non-Christian that a "hellfire and damnation" sermon expresses love?
7. Explain why John's baptism and Christian baptism appear to exclude infants.
8. How are all three members of the Trinity present in Matthew 3:15-17?
9. Why was Jesus baptized if He had no sin?
10. What is the difference between resolving to be good before salvation and resolving to obey God after salvation?

Triumph through Temptation

MATTHEW 4:1-11

Main Idea: As the sinless Son of God, Jesus' victory over temptation by relying on God the Father provides the basis and pattern for our own victory over sin and Satan.

I. **Six Realities**
   A. There is a spiritual world.
   B. We are involved in a spiritual war.
   C. Our enemy in this spiritual war is formidable.
   D. The stakes in this spiritual war are eternal.
   E. The scope of this spiritual war is universal.
   F. Our involvement in this spiritual war is personal.

II. **Two Pictures**
   A. Jesus is the new Man, stepping into the universal human story.
   B. Jesus is the true Son, suffering through the particular Israelite story.

III. **Two Questions**
   A. Does God tempt us?
      1. We are tempted by Satan (who is subordinate) for evil.
      2. We are tested by God (who is sovereign) for good.
   B. Could Jesus have sinned?
      1. Jesus is fully man.
      2. Jesus was fully tempted.
      3. Jesus is fully God.
      4. God cannot be tempted.

IV. **Three Temptations**
   A. The first temptation: self-gratification
      1. We are tempted to fulfill our wants apart from God's will.
      2. Jesus trusted the all-satisfying, all-sufficient goodness of the Father.
   B. The second temptation: self-protection
      1. We are tempted to question God's presence and manipulate God's promises.
      2. Jesus rested in the shelter of the Father's unshakeable security.

C. The third temptation: self-exaltation
1. We are tempted to assert ourselves in the world while we rob God of His worship.
2. Jesus refused to exchange the end-time exaltation by the Father for a right-now exaltation of a snake.

V. Three Conclusions
A. Christ will be crowned as King.
B. Satan will be cast down in defeat.
C. The church will rise up in victory.

Triumph through Temptation
MATTHEW 4:1-11

The temptation of Jesus in Matthew 4 is a familiar passage for many Christians. We may even be able to recite the three temptations Satan set before our Lord, along with Christ's responses. Yet, if we're not careful, there's a danger that we'll miss the meaning of this well-known story, a meaning that is crucial in our own battle against sin. We need to see the close tie between the temptations Jesus faced and the spiritual battles that all of us face.

Six Realities

As we consider the temptation of Jesus in Matthew 4:1-11, we'll begin by acknowledging six realities. These are really basic reminders that will help us wrap our minds around what is happening in this passage.

There is a spiritual world.

First, there is a spiritual world. When we see the Devil tempting Jesus, we don't know exactly how this actually played out, whether in some kind of physical form or just a spiritual form. We don't have all the answers, but what we do know is that the Devil is real, and he is active. And we know that there is an invisible, spiritual world that is just as real as the visible, natural world. Scripture teaches that there are vast numbers of angels, both good and bad, and that these spirits exist all around us. There are glorious beings that would take our breath away at this moment if we saw them, and there are evil beings that would horrify us if they were to appear before our eyes. We need to feel the weight of these supernatural realties.

We are involved in a spiritual war.

Second, followers of Christ need to be reminded that we are involved in a spiritual war. A battle is continually raging, and this battle is between conflicting kingdoms. The kingdom of Christ and the kingdom of Satan—a kingdom of light and a kingdom of darkness—are warring against one another. All of history is a story of spiritual warfare. This war begins with the first man and the first woman in Genesis 3, where the enemy, Satan, tempts man to sin and leads him into spiritual darkness and ultimate death. From that moment, the world and all its inhabitants are darkened with sin, under the rule of the prince of this world (Eph 2:1-3). Yet, just a few chapters later, God takes a people for Himself from the midst of the darkness to display His light, but even then His own people cannot overcome the darkness on their own. Abraham, a friend of God, lied about his wife (Gen 12:10-20; 20:1-18). Jacob, loved by God, deceitfully schemed to get God's blessing (Gen 25:29-34; 27:1-29). Moses, the prophet of God, was filled with pride (Num 20:10-13). David, a king after God's own heart, had an affair and committed murder (2 Sam 11). Over and over again in history, men and women have fallen prey to the evil one and experienced the punishment of sin, which is death (Rom 3:23; 6:23).

For every one of us, these conflicting kingdoms of Christ and Satan create a continual struggle. In actuality, this continual struggle is not just between Christians and demons, but between all people and demons, which brings us face-to-face with two realities. First, the Devil is not omnipresent like God is. So when you are being tempted, remember that Satan is only a creature, and although he is behind every temptation to do evil, our battle is not only against him, but against what Paul calls "the rulers . . . the authorities . . . the world powers of this darkness . . . the spiritual forces of evil in the heavens" (Eph 6:12). These powers Paul refers to are demons.

The second reality we need to come to terms with is the fact that temptation for the Christian is not simply about us and our own little kingdoms; it's about an all-out attack of the Devil and all his demons on the kingdom of Christ and every single person who associates with Christ. In attacking Christians, demons are attacking Christ. So trusting in Christ for salvation doesn't end the believer's battle against temptation. If anything, it takes the battle up a notch. The kingdom of darkness that sought to destroy the Messiah is absolutely committed to devouring the Messiah's followers. Therefore, when we talk about temptation, we're not simply talking about some psychological battle; we're talking about an intense spiritual war against cosmic powers of darkness who are dead set on destroying the kingdom of Christ and the children of God.

In addition to remembering these first two foundational realities—that there is a spiritual world, and we are involved in it—there are four more realities that we must keep in mind.

Our enemy in this spiritual war is formidable.

He is a lion looking to devour (1 Pet 5:8).

The stakes in this spiritual war are eternal.

Heaven and hell hang in the balance with this war.

The scope of this spiritual war is universal.

It is being waged in every nation, among every people, in every language, and in every individual life on the planet.

Our involvement in this spiritual war is personal.

Each one of us is involved in this battle in specific ways. There is a grand, over-arching realm in which this spiritual war is being waged, but there is also a specific, pointed way in which this battle is being fought right now where you are. You are being tempted right now, even if you don't realize it. Russell Moore stresses this point in his book, *Tempted and Tried,* an extremely helpful book on the topic of temptation (Moore, *Tempted and Tried,* 26).[9] Moore explains why we might be on the verge of wrecking our lives, especially if we don't know it. He uses the illustration of cows being led to the slaughter to make the point.

For a long time, cattle workers would forcefully push and prod cows into the slaughterhouse. For good reason, the cows would resist, and the whole operation would be extremely difficult to carry out. That's until one particular scientist came along and pointed out that the most efficient way to slaughter cows is to make them feel "contented and comfortable" as they enter into the slaughterhouse. In other words, keep the

---

[9] Moore's book was immensely helpful to me in my study of this text, and his observations, illustration, and application inform much of this section. I highly recommend this book for further study.

scenery the same as it is in the most peaceful moments of the cow's life. Moore continues,

> In this system the cows aren't prodded off the truck but are led, in silence, onto a ramp. They go through a "squeeze chute," a gentle pressure device that mimics a mother's nuzzling touch. The cattle continue down the ramp onto a smoothly curving path. There are no sudden turns. The cows experience the sensation of going home, the same kind of way they've traveled so many times before.
>
> As they mosey along the path, they don't even notice when their hooves are no longer touching the ground. A conveyor belt slowly lifts them gently upward, and then, in the twinkling of an eye, a blunt instrument levels a surgical strike right between their eyes. They're transitioned from livestock to meat and they're never aware enough to be alarmed by any of it.

Like the cattle in Moore's illustration, we too can be lulled into thinking that everything is all right, even as danger is approaching. Oh how we need to be aware of the forces that are afoot right now, working to lure us into places that we do not want to go! To repeat Russell Moore's warning, we *are* on the verge of wrecking our lives, *especially* if we don't know it.

I feel this temptation continually in my own life. At every point, I am prone to sin. My mind is susceptible to wandering, and I am tempted to think unmentionable thoughts when I see an attractive woman who is not my wife. My heart is bent toward pride, and I am tempted to compete with other pastors over who is more spiritual and more successful. I am tempted to cut moral corners in order to gain personal advantage over others. I am prone to pretense and hypocrisy, tempted to lie to make myself look better, and to call people to do what I am not willing to do myself. I am prone to value appearance over authenticity, my wants over other people's needs, and I am prone to desire the glory that is due God alone. I am keenly, if not frighteningly, aware that one wrong look, one inappropriate meeting, one rash decision, one fleeting moment could wreak spiritual havoc on my life, my family, and my church. I have the potential of bringing untold disgrace on my God.

My involvement in spiritual warfare is personal, and the same holds true for every follower of Christ. The battles may look different as they play out in other people's lives, but don't be fooled: the war is real, and the evil one is persistently plotting to subtly entice you with sin and ultimately to bring destruction upon your soul. So don't be caught unaware.

We are a part of a human race wherein every man and every woman has succumbed to sin, and thus every man and every woman has experienced death, except one. And that's the good news of Matthew 4:1-11. A new Man has come, a Man over whom Satan could gain no control. His name is Jesus, and Matthew gives us two pictures of Him.

Two Pictures

Jesus is the new Man.

First, Matthew shows us that **Jesus is the new Man, stepping into the universal human story**. There are deliberate parallels here between Jesus in the wilderness in Matthew 4 and Adam and Eve in the garden in Genesis 3. It's no coincidence that both Adam and Jesus are initially tempted to eat food apart from the Father's will. For Adam, it was fruit from a tree. For Jesus, it was stones becoming bread. And in both situations, the temptation begins by questioning God. For Adam, the serpent questions God's word, asking, "Did God really say . . . ?" (Gen 3:1). For Jesus, the serpent calls into question Christ's sonship, saying in effect, "If you are really the Son of God, why are you hungry like this?" (cf. Matt 4:3). Jesus steps into the same story that Adam stepped into, but Jesus is able to stand where Adam fell. Jesus is a new Man, unlike Adam and unlike all of us in the universal human story who have succumbed to sin.

Jesus is the true Son.

He is not only the new Man, but **Jesus is the true Son, suffering through the particular Israelite story**. There are some parallels between Matthew 4 and Genesis 3, but there are even more parallels between Jesus' temptation and the testing of God's people before they entered into the promised land in the Old Testament. When God commanded Pharaoh to let His people go, God told Moses, "Then you will say to Pharaoh: This is what Yahweh says: Israel is My firstborn son. I told you: Let My son go so that he may worship Me" (Exod 4:22-23). Notice that God refers to Israel as His son. Son language was also used in Matthew 2:15, where Matthew quoted from Hosea 11:1, saying, "Out of Egypt I called My Son." Both Israel and Jesus were tested in the wilderness; God's son, Israel, was tested for 40 years, while God's Son, Jesus, was tested for 40 days. It's fitting, then, that Jesus uses Scripture every time He wards off temptation, and the passages He uses are from Deuteronomy 8:3; 6:16; and 6:13—all passages related to Israel's wandering through the wilderness those 40 years. One last parallel is worth pointing out: right before they were tested, God delivered the people of Israel through the waters of the Red Sea, so that Paul is able to call this Israel's baptism (1 Cor 10:2). Then in the New Testament, right before Jesus' testing, we see His baptism in the Jordan by John the Baptist (Matt 3:16).

These parallels concerning Jesus' sonship are the key to understanding His temptations. Notice how the first two temptations begin with Satan saying, "If You are the Son of God" (Matt 4:3, 6), a clear reference back to Matthew 3:17, where God said of Jesus, "This is My beloved Son. I take delight in Him!" At the core, temptation to sin is an assault on sonship. Just as the Devil was trying to attack the relationship between the Father and the Son in the wilderness temptations, so the temptations you and I face today are really attacks on what it means to relate to God as Father. The Israelites' sin in the wilderness began when they started saying in effect, "Are we really the sons of God? We don't have bread or water! Is He really our Father?" That's exactly how Satan attacked Jesus in Matthew 4, and it's where he'll attack you today, Christian. He did it in the garden of Eden, tempting Adam and Eve to see God not as their Father, but as their rival. Every sin that we commit is tantamount to a rejection of God as our Father, as the One who knows what is best for us and is committed to providing it for us. How crucial it is, then, for us to see that Jesus is the true Man and the true Son.

Two Questions

When we consider Jesus' temptation in Scripture, there are two questions that often arise.

Does God tempt us?

Matthew 4:1 says that Jesus was led "by the Spirit" to be tempted by the Devil in the wilderness. But in what sense did the Spirit lead Jesus to be tempted? Did the Spirit of God tempt Jesus? The clear answer from Scripture is, "No." God never tempts us in the sense of enticing us to evil. James 1:13 says, "No one undergoing a trial should say, 'I am being tempted by God.'" Instead, Satan is seen in Scripture as "the tempter" (Matt 4:3). Therefore, we can say that **we are tempted by Satan (who is**

subordinate) for evil. Only the Devil and demons tempt us to evil, but even their tempting, though directly attributable to them, is ultimately under the sovereign control of God. *Nothing* happens in the universe apart from the sovereignty of God.

There is a flip side to Satan's temptations in Matthew 4: **We are tested by God (who is sovereign) for good.** If we put the two points together we can say that temptation by the Devil (who is subordinate) toward evil is ultimately a part of a testing by God (who is sovereign) for good. The book of Job teaches us that Satan is on a leash; he can do nothing that God does not allow him to do. Now to be sure, when Satan tempts, he intends it for evil, but God uses these temptations to refine His children and to teach them His faithfulness (Jas 1:2; 1 Pet 1:6-7). The apostle Paul experienced this when God gave him a "thorn in the flesh . . . a messenger of Satan" to torment him (2 Cor 12:7). The purpose of the trial was so that Paul would know the strength and sufficiency of Christ (2 Cor 12:9-10). Consider also Joseph in the Old Testament, who was sold into slavery and tempted in a number of ways. God used these trials to bring about good—for Joseph *and* for his brothers who sold him into slavery (Gen 50:20).

We can say definitively that God was not tempting Jesus, nor was He tempting Adam, Joseph, Israel, or Paul, toward evil. For that matter, He will never tempt you toward evil. Instead, in His sovereignty, God uses even Satan's temptations to evil in order to bring about good in your life (Rom 8:28).

Could Jesus have sinned?

The answer to the second question this passage raises is no . . . and yes. Pointing out four truths from Scripture may help explain the complex answer to this question. First, **Jesus is fully man.** He was and is fully human, as human as you and me. Second, **Jesus was fully tempted.** The Bible says He was tempted as we are (Heb 4:15), that is, He was tempted with things that are common to man (1 Cor 10:13). Now you may read these temptations in Matthew and think, "I'm not tempted in these ways." If you're honest, these temptations may even seem quite trivial; however, these temptations Jesus faced are at the core of every temptation that you and I face. There are no new temptations—just new ways of succumbing to old temptations.

The third truth we must keep in mind as we think about whether or not Jesus could have sinned is that **Jesus is fully God.** This is a truth we've already seen in Matthew, and one that will continue to unfold in the chapters ahead. Let it suffice to say, the One who is called Immanuel, "God is with us" (Matt 1:23), is more than just a man. Fourth, keep in mind that **God cannot be tempted**. James 1:13 says explicitly, "God is not tempted by evil." So here are the four truths that we must affirm: Jesus is fully man, Jesus was fully tempted, Jesus is fully God, and God cannot be tempted. The difficulty comes when you try to figure out precisely how these truths work together, which leads us back to the mystery of the Incarnation.

In an earlier chapter we saw that Jesus' human nature and divine nature are different, yet unified, leading to some wonderful mysteries.[10] As a picture of His humanity, Jesus was asleep on a boat in the middle of a storm (8:23). Then, as a demonstration of His deity, He stood up and calmed the wind and the waves (v. 26). He was (and is) fully human and fully God. So, in His humanity, Jesus was tempted as we are. Yet, in His deity He was not tempted, for God *cannot* be tempted (Jas 1:13). These are mind-boggling realities, for which an illustration from Russell Moore may help.[11]

Think of the person in this world that you love the most. Picture their face, and then ask yourself, "Could I murder that person?" Immediately you're thinking, "Absolutely not!" And in that response, what you're thinking is, "I don't have the *moral* capability of murdering that person." But if you understood my question, "Could you murder that person?" in terms of *physically* performing an action, though it's unfathomable to you, it would be *physically* possible. Even so, Jesus, in His deity, as the light of the world in whom there is no darkness, could not have sinned. He is *morally* incapable of such an action. Yet at the same time, Jesus could have sinned in the sense that He was *physically* capable of eating bread or throwing Himself off a temple or bowing the knee to Satan. In this way, Jesus was fully tempted as we are (Heb 4:15).

Three Temptations
MATTHEW 4:1-11

Having looked at some difficult questions related to Jesus' temptations, we now turn to the temptations themselves. When we look under the

---

[10] See the chapter on Matthew 1:18-23 for more on how to relate Jesus' humanity and His deity.

[11] This illustration is adapted from Russell Moore, *Tempted and Tried*, 43–44.

surface of each of these temptations to see their core, we will see that we are tempted in exactly the same ways. And most importantly, we will see how Jesus conquered each temptation on our behalf.

Self-Gratification

In verse 3 we see the first temptation: self-gratification. After 40 days of fasting, the Bible says Jesus was hungry. This seems like an understatement from Matthew. The Devil tempts Jesus to turn stones into bread as proof that He is the Son of God. He is sowing doubt by asking, "If You are the Son of God, the beloved of God, then why are You out here in the wilderness starving? You desire food. Is Your Father not providing and caring for You? Satisfy Your desires now." It's not difficult to see the self-gratification that every one of us craves in the depths of our own hearts.

We are tempted to fulfill our wants apart from God's will. All of us have desires that God has built into us, desires that are good—needs in our bodies and cravings in our souls. But God has also created us to look to Him as a good Father who satisfies those desires. That was the point of the garden of Eden, wasn't it? Satan suggested to Adam and Eve that God was withholding good from them, so they decided to fulfill their desire apart from God's will. That's when sin entered the world (Rom 5:12). It's the same story behind God's testing of Israel in the wilderness. In Deuteronomy 8:2-3, the passage that Jesus quotes from during His temptation, we read the following:

> *Remember that the LORD your God led you on the entire journey these 40 years in the wilderness, so that He might humble you and test you to know what was in your heart, whether or not you would keep His commands. He humbled you by letting you go hungry; then He gave you manna to eat, which you and your fathers had not known, so that you might learn that man does not live on bread alone but on every word that comes from the mouth of the LORD.*

This was a testing of the heart to see if the Israelites would trust the goodness of God to fulfill their desires according to His word and the counsel of His will. This same kind of testing accompanies every temptation in our lives. We have desires that are good and God-given, desires for food, water, sleep, sex, relationships, companionship, etc. This is the place where Satan works—at the level of our wants. You desire food, and he tempts you toward undisciplined overeating. You desire sleep, and he tempts you toward apathy and laziness. You desire sex, and he tempts you toward such sins as lust, pornography, adultery, and homosexuality. And at the core is a desire for self-gratification that says, "God is not providing for me in the way I want, so I will seek my own gratification apart from Him." Satan tempts you to fulfill God-given wants apart from God's will.

The Enemy is so deadly in the way he attacks our desires. He has convinced many followers of Christ that their desires for sin define who they are. But that is not true. Christian, you are a child of God. And just because you are His child does not mean that you will never want something that doesn't accord with God's will. You will fight with some temptations for 40 days, or in some cases 40 years; you may even have to battle your entire life. So how do you win, day after day, year after year? You do what Jesus did.

When He was hungry, **Jesus trusted the all-satisfying, all-sufficient goodness of the Father**. Don't tell God when and how your desires should be fulfilled; trust God to fulfill your desires in His way according to His Word. Trust that God your Father is good, and realize that any attempt to satisfy your wants apart from His will ultimately leads not to delight, but to destruction. As soon as Adam and Eve had eaten the fruit, they realized what they had done, and everything—around them, within them, and between them—changed for the worse. What they thought would lead to delight led to destruction.

We see foolish and deadly decisions similar to those made by Adam and Eve throughout Scripture. In Genesis 25:29-34 we read that Esau was so hungry that he sold his birthright for a bowl of soup. After filling his belly he realized the foolishness of his decision (see Heb 12:16-17). Or consider Judas, who betrayed Jesus for 30 pieces of silver. He got the money he wanted, and that money eventually led to his death (Matt 27:3-10). What Esau and Judas thought would lead to delight led to their destruction. Mark it down: The bread of demons always destroys. The will and Word of the Lord, on the other hand, always satisfy. So trust the goodness of the Father. Jesus did, and by the end of Matthew 4 Jesus' desire for food was supernaturally fulfilled.

Self-Protection

After looking at the temptation of self-gratification, we move next to the second temptation: self-protection. This temptation is probably the most difficult to understand because we struggle to see what is so enticing about the possibility of Jesus jumping off a tower. But this was no normal tower; this was the top of the temple, the place that was intended to be a visible demonstration of God's presence and protection among His people. Satan quotes from Psalm 91, a song about God's protection, and he tempts Jesus to prove that God will be faithful to Him as His Son: "If You are the Son of God, throw Yourself down" (v. 6). Once again, Jesus' reply helps us understand the core of the temptation here. He quotes from Deuteronomy 6:16, where Israel received the following command: "Do not test the LORD your God as you tested Him at Massah."

The reference to Massah in Deuteronomy 6:16 takes us back to Exodus 17, where the people of God put God to the test by demanding that He provide them more water. They asked, "Is the LORD among us or not?" (Exod 17:7). Their questioning proved a lack of trust in God. They didn't trust His presence with them or His protection of them. The same thing can often be said of us. Just as Israel was tempted in the Old Testament, and Jesus was tempted in the New Testament, **we are tempted to question God's presence and manipulate God's promises**. Jesus was tempted to put God to the test by manipulating Psalm 91 into forcing the Father to prove His [Jesus'] sonship by miraculously delivering Him. This would be tantamount to asking God for proof of His presence and protection. But that kind of callous experimentation with God is a clear example of a lack of trust, and it shows up in all kinds of ways in our lives.

We are tempted to twist God's Word around our personal preferences. We are tempted to question His plans for us when they don't go the way we would like. We are tempted to doubt His love for us when something goes wrong. We are tempted to ask for signs that He is still with us even though He has shown His faithfulness to us over and over and over again. We are tempted to complain to Him about the circumstances of our lives, boldly thinking (if not saying) just like the Israelites did, "God, are You with me or not?" So how did Jesus react to such temptation?

Jesus rested in the shelter of the Father's unshakeable security. Jesus knew He had no reason to test the Father. It's no wonder, therefore, that Jesus' message to us repeatedly in the book of Matthew is, "Don't worry" (6:25, 31). In the Sermon on the Mount, which starts in the next chapter, Jesus points to the Father's care for the flowers of the field and the birds of the air as evidence that His children need not worry (6:26-30). If God cares for plants and animals, He will surely provide for His children.

I love spending time with my kids, and I would do anything to protect them and care for them. Yet, according to what Jesus says in Luke 11:13, I am an evil father. That is, even with my good intentions and the kindness I show to my kids, I am a sinner who fails repeatedly to do what is right. Consider that God is a good Father, and *everything* He does in our lives is good. How much more, then, can we trust Him? Like Jesus, we can rest in the shelter of the Father's unshakeable security.

Self-Exaltation

Having looked at the temptations of self-gratification (4:3-4) and self-protection (4:5-6), consider now the third temptation: self-exaltation. In verses 8-9 Jesus is taken to a very high mountain, either a physical mountain or at the very least a very high vision, and He is shown all the kingdoms of the world and their splendor (France, *The Gospel of Matthew*, 134).[12] You may be wondering why this would be such a great temptation if Jesus already knew these kingdoms would be His. But remember, Jesus also knows that the road ahead leading to such authority is filled with sorrow, suffering, and ultimately a violent death. He was tempted to try and seize God's reward right then, apart from the path of pain. "You're a Son," the Devil said, "so why be a Servant? You're a King, so why be crucified? Take them now; they're yours."

That's precisely what Satan whispers in our ears today. He points to all the things of this world—the successes, the accomplishments, the pleasures, and the possessions—and he says, "Get them now." He promised Adam and Eve that they would be like God if they ate the fruit, and they believed him. They ascribed worth to Satan instead of worth to God.

We are tempted to do the same thing that Adam and Eve did. **We are tempted to assert ourselves in the world while we rob God of His worship.** Instead of a simple, humble, difficult obedience to God in this world, in our pride we seek to attain what we want in the way we want to do it. This pride is at the root of all our rebellion. We all struggle with pride, wherein we bow the knee to the prince of this world and seek to dethrone the one true God who alone is worthy of all worship. Once again, we need to see how Jesus resisted this temptation.

---

[12] France points to passages such as Deut 34:1-4 and Gen 13:14-17 as other places in Scripture where a mountain serves as a place to view "promised territory" (p. 134). France does not think the passage demands a literal mountain.

I'll quote directly from Russell Moore again, as I can't improve on his words: **Jesus refused to exchange the end-time exaltation by the Father for a right-now exaltation of a snake** (Moore, *Tempted and Tried*, 131). Jesus, the beloved Son, knew that the supreme duty of everyone and everything is to worship God, and He knew that everyone who humbles himself before God will be exalted (Matt 23:12). Jesus chose to live a life of suffering obedience to the Father instead of sinful submission to Satan, and in the end, all authority in heaven and on earth was given to Him (Matt 28:18).

Three Conclusions

Christ will be crowned as King.

The temptations Matthew records for us in this chapter are directly relevant to the battles we face every day. Self-gratification, self-protection, and self-exaltation are always trying to allure us. And we'll continue to face these battles until the day when finally and eternally Christ will be crowned as King. Two thousand years ago He conquered sin as our Savior. Each of these wilderness temptations is ultimately connected to the cross. This bout in the wilderness was just a picture of the temptation Christ would endure on the way to Calvary. The crowds taunted Him, "If You are the Son of God, come down from the cross!" (Matt 27:40). Jesus knew that He had authority to call down 12 legions of angels to save Him from the cross (Matt 26:53), yet He refused to bow the knee to Satan's temptations. In worship, He cried out, "Father, glorify Your name" (John 12:28), and then in obedience, He walked the hard Calvary Road on your behalf and mine. He died for sinners and rose again, conquering sin as our Savior. And His work on our behalf is ongoing.

Jesus now sits at the right hand of the Father in heaven where today He fights alongside us and for us through His Spirit. To use Paul's words, "We are counted as sheep to be slaughtered," yet "we are more than victorious through Him who loved us" (Rom 8:36-37). Paul puts it beautifully in Romans 8:31-34:

> *If God is for us, who is against us? He did not even spare His own Son but offered Him up for us all; how will He not also with Him grant us everything? Who can bring an accusation against God's elect? God is the One who justifies. Who is the one who condemns?*

Christ Jesus is the One who died, but even more, has been raised; He also is at the right hand of God and intercedes for us.

God has given us His Spirit, the same Spirit who led Jesus not only *into* the wilderness, but also *through* the wilderness unscathed. This same Spirit is alive in you! You cannot triumph over temptation, but Christ can. And Christ is in you, the hope of glory (Col 1:27).

We must consider the danger we are in as a part of this cosmic and very personal spiritual war. But we also need to see how empowered we are to resist the Devil, and when we do resist him, he will flee from us (Jas 4:7). There is a way of escape, Paul tells us in 1 Corinthians 10:13, and it is Christ. Therefore, live in Him until one day He will reign over all as our Sovereign.

Satan will be cast down in defeat.

On that last day, Jesus will once and for all assert His authority over all creation, and when He does, Satan will be cast down in defeat. Be assured that the accuser will be arraigned, the serpent will be sentenced, and the Devil will be destroyed. Revelation 20:10 says, "The Devil who deceived them was thrown into the lake of fire and sulfur where the beast and the false prophet are, and they will be tormented day and night forever and ever." Christ will be crowned as King. Satan will be cast down in defeat. So what about the church?

The church will rise up in victory.

God's Word makes clear that on the last day the church will rise up in victory. That's right, victory is assured. For all sons and daughters of God, it may be wartime now, but peacetime is coming. As children of God in Christ, let's trust the all-satisfying, all-sufficient goodness of our Father! Let His supreme love be the satisfaction of your soul. Trust Him—His Word, His will—for He knows what is best for you. He is not your rival; He is your Father. In light of this, as children of God in Christ, let's rest in the shelter of our Father's unshakeable security! We have no reason to fear, worry, doubt, or question God. We shouldn't complain or in any way be concerned about the Father's presence, power, and protection for us. Christ has secured all of these things for His people, so that we can now rest in Him.

All of this leads to the final encouragement: As children of God in Christ, let's refuse to exchange our end-time exaltation by the Father for a right-now exaltation of a snake (Moore, *Tempted and Tried*, 131)! You may ask, "What do you mean by our end-time exaltation?" Remember that there is coming a day when we will receive the ultimate reward of our salvation as we reign with Christ in His kingdom.

Reflect and Discuss

1. What images come to mind when you hear about demons and spiritual warfare? Are these thoughts biblical? If not, explain why.
2. List some things that distract us from seeing the spiritual battles all around us. What are some specific ways we can battle our ignorance and apathy toward spiritual warfare?
3. Which sins are especially prevalent in our culture today?
4. Explain how Jesus' triumph through temptation is both our example and the basis for our own victory in temptation. What is the danger if we only see Jesus as our example?
5. How would you answer the following question: "If Jesus was fully God, then how can His victory over temptation help a weak and sinful person like me?"
6. Of Satan's three temptations in this passage, which one do you struggle with the most? What promise from Scripture might help you battle that temptation?
7. Explain the following statement: Jesus triumphed where Adam and Israel failed.
8. What attributes of God strengthen you during temptation?
9. How do Satan's temptations seek to undermine the purpose of the cross?
10. How does the promise of eternal life and the believer's future reign with Christ affect your everyday battle with sin?

Two Simple Words

MATTHEW 4:12-25

Main Idea: Obeying Jesus' command to 'Follow Me' means that we must know who He is, and we must be willing to renounce everything for His glory.

I. **Me**
   A. Matthew 1
      1. Jesus is the Savior, the Messiah, the son of David, and the son of Abraham.
      2. He is fully human and fully divine.
   B. Matthew 2
      1. Jesus is the Sovereign over the wise and the Shepherd of the weak.
      2. He inaugurates the new exodus, ends the mournful exile, and loves His fiercest enemies.
   C. Matthew 3
      1. He is the Savior King and Righteous Judge.
      2. He is filled with the Spirit and loved by the Father.
   D. Matthew 4
      1. He is the new Adam and the true Israel.
      2. He is the light of the world and the hope for all people.
   E. Conclusion
      1. Jesus is worthy of far more than church attendance and casual association.
      2. He is worthy of total abandonment and supreme adoration.

II. **Follow**
   A. Live with radical abandonment for His glory.
      1. We leave behind all things.
      2. We live for one thing: to honor the King.
   B. Live with joyful dependence on His grace.
      1. He takes the initiative to choose us.
      2. He provides the power to use us.
      3. He gets the glory through us.
   C. Live with faithful adherence to His person.

      1. We are not casual listeners.
      2. We are not convinced listeners.
      3. We are committed learners and followers.
  D. Live with total trust in His authority.
      1. He is the Master of every domain in our lives.
      2. He is the Lord of every detail in our lives.
  E. Live with urgent obedience to His mission.
      1. Every follower of Jesus is a fisher of men.
      2. Every disciple is a disciple-maker.
      3. This is an unconventional plan that demands a universal response.

III. Will You Follow Jesus?
  A. Consider the cost of discipleship.
  B. Consider the cost of non-discipleship.

Two Simple Words
MATTHEW 4:12-25

Two simple words: Follow Me. This is the life-changing call of Jesus in Matthew 4:12-25. This passage helps us see what it means to follow Jesus at the most basic level. In response to this passage, we should be asking ourselves the question, "Am *I* following Him?" No more important question can be asked.

Me

Many people are familiar with Jesus' command to "Follow Me" in verse 19. The command is not complicated, but what do those two words actually mean? It will help to consider these words in reverse order, so that we first get a grasp of the "Me" we're called to follow.

This is where it may be helpful to quickly review the first four chapters of Matthew, because this Gospel has already given us a stunning and majestic picture of Jesus from a number of different angles. Consider what we've already seen.

Matthew 1

The first verse of Matthew's Gospel speaks of "the historical record of Jesus Christ, the Son of David, the Son of Abraham." From the very beginning Matthew makes clear that **Jesus is the Savior**, which is actually what

His name means. Jesus is also **the Messiah**, which is signified by the title "Christ." Christ is not simply Jesus' last name; rather, it designates Him as the Anointed One. Matthew also points out that Jesus is **the Son of David**, born into Israel's kingly line. Then, at the end of verse 1, Jesus is called **the Son of Abraham**, the father of the people of Israel. Matthew's genealogy helps us see that the whole Old Testament points to Jesus Christ. That's a theologically loaded first verse! In the second half of chapter 1, we considered the mystery of Christ's incarnation. **He is fully human and fully divine.** Jesus was born of the Spirit through a woman, something no other man can claim. The Incarnation is a miracle and a mystery. Jesus Christ is Immanuel, literally "God is with us" (1:23).

Matthew 2

In the second chapter Matthew shows us that **Jesus is the Sovereign over the wise and the Shepherd of the weak**. Wise men came looking for a King, a Sovereign, and they bowed before the child Jesus. Matthew quotes from Micah 5:2, where Jesus is prophesied as the "ruler" who would shepherd God's people. Using other Old Testament quotations, Matthew shows that Jesus **inaugurates the new exodus** (2:15 citing Hos 11:1) as God brings His Son out of Egypt, and He **ends the mournful exile** (2:18 citing Jer 31:15) by bringing hope to God's beleaguered people. Jesus also **loves His fiercest enemies**. The Son of God came for the despised and the destitute, even those committed to destroying Him.

Matthew 3

Jesus was proclaimed by John the Baptist, and John announced that **He is the Savior King and Righteous Judge**. "Repent," John said, "because the kingdom of heaven has come near!" (v. 2). In other words, the King is here and the King is coming to save all who will trust in Him. Yet, this will also bring judgment: "His winnowing shovel is in His hand, and He will clear His threshing floor and gather His wheat into the barn. But the chaff He will burn up with fire that never goes out" (v. 12). John also tells us that **Jesus is filled with the Spirit and loved by the Father**. In a rare glimpse into heaven, we hear the very voice of God declaring, "This is My beloved Son. I take delight in Him!" (v. 17).

Matthew 4

Jesus was led into the desert to be tempted by the Devil, where we find that **He is the new Adam and the true Israel**. Whereas the first Adam gave in to the temptation of the Devil in the garden, Jesus stood against that same serpent. He did what no one else in history has ever done or will ever do—He resisted temptation fully and completely, never giving in once to sin. Jesus is the true Israel, the faithful and obedient Son of God who passed the test of Satan's temptation and conquered sin.

Here, in the latter half of chapter 4, Matthew continues to paint a portrait of Jesus Christ, the One whom we're called to follow. In verses 12-25 **He is the light of the world and the hope for all people.** After hearing that John the Baptist had been thrown into prison, Jesus withdrew into Galilee. Once again Matthew shows how Jesus fulfilled Old Testament prophecy: "Land of Zebulun and land of Napthali, along the sea road, beyond the Jordan, Galilee of the Gentiles! The people who live in darkness have seen a great light, and for those living in the shadowland of death, light has dawned" (vv. 15-16). This quotation is from Isaiah 9:1-2, and the surrounding context of Isaiah helps us understand what Matthew is saying. Isaiah 8 contains a prophecy of coming judgment, but in chapter 9 God promised to deliver His people through a child who would be born, whose name would be "Wonderful Counselor, Mighty God, Eternal Father, Prince of Peace" (Isa 9:6). That promise was given particularly to Jews living in Galilee, a city far from the center of Jerusalem. These Jews were living in darkness among the nations, and to them Isaiah says, "A light has dawned" (Isa 9:2). All those who dwell among the despised, in the midst of darkness, enveloped in the "shadowland of death," are now being introduced to the One who is the light of the world and the hope for all people.

At the end of Matthew 4 we read that Jesus was "teaching in their synagogues, preaching the good news of the kingdom, and healing every disease and sickness among the people" (v. 23). Matthew describes His ministry as threefold: teaching, preaching, and healing. Jesus' teaching and preaching were accompanied by His healing ministry; He healed the sick, diseased, demon-possessed, epileptics, and paralytics (v. 24). This ministry consisted of both word and deed—proclamation of the good news of the kingdom alongside demonstrations of the greatness of the King.

Conclusion

In light of everything we know about Jesus from the first four chapters of Matthew, we should feel the wonder and weight of the One who gives this invitation, this command, to four fishermen to "Follow Me" in verse 19. This is Jesus, the Savior, the Messiah, the One promised to come in the kingly line of David and from Abraham, the father of Israel. He was fully human and fully divine, the One to whom wise men from the nations bow down, the One whose birth and life are the culmination of generations of prophecy and anticipation. He is the Savior King and Righteous Judge of the world, perfectly filled with God's Spirit and loved by God the Father. He is the only man who has conquered sin, and the true Son that Israel could never be.

There is only one conclusion to draw when we hear the invitation "Follow Me": **Jesus is worthy of far more than church attendance and casual association.** We have such a dangerous tendency to reduce Jesus to a poor, puny Savior who is just begging for you and me to accept Him into our lives. As if Jesus needs to be accepted by us! Jesus doesn't need our acceptance; He is infinitely worthy of all glory in the whole universe, and He doesn't need us at all. We need Him.

We dare not patronize Jesus, for **He is worthy of total abandonment and supreme adoration.** We're talking about the Savior King of the universe and Righteous Judge of all nations—God in the flesh— saying, "Follow Me." That thought alone is mind-boggling. There is no potential casual response to Jesus. It's either "turn and run" or "bow and worship." Luke's Gospel records that as soon as Peter caught a glimpse of Jesus' power and authority, He fell on His face, and then rose and followed (Luke 5:1-11). Everything is different once you meet this King. That's why we know that people who profess to be Christians but whose lives look just like the rest of the world are lying.

Many people claim to have made a decision, prayed a prayer, signed a card, walked an aisle, accepted Jesus into their hearts, but their lives don't look any different. These people say they're Christians, but the reality is that they've never met Jesus. Because when you do, everything changes.

Follow

After seeing the portrait of the One who used those two simple words, "Follow Me," we need to see what it means to respond. Having looked at the "Me," we turn to the "Follow."

Radical Abandonment

Matthew is clear that to follow Jesus means to **live with radical abandonment for His glory.** This word "abandonment" takes us back to Jesus'

call to repent in verse 17, and prior to that to the beginning of chapter
3 where John the Baptist said the exact same thing that Jesus now says:
"Repent, because the kingdom of heaven has come near!" (3:2; 4:17).
That word "repent" means to admit your sin (confession), to express
sorrow over your sin (contrition), and to turn from your sin (conversion). Repentance is illustrated in baptism, which is a picture of totally
renouncing your dependence on self. Consider how that "renouncing"
played out in the lives of the disciples.

Just as Jesus' invitation to those first disciples was a call to leave
behind all things, so also when we follow Him **we leave behind all things**,
including our comfort. The early disciples left behind everything that
was familiar and natural for them. They exchanged comfort for uncer-
tainty. They didn't know *where* they would be going; they only knew *who*
they would be with. All followers of Christ must respond to this same call
today: we may not always know all the details about *where* Christ is leading us, but we do know *who* we're following.

As followers of Jesus, we also leave behind our careers and our possessions. The disciples re-oriented their life's work, being willing to follow Jesus with nothing in their hands. Now to be sure, these guys may
not have been among the economically elite in society, but the fact that
they had this boat and a successful trade as fishermen shows that they
had much to lose in following Christ. When we follow Jesus, we also
lose our position. In Jesus' day, disciples would attach themselves to a
rabbi to promote themselves. Discipleship could be a step up the ladder
toward greater status and position. But this wasn't the case with these
early disciples; they were stepping down the ladder. They would eventually find this out when the One they were following was tried and killed.

In addition to leaving behind comfort, careers, possessions, and
position, we also leave behind our families, our friends, and our safety.
Jesus would later tell the disciples, "I'm sending you out like sheep
among wolves" (Matt 10:16); "If they persecuted Me, they will also persecute you" (John 15:20). Obedience to Christ is costly. Following Him
must be put even before our own physical security. Martin Luther's
hymn "A Mighty Fortress" says it well: "Let goods and kindred go, this
mortal life also; The body they may kill: God's truth abideth still, His
kingdom is forever."

While following Christ requires abandoning everything, at the core
it means that we must abandon our sin. That is, we admit our sin in
brokenness before God, and then we run from it. That's what it means

to abandon ourselves. This is the central message for any prospective disciple: "If anyone wants to come with Me, he must deny himself, take up his cross, and follow Me" (Matt 16:24). That's where following Jesus starts. In a world where everything revolves around self—protect yourself, promote yourself, preserve yourself, take care of yourself—Jesus says, "Slay yourself."

Now let me be very careful here: I am not saying, and I would not say based on the whole of the New Testament, that all followers of Jesus must lose their careers, sell or give away all their possessions, leave their families behind, and physically die for the gospel. But the New Testament is absolutely clear that for all who follow Jesus, comfort and certainty in this world are no longer your concerns. Your career revolves around whatever Jesus calls you to do and however He wants to use you to spread the good news of the kingdom. Your possessions are not your own, and you forsake material pleasure in this world in order to live for eternal treasure in the world to come. And this *could* mean that you sell or give away everything you have. After all, position is no longer your priority.

When it comes to family, the Bible is clear that you are to honor your parents (Eph 6:1-3; Exod 20:12), love your spouse (Eph 5:22-33), and provide for your children (1 Tim 5:8). So don't use a command like "Follow Me" to justify being a lousy husband, wife, or parent. Nevertheless, as we'll see in Matthew 10:37, your love for Christ should make love for your closest family members look like hate in comparison. God may call you to leave your family for His own purposes, perhaps to make His gospel known across the world.

The costly call to abandon everything for Jesus can be stated another way. We lay down all things so that **we live for one thing**: to **honor the King**. To follow Jesus means to hold loosely to everything else and to cling tightly to the person of Christ and the mission of His kingdom. This may sound extreme to some people, but we can't forget who the "Me" is here. To lay down everything in your life doesn't make sense until you realize who the King is. Once you realize this, leaving behind all things is the only thing that makes sense. Remember Matthew 13:44: "The kingdom of heaven is like treasure, buried in a field, that a man found and reburied. Then in his joy he goes and sells everything he has and buys that field." We have Someone worth losing everything for!

Joyful Dependence

It should be clear by now that following Christ is not easy. However, this is not a call to earn something from God by our sacrificial lifestyles. As we live with radical abandonment for Christ's glory, we are to **live with joyful dependence on His grace.** See the beauty and wonder of God's grace in those words, "Follow Me." **God takes the initiative to choose us.** While potential disciples in first-century Judaism would seek out a rabbi to study under, Jesus did the seeking in this passage. The disciples didn't come to Jesus—He came to them. Jesus does at the beginning of the New Testament what God did throughout the Old Testament. God always chooses His partners. He chose Noah, Abraham, Moses, and David. He also chose the prophets. And he chose Israel to be His people (Deut 7:6-7). Just as the Father chose His people in the Old Testament, so Jesus chose His disciples in the New Testament. Jesus will tell the disciples later, "You did not choose Me, but I chose you" (John 15:16). This choice was not because of anything in them; it was all because of grace in Him.

It's common to hear people give reasons for why Jesus would choose fishermen to be His disciples. It may be that four to seven of these men were actually fishermen, and, it is pointed out, fishermen have certain tasks and skill sets that make them likely candidates as disciples and disciple-makers. But if that's the direction we go, we'll miss the whole point of the text. Jesus did not call these guys because of what they brought to the table. These four guys, and the disciples that came later, didn't have many things in their favor. For starters, they were Galileans, deemed to be lower class, rural, and uneducated by many. They were hardly the cultural elite, and they certainly weren't the most spiritually qualified for this task. Instead, they were narrow-minded and superstitious, full of Jewish prejudices, misconceptions, and animosities. *These* are the ones Jesus chose.

This may sound like a harsh description of these 12 men, but the reality is that it's not just them; it's us too! You and I have nothing in us to draw Jesus to us, to elicit this invitation. We are sinners—rebels to the core—running from God. And the beautiful, gracious, glorious reality of the gospel is that Jesus comes running to us. He calls our name. He chooses us. To use the words of Ephesians 1:4-6,

> *For He [God] chose us in Him, before the foundation of the world,*
> *to be holy and blameless in His sight. In love He predestined us to be*

adopted through Jesus Christ for Himself, according to His favor and will, to the praise of His glorious grace.

God the Father sent the Son to bear the wrath you and I deserved on a cross so that we, by His grace, might be drawn to Him. Praise be to God that He takes the initiative to choose us! But why does He do this?

Right after telling us that He chose the disciples, Jesus gives us the purpose of their choosing: "I appointed you that you should go out and produce fruit" (John 15:16). Likewise, the command to "Follow Me" has a purpose: "Follow Me . . . and I will make you fish for people!" (Matt 4:19). So Jesus not only takes the initiative to choose us, but also **He provides the power to use us**. Notice that Jesus does not command the disciples to fish for people; rather, He says, "*I will make you* fish for people." In other words, "I am going to do a transforming work in your life that will enable you to spread the message of My kingdom around the world." The power to follow Christ and make Him known comes only as we rely fully on His strength. In John 15:4 Jesus tells His disciples, "Remain in Me, and I in you." The fruit we bear in following Jesus only comes as we remain in Him by faith. There's no way these men could carry out the commands given from Jesus, and so Jesus says, in effect, "I will enable you to do all that I command."

God takes the initiative to choose us, He provides the power to use us, and **He gets the glory through us**. Consider how God used this unlikely group of men:

- Peter, the disciple with the foot-shaped mouth, preached the first Christian sermon and led more than 3,000 people to Christ, literally increasing the church by 2,500 percent in one day (Acts 2).
- John wrote books contained in the NT that are still used to lead people to Christ 2,000 years later.
- Other disciples would scatter to the nations proclaiming the good news of God's kingdom, even at the risk of their own lives.

Human history was altered forever by this group of disciples, and it began with four local fishermen. Hardly a world-changing task force! But this is the beauty of God's design, namely, to take weak and lowly sinners and enable them to do far more than they (or anyone else) could ever imagine, all to the praise of His glorious grace! May He use us and our churches to change our own world today.

Faithful Adherence

Next, we see that to follow Jesus means to **live with faithful adherence to His person**. This is what the disciples did; their commitment wasn't perfect and their understanding was often cloudy, but they were loyal to their Lord. It's worth noting that the word "disciple" appears more than 250 times in the New Testament, but it doesn't always refer to these 12 men. Sometimes the word "disciple" refers to the crowds who were following Jesus and simply listening to Him (Luke 6:17). Other times, the word "disciple" refers to the people who seemed to be convinced of what Jesus was saying, but they weren't "all in." However, there were 12 guys, and a few women, who after these many days of teaching and preaching and healing in Galilee, would follow Jesus all the way to Jerusalem to the cross. As we'll see clearly in the upcoming Sermon on the Mount, nominal adherence to Jesus is not something new to the twenty-first century (Matt 7:21-23). It has been prevalent ever since the first century.

Throughout history, there have been crowds of people who were content to hear from Jesus, maybe even to agree with Jesus, but they didn't truly follow Him. In the place where I pastor, Birmingham, Alabama, it is no big deal to go to a church. In fact, so many people go to church that it becomes a game to see which church can draw the biggest crowd. But this is not New Testament Christianity. New Testament Christianity is a narrow road, a costly road of continual obedience. Anyone who wants to become a follower of Jesus needs to know what they are signing up for.

First, **we are not casual listeners**. True disciples don't simply listen to the words of Jesus week by week and then move on with their lives. Second, **we are not convinced listeners**, people who are content to merely *affirm* belief in Jesus. Even demons believe Jesus is who He says He is (Jas 2:19)! Intellectual belief alone ultimately damns. Followers of Jesus are not simply casual or even convinced listeners; **we are committed learners and followers**. In a world, even a church world, full of casual and convinced listeners, I want to invite you to yield your life as a learner and follower of Jesus, being willing to go wherever He asks and to do whatever He says, no matter what it costs.

Total Trust

Next we need to see that to follow Jesus means to **live with total trust in His authority**. We might put it this way: **He is the Master of every domain**

in our lives. Luke records that just before Jesus called these four fishermen (Peter, Andrew, James, and John), He was able supernaturally to determine where they should drop their nets for a massive catch (Luke 5:1-11). From the beginning, then, the disciples realized that Jesus was sovereign, even over the fish of the sea. For them and for us, it is important to realize that there is nothing in our lives or our professions that is outside Jesus' authority.

All of us have the dangerous tendency to compartmentalize Christianity. We relegate Jesus to the religious realm, not realizing that **He is the Lord of every detail in our lives.** He is Lord over politics and policies. He is Lord over budgets and bank accounts. He is Lord over houses and cars. He is Lord over words and thoughts, attitudes and actions. And to follow Him is to live with total trust in His sovereign, supreme authority in every domain and in every detail of your life.

Urgent Obedience

Finally, to follow Jesus is to **live with urgent obedience to His mission.** This is integral to why He called us in the first place. **Every follower of Jesus is a fisher of men.** Using imagery that was familiar to their vocation, Jesus was calling the disciples to a mission. Instead of searching for fish all over the lake, they would spread the gospel all over the world. At the close of this Gospel, this message remains front and center. Jesus met the disciples on a mountainside in Galilee, and He commanded them, "Go . . . and make disciples of all nations."

The theme of mission is prominent in Matthew's Gospel, for **every disciple is a disciple-maker.** This is admittedly an unconventional plan. With the good news of a kingdom to spread throughout the world, Jesus gathered a few men around Him for three years. He loved them, cared for them, taught them, and trained them, and when He left this earth, He only had a handful of people who were actually following Him. But each one of them knew that he (or she) had one mission—to fish for men and make disciples. The advancement of the gospel in the world came about as the Spirit of God used every single one of those early disciples to accomplish His grand and global purpose.[13]

---

[13] Judas was the lone exception among the disciples, as He betrayed Christ (Matt 26:47-50) and was thus never a part of the early church's worldwide mission in Acts. Matthias was chosen to take his place (Acts 1:15-26).

We desperately need to be reminded that the Great Commission and the call to fish for men are every Christian's privilege and responsibility. **This is an unconventional plan that demands a universal response.** This is one of the deepest burdens of my heart for the church I pastor. I want every member, every disciple, to see themselves as disciple-makers. So biblically, if we're not making disciples, then we have missed what it means to be a disciple in the first place. This is one of the reasons I encourage every member of our church to be a part of a small group, where the goal is not simply to meet, but to come alongside other believers and ask, "How can we make disciples?"

You may be thinking, "I can't do that." To which I say, "Yes, that's the point." *We* can't do it. That's why we need Jesus to make us what we cannot be in and of ourselves. This is the core of discipleship: we follow Him, and *He* makes us fishers of men.

Will You Follow Jesus?

A passage like Matthew 4:18-25 isn't intended simply to be analyzed. It's intended to confront us with the question of whether or not we will follow Jesus. Therefore, **consider the cost of discipleship.** That is, consider the cost of what it means to follow Jesus, to live with radical abandonment for His glory, to lay down and leave behind all things in order to live for the King. And this is to be done with joyful dependence on His grace, faithful adherence to His person, and total trust in His authority. Disciples of Jesus ought to live with urgent obedience to His mission.

Discipleship is undoubtedly costly, but as you consider the cost of discipleship, I beg you to **consider the cost of non-discipleship.** What if you choose to reject Jesus, to live for yourself and to die in your sin? What if you choose to settle for casual, cultural Christianity that never truly encounters Christ?

Consider what the cost will be for our lives. Eternity is at stake. The wages of sin is death (Rom 6:23), and death apart from a saving relationship with Jesus Christ means that an eternal hell is your destination. Don't be deceived: the cost of non-discipleship is far greater than the cost of discipleship.

And also consider the cost for our community. Your non-discipleship means that the people who know you get a picture of a half-hearted, lukewarm Christianity and a puny, pathetic Christ. Instead, we want to show people that Jesus is worthy of more than Sunday morning or even small group attendance; He's worthy of our lives and our possessions, our dreams and our ambitions. He's worthy of it all, and we gladly lay it all down for Him. Let's make known the good news of a King for whom it is worth losing everything.

Finally, consider the cost for the world if we aren't committed learners and followers of Christ. How is it that billions of people have still never heard this gospel? Surely it is at least in part because we have been content with business as usual in the church, instead of realizing what it means to really follow the Jesus of the Bible and to spend our lives spreading the gospel of the kingdom to the ends of the earth. Failing to follow Jesus truly has global consequences.

Reflect and Discuss

1. How would your friends and coworkers answer the question, "Who is Jesus?"
2. Why is an understanding of Matthew's teaching about Jesus' identity up to this point so crucial to understanding Jesus' command to "Follow Me"?
3. In light of who Jesus is, why do mere church attendance and casual association with Him not make sense?
4. How would you explain what it means to "repent" to someone who had never heard the term?
5. Following Jesus costs us everything. What might that look like practically in our own culture? How might this look different in a hostile Muslim context?
6. If we must abandon everything for Christ, then how does God's grace play a part in our salvation?
7. In what ways has the call to follow Jesus been watered down in our culture?
8. Explain the idea that every disciple is to be a disciple-maker. What might this look like for a mom with young kids? For an accountant? What about a college student?
9. Explain the following statement: "The New Testament pattern for discipleship is more about 'go and tell' than 'come and see.'"
10. What are some of the costs of non-discipleship that you see around you?

The King's Sermon

MATTHEW 5–7

Main Idea: Kingdom citizens must manifest a righteousness that exceeds the righteousness of the scribes and Pharisees, and this righteousness only comes about as we are changed by God's grace and power in the gospel of Jesus Christ.

I. **The Setting of the Sermon**
   A. We must remember the context of the sermon in the Gospel of Matthew.
      1. Matthew begins by calling attention to the sins of God's people.
      2. Matthew ends by calling attention to the death of God's Messiah.
   B. We must remember the context of the sermon in the history of redemption.
      1. Jesus is the long-awaited Messiah.
      2. His is the long-awaited kingdom.
II. **The Subject of the Sermon**
   A. Jesus demands a righteousness exceeding that of the scribes and the Pharisees.
      1. Not more righteous deeds by human effort . . .
      2. But more righteous hearts by divine grace.
   B. This exceeding righteousness should be evident in our
      1. Attitudes
      2. Desires
      3. Ambitions
      4. Relationships
III. **The Seriousness of the Sermon**
   A. The options are limited.
   B. The fruit is evident.
   C. The consequences are eternal.

The King's Sermon

MATTHEW 5–7

No matter how many times we've heard the Sermon on the Mount, there is still more to be gained from this most majestic sermon from the greatest preacher who ever lived. Here in Matthew 5–7—just 111 verses—is the fullest exposition of Jesus recorded in the Gospels. John Stott referred to it as "the nearest thing to a manifesto that [Jesus] ever uttered, for it is his own description of what he wanted his followers to be and do" (Stott, *Sermon on the Mount*, 5). To put it differently, the Sermon on the Mount teaches us what it means to be a citizen of Christ's kingdom.

Although few people have heard of him today, in the late nineteenth and early twentieth centuries Billy Sunday was a well-known evangelist.[14] Sunday was known for his unique, sometimes bombastic style of preaching. He would act out skits sometimes as he preached. He would use slang-filled language. As a former baseball player, he would sometimes slide across the stage as he was making a point. By the time of his death in 1935, he had preached to millions of people. And he was a forerunner of sorts to the Billy Graham evangelistic crusades and campaigns that were to come in the latter twentieth century.

Billy Sunday was also a vocal critic concerning certain vices that he perceived in the culture in his day. Two of those vices were card playing and dancing. Sunday warned, "I believe that cards and dancing are doing more to damn the spiritual life of the church than the bars." He also said, "The dancing Christian never was a soul-winner," and dance is "simply a hugging match set to music." Now, the twenty-first century Christian laughs at those seemingly antiquated notions. (If only our main worry were card playing!) Yet Billy Sunday thought them significant. He considered them matters of life and death. And it raises the question, "Why?" Why so much worry over things so incidental? Well, it's simply because in his mind activities like card playing, dancing, and theater were a separation point. There was to be a clear line of demarcation between believers and unbelievers. These were things that marked off the people of God—things that marked out holiness, godliness, and salvation. He had a certain picture of what it looks like to be a believer in Jesus, and anything outside that didn't fit.

---

[14] The information on Billy Sunday was taken from the following site: http://www.biblebelievers.com/billy_sunday/sun12.html.

While we may reject Sunday's picture of what it looks like to be a Christian, the truth is we do the very same thing. We have our own picture of what it looks like to be a Christian—certain behaviors that fit and certain ones that do not, or certain attitudes that we ought to possess to be a Christian in our particular culture. Perhaps that means being of a particular political persuasion, aligning ourselves with certain groups within the Christian subculture, and so on.

For Billy Sunday in his day, and for us in ours, Jesus repaints the picture. Better, Jesus has already painted the picture, and it's for succeeding generations to make sure their conception of the Christian life matches the one painted on the Galilean hillside long, long ago. And it's to that portrait we now turn.

Although the Sermon on the Mount certainly merits verse-by-verse consideration, here we'll take a 30,000-foot view of the sermon, seeking to get at the heart of Jesus' message. We'll begin with the setting of the sermon.

The Setting of the Sermon

Literary Context

First of all, we must remember the context of the sermon in the Gospel of Matthew. Both the beginning and end of this Gospel are especially important for this point. Consider: **Matthew begins by calling attention to the sins of God's people.** And we have in mind here that particularly crucial statement in the opening chapter of the Gospel: "She will give birth to a son, and you are to name Him Jesus, because He will save His people from their sins" (Matt 1:21). Very simply, the Gospel of Matthew is about Jesus granting salvation from sin, not our achievement of our own salvation.

Similarly, consider the close of the Gospel. **Matthew ends by calling attention to the death of God's Messiah.** The last eight chapters of the book of Matthew are all consumed with the very last week of Jesus. In other words, Matthew does not end his Gospel at chapter 7, as if the main point were: "This is what Jesus taught. This is how Jesus showed us what it means to be a disciple. This is what it looks like. This is how you ought to behave. This is how you ought to think. These are the attitudes that you are to have. Now go and do it."

No, the cross is absolutely necessary for understanding the Sermon on the Mount. In fact, the cross is predominant when you come to any of the four Gospels. Whether you're reading Matthew, Mark, Luke, or John, you can never read these accounts apart from the very end of the story. The cross is always looming; it's always lurking. The cross should always impact what we're reading, even though the crucifixion hasn't yet happened in the narrative. This is especially true for the Sermon on the Mount. The last thing we need to come away with is an imposing and crushing laundry list of things that we must do in order to be accepted by God.

When you read the Sermon on the Mount, you should not walk away thinking, "I must turn the other cheek in order to be accepted by God. I must love my enemies and pray for those who persecute me in order to be accepted by God. I must follow the Golden Rule perfectly in order to be accepted by God." We are not accepted by God because of anything that we do. We are accepted by God completely and totally because of a perfect Savior who has died a bloody death in our place and who has risen again in victory. Yes, we pray for our enemies, we love those who persecute us, and we follow the Golden Rule. But we do these things not in order to earn acceptance before our God, but *because* we have acceptance by God and we want to glorify Him in everything that we do.

Historical Context

In addition to considering how the Sermon on the Mount fits in the Gospel of Matthew, **we must remember the context of the sermon in the history of redemption**. In particular, how does Matthew's Gospel containing the Sermon on the Mount fit with the story of the Old Testament? Over and over in Matthew's Gospel we see phrases like, "Now all this took place to fulfill what was spoken by the Lord through the prophet" (1:22).[15] Matthew is deeply concerned to show the continuity between his Gospel and the Old Testament, a continuity that is highlighted in the life of Jesus. And we see that concern in at least a couple of ways here in this text.

First, we see that **Jesus is the long-awaited Messiah**. We've noted this in a couple of places in this Gospel already, and here in the Sermon on the Mount Matthew continues that theme by showing Jesus as the new

---

[15] For other fulfillment texts in Matthew, see also the following: 2:15, 17, 23; 3:15; 4:14; 5:17; 8:17; 12:17; 13:14, 35, 54; 21:4; 26:54, 56; 27:9.

and better Moses. Consider the following: as a child, Jesus was providentially delivered from a massacre of children in Bethlehem (2:13-18), a deliverance reminiscent of Moses' own rescue as a child in the midst of Pharaoh's mass murder of Hebrew children in Egypt (Exod 2:1-10). The parallels between Jesus and Moses continue in Matthew 5:1: "When He [Jesus] saw the crowds, He went up on the mountain, and after He sat down, His disciples came to Him." Notice that expression, "He went up on the mountain," as this very same wording is used in the Greek Old Testament when Moses went up onto the mountain to receive the law (Exod 19:3). Just as Moses went up on the mountain, Matthew is telling us, so Jesus went up on the mountain, and in the same way that Moses spoke with authority, so now Jesus speaks with authority. These parallels also extend to the very structure of Matthew's Gospel, for just as Moses authored five books—Genesis, Exodus, Leviticus, Numbers, and Deuteronomy—so Matthew's Gospel gives us five speeches of Jesus, or five main blocks of teaching material. The message resounds that a new authority is now on the scene, so much so that at the end of the Gospel, Jesus is able to say,

> All authority has been given to Me [not Moses] in heaven and on earth. Go, therefore, and make disciples of all nations, baptizing them in the name of the Father and of the Son and of the Holy Spirit, teaching them to observe everything I [not Moses] have commanded you. (28:18-20)

Matthew is showing us that Jesus is the One greater than Moses, the One who has come and delivered His people, and who has now given them the Word. Of course, Moses would not chafe at this idea, for he said, "The LORD your God will raise up for you a prophet like me from among your own brothers. You must listen to him" (Deut 18:15). Charles Quarles helpfully sums us this idea of Jesus as the new and greater Moses:

> Just like Moses, the Great Redeemer (speaking of Jesus) has cried out, "Let My people go." He has removed their shackles. He has killed their harsh taskmaster. He's buried his body in the sand. He has crushed the power of the dark Pharaoh with one plague after another, and He has led His people to freedom across the parted sea. (Quarles, *Sermon on The Mount*, 27)

After seeing that Jesus is the long-awaited Messiah, we must also see that **His is the long-awaited kingdom**. Again, this point is critical to understanding the Sermon on the Mount—there is indeed a new kingdom, a new people. It was God's intention all along not just to give commandments to His people, but to create a new people with new hearts, new affections, and new attitudes. This newness is what Isaiah, Jeremiah, Ezekiel, Daniel, and the rest of the prophets were anticipating. They looked forward to a new exodus—a greater and final deliverance from sin's penalty and power—for the people of God.

This Old Testament expectation of a people transformed by God's Spirit is critically important for our application of the Sermon on the Mount. The larger context of redemption is a reminder that we cannot dismiss Jesus' words because we think the standard too high, as if we can't truly love from the heart or resist our lusts and temptations. We cannot throw in the towel on praying like Jesus, giving freely of our resources, or fasting in the right spirit. And this means that loving our enemies, perhaps the most difficult of all commands, is within the reach of every Christ-follower by the grace and power of God.

The Subject of the Sermon
5:17-20

Matthew 5:17-20 serves as the interpretive key to the rest of the Sermon on the Mount. Therefore, understanding this particular section of the sermon is critical for understanding the sermon as a whole. Jesus says in verse 17, "Don't assume that I came to destroy the Law or the Prophets. I did not come to destroy but to fulfill." "The Law and the Prophets" is Jesus' way of referring to the entire Old Testament (7:12; 22:40), and He says that He didn't come to abolish the Old Testament, but to fulfill it. That word "fulfill" is the same one we noticed earlier, as we're reminded again that Jesus came to fulfill the intention of the Old Testament, that is, to bring it to its intended completion. And the fulfillment Jesus has in mind here in relation to the Old Testament is not simply external conformity to its commands, but rather a heart alive to God. This is what the law was calling for all along (Deut 30:6).

The Demand for Exceeding Righteousness

Jesus continues in verses 18-20:

> For I assure you: Until heaven and earth pass away, not the smallest letter or one stroke of a letter will pass from the law until all things are accomplished. Therefore, whoever breaks one of the least of these

*commands and teaches people to do so will be called least in the
kingdom of heaven. But whoever practices and teaches these commands
will be called great in the kingdom of heaven. For I tell you, unless
your righteousness surpasses that of the scribes and Pharisees, you will
never enter the kingdom of heaven.*

When in the last phrase of verse 20 Jesus says, "you will never
enter the kingdom of heaven," He is not referring to some elite club
for Christians or rewards for the extra-obedient. Instead, this is simply
another way Jesus speaks about salvation. **Jesus demands a righteousness exceeding that of the scribes and the Pharisees**. That reality ought
to shock us, and it should alert us that unless our righteousness exceeds
that of the scribes and the Pharisees, we will not enter the kingdom of
heaven but will remain forever in the kingdom of darkness. In other
words, this righteousness is the difference between heaven and hell.

In light of these truths, we're left wondering what kind of righteous-
ness the Pharisees had, given that our righteousness must exceed theirs.
Although we could look at other passages for help with this question,
Matthew 23:25-28 really captures the kind of righteousness that the
Pharisees possessed. In verse 25 Jesus says,

*Woe to you, scribes and Pharisees, hypocrites! You clean the outside of
the cup and dish, but inside they are full of greed and self-indulgence!*

Notice the contrast that Jesus draws between what is on the inside and
what is on the outside. The Pharisees were clean on the outside, but
they were full of greed and self-indulgence in their hearts. The same
reality is presented in verse 26:

*Blind Pharisee! First clean the inside of the cup, so the outside of it
may also become clean.*

Then in verses 27-28 Jesus gives perhaps the clearest and most pictur-
esque illustration of the Pharisees' righteousness:

*Woe to you, scribes and Pharisees, hypocrites! You are like whitewashed
tombs, which appear beautiful on the outside, but inside are full of
dead men's bones and every impurity. In the same way, on the outside
you seem righteous to people, but inside you are full of hypocrisy and
lawlessness.*

The righteousness of the scribes and the Pharisees was purely an
external righteousness. But Jesus says that it's not enough to be righteous

on the outside if you are not also righteous on the inside. What Jesus is demanding is **not more righteous deeds by human effort, but more righteous hearts by divine grace**. He is not saying that you must have a *quantitatively* greater righteousness, something like a righteousness that is numerically greater than the scribes or the Pharisees. To use an academic analogy, it's not that the Pharisees have scored in the low 90's on the holiness test, and entrance into the kingdom of heaven requires a score of 94, 95, or 96. This misses the point altogether. Rather, Jesus is talking about a *qualitatively* different righteousness—a righteousness of a different kind altogether. This is not an outer righteousness to show everyone how good we look, but an inner righteousness that shows how gracious and powerful God is.

Jesus spoke of this inner righteousness with Nicodemus in John 3. Nicodemus was a Pharisee, a teacher of Bible and theology according to John 3:10, yet he didn't understand what Jesus meant when He said that someone must be "born again" (John 3:3). Nicodemus was thinking in terms of externals, as in re-entering your mother's womb, but Jesus informed him that a man must be born of water and the Spirit (John 3:4-5). Man must be given a new heart by God, just as the Old Testament prophets foretold (Ezek 36:24-28; Jer 31:31-34). Like the wind, Jesus says, this work of God's Spirit is not something we can bring about. We can only see the effects (John 3:8).

This idea in John 3 of being born again is precisely what Jesus is getting at in Matthew 5:20 when He says that our righteousness must be greater than that of the scribes and the Pharisees. We must have a righteousness that extends beyond externals and legal conformity. And such an exceeding righteousness is only possible by God's gift of a new heart.

The Evidence of Exceeding Righteousness

So how do we know that we have this exceeding righteousness? Or a new heart? Is there instant obedience to every command in Scripture overnight? Of course not. But know this: there will be some evidence. There will be some change in our life if we have been born again. And this is, in some measure, what the remainder of Jesus' sermon is about.

First, **this exceeding righteousness should be evident in our attitudes**. Six different times in Matthew 5:21-48 Jesus says, "You have heard that it was said . . . but I tell you . . ." The Pharisees had created all kinds of ingenious ways of working around the intentions of God's Word. For example, they found ways to harbor bitterness and hatred toward their neighbor while remaining innocent in their own eyes with regard to murder. They may have lusted after their neighbor's wives, but so long as they didn't commit adultery, they felt themselves to be holy, technically speaking. In general, they felt justified in blurring the edges of the truth. They would swear by this or that object and then back out on their promise, but so long as they didn't swear by the wrong things, then they were somehow people of integrity (see also 23:16-22). But that's merely an external righteousness, not the kind of righteousness Jesus brings about.

Of course, it's all too easy to pile on the Pharisees, as if we don't also struggle with this kind of duplicity. For example, I can maintain hatred toward my wife, bitterness toward my children, and jealousy toward my neighbor, all while technically never killing them or harming in them in any physical way. But self-justification and good appearances are not what Jesus came to do for us and in us; that is not saving people from their sins. He came to give us a righteousness that works its way all the way down to the heart and then ushers forth in love, purity, and holiness. These are the new attitudes that Jesus is producing in His people by His Spirit.

The question we need to ask is this: "Do we see those new attitudes in our lives?" Is there genuine love, purity, integrity, and holiness? And this is where we desperately need the help of those around us. We need other Christians in our life who can say, "I see the grace of God in you," or, conversely, "I'm not sure I see the life of Christ evident in your life." The latter is difficult to hear, but it's far better to hear that today than on the Last Day.

Second, Jesus says that our exceeding righteousness should be evident in our **desires**. In Matthew 6:1-18 Jesus refers to three different kinds of behavior: giving (vv. 2-3), prayer (vv. 5-14), and fasting (vv. 16-18). Just to be clear, Jesus is not telling His disciples to abandon these things, but to do them in the right way, a way that manifests God-glorifying desires. Jesus' main concern in speaking of these subjects is stated in verse 1: "Be careful not to practice your righteousness in front of people, to be seen by them." So, yes, we give, pray, and fast, but we should not do these things in order to attract attention.

There's no denying that disciples of Jesus will continue to struggle with wanting man's approval. At times we desire the applause of men and we seek to win their approval, but there should at least be combat against those sinful desires in a heart changed by God. Our ultimate desire should be for God's recognition, regardless of what man says. We shouldn't give in order to impress others, we shouldn't pray in a way that highlights our spirituality, and we shouldn't fast so that others are aware of our supposed humility. Rather, new desires are part and parcel of the exceeding righteousness Jesus is bringing about in His people.

Third, in Matthew 6:19-34 Jesus says that we must have new **ambitions**. He gives the following instructions in verses 31-33:

> So don't worry, saying, "What will we eat?" or "What will we drink?"
> or "What will we wear?" For the idolaters eagerly seek all these things,
> and your heavenly Father knows that you need them. But seek first the
> kingdom of God and His righteousness, and all these things will be
> provided for you.

Those who have a qualitatively different kind of righteousness, that is, a righteousness that flows from a heart changed by God, should no longer be consumed with the things of this world. Now, this does not mean that if we ever struggle or give in to the pull of the world, that we are not disciples of Jesus. There is an "already–not yet" aspect to the Christian life. We are already saved, but we are not yet in heaven. We are not perfected. We are not glorified. There will always be a struggle in this life. Nevertheless, Jesus' point is that even though we will still battle these ungodly ambitions, and even fail many times, there ought to be at least a competing desire in our hearts for the glory of God and for the kingdom of righteousness. On some level, we should be able to pray with sincerity, "Our Father in heaven, Your name be honored as holy. Your kingdom come. Your will be done on earth as it is in heaven" (Matt 6:9-10).

The fourth evidence of an exceeding righteousness concerns new **relationships**. Jesus warns us in Matthew 7:1, "Do not judge, so that you won't be judged." Now clearly Jesus is not saying here that we never judge, that we never point out sin in our brothers and sisters, or that we never receive correction from others. In fact, He goes on to indicate that's exactly what we ought to be doing (vv. 2-5)!

> For with the judgment you use, you will be judged, and with the
> measure you use, it will be measured to you. Why do you look at the
> speck in your brother's eye but don't notice the log in your own eye?
> Or how can you say to your brother, "Let me take the speck out of your
> eye," and look, there's a log in your eye? Hypocrite! First take the log

*out of your eye, and then you will see clearly to take the speck out of
your brother's eye.*

Jesus is not telling us to overlook sin in one another. Rather, Jesus is
responding to Pharisees who have elevated themselves and demeaned
others who didn't live up to their own particular standards. This was the
Pharisees' way of life, their program of holiness. And Jesus' response
to that is not to tell them to forget about holiness or to stop pointing
out sin; rather, His response is to exhort them to consider their own sin
before they begin pointing out sin in others. Undoubtedly, we should be
willing to encourage one another and point out sinful habits in others,
but only after a time of reflection on the ways that sin is present in our
own life. And then, even when we do that, all of our correction, all of
our admonition, and all of our encouragement should be seasoned with
love, grace, and evident humility.

The bottom line is this: There should be something different about
the lives of Jesus' disciples. Life in the kingdom will look different from
life in the world. This is the exceeding righteousness of which Jesus
speaks. So, do we see this difference in our lives? And do we see this difference in our churches?

The Seriousness of the Sermon

Like every good preacher, Jesus puts us on the spot and He calls for us
to respond. He impresses on us here at the end of the Sermon on the
Mount the seriousness of what He has said. Below we'll look at three different realities we are faced with in this text.

The options are limited.

First, Jesus makes clear that the options are limited. There is one road
that leads to life, and there is one road that leads to destruction. You see
this point in a very familiar passage in Matthew 7:13-14, where Jesus says,

*Enter through the narrow gate. For the gate is wide and the road is
broad that leads to destruction, and there are many who go through it.
How narrow is the gate and difficult the road that leads to life, and
few find it.*

Scholars have disagreed about whether it is a road that leads to a gate
or a gate that leads to a road, but the bottom line is the same: there are

only two ways. Just as Paul tells us in Romans 5:12-21 that there are only two kinds of people (those in Adam and those in Christ), Jesus tells us that there are only two kinds of roads, and everybody on the planet is on one of them. You're either on a road that leads to life, or you are on a broad way, an easy road—the way of the world—which leads to destruction.

The fruit is evident.

Next, Jesus says that the fruit is evident. In verses 15-23, He says that one tree bears good fruit and one tree bears bad fruit. Everyone falls into one of those two categories. Either you have repented of your sins and Christ has changed your heart, and you're producing love, joy, peace, and other good fruit (Gal 5:22-23); or you're still trusting in yourself and rejecting Christ. Those in the latter category bring forth the works of the flesh (Gal 5:19-21).

The consequences are eternal.

Finally, Jesus says that the consequences are eternal. This is not a temporal reality or a game. Nothing else in our lives is on par with this. In verses 24-27 He says that when the storm hits, one house stands upon the rock and one house crashes upon itself.

We must hear Jesus. When He says that there is a storm coming, He is not talking about what we so often identify as the "storms of life." Those storms are real and they are painful—storms like cancer, divorce, and losing a loved one—and the Bible certainly addresses them. However, Jesus is referring to a cataclysmic reality, a final and utterly devastating storm of the future judgment of God. It may be tonight or it may be 10,000 years from now. But it will come. And Jesus reminds us that it doesn't matter how we've propped up our house or how we've fixed it up or what other people think of it. Unless that house is founded upon the Rock, its fall will be stunning.

In response to Jesus' teaching, do you see an "exceeding righteousness" to your life? Do you have a new heart? If not, God's judgment now hangs over you. But the good news—the gospel—is that it doesn't have to be that way. The good news is that you can withstand the judgment of God so long as you are in Christ, who has already been judged (Rom 8:3). Place yourself totally, completely in Him. Don't rest in yourself; rest wholly in the Savior. That is the gospel.

Reflect and Discuss

1. How is the Sermon on the Mount different from a simple code of ethics?
2. How does the larger context of Matthew, including Jesus' death and resurrection, affect your understanding of the Sermon on the Mount?
3. Explain what Jesus means when He says our righteousness must exceed that of the scribes and Pharisees.
4. How would you respond to an unbeliever who asks, "How can I live out the kind of righteousness Jesus is talking about in this sermon?"
5. How should the career ambitions of a kingdom citizen differ from those of an unbeliever?
6. As a believer, does the Sermon on the Mount ever sound too daunting? How should the work of the Spirit and the truths of the gospel shape your thinking?
7. How does the close of this sermon speak to the uniqueness of Jesus?
8. We cannot see anyone's heart, but are there indications that someone is or is not a citizen of Christ's kingdom?
9. Is the Sermon on the Mount meant to be obeyed now, or is it a set of ideals only to be achieved in eternity? Explain your answer.
10. In what areas of your life are you failing to manifest a righteousness that differs from the world?

The King's Authority (Part 1)

MATTHEW 8

Main Idea: Jesus possesses absolute authority in the world and warrants absolute allegiance from the world.

I. **The Basic Outline of Matthew 8–9**
    A. Three Miracle Stories (8:1-17)
    B. Two Descriptions of Discipleship (8:18-22)
    C. Three Miracle Stories (8:23–9:8)
    D. Two Descriptions of Discipleship (9:9-17)
    E. Three Miracle Stories (9:18-34)
II. **The Bottom Line of Matthew 8–9**
III. **The Portrait of Jesus in Matthew 8**
    A. Jesus has authority over disease.
        1. He cleanses the physically unclean.
        2. He heals the ethnically outcast.
        3. He restores the culturally marginalized.
    B. Jesus has authority over disciples.
        1. Jesus is worthy of unconditional trust.
        2. Jesus is worthy of undivided affection.
    C. Jesus has authority over disaster.
        1. The point of the story: Jesus is God.
        2. The promise in the story: You will never be alone.
    D. Jesus has authority over demons.
        1. The demons have fear because of their belief.
        2. We often have fear because of our unbelief.
IV. **A Pause after Reading Matthew 8**
    A. Let's trust wholeheartedly in Jesus' authority.
    B. Let's rest peacefully in Jesus' authority.
    C. Let's submit completely to Jesus' authority.
    D. Let's rejoice gladly in Jesus' authority.

The King's Authority (Part 1)
MATTHEW 8

Chapters 8 and 9 of Matthew's Gospel stand together as one unit, so it may be best to think of them as a two-part treatment of the authority of Jesus. As we saw earlier, Matthew is arranging his material intentionally, but not necessarily chronologically. In these two chapters, Matthew arranges his material around certain themes, and in particular a theme he introduced in Matthew 4:23—the words and works of Jesus.

Matthew 4:23 says, "Jesus was going all over Galilee, teaching in their synagogues, preaching the good news of the kingdom, and healing every disease and sickness among the people." This is a summary of Jesus' ministry, carried out in both word (teaching/preaching) and deed (healing). In the Sermon on the Mount, the passage that follows Matthew's summary statement in 4:23, we saw Jesus' ministry in word. Then, right after this grand teaching section in chapters 5–7, you get several stories in chapter 8 of Jesus' healing or showing His power in various ways. We might put it this way: Matthew has shown us the words of Jesus in chapters 5–7; now in chapter 8 he's going to show us the works of Jesus.

The Basic Outline of Matthew 8–9

It will be helpful to understand the basic outline of Matthew 8–9 as we examine these miracle stories and descriptions of discipleship. Here is a general guide to these chapters:

- Three Miracle Stories (8:1-17)
- Two Descriptions of Discipleship (8:18-22)
- Three Miracle Stories (8:23–9:8)
- Two Descriptions of Discipleship (9:9-17)
- Three Miracle Stories (9:18-34)

In these two chapters alone there are nine miracle stories that contain a total of ten miracles. It's as if Matthew is giving us back-to-back-to-back highlights demonstrating the authority of Jesus. At the end of the Sermon on the Mount in chapter 7, Matthew says, "When Jesus had finished this sermon, the crowds were astonished at His teaching, because He was teaching them like one who had authority, and not like their scribes" (7:28-29). Now in chapter 8 that same authority is put into action as Jesus rules over sickness, nature, demons, and death. So what is Matthew's point in telling us all this?

The Bottom Line of Matthew 8–9

Matthew shows us in these chapters that **Jesus possesses absolute authority in the world and warrants absolute allegiance from the world**. This is good news, for in this sin-stricken world we are familiar with sickness and struggle and disease and suffering. The National Cancer Institute reports that one out of every two people who are born in the United States today will be diagnosed with cancer at some point in their lifetime. Even if it's not cancer, there are any number of sicknesses and struggles that we have to deal with. Right here in Birmingham, the city where I minister, we have recently experienced the deadly force of a natural disaster in the form of a tornado. So whether it's cancer, tornadoes, disease, or death, Matthew wants us to see that Jesus has authority over it all. And once we see this, then it's only logical to conclude that Jesus has authority over our lives as well. For those who know they are sinful and weak, this is *really* good news.

The Portrait of Jesus in Matthew 8
MATTHEW 8:1-34

Jesus has authority over disease.

Immediately in the opening verses of chapter 8, we see that Jesus has authority over disease. This authority is revealed in three different ways in three different stories. In verses 1-4, **He cleanses the physically unclean**. This term "cleanses" is a key term for Matthew, for this story is not simply framed as a story of healing. Leprosy, also called Hansen's disease, is probably the "serious skin disease" in view here. Leprosy was not simply looked at as a physical condition in first-century Judaism. To be sure, leprosy *is* a physical disease that attacks the nerve system, sometimes to the point where a victim can no longer feel pain. Those with leprosy experience infection easily, which leads to the degeneration of tissues, organs, and limbs, to the point where limbs become deformed and then eventually fall off. So leprosy is definitely a physical condition—brutally physical; but it is more than that.

Leviticus 13–14 describes skin conditions not simply as physical illnesses, but as spiritual contagion. Lepers were seen as repulsively

unclean, cursed by God (Num 12:10). They were required to stay a
certain distance from everyone around them. If someone began to
approach them, or if they began to approach someone else, they were to
yell out, "Unclean, unclean!"—even to touch a leper would be to make
yourself unclean (Lev 13:45; 22:4-6). With this background, we are better able to grasp the significance of this first miracle in Matthew 8. Jesus
is coming into contact with the physically, spiritually, and ceremonially
unclean. The leper approaches Jesus, which immediately creates a sense
of tension in the story. He says, "Lord, if You are willing, You can make
me clean" (Matt 8:2).

Consider what the leper does know: Jesus is able to heal. The leper
didn't question Jesus' ability or power; he knew that Jesus was *able* to
heal. The issue becomes what the leper doesn't know: Is Jesus *willing* to
heal? Will Jesus *choose* to heal him?

We must understand the distinction between Jesus' sovereign power
and Jesus' sovereign will. Both of them are extremely important, especially when it comes to praying for healing in our lives. For example, if
you have cancer or any other sickness or disease, you shouldn't doubt
Jesus' sovereign power. He is absolutely able to heal you, no question
about it. He has authority over disease.

The question then becomes, "Is Jesus *willing* to heal?" In other
words, is it His will for you to be made well? That's a different question
altogether. In this instance in Matthew 8, the answer is "yes," Jesus is willing. However, in the case of Paul's struggle with "a thorn in the flesh"
(2 Cor 12:7), the Lord was not willing to heal in that instance. He told
Paul the reason He refused to heal him, namely, so that Paul would
know the strength and sufficiency of Christ (2 Cor 12:9). In such situations, we too have to trust both the power and the wisdom of God. The
One who is *able* to heal also knows *when* to heal. The Lord knows what
will bring Him the most glory and what will bring us the most good.

In the spring of 2000, James Montgomery Boice, the well-known
pastor of Tenth Presbyterian Church in Philadelphia, was diagnosed
with cancer. He shared with his congregation about how they should
pray for him:

> Should you pray for a miracle? Well, you're free to do that,
> of course. My general impression is that the God who is able
> to do miracles—and he certainly can—is also able to keep
> you from getting the problem in the first place. So although
> miracles do happen, they're rare by definition. A miracle has

to be an unusual thing. Above all, I would say pray for the glory of God. If you think of God glorifying himself in history and you say, where in all of history has God most glorified himself? He did it at the cross of Jesus Christ, and it wasn't by delivering Jesus from the cross, though he could have. Jesus said, "Don't you think I could call down from my Father ten legions of angels for my defense?" But he didn't do that. And yet that's where God is most glorified. God is in charge. When things like this come into our lives, they are not accidental. It's not as if God somehow forgot what was going on, and something bad slipped by. God is not only the one who is in charge; God is also good. Everything he does is good.

Boice's testimony is a model in terms of what it means to have confidence in the sovereign power of God and to trust in the sovereign will of God. Like Boice, we too must trust that God will do what is good. Boice died eight weeks after sharing those words with his congregation, but he died trusting in the sovereign power and sovereign will of God. He knew that Jesus was able to heal, yet He submitted to Jesus' will—His good, pleasing, and perfect will (Rom 12:1-2).

In the case of the leper in Matthew 8, it was Jesus' will to heal him. He reached out and touched the man, saying, "I am willing; be made clean" (v. 3). Have you stopped to realize the beauty of Jesus' response? To touch a leper is to take his uncleanness upon yourself, and yet we know from the healing of the centurion's servant in the next story that it was not at all necessary for Jesus to touch this leper in order to heal him (v. 8). He could have spoken a word, and the leprosy would be gone. But Jesus touched him. Don't miss the point: Jesus identifies with the uncleanness of the leper in order to make the leper clean.

In this brief scene we get a foretaste of what Jesus will do, ultimately on the cross, with the uncleanness in the lives of every one of us. All of us stand before Christ dirty and stained with the shame of sin. We have things in our lives, either past or present, that make us feel untouchable—sins we've struggled with or sins others have committed against us. In and of ourselves, we are unclean before a holy God. But on the cross, Jesus identifies with our uncleanness, taking the shame and filth of our sin upon Himself in order to make us clean. Praise God for such a compassionate Savior!

In verse 4 Jesus tells the man not to say anything to anyone, but to go and present himself to the priest to show that he is clean, which is what the law prescribed.[16] Have you ever wondered why in certain instances Jesus tells people to stay quiet?[17] Several explanations have been offered, but we can at least see in this first miracle story in Matthew 8 that Jesus' goal was not to advertise Himself as a wonder worker who would miraculously overthrow the Roman government, which is what some thought the Messiah would do. Jesus had not come to impress the crowds; He had come to die for sinners (Carson, *Matthew*, 199).

After seeing Jesus heal the physically unclean in verses 1-4, now in verses 5-13 we see that **He heals the ethnically outcast.** The centurion in this story and his servant would have been Gentiles, likely brought in for military service from somewhere outside Galilee, like Lebanon or Syria. As a Roman centurion, he was not only viewed as an ethnic outsider by the Jewish people, but also as one who was deliberately opposed to the people of God. This context makes Jesus' reply in verse 7 surprising, because a devout Jew would likely not even go into the home of an unbelieving Gentile. Yet, as soon as Jesus surprisingly offered to come to this Gentile's home, the centurion confessed that he was not worthy to have Jesus come under his roof. He knew that Jesus only needed to speak the word for the healing to occur.

When Jesus hears the centurion's reply, He says, "I have not found anyone in Israel with so great a faith!" (v. 10). This should cause us to ask, "What kind of faith is this?" Here's the picture Matthew gives us: faith is humble trust in the authority of Jesus. See the humility of this Gentile centurion calling Jesus, a Jewish teacher, "Lord." He is too overwhelmed to even have Jesus in his home, so he implores Jesus to merely speak the word. The centurion's explanation for such faith in verse 9 is astounding. He knew what it was like to have authority over soldiers and servants, since Rome's authority had been bestowed on him. The centurion perceived that Jesus had this kind of authority over disease. Jesus says "Go," and sickness will go; He says "Do this" to paralysis, and it is done. Jesus has absolute authority over disease.

We have no evidence before this in Matthew that Jesus had ever performed a miracle in this manner. So this man, this Gentile centurion, wasn't leaning on prior information. He simply and humbly

---

[16] See Leviticus 13–14 for more on the law's instructions about leprosy and cleansing.

[17] D. A. Carson lists several other examples in Matthew's Gospel of Jesus telling someone not to make known either His miraculous works or His identity: 9:30; 12:16; 16:20; 17:9. Carson, *Matthew*, 199.

had absolute trust in the authority of Jesus in a way that no one else
among the Jewish people, including the disciples, had displayed up to
this point. In verses 11-12 Jesus goes on to talk about how the "sons of
the kingdom"—a reference to Jewish men and women who assumed
they had a biological right to be part of the people of God—would be
cast out of God's presence into hell for eternity because of their lack of
faith. The example of the centurion's faith, then, is not only important
because it displays humble trust, but also because such faith is the essential determinant of a person's eternal destiny.

Jesus' words about Gentiles being a part of the kingdom in verses
11-12 would have been shocking to Matthew's Jewish readers, essentially
saying to them that their Jewishness guaranteed them nothing in eternity. The only thing that mattered was whether or not they had faith.
This same truth applies to every human being alive today. Your eternal
destiny is dependent on humble trust in the authority of Jesus to save
you from your sins and to rule over you as the Lord of your life. And all
who trust in Him like this, regardless of ethnicity or background, will be
welcomed by the King at His table forever.

Finally, in relation to Jesus' authority over disease, He not only
cleanses the physically unclean and heals the ethnically outcast, but
also **He restores the culturally marginalized**. In verses 14-15 Jesus healed
another unlikely candidate from the outskirts of Jewish society and culture: "When Jesus went into Peter's house, He saw his mother-in-law
lying in bed with a fever. So He touched her hand, and the fever left her.
Then she got up and began to serve Him." After healing a leper and a
Gentile, Jesus now heals a woman, Peter's mother-in-law. Jesus heals her
with a simple touch. Again, in His extravagant grace, Jesus defies the
traditions and practices of His day (Osborne, *Matthew*, 298).

Matthew concludes this first section in verses 16-17 by telling of
Jesus' healing of "many" who were demon-possessed and sick, followed
by another fulfillment saying:

> When evening came, they brought to Him many who were demon-
> possessed. He drove out the spirits with a word and healed all who
> were sick, so that what was spoken through the prophet Isaiah might be
> fulfilled: He Himself took our weaknesses and carried our diseases.

Matthew's quotation in verse 17 is from Isaiah 53:4, a part of the prophecy of Jesus as the suffering servant in Isaiah 53. In the verses that immediately follow, Isaiah prophesies,

But He was pierced because of our transgressions,
crushed because of our iniquities;
punishment for our peace was on Him,
and we are healed by His wounds.
We all went astray like sheep;
we all have turned to our own way;
and the Lord has punished Him
for the iniquity of us all. (Isa 53:5-6)

Isaiah's prophecy concerns Jesus' substitutionary death in the place of sinners, which causes many to wonder how this prophecy relates to Jesus' physical healing ministry. Does Christ's death on the cross ensure that believers won't have to endure sickness in this world anymore? This is an important question, for we can't afford to be confused concerning what it means that Jesus has authority over disease.

Some people have read these verses and concluded that as a Christian, God's will for you is to be healthy (even in this world), because Jesus has taken away your sicknesses. This kind of thinking is at the core of health-and-wealth teaching, or prosperity doctrine as it is sometimes called, both here in the United States and around the world. For example, here's well-known pastor and author Joel Osteen's advice:

Maybe Alzheimer's disease runs in your family genes, but don't succumb to it. Instead, say every day, "My mind is alert. I have clarity of thought. I have a good memory. Every cell in my body is increasing and getting healthier." If you'll rise up in your authority, you can be the one to put a stop to the negative things in your family line. . . . Start boldly declaring, "God is restoring health unto me. I am getting better every day in every way." (Osteen, *Becoming a Better You,* 45, 114)

Osteen is not the only person putting out this kind of unbiblical teaching. Health, wealth, and prosperity teachers are all too common in Christian circles today, as people flock to hear these men and women speak, and they buy their books by the millions. This is most certainly *not* what Matthew 8:17 or Isaiah 53:4 is teaching.[18]

---

[18] For a critique of the prosperity gospel, see David W. Jones and Russell S. Woodbridge's *Health, Wealth & Happiness: Has the Prosperity Gospel Overshadowed the Gospel of Christ?* (Grand Rapids: Kregel Publications, 2011).

By connecting Jesus' healing authority to Isaiah's prophecy, Matthew is showing that He has the power to overcome all our suffering. In light of the larger context of Isaiah, Matthew attributes this power and authority to Jesus because He paid the price to overcome all our sin. That is the point of the cross. And this truth makes sense if we consider the larger context of redemptive history.

All suffering in the world ultimately goes back to sin, for before sin came into the picture, there was no suffering, according to Genesis 1–2. But when sin entered the world in Genesis 3, suffering entered the world, and as a result, we live in a world marked by evil and suffering, sickness and pain. So when Jesus came to die on a cross, He came to address the root problem, which is not *suffering*; the root problem is *sin*. And He paid the price with His life to overcome our *sin*, so that you and I could be free from sin's penalty.

If, therefore, God has dealt with the root of sin through the death of His Son, does that mean His will for us in this world is that we would no longer experience pain, sickness, and suffering? Absolutely not! The miracles in Matthew's Gospel are intended to give us a picture of what is to come in the fullness of God's kingdom, that is, when Christ fully and finally asserts His authority and reign over the earth. But that time is not yet. In the meantime, we still live in a world of suffering and pain, and we will see later on in this Gospel that our suffering actually increases in this world as a result of trusting in Jesus for salvation. Two chapters later, Jesus is going to tell His disciples that they will be flogged, betrayed, hated, and persecuted in this world for following Him (10:16-25). And this is not just an isolated verse or theme. Listen to Paul's consistent testimony to suffering in the lives of believers:

> For it has been given to you on Christ's behalf not only to believe in Him, but also to suffer for Him. (Phil 1:29)

> Now I rejoice in my sufferings for you, and I am completing in my flesh what is lacking in Christ's afflictions for His body, that is, the church. (Col 1:24)

> We are pressured in every way but not crushed; we are perplexed but not in despair; we are persecuted but not abandoned; we are struck down but not destroyed. We always carry the death of Jesus in our body, so that the life of Jesus may also be revealed in our body. (2 Cor 4:8-10)

My goal is to know Him and the power of His resurrection and the fellowship of His sufferings. (Phil 3:10)

For we know that the whole creation has been groaning together with labor pains until now. (Rom 8:22)

We could list a host of other verses on the theme of suffering, but let it suffice to say, the Bible nowhere says that because you have been saved from your sins, you will not get cancer or some other illness. Instead, the Bible says that Jesus has overcome the root of all suffering—sin itself—and that He has paid the price to conquer sin so that you don't need to be afraid of cancer or tumors or Alzheimer's or anything else. Regardless of what happens in this decaying world, there is a day coming when death, mourning, crying, and pain will be no more (Rev 21:4). As we wait for that day, we don't run *from* suffering; we rejoice *in* suffering. Paul, the same apostle who wrote so much about the reality of suffering in the lives of Christians, also wrote about the joy that we can experience in the midst of suffering.

And not only that, but we also rejoice in our afflictions, because we know that affliction produces endurance, endurance produces proven character, and proven character produces hope. This hope will not disappoint us, because God's love has been poured out in our hearts through the Holy Spirit who was given to us. (Rom 5:3-5)

For I consider that the sufferings of this present time are not worth comparing with the glory that is going to be revealed to us. (Rom 8:18)

For our momentary light affliction is producing for us an absolutely incomparable eternal weight of glory. (2 Cor 4:17)

Before moving to the next section, it's important to recognize at least two kinds of suffering. Some suffering is simply due to the general effects of sin in the world. Job experienced this kind of suffering, which was not directly tied to a particular sin in his life. God brings about suffering like this for His own purposes, though those purposes are often hidden from us, and we should humbly embrace this kind of suffering with trust in God. But there's another type of suffering in the Bible, and that's suffering that happens due to a particular sin in someone's life. When a Christian continues in sin, he will inevitably suffer, for God disciplines those whom He loves (Heb 12:5-11). A person may suffer physically, emotionally, relationally, or in other ways, but in the end sin inevitably leads to suffering. The proper response in that kind of situation is not to rejoice in suffering, but to run from your sin.

Jesus has authority over disciples.

Following this section on Jesus' authority over disease, Matthew inserts a story of two potential disciples in verses 18-22. A similar passage is found in Luke 9:57-62, where three men approach Jesus, and there too we find out the steep cost of what it means to follow Jesus. It may not be immediately obvious how this teaching on discipleship relates to Jesus' healing in the previous section, but Matthew purposefully places these events alongside one another. Jesus has authority over disease *and* Jesus has authority over disciples.

The first man comes to Jesus in verse 19 in seeming over-eagerness, saying, "Teacher, I will follow You wherever You go!" but Jesus knows this man hasn't counted the cost of what is involved in discipleship. Jesus tells the man that following Him will not even guarantee a roof over the man's head. In other words, "If you follow Me, I'm all you've got." This potential disciple needs to learn that **Jesus is worthy of unconditional trust**, even if it means giving up earthly security and comforts. We too must know this if we want to follow Jesus.

Following Christ may mean losing everything in this world. This is another problem with the prosperity gospel—it makes Jesus a means to an end. You come to Jesus to get health, wealth, or anything else you want; just fill in the blank. The problem is that you shouldn't come to Jesus to get stuff; you come to Jesus to get Jesus. You may lose everything in this world, but He is enough.

The second potential disciple learned an equally valuable lesson in verses 21-22: **Jesus is worthy of undivided affection**. This man said to Jesus, "First let me go bury my father." Commentators disagree over what is actually being requested here. Does the man just want to give his father (who is deceased) a proper funeral, or does he want to wait until his father (who is alive) dies and he gets his inheritance before he agrees to follow Jesus? Regardless of the precise meaning of the request, Jesus' response is direct: "Follow Me, and let the dead bury their own dead." More important than honoring your father or receiving an inheritance is following Jesus. The Savior wants undivided affection.

Recognizing Jesus' sovereign authority in the world should lead to giving Jesus total allegiance in your life. His authority is not to be toyed or trifled with. J. C. Ryle once said, "Nothing, in fact, has done more harm to Christianity than the practice of filling the ranks of Christ's army with every volunteer who is willing to make a little profession" (Ryle, *Matthew*, 59). Remember, Jesus is not begging for followers in Matthew 8. He's actually turning them away because He warrants unconditional trust and undivided affection from those who follow Him. When Jesus speaks, leprosy, paralysis, and fever obey. The question is, "Do *you* obey?"

Jesus has authority over disaster.

Jesus' authority over His disciples sets the stage for three consecutive miracle stories that come next in chapters 8–9, the first of which appears in 8:23-27. In this brief and miraculous account, we see that Jesus has authority over disaster. It's at this point that many sermons on this text launch into extravagant promises about how Jesus will calm the storms in your life. As the question usually goes, "What storms are you facing in your life—in your marriage, in your home, or in your health?" We are then assured, "Jesus will calm those storms." The only problem is that's not the point of this story. The point is much deeper than that, which becomes obvious when you pay attention to the question the disciples ask at the end of the story in verse 27: "What kind of man is this?—even the winds and the sea obey Him!"

The disciples were good Jewish men, and they knew that only God (Yahweh in the Old Testament) is able to direct the wind and the waves. Psalm 89:9 says, "You rule the raging sea; when its waves surge, You still them." Likewise, in Psalm 107:29 the psalmist announces, "He stilled the storm to a murmur, and the waves of the sea were hushed." Jesus' disciples marveled because they began to realize that the man in the boat with them was not just a man. God Himself was in the boat with them! **That's the point of the story: Jesus is God**. The authority that belongs to God is the authority that belongs to Jesus.

Having seen the point of the story, we also need to see **the promise in the story**. The promise is not that all the storms in your life will end soon. The Bible does not guarantee this, nor can anyone else. Your cancer may not go away, and that struggle in your marriage may not end this week, or even this year. As a believer, your confidence is not that these storms will end very soon, but that in the midst of the storms in your life, you will never be alone. God Himself, in the person of Jesus Christ, will be with you every step in the midst of the storm.

Faith is not confidence that trials won't come your way. Faith is confidence that no matter what wind and waves come your way in this world, the God of the universe will be right there in the boat with you. His power and His presence will see you through. Christian, you are not alone, and ultimately you are safe in the presence of the One who has ultimate authority over all disaster.

Jesus has authority over demons.

The second miracle story that occurs at the end of chapter 8 occurs in verses 28-34. Jesus has authority over disaster, and Jesus has authority over demons. In this fascinating account, we have a portrait of demons who violently possess two men, yet they are deathly afraid of the Son of God. Knowing that Jesus has absolute authority over them, the demons plead for Him to cast them into a herd of pigs, and He does. It's quite telling that these demons hate and loathe everything about Jesus, yet they are powerless to do anything apart from His permission! Satan can do nothing in this world, and nothing in your life, apart from the sovereign permission of God. Satan is a lion (1 Pet 5:8), but he is a lion on a leash. And God holds the leash. Demons decidedly do not have all authority; Jesus does.

Do you see how passages like this encourage us not to fear? We don't have to be afraid of what may happen in this world, because Jesus has authority over it all. Many Christians, in the midst of a world of pain and suffering, live in fear and anxiety and worry, wondering what will happen in this or that situation. This tendency to fear is why we must remember the authority of Jesus. Sometimes we lack even the faith of demons, for **the demons have fear because of their belief**. They know who Jesus is, and they are scared out of their minds (Jas 2:19). But we are just the opposite: **We often have fear because of our unbelief**. If we realized what the demons realize, we would know that we have no reason to fear.

Jesus is the Son of God, with all authority over disease, disaster, and demons, and nothing can touch us apart from His sovereign power and in accordance with His sovereign will. We, as followers of Christ, are the most secure people in the world, and our security is not based on how big our house is, how good our job is, how stable our economy is, or who our president is. We are secure simply because we are in the hands of the One who has all authority in the whole world, and because this One with all authority loves us and cares for us. God is committed to providing for us in the midst of struggles with sin, demons, natural disasters, and various diseases. Hear, then, Christ's question in verse 26: "Why are you fearful, you of little faith?" How can we not trust such a Savior?

Did you notice the question the demons shouted out in verse 29? They said, "What do You have to do with us, Son of God? Have You come here to torment us before the time?" Notice that phrase, "before the time." The demons know that there is coming a day when they will be fully and finally judged by the Lord and cast out completely into utter darkness (Matt 25:41). As believers, we look toward that day with great anticipation. Leprosy, paralysis, fever, and natural disasters will be no more. Demons will no longer tempt or torment God's people. The authority of Jesus will be fully and finally asserted; His kingdom will come and His will be done on a new earth as it is in heaven. And all of this is possible, all of this is guaranteed, because of what Jesus has done on the cross. This is our great hope.

A Pause after Reading Matthew 8

Jesus' power and sovereignty are not simply there to be observed, but to be relied on and rejoiced in. In light of the realities of Jesus' authority in this text, we should respond in a number of ways:

- Let's *trust* wholeheartedly in Jesus' authority.
- Let's *rest* peacefully in Jesus' authority.
- Let's *submit* completely to Jesus' authority.
- Let's *rejoice* gladly in Jesus' authority.

Reflect and Discuss

1. How does Jesus' absolute authority contrast with the relativism of our day?
2. Why is a privatized, keep-it-to-yourself faith incompatible with Jesus' authority?
3. Jesus heals three unlikely characters in this chapter. How might this impact those with whom you seek to share the gospel?
4. How does the account of the centurion highlight the centrality of faith in our response to Jesus?
5. Does Jesus' healing ministry guarantee the healing of those for whom we pray? Why or why not?
6. How would you counsel someone who wanted to follow Jesus as long as they could maintain their current lifestyle?

7. Explain how Matthew 8 speaks against the prosperity gospel.
8. How can Jesus' calming of the storm give you comfort in your own trials and suffering?
9. How do verses 28-34 speak to Jesus' authority in regard to Satan?
10. List five ways Matthew 8 demonstrates that Jesus was more (though not less) than a mere man?

The King's Authority (Part 2)

MATTHEW 9

Main Idea: Jesus meets our greatest need by providing for the forgiveness of our sins and by defeating death on our behalf.

I. **The Portrait of Jesus in Matthew 9**
   A. Jesus has authority over sin.
      1. Jesus' authority penetrates to the root of all suffering, which is sin.
      2. Our ultimate need is never physical; it's always spiritual.
      3. The good news of the kingdom: Jesus will forgive you of all your sins.
      4. Forgiveness is God's greatest gift because it meets our greatest need.
   B. Jesus has authority to save.
      1. The call of Matthew
      2. The question about fasting
   C. Jesus has authority over death.
      1. He gives hope in the midst of despair.
      2. He brings life in the midst of death.
   D. Jesus has authority over disability.
      1. He is gently merciful.
      2. He is the promised Messiah.
   E. Jesus has authority over the Devil.
      1. Jesus' ministry on earth: Satan has been defeated.
      2. Jesus' promise for eternity: Satan will be destroyed.
II. **The Bottom Line of Matthew 8–9**
   A. Jesus possesses absolute authority in the world.
   B. Jesus warrants absolute allegiance from the world.
      1. The crowds revere him.
      2. The proud reject him.
      3. The faithful renounce everything to follow him.
III. **The Personal Question from Matthew 8–9**

The King's Authority (Part 2)
MATTHEW 9

In the previous chapter, we saw that Matthew has arranged chapters 8–9 to work together. By seeing this relationship, we can understand better what Matthew is trying to tell us. There are three sections containing three miracle stories each (8:1-17; 8:23–9:8; 9:18-34) and two sections that each contain two descriptions of discipleship (8:18-22; 9:9-17). Chapter 8 ends two-thirds of the way through the second section of miracle stories.

Matthew has already shown us in chapter 8 that Jesus has authority over disease—leprosy, paralysis, and fevers are all His servants. He also has authority over disciples, disasters, and demons. And all this is good news for followers of Christ. We trust in His authority over all these things and we rejoice in it. Now in chapter 9, this portrait gets more beautiful, for we realize that we have only been touching on the surface of the real problem. The real problem of the human condition is much deeper and much more severe than a cancer diagnosis or a tornado coming through your neighborhood. And the magnitude of this fundamental problem serves to magnify our great God and Savior Jesus Christ.

The Portrait of Jesus in Matthew 9
MATTHEW 9:1-34

Matthew begins his third miracle story cycle in 9:1-8. This story is the only record we have in the entire Gospel of Matthew where Jesus forgives a specific individual, and it happens to a man who didn't ask for forgiveness! The man was paralyzed, so his friends brought him to Jesus for healing, but we don't hear anything about a request for forgiveness. Try to put yourself in this man's shoes (or on his mat) and imagine what would be going through your mind if the first thing Jesus said to you was, "Have courage, son, yours sins are forgiven" (v. 2). Forgiveness may not have been what he was looking for, and therein may be the key to the whole story. The text doesn't specifically say, but it seems as if this man and his friends were hoping that Jesus would heal his paralysis. Jesus astounds everyone when He says, in effect, that the man had a much deeper issue than paralysis.

Jesus has authority over sin.

Matthew makes plain that Jesus has authority over sin. A lot of people in the first century would have equated this man's disability with sin. In John 9 people basically assumed a certain man was blind due to either his sin or his parents' sin; therefore, it is likely here that people, maybe even the paralytic himself, thought he was paralyzed due to sin. To be fair, that's a possible explanation, since the Bible does give us pictures of physical penalties for sin in our lives (see 1 Cor 11:29-30). However, the text doesn't tell us whether or not *this* man's sickness was due to a particular sin in his life. Nevertheless, the point still stands: all suffering is ultimately caused by sin in the world.

This miracle story teaches us that **Jesus' authority penetrates to the root of all suffering, which is sin**. As we saw in the previous section (8:16-17, pp. 108–12 above), all of our spiritual and physical struggles, including suffering and pain, can be traced back to sin and separation from our Creator. This sin can be either in your life, as in sins that you have committed and are suffering for, or in the world. This latter category refers to sins that occur as a result of living in a fallen, diseased, decaying world. Unlike sin in your own life, which can bring suffering and other negative consequences, including God's fatherly discipline (Heb 12:5-11), sin in the world leads to suffering that is not necessarily connected to a particular wrongdoing. The point of this passage is that Jesus came to deal with the root of all suffering: sin.

Jesus' approach to this paralytic teaches us that **our ultimate need is never physical; it's always spiritual**. This holds true no matter what type of suffering we are experiencing. If we are suffering as a result of our own sin, the need that we address is spiritual—we go to the core of where we are in our relationship with God. On the other hand, even if we are suffering simply as a result of living in a sinful world, our ultimate need is still spiritual. Like Paul in 2 Corinthians 12:9, we desperately need to know in the midst of our suffering that the Lord's grace is sufficient.

Jesus' authority over sin infuriated the scribes (the teachers of the law) because they knew only God can forgive sins. Jesus was thus claiming to be God, which brings us to **the good news of the kingdom**. Chapters 8–9 continue to put Jesus' deity on display. Only God is able to calm the wind and the waves. Only God is able to command disease. Only God can forgive sins. Therefore, since Jesus does all these things, we conclude that Jesus is God. In other words, the King is here.

Recall from chapter 8 the error that many people fall into at this point. The great hope you have due to the King's arrival is not that Jesus will heal you of all your sicknesses. After all, we don't send missionaries across the globe and say, "Trust in Christ, and your cancer will be gone." The good news is not that you will instantly be given better health, but that Jesus will forgive you of all your sins.

This is what we need most. For when our sins are forgiven, the root problem is severed. All other struggles we have in this world are temporary. To use Paul's language in 2 Corinthians 4:16-17, "Even though our outer person is being destroyed, our inner person is being renewed day by day. For our momentary light affliction is producing for us an absolutely incomparable eternal weight of glory."

God gives us many good things, but **forgiveness is God's greatest gift because it meets our greatest need**. The central message of Christianity is that God will forgive your sins through Jesus. There is no greater news in the whole world than this. The idea that by trusting in Jesus you will receive health and wealth is no gospel at all. The gospel is so much greater than that: Trust in Jesus, and you will be made right before God. That's the news we need to hear, and that's the news we need to spread around the world. No matter what you've done against God, no matter how sinful your past or present might be, God is gracious, and through Christ He will wipe your sins away.

Jesus has authority to save.

Matthew recounts the story of his own call to discipleship in verses 9-13. Jesus has declared His authority over sin, and now He demonstrates that authority with a sinner named Matthew (or Levi, as he is referred to in Mark 2:14 and Luke 5:27). Jesus has authority to save, even in the case of tax collectors. This was Matthew's profession before becoming one of the 12 apostles and before recording this very Gospel. Tax collectors were constantly interacting with unclean Gentiles (non-Jews), and they were known for taking advantage of Jewish people for the sake of Rome and for the sake of their own pockets. Nevertheless, Jesus goes straight to this despised man.

The call of Matthew is a wonderful demonstration of the fact that Jesus pursues sinners. After all, why would He choose Matthew? Jesus was surrounded by tons of people, and His miracles were attracting quite a crowd. Yet, He pursues Matthew and calls him as a disciple. It is incredibly good news that Jesus summons sinners to Himself. His call to Matthew in verse 9—"Follow Me!"—is the same weighty call He gave to Peter, Andrew, James, and John earlier (4:18-22). Matthew was summoned to leave his post, his position, and his possessions. Tax collectors were usually fairly wealthy because there was so much room for profit in their business, so this was a significant financial and career sacrifice. If following Jesus didn't work out for Matthew, what job could a former tax collector get? Undoubtedly, this was a decisive moment in Matthew's life as he dropped everything to follow Jesus. May God help us to be done with casual discipleship—as if there were such a thing!

Notice that Matthew didn't leave his tax booth in a spirit of grim resignation. Immediately after stepping out to follow Jesus, he threw a banquet, a feast for sinners! We've already seen that Jesus pursues and summons sinners, and now we see that Jesus satisfies sinners. This upset the Pharisees, because they ignored sinners. They stayed away from the tax collectors and other people who weren't ceremonially and culturally clean like themselves.

It is my hope that the church I am a part of will not be like the Pharisees as we consider the people around us. I want the church I pastor to be a people who come alongside and minister to prostitutes and drug pushers, to homosexual men and women, and to the outcasts. This doesn't mean we join them in their sin, but we do reach out to them because we love sinners. We realize what these Pharisees didn't realize— that we are all sinners in need of God's grace and mercy. We take seriously the words of Jesus: "Those who are well don't need a doctor, but the sick do" (v. 12). Sick people clearly need a doctor, but sinful people desperately need a Redeemer. This is why Jesus came. He quotes from Hosea 6:6, "I desire mercy and not sacrifice" (Matt 9:13), to make clear that He has come to change sinners' hearts, not to prop up people who think they are righteous through their religious traditions and ritualistic worship.

Jesus' interaction with the Pharisees in verses 9-13 leads directly into **the question about fasting** in verses 14-17. We can split this section up into two parts. First, we need to understand why Jesus' disciples didn't fast then, in the time of Jesus' earthly ministry. That's the big question posed by John's disciples, to which Jesus replies, "Can the wedding guests be sad while the groom is with them?" (v. 15). This loaded statement from Jesus is worth reflecting on.

Fasting is related to sadness or mourning. Fasting is a picture of mourning, of broken-heartedness. Oftentimes, people fast when things aren't going the way they are supposed to. But Jesus here uses the imagery of a wedding feast with wedding guests and a bridegroom. Throughout the Old Testament, God had pictured Himself as the husband, the groom, of His bride Israel. For instance, Hosea says,

> In that day—this is the Lord's declaration—you will call Me, 'My husband.'. . . I will take you to be My wife forever. I will take you to be My wife in righteousness, justice, love, and compassion. I will take you to be My wife in faithfulness, and you will know Yahweh. (Hos 2:16, 19-20)[19]

These were promises that God would draw His people to Himself like a groom seeks after a bride. With this beautiful imagery, Jesus is making the incredible claim, "The groom is with you!" In other words, "I am the groom!" Jesus is saying that He is God, and that He has come to betroth His people to Him forever.

In light of the fact that Jesus is claiming to be present as the groom, it makes sense that His disciples would not be fasting. You don't sit around at a wedding mourning and fasting. This is a time for feasting, not fasting. For generations God's people longed for the groom to come, for God to come and save them. They had prayed and mourned and fasted, waiting for that day. And now, Jesus says, the day is here. After a thousand years of waiting, the King had finally come! And that changed everything.

In verses 16-17, Jesus uses two more illustrations to make a similar point. You don't put an unshrunk patch on an old garment, He says, for it will make a tear worse. And you don't put new wine into old wineskins, for the old containers can't hold the new wine. God was also doing something new with the coming of Jesus, and this was not just a revision or an update of the Jewish religious system. Christ's coming was a transformation of everything. This royal bridegroom was making a way for people to come to God. This was a time for celebration.

Although the present hour was a time for celebration, Jesus spoke of a time when fasting would be appropriate. He says in verse 15, "The time will come when the groom will be taken away from them, and then they will fast." We see here why Jesus' disciples do fast now. The time for fasting began immediately after Jesus died on the cross, rose from the grave, and ascended into heaven. The bridegroom was gone, so there's a sense in which we would expect to see disciples of Jesus fasting in the

---

[19] Two other examples of similar language include Isa 62:5 and Jer 31:32.

book of Acts (Acts 13:2; 14:23).[20] However, in light of His death and triumphant resurrection, what reason did they still have to mourn?

It's crucial that we understand the difference between Old Testament fasting and New Testament fasting. Old Testament fasting was a longing and a waiting for the King to come. It was purely a future hope. New Testament fasting, on the other hand, has both a *past* and a *future* element to it. The *past* element has to do with looking back to the life, death, and resurrection of Christ, believing firmly that the King has come. Followers of Christ have tasted the new wine of His presence. We have been forgiven of our sins, and we have been satisfied by our Savior. So in that sense, there is not mourning; there is rejoicing.

Yet, at the same time, we have been promised that there is more to come; this is the *future* element to our fasting. Although the King has come, we know that our world is still full of sickness, disease, suffering, and pain. The effects of sin and the fall are all around us: paralysis, fevers, malaria, HIV/AIDS, cancer, tornadoes, hurricanes, etc. Based on the entire context of Matthew 9, we know that Jesus has authority over all these things; therefore, what we are longing and fasting for is the day when the King will put an end to these menaces once and for all. We'll live in a new heaven and a new earth where we will dwell forever with our King (Rev 21).

In Acts 1:11 those early disciples were told to look for Christ's coming. The angel said to them, "This Jesus, who has been taken from you into heaven, will come in the same way that you have seen Him going into heaven." This should continue to be our eager expectation—it's why we fast now. Those who celebrate the ascension of the King now crave the consummation of the kingdom. We fast and we pray and we crave the day when what we have tasted and seen in Christ will be complete.

Jesus has authority over death.

In Matthew 9:18-26 the picture we get of Jesus' authority gets even better. Not only does Jesus have authority to save, but also Jesus has authority over death. Matthew gives us two miracle stories in one episode.

---

[20] On a similar note, Paul speaks of the new day that had arrived as a result of the Lord's coming in 2 Cor 6:2: "Look, now is the acceptable time; now is the day of salvation." He also picks up the wedding/marriage imagery in 2 Cor 11:2 in describing his ministry to the Corinthians: "For I am jealous over you with a godly jealousy, because I have promised you in marriage to one husband—to present a pure virgin to Christ."

Notice the faith of those who approach Jesus in this passage. First, you have a leader named Jairus who came and knelt before Jesus. Jairus confessed that Jesus had the authority to save His daughter (v. 18). Then, on the way to see Jairus's daughter, a woman who had been sick, unclean, and socially ostracized for 12 years touched Jesus. Matthew lets us in on what she was thinking: "If I can just touch His robe, I'll be made well!" (v. 21). Jesus' authority is comforting, then, because **He gives hope in the midst of despair**. Just picture this lady: for 12 years she had lived with this health problem and no one had been able to help her. To add insult to injury, this was not just a physical problem; it was also spiritual. According to Jewish law, this lady was ceremonially unclean, so she was not allowed to go to the temple and participate in Jewish religious life. It's all but certain that she couldn't have a social life, since people could not touch her for fear of defilement (Lev 15:19). Yet, she believed that she would be made well if only she could touch Jesus' garment, which is exactly what she did (Matt 9:20-21).

When Jesus was touched, He stopped immediately in the middle of a crowd of people. He looked at the woman and said, "Have courage, daughter. . . . Your faith has made you well" (v. 22). Even in a crowd, Jesus gives hope in the midst of despair. What good news to those who are hurting, to those who are walking through pain or struggling in some area of life. You are not lost in the crowd before Jesus. He is intimately aware of every single detail of your life. He knows your struggle, and His love for you is extremely personal. In the middle of the crowds, you have His attention, though not in some self-centered way, as if the world revolves around you. But because you are a child of God, Jesus is attentive to your deepest needs, and you have His affectionate attention.

After healing this unclean woman, Jesus demonstrated His authority over death by raising the daughter of Jairus (vv. 23-26). Jesus not only brings hope in the midst of despair, but **He brings life in the midst of death**. The traditional funeral had already begun, with the flute players brought in and the mourners assembled. But Jesus said, "Leave . . . because the girl isn't dead, but sleeping" (v. 24). Those present laughed at Jesus. Of course, He knew she was dead, but He also knew that her death was only temporary. Can you imagine being at a funeral with a body in a coffin and someone arriving and saying, "Stop the funeral," and then taking the corpse by the hand and saying, "Rise"? What boldness! And yet it was *humble* authority, as Jesus cleared the crowd outside, took the girl by the hand, and raised her up. With Jesus, death is temporary.

When we put Matthew 8–9 together, this life-giving miracle actually makes sense. The One who has authority over disease, natural disasters, and demons, and the One who has severed the root of all suffering with His authority over sin, has authority over death itself. This authority will ultimately be shown when Jesus dies on the cross. And make no mistake, as the One with power over death Jesus *really* died and was placed in a tomb. His heart flat-lined for three days before He walked out of the tomb on His own authority. Death does not have the last word; Jesus does. The Canadian scientist G. B. Hardy once said,

> When I looked at religion, I said, I have two questions. One, has anybody ever conquered death, and two, if they have, did they make a way for me to conquer death? I checked the tomb of Buddha, and it was occupied, and I checked the tomb of Confucius and it was occupied, and I checked the tomb of Mohammed and it was occupied, and I came to the tomb of Jesus and it was empty. And I said, There is one who conquered death. And I asked the second question, Did he make a way for me to do it? And I opened the Bible and discovered that He said, Because I live, ye shall live also. (As cited in MacArthur, *Matthew 8–15*, 75)

In our superficial culture, we need to hear that death is real, that it's difficult and painful. But with Jesus, death is only temporary. So we say with Paul, "For me, living is Christ and dying is gain" (Phil 1:21). Dying is gain when you're with the One who has authority over death.

Jesus has authority over disability.

Matthew includes two more healing stories in chapter 9. The first occurs in verses 27-31 involving two blind men. This encounter teaches us that Jesus has authority over disability. Eager to see, these blind men cried out, "Have mercy on us, Son of David!" (v. 27). This brief plea tells us two things about Jesus. First, **He is gently merciful**, even in the midst of our suffering. Second, **He is the promised Messiah**. This is the first time in the book of Matthew that someone besides Matthew calls Jesus the "Son of David," a title that takes us all the way back to Matthew 1:1, where Matthew introduced Jesus as "the Son of David, the Son of Abraham." There is no question that these blind men realize who Jesus is.

Isaiah 35:5 had promised that with the coming of the Messiah the "eyes of the blind will be opened." These men may well have known of such a prophecy and taken from it great hope in the Messiah. Notice that even in their blindness, these two men were able to see what all the Pharisees and scribes and teachers of the law around them could not see. May the Lord give us eyes to see Jesus as well.

Jesus has authority over the Devil.

Finally, in verses 32-34 we see that Jesus has authority over the Devil. A demon-oppressed man who was mute was brought to Jesus. Many believe the man was deaf as well, being unable to speak and unable to hear specifically because of demonic oppression. We shouldn't conclude from this passage that anyone who is mute or deaf (or has any disability) is oppressed by a demon. Rather, Matthew is using this story as one piece of evidence that Jesus is indeed the Messiah. Jesus' response to John the Baptist in Matthew 11:2-5 is instructive here:

> When John heard in prison what the Messiah was doing, he sent a message by his disciples and asked Him, "Are You the One who is to come, or should we expect someone else?"
>
> Jesus replied to them, "Go and report to John what you hear and see: the blind see, the lame walk, those with skin diseases are healed, the deaf hear, the dead are raised, and the poor are told the good news."

The very things predicted of the Messiah in the Old Testament were being fulfilled in Jesus' ministry. We saw earlier from Isaiah 35:5 that the Messiah would open the eyes of the blind; here is the fuller context, which is extremely relevant for Jesus' healing in Matthew 9:

> Strengthen the weak hands,
> steady the shaking knees!
> Say to the cowardly:
> "Be strong; do not fear!
> Here is your God; vengeance is coming.
> God's retribution is coming; He will save you."
> Then the eyes of the blind will be opened,
> and the ears of the deaf unstopped.
> Then the lame will leap like a deer,
> and the tongue of the mute will sing for joy,

for water will gush in the wilderness,
and streams in the desert. (Isa 35:3-6)

According to Isaiah, the Messiah would usher in a new day, and in the fullness of His kingdom (something which is still future) the blind will see, the deaf will hear, the lame will leap, and the mute will sing for joy.

How do we know this for sure? The response of the Pharisees in verse 34 gives us a clue. They say, "He drives out demons by the ruler of the demons!" They were claiming that Jesus was demonic, and that demonic power was the source behind His miracles. Jesus makes clear in Matthew 12 that that was not the case. Instead of being in league with Satan, there was another reality at work in **Jesus' ministry on earth: Satan has been defeated**. Jesus casts out demons, not because He is of the Devil, but because He has overcome the Devil. Jesus has authority over sin, death, and the Devil himself. Therefore, we can rejoice in **Jesus' promise for eternity: Satan will be destroyed**. The enemy will be cast down, and his sting will never be felt again, because Jesus has all authority over the enemy (1 Cor 15:56-57).

The Bottom Line of Matthew 8–9

After seeing Jesus' miracles and His teaching on discipleship in chapters 8 and 9, several points of application are especially relevant. First and foremost, we must see that **Jesus possesses absolute authority in the world**. This means that He reigns over us supremely. Who are we to tell Him what He should do with our lives? Surely we don't think that we're wiser than the King? He is wise, He is good, and He is in control; therefore let us rest in the security of His supreme authority.

When we think of Jesus' authority, we should not imagine a raw, lifeless power, for that is not the picture the Bible gives us. Right here in Matthew 9 we've watched Jesus in action and we've seen that **He loves us deeply**. His showcase of authority is not self-ish; it's self-less. He even commands certain people that He heals not to tell anyone. He is doing what He's doing because He wants to save sinners from hell. This is why He came. It's why He pursues you, summons you to Himself, and then satisfies you—because He loves you deeply.

Next, we see that in light of His absolute authority in the world, **Jesus warrants absolute allegiance from the world**. Recall the three types of people who responded to the authority of Jesus in this passage. First, you have many people on the outside observing all these miracles, and **the crowds revere Him**. In the first miracle in chapter 9, the healing of the paralytic, the crowds were afraid (v. 8). In response to the last miracle, they marveled (v. 33). So there's a following attached to Jesus, and it consists largely of people who are amazed by His miracles; however, they only admire Him from a distance. The praise of man is passing, and the crowds are fickle. When Jesus walks a long, dusty, difficult road to the cross, few of them will still follow Him.

On the other hand, we see **the proud reject Him**. The scribes, the Pharisees, and the teachers of the law all thought they were counted among the righteous, yet they rejected the Righteous One. This same spirit is reflected all around the world today, even in our own conservative evangelical churches. It's a spirit of self-sufficiency, where we communicate (often implicitly) that we don't need Jesus. We refuse to humble ourselves before Him and trust in Him. That's a foolish response to Jesus, and it's ultimately dangerous. The only proper response is to bow before this glorious King and receive His mercy.

The appropriate response to Jesus in this passage can be seen as **the faithful renounce everything to follow Him**. This response is reflected in two main ways. First, we see those who believed that Jesus had merciful authority to meet their need: a leper (8:2), a centurion (8:5-9), a paralyzed man and his friends (9:2), a sick woman (9:20-21), a grieving dad (9:18-19), and blind men (9:27-28). These individuals renounced themselves and trusted in Christ. Second, in a similar way, we see Matthew abandon his livelihood to follow Jesus (9:9). The faith-full—those full of faith—gladly renounce themselves and the things of this world to follow Jesus. They trust in His mercy.

What about you—will you humbly and gladly submit to the authority of Jesus? Or will you instead revere Him from a distance like the crowds? Would you even dare to proudly reject Him like the Pharisees? May God give us the faith of the unclean woman who said to herself, "If I can just touch His robe, I'll be made well!" (9:21).

Reflect and Discuss

1. What would you say if someone asked you, "What is your greatest need?" Explain your answer.
2. Explain the difference between suffering that is directly related to your own sin and suffering that comes as a result of living in a fallen world.

3. If someone said that Jesus never claimed to be divine, how could you respond by using the account of the paralytic?

4. How might Jesus' calling of Matthew give us hope for unbelievers we know who seem unreachable with the gospel?

5. Why do disciples of Jesus fast now? What does this say about our ultimate hope?

6. How does the account of the woman touching Jesus' robe speak against the idea of earning God's favor?

7. How does the blindness of the two men in verses 27-31 serve as an indictment of the Jewish leadership?

8. Explain the following statement: Satan's defeat is in the past, but his final destruction is in the future.

9. What is the danger of merely admiring Jesus' supernatural abilities?

10. What two or three aspects of Jesus' character stand out in this passage? Do these things come to mind when you think about Jesus?

Sent by the King

MATTHEW 9:35–10:42

Main Idea: Christ calls His followers to a costly mission that will involve suffering and opposition, but the sovereign care and protection of God are sufficient to sustain our faith.

I. **The Condition of the Lost**
   A. See their size.
   B. Feel their suffering.
   C. Realize their separation.

II. **The Commission of Christ**
   A. Jesus beckons us to pray.
   B. Jesus summons us to go.
      1. Go to great need.
      2. Go to great danger.
      3. We will be betrayed.
      4. We will be hated.
      5. We will be persecuted.
      6. Fear will tempt us.
      7. The Father will take care of us.
      8. Confess Him publicly.
      9. Love Him supremely.
      10. Take the ultimate risk.
      11. Find the ultimate reward.

III. **The Prayer of the Church**
   A. God, give us supernatural awareness of the condition of the lost.
   B. God, give us sacrificial obedience to the commission of Christ.

A little more than two hundred years ago, Adoniram and Ann Judson boarded a ship and set sail for India on a journey that would eventually lead them to Burma (modern-day Myanmar). Along with William Carey, the Judsons are considered pioneers in the modern missions movement. These converted Baptist missionaries (they were previously Congregationalists) were and continue to be used by God in some extraordinary ways for the cause of global missions; however, their journey looked anything but successful on the outside.

The intense suffering the Judsons endured on the mission field was foreshadowed by a letter written from Adoniram to Ann's father asking for permission to marry his daughter. The following is Adoniram's candid request:

> I have now to ask, whether you can consent to part with your daughter early next spring, to see her no more in this world; whether you can consent to her departure, and her subjection to the hardships and sufferings of missionary life; whether you can consent to her exposure to the dangers of the ocean, to the fatal influence of the southern climate of India; to every kind of want and distress; to degradation, insult, persecution, and perhaps a violent death. Can you consent to all this, for the sake of him who left his heavenly home, and died for her and for you; for the sake of perishing, immortal souls; for the sake of Zion, and the glory of God? Can you consent to all this, in hope of soon meeting your daughter in the world of glory, with the crown of righteousness, brightened with the acclamations of praise which shall redound to her Savior from heathens saved, through her means, from eternal woe and despair? (Anderson, *To the Golden Shore*, 83)

Gratefully, Ann's dad said "yes," the couple was married, and a year later they set sail. Ann's dad would never see his daughter or son-in-law again. In fact, Ann would lose her life sharing the gospel with people who had never heard the good news of Jesus Christ. As a result of the Judson's service, today there are nearly 4,000 Baptist churches with more than a half a million followers of Christ in the heart of Buddhist Burma/Myanmar.

This story seems unusual to us, yet it should be more normal in light of the truths contained in Matthew 9:35–10:42. After having looked at the truly encouraging news of the authority of Jesus in His teaching, preaching, and healing in the last several chapters, it would be a mistake to conclude that this good news is meant solely for us. The reality is that there's a world around us suffering amid sin and trials of various kinds. This world needs to hear the good news of the kingdom. They need to know that Jesus has authority over sin, sickness, cancer, disease, natural disasters, and even death itself, and they must hear the gospel in order to be saved. Therefore, it is incumbent upon us to spread this good news.

The good news is for everyone you work with and live around. It's for your own neighborhood and for the unreached people groups of the world. We don't just live to *celebrate* this good news; we live to *spread* this good news. But when we do, we must realize that just as Jesus faced opposition, so we will face opposition. That's what Matthew 9:35–10:42 is about. May God use this passage to so grip our hearts with the good news of Christ that students will risk their reputations at school, that brothers and sisters in Christ will risk their reputations at work, that the church will throw aside the fear of man, and that every one of us will give our lives—lose them, if necessary—spreading the good news of Christ's kingdom everywhere we go. This is, after all, what it means to be a disciple of Jesus.

The Condition of the Lost
MATTHEW 9:35-36

The kind of risk-taking discipleship that Scripture calls for will not be a reality in our lives until we see the lost as Jesus sees them. At the end of chapter 9, Matthew closes out a section of Jesus' miracle stories and teaching on discipleship by pointing to Jesus' compassion for those who needed Him. Verses 35-36 give us a glimpse into His heart.

To understand what compelled the compassion of Jesus, there are at least three different factors we need to see. First, with regard to the crowd, we need to **see their size**. Verse 36 says, "When He saw the crowds, he felt compassion for them." There may have been around 200 cities and villages in Galilee at this point, with a possible population of about three million people. When Jesus saw them, the text indicates that He literally felt agony. He was not just emotionally moved, but physically affected with compassion when He saw the crowds. Think about seeing someone you love hurting or suffering, so much so that your heart physically feels like it's going to burst for them. That's the kind of language used here.

To have the compassion of Jesus for the crowds, we not only need to see their size, but we also need to **feel their suffering**. Matthew describes the crowds as "weary and worn out, like sheep without a shepherd" (v. 36). They were running after pleasures, pursuits, and people in this world, thinking that they could be satisfied apart from God, but they couldn't. Every road to satisfaction that this world offers—the road of success or sex or money or relationships or pleasures—is ultimately empty. Jesus knew this. These crowds desperately needed Him as a merciful shepherd.

Third and finally, when we look at the crowds we need to **realize their separation**. In verse 37, Jesus said to his disciples, "The harvest is abundant, but the workers are few." This "harvest" language in Scripture is often associated with judgment. For example, the prophet Joel says,

> *Swing the sickle*
> *because the harvest is ripe.*
> *Come and trample the grapes*
> *because the winepress is full;*
> *the wine vats overflow*
> *because the wickedness of the nations is great.*
> *Multitudes, multitudes*
> *in the valley of decision!*
> *For the Day of the LORD is near*
> *in the valley of decision.* (Joel 3:13-14)

Jesus also speaks of the harvest as a time of judgment in Matthew 13. At the end of the age, Jesus will bring the wheat (the righteous) to eternal blessing, and He will cast the tares (the unrighteous) into the "blazing furnace" where there will be "weeping and gnashing of teeth" (v. 42).[21]

In light of God's coming judgment, Jesus knew the desperate condition of those to whom He ministered. These were people who were separated from God and who, if nothing changed, would one day stand before God in their sin and be cast into eternal darkness. *This* is why Jesus had such compassion on them. How much more so should this be true in our day? We live in a world of approximately seven billion people, with most liberal estimates labeling about one-third of this seven billion "Christians." That leaves more than 4.5 billion people without Christ—that's more than 4.5 billion people on a road that leads to an eternal hell. This is the condition of the lost.

Do we realize the gravity of eternity? Far more important than sports, money, sex, or success in this world, there are people around us today (and every day) who are eternally lost. Do we sense the urgency?

---

[21] A similar image of God's end-time judgment harvest is pictured in Rev 14:14-20.

Do we see the world with the eyes of Jesus? We don't have time to play games with our lives or play games in the church. And we don't have time to waste our lives on the pursuits, pleasures, and possessions of this world, when there is something infinitely more important for us to do. But what exactly is that purpose? What is more important than all that this world offers? Answer: The commission of Christ.

The Commission of Christ
MATTHEW 9:37–10:42

At the end of chapter 9, Jesus mentions two main things that we must do with urgency. First, in light of the abundant harvest of people who are separated from God, **Jesus beckons us to pray**. He says, "Therefore, *pray* to the Lord of the harvest to send out workers into His harvest" (v. 38; emphasis added). Notice that Jesus doesn't say, "Here's the harvest, now *go!*" Instead, He says, "Here's the harvest, now *pray.*" Jesus will eventually get to the "go" part, but first His followers must be on their knees, asking and pleading with God to send out workers. This is precisely what we should be doing in our churches as we seek to send people out regularly into this dark world to proclaim the gospel. We should actually pray for people to leave . . . on mission! God *loves* to answer prayers like this. Our churches ought to be sending bases of laborers for the harvest of souls. No one is to be a spectator.

Many believers don't even consider the possibility that God could call them to proclaim the gospel in another location. Or if they do, they often have a distorted view of what such a call would look like. Jim Elliot, the missionary martyr to the Auca Indians of Peru, lamented the fact that so few were willing to go to the mission field in his own day. He said, "Our young men are going into [other] fields because they don't 'feel called' to the mission field. We don't need a call; we need a kick in the pants" (Elliot, *Shadow of the Almighty*, 150). As followers of Christ, our lives should be "on the table" before the Lord. Wherever He says to go, we go. None of us is intended simply to coast through life until we get to heaven.

And when we pray, God will send us out in different ways to different places. For some, this will simply mean going into the workplace, not simply to provide for your family, but also to spread the gospel. For others, this will mean being a part of a church plant in an area that's difficult to reach with the gospel. Still for others, this will mean going to live with an unreached people group. Jesus beckons us to pray to the

Lord of the harvest for the glorious goal of spreading His gospel to the whole world.

As the first part of Christ's commission, then, we are beckoned to pray. Then in Matthew 10:1-7, **Jesus summons us to go**. In verse 1, Jesus calls these 12 disciples to Himself. The language Matthew uses of "summoning" might be compared to a military commander calling soldiers together to give them orders. The rest of the chapter is then filled with those orders. We can group those orders into 11 basic directives that Jesus gives to these men.

As a word of caution in understanding this passage, Jesus' words at the beginning of the chapter are specifically aimed at *these* particular disciples on *this* particular occasion. For example, the command not to go to the Gentiles (v. 5), but only to the "lost sheep of the house of Israel" (v. 6), had a specific purpose in Jesus' day concerning speaking the gospel to Jewish people. However, we know that Jesus later commanded these same disciples, and by implication all disciples, to go to "all nations" (28:19) with the good news of the gospel. As chapter 10 progresses, the marching orders become more general, applying to all disciples at all times. In verse 24, for instance, Jesus says, "A disciple is not above his teacher, or a slave above his master." Based on the rest of this Gospel and the New Testament more broadly, we know this truth applies to all believers.

As we step back and take a look at the overall picture of Matthew 10, we begin to see what Jesus' summons to "go" actually looks like, including the kind of reception we should expect as people who are commissioned by Christ the King. In verses 7-8 He calls us to **go to great need**: "As you go, announce this: 'The kingdom of heaven has come near.' Heal the sick, raise the dead, cleanse those with skin diseases, drive out demons. You have received free of charge; give free of charge." By the world's standards, this is an unlikely group for the disciples of Jesus to target—the diseased, dying, despised, and dirty. But these were precisely the King's orders.

First, Jesus says to **go to the diseased**. Our mission is not to the healthy, but to the sick. Second, we **go to the dying**. Jesus tells the disciples to "raise the dead" (v. 8). Third, **go to the despised**. In other words, cleanse those who have leprosy, those who are unclean.[22] And

---

[22] In verse 8, the HCSB refers to "those with skin diseases." See the discussion in chapter 8 concerning leprosy and its association with uncleanness.

fourth, **go to the dirty**. The disciples were commanded to engage the demon-possessed, the people most tainted by sin. In essence, Jesus told His disciples to go to the people that the world ignored or oppressed. The result of such action is that we will grow in faith, for **as we go to the needy, we will learn to trust His provision**. Jesus commanded them, "Don't take along gold, silver, or copper for your money-belts. Don't take a traveling bag for the road, or an extra shirt, sandals, or a walking stick, for the worker is worthy of his food" (vv. 9-10). As they reach out to the needy, the disciples will find that Jesus is sufficient for all their needs. In other words, when they go to great need, He will meet their needs along the way.

Not only do followers of Jesus go to great need, but they also **go to great danger**. Jesus' gives instructions in verses 11-16. The phrase "sheep among wolves," in verse 16 is startling. After all, the responsibility of the shepherd is to protect the sheep from wolves. But Jesus, the Good Shepherd (John 10:11), tells His disciples to hang out with the wolves! He instructs them to **be as foolish as sheep**. Sheep are some of the most helpless and foolish of all domesticated animals. Harmless noises can send sheep into a frenzy, and when they face danger, they've got no defenses. All sheep can do is run, and they're really slow. That's why the dumbest thing a sheep can do is to go wandering into a pack of wolves; yet Jesus tells His followers to do precisely that.

In these verses, Jesus tells His 12 disciples—and by implication, He tells us—to go into dangerous places where they will find themselves among evil, rapacious people. But they will be there by His design. We often think that if something is not safe, it must not be of God. If it's dangerous, risky, or if it may cause us harm, we must not be in God's will. But those are not not the criteria by which we determine God's desire for us. As we go like sheep among wolves, people may think we're foolish or clueless, but we're actually being obedient, which is most important.

Jesus also tells His disciples to **be as smart as snakes** (v. 16). But is it possible to be as foolish as sheep *and* as smart as snakes? If so, how? Jesus tells them go to danger without reservation or hesitation, and when they're there, to be smart. It's similar to Jesus going boldly into the presence of Pilate and the Roman officials, like "a lamb led to the slaughter" (Isa 53:7), yet while He's being beaten and taken off to be crucified, Jesus speaks with wisdom. He doesn't needlessly incite anger or trouble. The command to be wise leads to Jesus' third instruction with regard to *how* His disciples should conduct themselves as they follow His summons to go: they are to **be as pure as doves**. When you're with the wolves, don't let them have anything against you when it comes to your purity. Do not be abrasive, inconsiderate, or belligerent. Be innocent in the middle of difficult situations and thereby demonstrate what purity looks like in action.

In verses 17-20, Jesus talks about the fact that as we go to the needy, we will learn to depend on His presence. If we follow Christ for the spread of the gospel into the midst of danger, we will never be alone. He'll be with us and give us everything we need to stand and to speak and to preach. This is where the presence of Christ is most powerful. We live in presumptive safety in this world, being surrounded by its comforts. Christ's presence and power aren't needed in such situations, or so we think. But when you go to danger, when you're a sheep in the midst of wolves, you need His presence and power more than anything else. You're acutely aware of your utter dependence on Him.

Next, as we're summoned to go, Jesus tells us that **we will be betrayed**. Verse 21 says, "Brother will betray brother to death, and a father his child. Children will even rise up against their parents and have them put to death." It may be shocking to hear, but the kingdom of God is divisive. Jesus will say something similar in verses 34-36, where He talks about bringing a sword to divide believers from unbelievers. If you follow Christ, you will almost certainly be misunderstood, and the people you least suspect, even family members, may turn on you.

In addition to being betrayed, Jesus says in verse 22 that **we will be hated**. He warns His disciples, "You will be hated by everyone because of My name. But the one who endures to the end will be delivered." The term "everyone" in this verse obviously doesn't mean every person on the planet, because many people will come to faith in Christ. However, whether it's your family, the government, or the religious establishment, you will be hated from all corners. People simply will not like you when you proclaim Jesus. But why will they hate you? Because the world hated Jesus, and our lives are identified with Him.

When we go into the world doing good deeds and helping people with their needs without saying anything about Jesus, the world is fine with that. But when we go into the world doing these same things *and* telling people that Jesus is the only way to be saved from sin, death, and hell, then the world will respond much differently. We will be betrayed, we will be hated, and **we will be persecuted**. Notice in verse 23 that Jesus doesn't say, "*If* you are persecuted." He says, "*When* they persecute you." This is one of the places in this passage where we know that these instructions weren't just for these disciples at this particular time, for Paul later says in 2 Timothy 3:12, "In fact, all those who want to live a godly life in Christ Jesus will be persecuted." This warning doesn't mean that we seek persecution, or that we foolishly or heroically pursue danger; we don't seek to be hated. Instead, we seek Christ and proclaim Him, knowing that opposition will come. And how do we know this? Listen to 10:24-25:

> A disciple is not above his teacher, or a slave above his master. It is enough for a disciple to become like his teacher and a slave like his master. If they called the head of the house "Beelzebul," how much more the members of his household!

Follow the logic here: If Jesus was persecuted, and He is our teacher and master, then do we think that we're above Him, that we won't endure what He has endured? Peter tells us that we are to follow in Jesus' steps in the path of suffering (1 Pet 2:21). If you proclaim the name of Christ, people will betray you, the world will hate you, and you *will* be persecuted, and it's all because Jesus Himself was betrayed, hated, and persecuted. People called Jesus "Satan,"[23] so if your life is identified with Him, they'll call you the same thing. **The reality we must face** is this: **The danger of our lives increases in proportion to the depth of our relationship with Christ**. That is an unavoidable conclusion from what Matthew is telling us.

Everyone who wants a safe, carefree life free from danger should stay away from Jesus. The world responds with hostility to Him. So as we are conformed to Christ more and more, the world will respond to us more and more as they responded to Him. If you want to avoid being betrayed, hated, or persecuted, then don't become like Christ! We are so prone to sit back and settle for religious routine and comfortable Christianity, because it's safe. And the world likes us in that mode. As long as we live lives just like everyone else—going to church on Sunday and keeping our faith to ourselves—we will face little risk in this world. The only problem is that we will know so little of Christ. But when we do know Christ, and when we're becoming like Him and proclaiming

---

[23] When Jesus uses the name "Beelzebul" in Matt 10:25, this term likely meant "lord of the high abode," a reference to "the home of pagan deities." Jews believed these deities to be demons. Blomberg, *Matthew*, 176.

Him, things will not be easy for us. The more Christ is manifest in your life and in your family, the harder it will get for you in this world. This is what Jesus said in Luke 6:40: "Everyone who is fully trained will be like his teacher." Does that frighten you?

You will become like the One who was mocked, beaten, scourged, spit on, and nailed to a cross. And all of this brings us **to the question we must ask**, namely, **do we really want to be like Christ?** I mean, *really?* Because if we really do want to be like Him, then our lives won't stay the same, and they won't be easy; they will be dangerous. Christian, this is what Jesus—your Savior, Lord, and King—is saying. So do you really want to be like Christ?

As we are betrayed, hated, and persecuted, Jesus says that **fear will tempt us**. This is where Jesus' words in verses 26-31 are so comforting. Three times in these six verses Jesus says not to be afraid (vv. 26, 28, 31). Fear is a real temptation, particularly when it comes to sharing the gospel. Whether we're in an area of the world where it's illegal to share the gospel, or even if we're in an area of the world where we're free to speak of Jesus, like our own workplace, fear is probably one of the biggest obstacles to obeying Christ's commission. Therefore, we need to know what Jesus says about overcoming fear.

First, as we face fear, we must **see with an eternal perspective**. We shouldn't be afraid of this world and its ways, because one day in the future, the sin and evil of this world will be exposed and God's justice will prevail. You don't need to vindicate yourself; God will vindicate you. Instead of worrying about what the world says now, we should worry about what God will say in eternity. He will uncover all that is true and right on the last day, so give yourself to righteousness, and trust God.

Second, we need to **speak with a holy boldness**. Whatever God whispers to us through His Word is to be proclaimed on the housetops (v. 27). We're reminded of the Sermon on the Mount, where Jesus says not to light our lamps and then put them under a basket; rather, we are to let them shine (5:15-16). Speak the truth of God everywhere—speak it often, speak it clearly, and speak it boldly.

The third thing we must do if we want to follow Christ's pattern in the face of fear is to **sacrifice with reckless abandonment**. Verse 28 gives us the reasoning behind such courage: "Don't fear those who kill the body but are not able to kill the soul; rather, fear Him who is able to destroy both soul and body in hell." Jesus knows that we will be tempted to fear man and to be intimidated by what people can do to us.

However, it's not man that we need to fear; God is the ultimate judge, and *He* holds our eternity in His hand, not men. This may sound like a strange way to encourage disciples, essentially telling them, "Don't be afraid of men—the worst thing they can do is kill you!" We may tremble to think that by going on mission to a certain region of the world we will be killed, but Jesus encourages us by telling us that that's all they can do. The only way that can sound comforting is if you realize that you have already died with Christ (Col 3:3). Your focus must be on eternal things, so that nothing man can do to you matters. It has been said that saints of old feared man so little because they feared God so much. Likewise, when you and I fear God alone, then we can stand boldly in front of people that we would previously have been afraid to share the gospel with, even those who would take our lives. For in the end, death for the follower of Christ is actually gain (Phil 1:21)!

Jesus' instructions in Matthew 10 are not easy, but thankfully we are not left to fend for ourselves in this life. Fear will tempt us, but **the Father will take care of us**. In verses 29-31 we have a wonderful picture of the Father's care. **He rules us sovereignly**, for He is in control of the smallest sparrow falling to the ground. He is, therefore, more than able to sovereignly direct our every step amid the danger of our mission. We can also be comforted that **He knows us completely**; every hair on your head is accounted for. God knows every detail of your life, more than you know yourself. Finally, we learn that **He loves us deeply**. The One who calls us to go as sheep in the midst of wolves is good, so there is no reason to fear.

In verses 32-39 Jesus talks about the importance and the cost of identifying with Him. As disciples of Jesus we must **confess Him publicly** (vv. 32-33). To confess means to affirm, to agree, or to identify with. When we follow Christ, we don't sit back in silence; we make it known to others that we belong to Him. What about you—do people around you at work or at school know that you are identified with Christ? Are you publicly identifying with Christ on a daily basis? It's incredible to think that one day all those who *publicly* identify with Christ will stand before the Father in heaven and Jesus will *publicly*, before the Father, identify with them.

Not only should we confess Jesus publicly, but we should also **love Him supremely**. This is Jesus' point in verses 37-38, where he speaks of loving Him more than our own family members. Love for Jesus should be superior to love for a parent, or even the love one has for a spouse. These loves are temporal, but a relationship with Christ is eternal.

Finally, at the end of this paragraph, we are urged to **take the ultimate risk**. In verse 39 Jesus says that we must lose our life in order to find it. Pick up your cross, Christ-follower, and die. The end result is more than worth it.

In verses 40-42 Jesus talks about the promise that awaits all who follow Him. Jesus' commission is not a summons to gloom and misery; it's a summons to joy and satisfaction. You take the ultimate risk, and in the process you **find the ultimate reward**. Contrary to what this world believes, we do not find our lives by indulging in the pleasures, the stuff, the safety, and the security of this world. That's a recipe for losing your life. We find our lives in sacrificing these things for the sake of the pleasure, safety, and security to be found in Christ. And when we live like that, the reward is not just for us. Yes, it is for us—we find joy, peace, and life as we live in and with Christ for the spread of the gospel—but it's also for those who hear our proclamation of Christ. When they believe in the gospel, they too experience eternal reward! Isn't that worth it?

Recently, the story was relayed to me by one of our church's mission teams to North Africa about a lady in that region who was brought to a medical clinic in a wheelbarrow. She was sick and about to die, until she received care from Christians. These Christians later shared the gospel with her, and the lady trusted in Christ and then went back home to her own family. When she shared her new faith in Christ with her household, her own father beat her. This kind of reaction is all too common in that region, as most of persecution happens in the household, not primarily from any government. Nevertheless, this lady stood strong and shared the gospel, and her own father, the man who had beaten her, came to faith in Christ. He's now an evangelist, going from village to village sharing the gospel. This story is one of many in that region of the world; however, when you talk with these believers, as some of our church members have, it's not the suffering they talk about. It's the joy. In Christ, the reward far outweighs the risk. And all of this is happening because believers are sharing Christ in their daily lives.

The Prayer of the Church

In order to move from comfortable Christianity to a Matthew 10 kind of Christianity, I want to suggest two prayers that we ought to be praying. First, **God, give us supernatural awareness of the condition of the lost**. We need help to see what God sees. We need to see it in the people right around us, the people we work with and live among, and the people who surround us in the world. All of them—every single person around us and around the world—will spend the next trillion years either in heaven or in hell. God, give us a supernatural awareness of the condition of the lost.

Our second prayer should be this: **God, give us sacrificial obedience to the commission of Christ**. Obedience to the commission of Christ is the only proper response of those who celebrate communion with Christ. This commission requires great risk, but the reward is more than worth it—both for us and for countless others who come to know Christ through us.

Reflect and Discuss

1. Share a ministry opportunity you've had that opened your eyes to the great spiritual needs around you. How might you pursue such opportunities in the near future?
2. Do the massive spiritual needs of the world compel you to action or make you feel helpless? How might Jesus's call to pray in 9:38 impact your reaction?
3. How would you describe your attitude toward unbelieving coworkers and neighbors? What factors keep you from feeling compassion for them?
4. Why is the Bible's teaching on God's wrath and the final judgment essential to our motivation for making disciples?
5. How will you practically apply Jesus' summons to pray and go in this chapter?
6. What ministry situations tend to be the most difficult for you? Jesus speaks of being like sheep, snakes, and doves in Matthew 10. How would this apply to your current context?
7. What aspects of being like Christ cause you the most fear and anxiety? What promises in God's Word might bolster your security and joy? Name two fellow believers you might reach out to for strength.
8. What aspects of God's character in this chapter ground our confidence in Christ's mission?
9. In what situations have you been reluctant to confess Christ publicly?
10. How does God's promised reward help fuel our faith and the carrying out of our mission?

When Faith Is Hard and the Burden Is Heavy

MATTHEW 11

Main Idea: Although followers of Christ may experience doubt, we must trust in and submit to the truths of God's Word concerning who Jesus is and what He has provided for us in the gospel.

Four Portraits of Jesus

I. **Jesus Is the Promised Messiah.**
   A. John doubts Jesus.
      1. The anatomy of doubt
      2. The answer to doubt
   B. Jesus defends John.
      1. John was the greatest prophet.
      2. We have a greater privilege.
   C. Like Jesus and John
      1. we will be opposed by this world.
      2. we will be criticized in this world.

II. **Jesus Is the Authoritative Judge.**
   A. Jesus will condemn the unrepentant.
   B. Jesus will damn the indifferent.

III. **Jesus Is the Sovereign Son.**
   A. Jesus alone knows the Father.
   B. Jesus alone reveals the Father.

IV. **Jesus Is the Gracious Master.**
   A. An explanation of Christianity
      1. We give all we have to Jesus.
      2. Jesus gives all He has to us.
   B. The invitation of Christ: When faith is hard and the burden is heavy
      1. repent of sin.
      2. renounce yourself.
      3. rest in Christ.
      4. rejoice forever in Him.

Have you ever doubted what the Bible says about God? What about the gospel? When you're alone, do you ever sit and wonder whether the things that we believe as Christians are actually real? I got an email recently from an old friend whom I respect greatly, and he is going through a very challenging time in his life. I was struck when he told me that faith is harder to come by than ever before. Do you ever feel like that?

If you've wrestled with doubts about God and His Word, take heart, because you're not alone. Alister McGrath said, "Doubt is natural within faith. It comes because of our human weakness and frailty." McGrath contrasts this doubt with unbelief:

> Unbelief is the decision to live your life as if there is no God. It is a deliberate decision to reject Jesus Christ and all that he stands for. But doubt is something quite different. Doubt arises within the context of faith. It is a wistful longing to be sure of the things in which we trust. (McGrath, "When Doubt Becomes Unbelief," 8–10)

Likewise, John MacArthur observed,

> When the New Testament talks about doubt, whether you're talking about the gospels or the epistles, it primarily focuses on believers. That's very important. It's as if you have to believe something before you can doubt it; you have to be committed to it before you begin to question it. So doubt is held up as the unique problem of the believer. (MacArthur, "Solving the Problem of Doubt")

Even Charles Spurgeon, one of my favorite pastors in history, said,

> Some of us who have preached the Word for years, and have been the means of working faith in others and of establishing them in the knowledge of the fundamental doctrines of the Bible, have nevertheless been the subjects of the most fearful and violent doubts as to the truth of the very gospel we have preached. (Charles Spurgeon, "Psalm 69:14")

The reality is that even for those who seem to be the most faithful, faith is sometimes hard, particularly when the burdens of life feel heavy. But the good news is that even in our doubts, the God whom we seek to be sure of is certain to meet us where we are. He desires to assure us of His faithfulness. In the words of J. C. Ryle, "Doubting does not prove that a man has no faith, but only that his faith is small. And even when our faith is small, the Lord is ready to help us" (Ryle, *Expository Thoughts on the Gospels*, 170). John the Baptist, the greatest prophet who ever lived, struggled with doubt. This prophet whom Jesus called the greatest man ever born up to that time (Matt 11:11) wavered over the identity of the Messiah. He needed to see afresh that Jesus is worthy of our faith and our worship. This is at the heart of the message of Matthew 11, one of the most beautiful passages in this Gospel. Jesus invites us to rest in Him when faith is hard and burdens are heavy.

Below we'll consider **four portraits of Jesus** that should help to combat doubt and strengthen our trust in Him.

Jesus Is the Promised Messiah
MATTHEW 11:1-19

Matthew has already mentioned the fact that John was arrested (4:12), and in just a few chapters he'll tell us why (14:1-12). By the time John began asking questions in Matthew 11, he had likely been in prison for a while. This may help explain why he was perplexed. **John doubts Jesus**, so he sends some of his disciples to ask Jesus a question. Matthew also tells us in verse 2 that John was hearing about the deeds of the Christ, another indication that John was in touch with his disciples during his imprisonment. He had believed that Jesus was the Messiah, but now he was starting to wonder. This leads us to ask, What exactly is causing John to doubt Jesus at this point?

Because we often find ourselves doubting for reasons similar to John, we need to consider **the anatomy of doubt**. There are at least three things we learn about doubt in this passage. First, doubt often arises during **difficult situations**. We've already seen John, a prophet in the wilderness who had proclaimed God's Word with boldness, preparing the way for the Messiah and pointing people to Him (Matt 3:1-12). But now, as a result of his bold and faithful proclamation, John was experiencing shame, hunger, physical torment, and emotional struggle as he sat there alone in prison. We're reminded again of Elijah, a tired prophet who was running from Jezebel and ready to give up (1 Kgs 19). Such difficult situations tend to produce doubt.

Second, accompanying the difficult situations were **unmet expectations**. After all, this is the Messiah of whom it was prophesied, "He has

sent Me . . . to proclaim liberty to the captives and freedom to the prisoners" (Isa 61:1). It was becoming clear by this point that Jesus was not
meeting many of the expectations that a lot of Jewish people had for
the Messiah. John the Baptist had prophesied about the judgment that
the Christ would bring about (Matt 3:11-12), but Roman rule was still in
place—and John was in jail because of it! It must have been confusing
for the prophet to see Rome in charge, sin still rampant, and political and religious corruption still ruling the day. Everything seemed to
be just as it had been for generations. Instead of overthrowing Rome,
Jesus was spending time with irreligious sinners, teaching them about
forgiveness, and to the great surprise of some, He wasn't even fasting.
Surely John was thinking, "Isn't the Messiah the One who is going to
deliver us?"

Third, in the midst of his struggles, John suffered from **limited perception**. He simply didn't understand everything that was happening, or
not happening, around him, so he sent his disciples to question Jesus.

In reality, many of our questions and doubts often spring from
these same factors. It's often in the midst of challenging circumstances
that faith is hardest to come by, especially when we have been walking
with the Lord, faithfully serving and worshiping Him, and then tragedy
hits, maybe even multiple tragedies. We think, "God, where are You?"
We don't understand why certain things are happening, especially
when our trials seem to be getting in the way of our desire to serve
God. We know He's good, but we can't understand why the struggle
won't end.

Oftentimes, trials come as a result of sin in our lives or sin in the
lives of others around us. However, even when our trials are not a direct
result of our own disobedience, we must remember that our perception
is limited. For example, John the Baptist had no idea how this story of
Jesus the Messiah was going to play out. God was ushering in a totally
different type of kingdom than most Jewish people expected. This was
more than just a political regime change; God was ushering in redemption of the entire world. John likely understood much of this when
many people didn't, yet he was almost certainly perplexed regarding the
timing of it all. Wasn't the Messiah supposed to bring imminent blessing and judgment? When would this kingdom come? John's perspective
was limited, and so is ours. Whenever we go through difficult situations
with unmet expectations and questions rising up within us, we need to

remember that our perspective is always limited. In the end, we must trust that God knows what He is doing.

Now that we've seen the anatomy of doubt, we need to see something even more important—**the answer to doubt**. In this text and in our lives, the answer to doubt seems to be (at least) twofold. First and foremost, we confront doubt with **biblical revelation**. When John's disciples questioned Jesus, Jesus answered them in verse 4 by saying: "Go and report to John what you hear and see." Then Jesus used phrases taken from Isaiah 35:5-6 and 61:1 to describe the miraculous works He had been doing and to show that He was indeed the Promised One.[24] He tells John, for instance, that the blind were receiving their sight. In the entirety of the Old Testament, no blind person ever received sight, nor is there any story in the New Testament, apart from Saul's conversion (Acts 9:17-18), where Jesus' followers restored a blind man's sight. Jesus was fulfilling what Isaiah had long ago prophesied, "Then the eyes of the blind will be opened" (35:5).

Interestingly, the passages that Jesus alluded to in Isaiah refer not only to healing but also to the judgment that the Messiah would bring. Jesus' miraculous works were evidence of the in-breaking kingdom; therefore John needed to trust that Jesus would indeed bring full and final judgment, a judgment that comes to the fore in verses 20-24. God will be true to His Word, and to try to fight doubt without a foundation in the truth of His Word is futile. God's Word is a rock, not because it makes everything easy, but because it keeps your feet out of sinking sand amid difficult situations and unmet expectations.

So the first antidote to doubt is biblical revelation. Second, we battle doubt with **joyful submission**. After Jesus recounts His great works to John's disciples, He closes by saying, "And if anyone is not offended because of Me, he is blessed" (v. 6). To not be offended because of Jesus is essentially to trust Him. Even when it's not easy and trusting Christ seems contrary to reason, we need to remain grounded in biblical revelation and look to Him in faith. The reward is blessing, and that's a promise from God.

As John's disciples leave to take this message back to him, **Jesus defends John** in verses 7-19. We may wonder, based on the first part of

---

[24] Jesus may also be alluding to Isa 26:19; 29:18-19. Carson, *Matthew*, 262.

this chapter, if tension was developing between John the Baptist and
Jesus, but Jesus took this opportunity to defend (and affirm) John for
who he was and what he had done. Jesus told the crowds that **John was
the greatest prophet**. More than that, John was also the greatest person born of woman. That is quite a statement! Even compared to Old
Testament spiritual giants like Abraham, Moses, Elijah, and King David,
Jesus says that none of them was greater than John. So what are we to
make of this shocking claim?

Jesus' statement about John had to do not primarily with John's
person, but with his position in redemptive history. He was a prophet,
a position of highest honor as a spokesman for God, but he was not
just any prophet. John was *the* prophet whom God had promised would
come and announce the Messiah (Isa 40:3; Mal 4:5-6). So many prophets had come before him—Elijah, Isaiah, Jeremiah, and a host of others—but none of these holy men of God had the distinct privilege of
announcing the arrival of the King. John's ministry was the prophetic
climax of all pre-Christian revelation. The greatness of John's position
in redemptive history sets the stage for the absolutely astounding statement that Jesus makes next: "but the least in the kingdom of heaven is
greater than he" (Matt 11:11).

While John was the climax of all who had come *before* and pointed to
Christ, none of them, not even the highest of them, had the position and
privilege that is reserved for all believers who would come *after* Christ.
That's because all men, including John the Baptist, had an incomplete
picture of the Messiah. Their perspective was limited in terms of what
to expect from the Messiah. However, even the least person who comes
into the kingdom after Jesus has a greater understanding of the Messiah
than everyone who came before Him. As followers of Christ today, we
should be amazed and grateful that **we have a greater privilege** and position than John the Baptist did. While John was unclear on all that the
Messiah would do, we know all that Christ has done. Furthermore, we
have the privilege of proclaiming the crucified and resurrected King to
the ends of the earth. What a position in redemptive history we have!
Therefore, let us take hold of this truth and be faithful to our task, a task
that is greater than all the prophets of the Old Testament. D. A. Carson
writes about our privilege:

> So often Christians want to establish their "greatness" with
> reference to their work, their giving, their intelligence, their

preaching, their gifts, their courage, their discernment. But Jesus unhesitatingly affirmed that even the least believer is greater than Moses or John the Baptist, simply because of his or her ability, living on this side of the coming of Jesus the Messiah, to point him out with greater clarity and understanding than all his forerunners ever could. If we really believe this truth, it will dissipate all cheap vying for position [in this world] and force us to recognize that our true significance lies [simply] in our witness to the Lord Jesus Christ. (Carson, *God with Us*, 65)

Followers of Christ today should rejoice in their privileged position. However, just because we have this privilege does not mean that things will be easy. **Like Jesus and John, we will be opposed by this world**. In verse 12 Jesus says, "From the days of John the Baptist until now, the kingdom of heaven has been suffering violence, and the violent have been seizing it by force." The kingdom of heaven experiences opposition as it advances, a truth we've already seen in Matthew 10 in Jesus' instructions to His disciples. This opposition was present in John the Baptist's ministry, and it will become increasingly evident in Jesus' ministry in the chapters ahead. This greater privilege of proclamation comes with a price: persecution.

Just as John and Jesus were opposed, so our message about the Messiah will be met with hostility. **We will be criticized in this world**, regardless of how we present the truth of the gospel. In verses 16-19 Jesus speaks of how different His ministry was from that of John the Baptist. John barely ate or drank anything, and it was claimed that he was demonic (v. 18); Jesus, on the other hand, ate with sinners and they called Him a "glutton and a drunkard" (v. 19). While John sounded a warning of repentance similar to a funeral dirge, Jesus had sounded a promise of forgiveness similar to a celebration; yet sinful hearts rebelled against both of them. The world will react similarly to you and me when we speak the truth, but wisdom—right living before God—is "vindicated by her deeds" (v. 19).

Even in the middle of difficult situations, unmet expectations, and limited perception, Jesus is worthy of our trust. Telling others about Him won't be easy, but it is a calling worth giving our lives to. We fight doubt *in* this world and fight fear *of* this world with faith in the promised Messiah.

Jesus Is the Authoritative Judge
MATTHEW 11:20-24

After the first portrait of Jesus as the promised Messiah, Matthew shows us next that He is the authoritative Judge. The words, "Woe to you" in verse 21 literally mean, "Warning of doom upon you." Jesus is speaking to these Galilean cities—Chorazin, Bethsaida, and later Capernaum—where He had performed most of His miracles, and the reason for the woe is because they did not repent. The message is clear: **Jesus will condemn the unrepentant.** People had seen the Messiah and been amazed by Him, and some had even admired Him. However, they did not turn from their sin in response to His summons, "Repent, because the kingdom of heaven has come near" (Matt 4:17). Tyre and Sidon were Gentile cities on the Mediterranean Sea known for their godless idolatry and immorality, and God had previously destroyed them in Ezekiel 28. Yet in verse 21 Jesus says that if He had done in Tyre and Sidon the miracles that He did in Chorazin and Bethsaida, those wicked cities would have repented in grief and sorrow over their sin, which is what it means to repent in "sackcloth and ashes" (v. 22). This was a stunning indictment, and it continues when Jesus speaks about Capernaum.

Jesus tells self-righteous Capernaum that though they think they will be exalted to heaven, in fact, they will "go down to Hades" (v. 23). Capernaum, then, teaches us a lesson: **Jesus will damn the indifferent.** The city where Jesus did more miracles than any other place during His earthly ministry, the place where He gave sight to the blind, healed demon-possessed men and paralytics, and even brought the dead to life, did nothing in response to Him. And Jesus says that that is worse than the immorality of Sodom, for the people of Sodom would have turned from their sin and the city would have been spared. We must be warned not to be indifferent to Christ, or we too will be damned forever. Don't close your eyes to Christ, the authoritative Judge.

Jesus Is the Sovereign Son
MATTHEW 11:25-27

Matthew's third portrait of Jesus is portrayed in a dialogue between the Son and the Father, wherein we get a glimpse into their relationship with one another. Reading these verses, you sense yourself treading on holy ground as you glimpse the inner workings of the Trinity. In the process, we discover several things about these trinitarian relationships.

First, in verse 27 we learn that **Jesus alone knows the Father**. When Jesus speaks of "knowing" here, He has in mind more than mere mental recognition, as when we speak of knowing an acquaintance. Jesus knows the Father in a unique and intimate sense, a kind of knowledge that only the divine Son possesses.[25]

Jesus' exclusive knowledge of the Father is closely connected to another important truth in this passage: **Jesus alone reveals the Father**. The only people who know the Father are those "to whom the Son desires to reveal Him" (v. 27). Revealing God was part of the purpose of Jesus' coming. He didn't come merely with a word *from* God; He came as the Word *of* God made flesh (John 1:14), and as such He was God revealed to man. We know the Father not through worldly wisdom and understanding, but through the revelation of the Son.

The fact that the only way to know the Father is through the Son means that knowing God comes only **by divine grace**. Verse 25 says that God has "hidden these things from the wise and learned and revealed them to infants." In His mercy, God must reveal Himself to us, which He does through the Son. And as God reveals Himself, we respond, not with unrepentance and indifference, but **through human faith**. We receive God's truth not with self-righteousness nor with intellectual pride, but with the humble trust of a child, acknowledging our total dependence on the Father. This truth leads to the fourth and final portrait of Jesus in this passage.

Jesus Is the Gracious Master
MATTHEW 11:28-30

Jesus is the promised Messiah, the authoritative Judge, the sovereign Son, and the gracious Master. This text is full of wonder: the Son of God, the revelation of the Father, the One who represents the Trinity before man, says, "Come to Me" (v. 28). We have here **an explanation of Christianity** that is radically different from every other religious system in the history of the world. With such an amazing invitation, we need to understand exactly what it means to come to Jesus.

To begin with, it means **we give all we have to Jesus**. The imagery in this passage is of a "yoke" (v. 29), a heavy wooden bar that fits over the

---

[25] Jesus makes similar claims to deity in passages like John 10:30: "The Father and I are one."

neck of an ox so that it can pull a cart or a plow. The yoke could be put on one animal or it could be shared between two animals. In a shared yoke, one of the oxen would often be much stronger than the other. The stronger ox was more schooled in the commands of the master, and so it would guide the other according to the master's commands. By coming into the yoke with the stronger ox, the weaker ox could learn to obey the master's voice.

In verses 28-30 Jesus was speaking to self-righteous people who were burdened down with laws, rules, regulations, and commandments. Many of these laws had come from God in the Old Testament, while others had been added on by religious teachers of the day. In Matthew 23:4 Jesus says that these religious teachers "tie up heavy loads that are hard to carry and put them on people's shoulders, but they themselves aren't willing to lift a finger to move them." In contrast to these scribes and Pharisees, Jesus called the weary and burdened to come to Him. This is Christianity explained: **we give Him the full weight of all our sin**. These people were so burdened because they had failed over and over again to keep the law, and as leaders poured on more laws, the people felt more guilty. The weight of their sin became heavier, and they could not stand up under it.

When Jesus calls us to give Him the weight of our sin, we don't merely give Him some of it, but rather all of it. And it's not just the weight of our sin that we give to Jesus; **we give Him our complete and utter inability to obey God**. To be sure, it's not that the commands of God are bad; they are good (Matt 5:17; Rom 7:12). But the commands cannot be carried out by men in their own strength. We are imperfect, sinful people, and we cannot obey the Master's voice. The call to come to Christ is definitively *not* a call to try and reform your life and to be a better person—that's not Christianity. That kind of self-righteousness is what Ian Thomas called "the curse of Christendom" (Thomas, *The Saving Life of Christ*, 104). Thomas talks about the danger of the result of that kind of effort for the life of the church:

> [It's] what paralyzes the activity of the church of Jesus Christ on earth today! In defiance of God's Word, God's mind, God's will, and God's judgment, men [and women] everywhere are prepared to dedicate to God what God condemns—the energy of the flesh! There is nothing quite so nauseating or pathetic as the flesh trying to be holy! (Thomas, *The Saving Life of Christ*, 85)

Rather than calling us to greater moral effort, Jesus says, "Come to Me" (v. 28). The good news is that when we submit to Him, **Jesus gives all He has to us**. Remember as you hear Jesus' invitation that He is the stronger One, the One who alone is able to bear the weight of the Father's commands. This is the One who invites us into the yoke with Him. We give Him the full weight of all our sin, and **He gives us full pardon for all our sin**. We are counted righteous in Christ because He has obeyed the very law we could not obey. Therefore, when we come to Him, **we rest with peace before God**. Jesus says in verse 29 that we will find rest in Him, or in other words, "relief from bearing the load." Praise God that in Christ we are free from self-effort, self-improvement, and a constant struggle to overcome the guilt and shame of our sin.

Having peace with God and the forgiveness of sins is an unspeakable privilege, but amazingly enough, that's not where Christianity stops. When we come to Jesus **He gives us His complete ability to obey God**. In exchange for our inability, Jesus says, "Take up My yoke and learn from me" (v. 29). That word "learn" is important—it's similar to the word that is translated "make disciples" in the Great Commission later in Matthew (28:19). Jesus is essentially saying, "Learn what it means to be My disciple, and you will find rest for your soul." And how is it that we find rest for our souls? Because, Jesus says, "My yoke is easy and My burden is light" (11:30).

Jesus alone knows the Father, reveals the Father, and perfectly obeys the Father; therefore when we come into the yoke with Him, He leads us in terms of how to walk with the Father. He enables us to do what we could never do on our own. And when we are in the yoke with Christ, **we work in peace with God**. In other words, we obey God, not by our own strength, but with the very strength of Christ. In everything we do, it is Christ who is leading us, guiding us, enabling us, teaching us—literally living through us. Speaking of our utter dependency on Christ, Martin Luther said, "Here the bottom falls out of all merit. . . . Christ must do and must give everything." When Hudson Taylor, the well-known missionary to China, came to this realization in his Christian life, it was said of him,

> He was a joyous man now, a bright happy Christian. He
> had been a toiling, burdened one before, with not much
> rest of soul. It was rest in Jesus now, and letting Him do the
> work—which makes all the difference. Whenever he spoke in
> meetings after that, a new power seemed to flow from him,

and in the practical things of life a new peace possessed him. How was his faith strengthened? Not by striving after faith, but by resting on the Faithful One. (Taylor, *Hudson Taylor's Spiritual Secret*, 159)

At the end of the day, the Christian life is not about what you and I can do in and for the kingdom in our own effort; that's a recipe for failure. Following Christ is about Jesus the Christ living in and through and for us on a daily basis. He helps us in our struggles with sin, in our battles with temptation, and in our suffering in trials. Believers are in the yoke with Jesus, and the One who calls us to righteous living is the One who enables us to live a righteous life. The One who beckons you to trust the Father is the One who enables you to trust the Father. And the One who calls us to preach the gospel to the nations is the One who empowers us to preach the gospel to the nations.

We desperately need to hear **the invitation of Christ: When faith is hard and the burden is heavy**, several responses are appropriate. First and foremost, **repent of sin**. Don't be indifferent or unrepentant when you become aware of your disobedience, but instead confess it and run from it. You do not need to bear its burden any longer. Second, **renounce yourself**. Like a child, come to the Father and throw aside your pride. Third, **rest in Christ**. Come to the One who is gentle and lowly in heart, and find rest for your soul. And when you do come to Christ, **rejoice forever in Him**. The rest that He offers is eternal.

Reflect and Discuss

1. How has doubt been a struggle in your own relationship with God? What truths from God's Word were the most difficult to believe in the midst of your doubts?
2. How can difficulties, disappointments, and suffering feed into our doubts? How did this play out in the life of John the Baptist?
3. Why is it futile to fight doubt apart from the foundation of God's Word?
4. How is joyful submission to Jesus an antidote to doubt? Explain.
5. Many Christians wish they had lived in the time when Scriptures were recorded. How does this passage correct such a notion?
6. How might the expectation of opposition and criticism from the world help you persevere in the faith? What is the danger to your faith of *not* expecting trials?

7. How does Jesus' role as your authoritative Judge affect how you relate to Him? How might it affect your approach to sharing the gospel with others?
8. Jesus is presented as the sovereign Son in Matthew 11. How does this portrait of Jesus correct our culture's understanding of Him? How about your own?
9. In your own words, explain why Matthew 11:28-30 speaks against the idea of works-righteousness. How does it speak to the notion that the Christian life is burdensome?
10. How would you respond to the following questions: "What is my role and responsibility in responding to the gospel? What is God's role in this process?"

Will Your Heart Be Hardened or Humbled by This King?

MATTHEW 12

Main Idea: When we see Jesus for who He is, we can either repent and receive His mercy, or we can reject Him and experience eternal judgment.

Six More Portraits of Jesus

I. **He Is the Lord of the Sabbath.**
   A. As legalists, the Pharisees
      1. added to the requirements of the law.
      2. ignored the exceptions to the law.
      3. missed the heart of the law.
   B. As Lord, Jesus
      1. is greater than the tabernacle.
      2. is greater than the temple.
      3. is God.

II. **He Is the Servant of God and Sinners.**
   A. Of God: Jesus is loved by the Father and filled with the Spirit.
   B. Of sinners: Jesus is hope for the hurting.

III. **He Is the Power of God.**
   A. An unreasonable accusation
   B. Undeniable conclusions
   C. The unforgivable sin
   D. Two unforgettable reminders

IV. **He Is the Greater Prophet.**
   A. Jonah was alive after three days in a fish; Jesus would be alive after three days in a grave.
   B. The Ninevites responded with repentance; the Israelites were responding with rejection.

V. **He Is the Wiser King.**

VI. **He Is our Elder Brother.**
   A. What we don't need: an empty religion consumed with outer reformation
   B. What we do need: an intimate relationship compelled by inner transformation

---

In Matthew 12 we get another stunning picture of King Jesus. Many people in the first century who saw Jesus in the flesh, including most of the religious people, were hardened by their encounter with Him. Due to the fact that our hearts are naturally sinful, this is how all of us would respond to Jesus apart from the grace of God. In reality, when anyone sees Christ for who He is, there are really only two options: (1) we will humble ourselves before Him, or (2) we will harden our hearts toward Him. After reading chapter 12, we should have a fuller and more glorious picture of Jesus than we previously had. And by God's grace, we will be humbled and overwhelmed at what we see.

In many ways, chapters 11 and 12 of Matthew's Gospel go together (much like chapters 8 and 9). In Matthew 11 we saw four portraits of Jesus: He is the promised Messiah, the authoritative Judge, the sovereign Son, and the gracious Master. To that impressive picture, we will add six more portraits of Jesus from chapter 12. At the end of these portraits, we are confronted with the ultimate question: Are you for or against Jesus?

He Is the Lord of the Sabbath
MATTHEW 12:1-14

Verses 1-14 give us the first portrait of Jesus in Matthew 12. You may be wondering what in these 14 verses incited murder in the minds of the Pharisees. Jesus' disciples simply picked grain to eat on the Sabbath, and then on that same day, Jesus healed a man's hand. These are hardly actions that necessitate murder, at least in our minds. To understand what is going on here, we need to get into the minds of the Pharisees. Pharisees were religious students, teachers, and defenders of God's law who sought to apply that law in every single detail of life. They believed that their obedience to the law helped them earn the favor and righteousness of God. We might refer to Pharisees as legalists, a term that needs some explanation.

Legalism involves working in our own power (sometimes according to God's law and other times according to our own rules) in order to earn God's favor. We think that if we can do certain things—good things no doubt—we can be righteous before God. Lest we too quickly disconnect ourselves from the Pharisees, we need to be reminded that we are all born with a legalistic heart, a heart that thinks there is something we can do to merit our way to God. It's the foundation of all the

religions of the world, whether it's paying homage to Hindu gods at
Sikh temples or bowing to Allah in a Muslim mosque. At their core all
other religions call us to follow religious rules and regulations. And if
we're not careful, this kind of thinking becomes the foundation for how
we live as Christians; we begin to think that if we pray enough, if we
study the Bible enough, if we avoid certain sins, if we come to worship,
if we help other people, if we go overseas in missions, if we do any number of things, we will become more acceptable to God. This is what the
Pharisees had done: they took the law of God, and not only had they
used it as a basis for righteousness before God, but they had added all
kinds of other rules and regulations to it.

As legalists, the Pharisees were in serious error in at least three
different ways. First, they **added to the requirements of the law**. For
example, the law said you couldn't travel on the Sabbath (Exod 16:29),
which leads us to ask, What is considered traveling? Can you travel
around your house? Can you travel to someone else's house? If you
travel beyond someone else's house, how far can you go? The Pharisees
answered such questions by saying that someone was permitted to travel
up to three thousand feet from their house, a permissible Sabbath day's
journey. That is, unless you have some food that is within 3,000 feet of
your house, and if that's the case, then that food is an extension of your
house, thus allowing you to journey another 3,000 feet. If you went any
further than that, it was sin (MacArthur, *Matthew 8–15*, 282).

Another example of the Pharisees' approach to the law concerned
God's command not to carry a load on the Sabbath (Exod 20:8-11; Jer
17:21-22). The question naturally arose, What constitutes a load? For
instance, are your clothes a load? The Pharisees said no, not if your
clothes are worn; only if you are carrying your clothes are they considered
a load. So it would be okay to wear a jacket on the Sabbath, but it would
be a sin to carry a jacket. John MacArthur describes the absurdity of it all:

> Tailors did not carry a needle with them on the Sabbath
> for fear they might be tempted to mend a garment and
> thereby perform work. Nothing could be bought or sold, and
> clothing could not be dyed or washed. A letter could not be
> dispatched, even if by the hand of a Gentile. No fire could
> be lit or extinguished—including fire for a lamp—although
> a fire already lit could be used within certain limits. For that
> reason, some orthodox Jews today use automatic timers to
> turn on lights in their homes well before the Sabbath begins.

Otherwise they might forget to turn them on in time and have to spend the night in the dark. Baths could not be taken for fear some of the water might spill onto the floor and "wash" it. Chairs could not be moved because dragging them might make a furrow in the ground, and a woman was not to look in a mirror lest she see a gray hair and be tempted to pull it out. (MacArthur, *Matthew 8–15*, 282)

With such strict regulations, we can begin to understand why Jesus and His disciples came under fire from the Pharisees in Matthew 12 for some seemingly harmless acts. MacArthur observes, "According to those hair-splitting regulations, a Jew could not pull off even a handful of grain to eat on the Sabbath unless he was starving" (MacArthur, *Matthew 8–15*, 282). This was exactly the kind of approach to God that Jesus had addressed at the end of Matthew 11 when He said, "Come to Me, all of you who are weary and burdened" (v. 28). The weary and burdened were those who had the law heaped upon them, with the idea that their righteousness depended on keeping certain rules and regulations.

In addition to adding to the requirements of the law, the Pharisees **ignored the exceptions to the law**. In order to justify His disciples' act of plucking heads of grain on the Sabbath, Jesus cited the Old Testament story of David entering into the tabernacle and eating a piece of bread with his men on the Sabbath (1 Sam 21:1-6), something only the priests were permitted to do (Lev 24:5-9). Jesus then noted how the priests were, according to the law, allowed to work on the Sabbath without dishonoring God (Num 28:9-10). In other words, the rules that the Pharisees were making would not even stand up with precedent in the Old Testament, the very same Old Testament they were seeking to uphold.

The third serious error the Pharisees committed was that they **missed the heart of the law**. We can see this error clearly in the Pharisees' response to Jesus' healing of a man with a withered hand on the Sabbath. The Pharisees believed—and enforced—a rule that it was only lawful to heal someone on the Sabbath if that person's life was in danger, which for the man in this story was clearly not the case. So they asked Him, "Is it lawful to heal on the Sabbath?" (v. 10). You can almost imagine the intensity of this scene as Jesus looked them in the eye and said, "If you had a sheep, and it fell into a pit, wouldn't you save it? And since people are more valuable than sheep, it is lawful to do good, to show mercy, on the Sabbath" (vv. 11-12, paraphrased). Jesus touched the man with the withered hand, and in response the Pharisees went out and began conspiring to kill Him (v. 14). What an amazing picture, as those most devoted to the law turned completely against the One who gave the law in the first place!

Jesus' actions and claims in this passage upset the Pharisees on multiple levels. They were infuriated that, **as Lord, Jesus** was telling them that He **is greater than the tabernacle**. If exceptions were made for King David and his men to eat in the tabernacle, surely they would be made for the Messiah King who had come in the line of David, who was Himself greater than David. Just as David and his men could eat in the house of God, so it is okay for Jesus' disciples to eat in the presence of God. For Jesus is not only greater than the tabernacle; He **is greater than the temple**. Just as the temple represented the dwelling place of God, so Jesus was present as God's dwelling place in an even greater way. Since there were clear exceptions for working on the Sabbath in the presence of God, it follows that it is permissible to work on the Sabbath in the presence of the Christ.

Don't miss the underlying point here: Jesus is making clear that as Lord of the Sabbath, He **is God**. He is God in the flesh, and as God, He has the authority to determine Sabbath regulations for His disciples. This authority goes beyond the mere exceptions to the law that gave David the right to eat in the tabernacle or priests the right to work on the Sabbath. It was absolutely right, then, for Jesus to show mercy to a man on that day. By claiming to be Lord of the Sabbath, Jesus was implicitly saying to these legalistic Pharisees that the way to become right before God is not through following certain rules and regulations; the way to become right before God is through faith in Him. This is the same message we proclaim to every single person on the planet: you cannot become right before God by following certain laws; you can only become right before God by trusting Jesus as Lord.

He Is the Servant of God and Sinners
MATTHEW 12:15-21

In the second portrait of Jesus, notice the contrast between the Pharisees, who ignored the needs of men and plotted to kill the Messiah, and Jesus the Servant. This passage contains the longest quotation of the Old Testament in the book of Matthew. Matthew is quoting Isaiah, one of his favorite authors, and in particular the prophecy of a Suffering Servant in Isaiah 42:1-3. Knowing that the Pharisees were plotting to kill Him,

Jesus didn't try to fight against them; instead, He withdrew, and as He healed the crowds at this time, He tried to keep a low profile. Jesus was intent on His mission: He is the Servant of God and sinners. Consider both of these aspects of Christ's service. First, He is the servant **of God: Jesus is loved by the Father and filled with the Spirit**. He alone is pleasing before the Father and He alone is perfectly and fully under the influence of God's Holy Spirit.

Second, the Promised One of Isaiah is the servant **of sinners: Jesus is hope for the hurting**. As a picture of Jesus' refusal to fight or shout against the Pharisees, Matthew (citing Isaiah) says that Jesus "will not argue or shout, and no one will hear His voice in the streets" (v. 19). Jesus is a meek and gentle Savior who "will not break a bruised reed" and "will not put out a smoldering wick" (v. 20). What imagery for the One who is Lord of the Sabbath, the One with authority over the law, and the promised King to come! Christ comes to people who are bruised and battered, whose flame is flickering out. He comes to the spiritually broken, those so bruised by sin and all its effects that they are unable to stand up under it. Richard Sibbes, the Puritan pastor who wrote *The Bruised Reed*—a classic book taken from the text of Isaiah 42:3—writes the following of Christ's compassion:

> Are you bruised? Be of good comfort, he calls you. Conceal not your wounds, open all before him and . . . go to Christ. . . . There is more mercy in [Him] than sin in [you].

He Is the Power of God
MATTHEW 12:22-37

Matthew's third portrait of Jesus in this passage comes in the context of another healing. After Jesus healed a demon-oppressed man who was both blind and mute, the crowds responded by saying, "Perhaps this is the Son of David!" (v. 23). They wanted to know if Jesus was the Messiah. This question enraged the Pharisees, causing them to make the outlandish accusation that Jesus was performing miracles by the power of "Beelzebul, the ruler of the demons." This is **an unreasonable accusation** that Jesus addresses on two primary levels. First, He points out that **it is illogical**. After all, why would the Devil want demons cast out? That would be like casting himself out, destroying his own work. A kingdom divided against itself will not stand (v. 25).

The second flaw Jesus points out about the Pharisees' accusation is that **it is inconsistent**. If casting out demons were a demonic activity, then why didn't the Pharisees criticize their own followers for casting out demons? These "sons" of the Pharisees, likely a reference to their followers, claimed to have cast out demons, and we know from Matthew 7 that people who were not followers of Jesus had cast out demons. Jesus points out the inconsistency in all of this, and this leads to three **undeniable conclusions**.

First and foremost, **if this is not by the power of Satan, then this is by the power of God**. If Jesus is not casting out demons by the power of the Devil—which would be both illogical and inconsistent—then there's only one other possibility: He is casting out demons "by the Spirit of God," which means that "the kingdom of God has come" (v. 28). More specifically, the King is here.

This leads to a second undeniable conclusion, which Jesus points out: **The One who is stronger than Satan is here**. Jesus claimed that He was tying up the "strong man," i.e., Satan (v. 29). Because Jesus is stronger than Satan, He is plundering his house, the domain where he has temporary rule. The book of Matthew has been making this point repeatedly. Jesus is healing people of diseases, delivering people from demons, raising people from the dead, and forgiving people of sins. And all of these things are shouting one reality: One who is stronger than the Devil is here!

As Jesus manifests the kingdom, we see a third undeniable conclusion: **Neutrality toward Jesus is impossible**. Verse 30: "Anyone who is not with Me is against Me, and anyone who does not gather with Me scatters." What Jesus said to the Pharisees applies equally to us. We too must decide whether Jesus is evil, which leads to prideful opposition, or else that He is good, which means that we follow Him wholeheartedly. There is no middle ground.

The fact that we must be either for or against Jesus leads directly into His discussion of **the unforgivable sin** in verses 31-32. This is surely one of the most misinterpreted and misunderstood passages in the whole Bible, and given the seriousness of Jesus' words, it is imperative that we understand them rightly. A right interpretation begins by looking at these verses in light of the *overall* biblical context, and then in light of this *specific* biblical context. In terms of the broader context, we know from Scripture that God is a forgiving God. That reality is all over both the Old and New Testaments. Exodus 34:6-7 is one clear example, where the Lord proclaims His name to Moses: "Yahweh—Yahweh is a compassionate and gracious God, slow to anger and rich in faithful love and truth, maintaining faithful love to a thousand generations, forgiving wrongdoing, rebellion, and sin." This is the God who forgave Adam and Eve, Abraham, Isaac, Jacob, Moses, Israel, King David, and countless others throughout the Old Testament. God even forgave His people for heinous and rebellious sins. We see the same thing in the New Testament, as forgiveness is extended to tax-collectors (like Matthew) and sinners, as well as anti-Christian terrorists like Paul (Acts 9). God's grace and compassion are consistent themes throughout Scripture.

Keeping in mind God's merciful character, we turn to consider Jesus' words in Matthew 12. Jesus is speaking to Pharisees who are showing themselves to be completely opposed to Him. They were saying that Christ's works were not through the power of the Spirit, but through the power of Satan. This context helps us to understand why Jesus uses the term *blasphemy* here instead of the more common term, *sin*. To blaspheme is to speak against or to slander, and that's what the Pharisees were doing. With this in mind, consider two aspects of Jesus' words in verses 31-32.

First, Jesus says that **blasphemy against the Son is forgivable, and the avenue to forgiveness is repentance**. Jesus will graciously pardon those who deny and mock Him, for we see this all over the New Testament. For example, Peter denied Christ three times and he was forgiven (Matt 26:69-75; Mark 14:66-72). Paul tells us that he was "formerly a blasphemer," yet "the grace of our Lord overflowed" (1 Tim 1:13-14). There's a sense in which all of us are guilty of blasphemy: we deny Christ by our silence or cowardice, or we defame Him by questioning His goodness toward us. Gratefully, all of these sins are forgivable by God's grace. He will forgive blasphemy against the Son for those who repent of their sins.

Second, **blasphemy against the Spirit of God is unforgivable, because the avenue to forgiveness is rejected**. Jesus is speaking to people who He knows were in serious danger, if not already guilty, of hardening their hearts completely against Him. In attributing the work of the Spirit to the person of Satan, they were setting themselves in total opposition to the Spirit of God, the only Spirit who can draw them to salvation through repentance. They were rejecting even the thought of repentance. Such sin involves willful unbelief, persistent rebellion, and final denial. It's worth considering each of these aspects of sin further.

The Pharisees had seen Jesus heal every kind of disease, cast out every kind of demon, forgive every kind of sin, yet they chose to charge Him with deceit and demonism. Theirs was **willful unbelief**. In the face of the undeniable evidence of Jesus' deity and messiahship, they rejected Him. They did not reject the Spirit's work in Jesus' life and ministry for lack of evidence, but rather for lack of humility. The Pharisees were also guilty of an ongoing pattern of sin, and not merely a spur-of-the-moment reaction. This was **persistent rebellion** that proudly refused to submit, regardless of what Jesus said or did.

In the end, the Pharisees' willful unbelief and persistent rebellion led to **final denial**. Theirs was a permanent refutation of the work of the Spirit in the Son of Man, and **permanent refutation leads to permanent condemnation**. Of such sin, Jesus says, "it will not be forgiven him, either in this age or in the one to come" (v. 32). One commentator described the Pharisees like this:

> For penitence they substitute hardening, for confession plotting. Thus, by means of their own criminal and completely inexcusable callousness, they are dooming themselves. Their sin is unpardonable because they are unwilling to tread the path that leads to pardon. For a thief, an adulterer, and a murderer there is hope. The message of the gospel may cause him to cry out, "O God be merciful to me, the sinner." But when a man has become hardened, so that he has made up his mind not to pay any attention to the promptings of the Spirit, not even to listen to His pleading and warning voice, he has placed himself on the road that leads to perdition. He has sinned the sin "unto death." (Hendriksen, *The Exposition of the Gospel According to Matthew*, 529)

In the end, no one can be saved if they pridefully and permanently reject the Spirit of God. This is the Spirit who draws us to salvation, who alone leads us to repentance and applies God's forgiveness. We dare not reject His testimony to the Son. Even as we consider the danger of blaspheming the Son and the Spirit, we must be careful not to completely disconnect the two from one another, for ultimately to reject the Spirit is finally to reject the Son. As 1 Corinthians 12:3 says, "No one speaking by the Spirit of God says, 'Jesus is cursed,' and no one can say, 'Jesus is Lord,' except by the Holy Spirit."

These sobering verses leave us with **two unforgettable reminders**. First, **we must avoid labeling anyone as guilty of the unforgivable sin**. The reality is that in all of our hearts, there was a time when we spurned the work of the Spirit. All of us were at one time opposed to Christ and His Spirit in some sense; yet God patiently pursued us. Jesus knew the thoughts of these Pharisees (v. 25) in a way that we do not, so we should be slow to make pronouncements on someone's spiritual condition. **We trust that God alone knows a person's heart**. Who are we to say that a person has committed willful unbelief, persistent rebellion, and final denial of the Spirit's invitation to repent? Because God has not enabled us to see perfectly into a person's heart, and because His mercy is so lavish, **we work and we pray with a constant hope** that God will soften even the hardest of hearts, that He will save even the most prideful of sinners.

Sometimes Christians wonder if they have committed the unforgivable sin. Based on all we've seen in this passage, it's pretty safe to conclude that if you're worried about having committed this sin, you are showing by your concern that you have not fully and finally rejected the Spirit's testimony. Some people have labeled suicide or other particular sins as ultimately unforgivable, but this passage definitively does not teach that. Blasphemy against the Spirit of God is unforgivable because the avenue to forgiveness—repentance—has been thoroughly rejected.

The second unforgettable reminder in this passage is in verses 33-37: We must realize that **the unforgivable sin is primarily a sin of the heart, not the lips**.

Based on verse 32 in the previous paragraph, blasphemy involves speaking against the Spirit of God. This causes people to wonder, "Have I ever said something against the Spirit of God?" In verses 33-37 Jesus spoke of a principle that we see all over Scripture: **Our words reveal our hearts**. The unforgivable sin, therefore, is not ultimately about what is spoken, but rather about what lies underneath what is spoken. A heart that rejects humble repentance speaks like the Pharisees and reveals a dangerous condition.

It's a sobering reality to think that what we say, and what we don't say, is a reflection of what is in our hearts. Jesus says in verse 33 that a good tree bears good fruit, and a bad tree bears bad fruit. The fruit that pours from our lips is evidence of what lies within our hearts. To put it another way, **faith results in good works, which includes good words**. This truth goes back to the reality that Jesus is the Power of God. He changes us so that what we believe actually makes a difference in terms of the words that we speak. It makes sense, then, for Paul to describe salvation as he does in Romans 10:9-10:

> If you confess with your mouth, "Jesus is Lord," and believe in your heart that God raised Him from the dead, you will be saved. One believes with the heart, resulting in righteousness, and one confesses with the mouth, resulting in salvation.

He Is the Greater Prophet
MATTHEW 12:38-41

Matthew gives us three more portraits of Jesus in the rest of Matthew 12. In the fourth portrait of Jesus we see that He is the Greater Prophet. The scribes and Pharisees asked Jesus for a sign, as if they hadn't seen enough already. Jesus had shown them many signs, but they wanted something else, something more sensational. Jesus called them out in their wickedness, knowing that even His own resurrection from the dead would not convince their hardened hearts. He points back to the prophet Jonah.

Consider the parallel: **Jonah was alive after three days in a fish; Jesus would be alive after three days in a grave**. There's some debate about Jesus' reference to three days and nights, because technically He died and was buried on a Friday and then He rose on a Sunday. That timeframe doesn't allow for three full nights (or three full days, for that matter). However, it was very common at that time to count any part of a day as a complete day. Three days and three nights could easily refer to parts of three days and parts of three nights (Carson, *Matthew*, 296). The point is that just as a fish swallowed up Jonah, a prophet who was shortly thereafter delivered from death, so the grave will swallow up Jesus, and He will be delivered from death too. But there's also a contrast here: Upon Jonah's deliverance, **the Ninevites responded with repentance; the Israelites** in Jesus' day **were responding with rejection**. Even in the face of the resurrection, Jesus' contemporaries refused to believe in Him.

He Is the Wiser King
MATTHEW 12:42

Fifth, Jesus continues His response to the scribes and Pharisees. Not only is He the Greater Prophet, He is the Wiser King. Jesus points out that a pagan queen from of old would condemn these Pharisees, for when the Queen of Sheba came to visit Solomon, seeing His wealth and wisdom, she marveled that God had given such wisdom to man (1 Kgs 10). Yet the Pharisees had the very wisdom of God standing in front of them, and they rejected everything He said.

He Is Our Elder Brother
MATTHEW 12:43-50

The sixth portrait of Jesus in Matthew 12 may be the most amazing. In light of Jesus' greatness, it is simply stunning to consider that He is our Elder Brother. As we hear the term *elder brother*, we need to guard against a misunderstanding related to certain cultic teachings in our day. Mormons, for instance, do not believe the Bible's teaching on Christ's divinity, though they do claim that certain people will actually attain unto godhood after the final resurrection based on certain religious requirements.[26] However, Scripture clearly presents Jesus Christ as God the Son, fully divine (Col 2:9), and although believers will one day receive a glorious resurrected body, we will never become gods. Our part will be to serve and worship the one true God (Rev 7:9-10). Referring to Jesus as our Elder Brother reminds us that, as God, He took on human flesh (John 1:14), and because He is both fully God and fully man, His death and resurrection make it possible for sinful human beings to be a part of His family. We see similar language in places like Romans 8:29, where Jesus is called the "firstborn among many brothers," or in Hebrews 2:11, where it says of believers that Jesus is "not ashamed to call them brothers."

After responding to the scribes and Pharisees, Jesus then tells a story about an unclean spirit and applies it to the present evil generation. At first glance, the point of Jesus' story in verses 43-45 is not altogether obvious. Jesus is telling us here **what we don't need: an empty religion consumed with outer reformation**. All kinds of fanciful explanations have been offered regarding what this passage teaches, including how to deliver demons out of people and what must be done to ensure demons don't come back. However, this kind of speculation about tactics in spiritual warfare misses the entire point of the passage. Jesus was

---

[26] For these and other false teachings by the Mormon Church (also known as the Church of Jesus Christ of Latter-day Saints), see Walter Martin's *The Kingdom of Cults* (Minneapolis: Bethany House Publishers, 1997), 179–243.

still addressing these Pharisees who had hardened their hearts toward Him and who were leading the Jewish people away from Him. He describes them as people who had sought to get their house in order, likely a reference to their attempt to follow God's laws and a variety of other rules and regulations. The Pharisees had tried to sweep evil out of their lives and put things in order in their own strength. But their religious devotion had ultimately left their hearts empty. They were so focused on outer reformation when their greatest need was a new heart. And as a result, they were even more susceptible to the advance of the Evil One than they had been before.

The Pharisees were classic moralists, thinking they could reform their own lives. This kind of self-righteous moralism is empty; it only drives you further away from God, making you worse off than you were previously. Ultimately, this kind of approach to God damns you. Legalism gets progressively worse in our lives from year to year and from generation to generation. The more we convince ourselves that we can reform our lives, the more we find ourselves working harder and harder; yet we come up empty every time. That is a recipe for hopeless living and eventual condemnation. Make no mistake about it: legalism is demonic.

Rather than legalism, in verses 46-50 Jesus points in another direction for the answer to our great need. So if we don't need empty religion consumed with outer reformation, then what *do* we need? **What we do need is an intimate relationship compelled by inner transformation**. Jesus says that those who do God's will are part of His family, a family united around the gospel.

We come to God the Father through God the Son, knowing that Christ Jesus is our Brother. In His humanity, Jesus is like us in every way, only He is without sin (Heb 4:15). He alone is righteous. He alone is able to obey the law that we cannot obey. He alone is stronger than Satan, which enabled Christ to overcome sin in His life and in His death. And finally, only Jesus was able to rise from the grave. On that basis, Jesus invites us into His family. He makes it possible for us to be called sons and daughters of God. When we turn aside from sin and self and trust in Jesus, we are brought into God's family by the power of His Spirit. This is the kind of relationship that brings about inner transformation.

Hear the **humbling invitations** given throughout this chapter in Matthew. For all who have worked hard to try to be righteous, rest in the Lord of the Sabbath who is righteous for you. To all who are bruised and broken, whose light is struggling to find life, humble yourself before the One who brings hope to the hurting and ask Him to heal you. To all who are struggling under the weight of sin, come to the One who is the Power of God—to the One who is stronger than your enemy. To all who fear death, come to the greater Prophet who conquers death. To all who seek wisdom, come to the only wise King. And to all who long to be loved, come to your Elder Brother, who brings you into the family where God is Father.

Reflect and Discuss

1. Why are legalistic hearts so resistant to Jesus?
2. How does legalism and a desire to earn your standing before God manifest itself in your own life?
3. Explain what it means to say that Jesus is greater than the temple.
4. Matthew presents Christ as merciful in this passage. How is the mercy of Jesus different from a "live and let live" mind-set?
5. In an effort to make the cost of following Christ clear, what is the danger of downplaying His mercy?
6. How might the portrait of Jesus' power in this passage impact our view of spiritual warfare?
7. How would you counsel someone who feared that they had committed the unpardonable sin because of a sinful thought or word toward God?
8. Matthew compares Jesus to Jonah and Solomon. How do these comparisons speak to the seriousness of rejecting Christ?
9. It's common to hear unbelievers refer to everyone as "God's children." How does Matthew 12:50 help us rightly define God's family?
10. Some sermons only emphasize moral lessons for believers. How does an emphasis on the person of Christ as we see in Matthew 12 help correct such an approach? What is the danger of not presenting Jesus as central in our teaching and preaching?

Parables of the Kingdom

MATTHEW 13:1-52

Main Idea: Jesus' parables tell of a kingdom that, despite being unrecognized and rejected by some, is already accomplishing its purpose in the world, and it will one day be gloriously consummated, resulting in eternal judgment for those who reject the gospel and eternal life for those who genuinely trust in Christ and treasure His reward.

I. **Four Questions**
    A. What is a parable?
        1. A practical story
        2. Often framed as a simile
        3. Illustrates a spiritual truth
    B. How do we understand parables?
        1. Listen from the hearer's perspective.
        2. Look for the main point.
        3. Let the truth change your perception.
    C. Why do we have parables?
        1. Jesus was revealing truth to those who were believing the mysterious—this was evidence of God's mercy.
        2. Jesus was concealing truth from those who were denying the obvious—this was evidence of God's judgment.
    D. What is the kingdom of heaven?
        1. The redemptive rule or reign of God in Christ
        2. A present reality: The King is here, and His kingdom is advancing.
        3. A future realization: The King is coming back, and His kingdom will one day be complete.

II. **Eight Parables**
    A. The parable of the Sower
    B. The parables of the Weeds and the Net
    C. The parables of the Mustard Seed and Yeast
    D. The parables of the Treasure and the Pearl
    E. The parable of the Homeowner

III. Two Primary Applications
  A. Humbly and joyfully receive the message of the kingdom.
  B. Confidently and urgently spread the message of the kingdom.

For many people, Matthew 13 is a confusing and perplexing chapter. Parables about sowing seeds and nets drawing fish to the shore can leave us scratching our heads. However, this chapter contains several keys to understanding our lives and the place where we find ourselves in history. These parables of the kingdom need to be understood and believed so that we might follow Jesus more faithfully and live for His kingdom.

Rather than treating each parable separately, taking each apart in great detail, we'll consider the parables in Matthew 13 collectively and then conclude by asking, "What does this mean, and why is it important?" Matthew 13:1 begins the third major teaching section from Jesus in this Gospel. The first major teaching section was the Sermon on the Mount in Matthew 5–7, and the second was Jesus' speech, or summons, to His disciples in Matthew 10. Here in Matthew 13, Jesus' teaching largely takes the form of parables.

In order to understand Matthew 13, we need to place ourselves in the broader context of Matthew's Gospel. In Matthew 3:2 John the Baptist announced, "Repent, because the kingdom of heaven has come near!" He had proclaimed that the King, Christ, would "baptize you with the Holy Spirit and fire" (v. 11) and that a "winnowing shovel is in His hand" (v. 12). As Judge, Jesus would separate the wheat from the chaff. Then John baptized Jesus, the anointed Messiah, the One who had come to usher in the kingdom of God (vv. 13-17). Drastic changes looked to be imminent.

But now in Matthew 13, ten chapters later, very little substantive change has happened. Sure, Jesus has healed and taught some people, but most were keeping a safe distance from Him. Religious people in particular were standing up against Him, even plotting to kill Him (Matt 12:14). Following these parables in chapter 13, Jesus' neighbors were ready to disown Him (vv. 53-58). Needless to say, there were a lot of people very confused about whether Jesus really was the Messiah, including the crowds (chap. 12) and John the Baptist himself (chap. 11). Even the disciples must have been a little perplexed, as things weren't shaping up the way they had hoped.

Many Jews expected all of Israel to flock to the Messiah and rally around Him, yet only a few people were rallying around Jesus. And it certainly didn't look like He was ushering in a whole new kingdom. As chapter 13 begins, interest had grown and the crowds were gathered around Jesus, even to the point where He had to get into a boat and go out into the water in order to see all of them (vv. 1-2). And what did Jesus do? He decided to tell them some stories about farmers, seeds, weeds, bread, pearls, and homeowners. How's that for a message from the Messiah! We need to see what these words that confused crowds two thousand years ago mean to our lives today. To do this, we need to start by asking four questions.

Four Questions

What is a parable?

This is the first question we must answer as we approach Matthew 13. A parable is **a practical story, often framed as a simile** (a comparison using "like" or "as"), **that illustrates spiritual truth**. There are all kinds of parables in the Gospels, and some of them are famous, such as the Prodigal Son (Luke 15:11-32), the Good Samaritan (Luke 10:25-37), and the Lost Sheep (Matt 18:10-14). These stories draw a comparison in order to illustrate a spiritual truth.

How do we understand parables?

This question is important because different parables have been interpreted (and misinterpreted) in different ways throughout the history of the church. Some people have tried to figure out the meaning of a parable by finding parallels for every detail. For example, one understanding of the parable of the Good Samaritan makes the following connections: the man who was beaten is a sinner; the priest stands for the law; the Levite stands for the sacrifices; Jesus is the Samaritan who pays the bill; the inn is the church where believers are cared for; the two silver coins are baptism and the Lord's Supper; the innkeeper is the apostle Paul. Now that's certainly a creative interpretation, but there's only one problem: neither Jesus nor the Bible ever tells us that this is what the parable means. So how *do* we understand parables so that we are not abusing or misunderstanding them?

We should keep at least three principles in mind as we seek to understand parables: **listen from the hearer's perspective, look for the**

main point, and then let the truth change your perception. We'll take those principles in order.

In terms of listening from the hearer's perspective, we've got to put ourselves in the shoes of people who first heard parables in order to understand what they were hearing. Jesus uses pictures and stories that are far more familiar to first-century Jews than twenty-first-century Americans. We need to ask ourselves questions such as, What would they hear? What would stick out to them? How would they respond at different points in the story? What kind of emotions would rise up when they heard the word "Samaritan?" I recall sitting in a Middle Eastern country sharing the story of the prodigal son with a Muslim man, and his eyes perked up when I said that the father went running to his son. He claimed that a father who had been offended like that would never run to his son. This man's reaction taught me more about the parable.

Next, in order to understand a parable, we need to look for the main point. There's usually one main point in any parable, or at most two or three, depending on the various elements in the story. As we read the parable, we should try to identify the primary truth the author is communicating.

Once we are able to discern the main point, we need to let that truth change our perception. After all, the whole point of parables is to challenge the way people think about something by using a kind of backdoor route—through story. This is exactly what Jesus was doing in Matthew 13.

Why do we have parables?

So far we've answered the questions "What is a parable?" and "How do we understand parables?" The third question we need to answer is, "Why do we have parables?" In other words, why not just state the main point instead of telling a story? This is exactly the question that the disciples ask Jesus in verse 10: "Why do You speak to them in parables?" He answers them in the next verse: "Because the secrets of the kingdom of heaven have been given for you to know, but it has not been given to them" (v. 11). Jesus points to two purposes for parables, and these purposes are different based on two different kinds of audiences. This twofold purpose is clear even in the way this chapter is structured, as these first four parables are told to the crowds, while the last four parables and their explanations are told only to the disciples.

First, **Jesus was revealing truth to those who were believing the mysterious**. For the disciples, the secrets of the kingdom of heaven had been given for them to know by God. These "secrets" of the kingdom may also be referred to as "mysteries" (NKJV). That word *mystery* or *secret* refers to something that was hidden in the Old Testament and now made known in the New Testament. It was no secret that God was going to send the Messiah to usher in a kingdom; what *was* a secret was what kind of Messiah God would send, and how that Messiah would conquer—not through political struggle or physical force, but through selfless love and a sacrificial death on a cross. So for those who were trusting that Jesus was indeed the promised King, the parables were helping them understand what kind of King He was and what kind of kingdom He was ushering in.

The disciples were greatly privileged to hear and understand the mysteries of the kingdom of heaven, for **this was evidence of God's mercy**. Jesus says, "But your eyes are blessed because they do see, and your ears because they do hear! For I assure you: Many prophets and righteous people longed to see the things you see yet didn't see them; to hear the things you hear yet didn't hear them" (vv. 16-17). God's grace is all over this passage. To the disciples it had been "given" to know these things (v. 11). Given by whom? By God! And more would be given by God (v. 12). If we ask why the disciples understood and believed while so many others didn't, the answer is that it was purely the mercy of God.

Have you ever wondered why you as a follower of Christ see forgiveness in the cross, when so many other people in the world see foolishness (1 Cor 1:18)? Is it because you are better, smarter, more humble, or more religious? No, it is only because God is merciful. He has opened your eyes to see and your ears to hear. You are also blessed to live in a time when we have the full revelation of God's Word as it points to Jesus Christ. Something Old Testament saints only could have longed for, believers now possess.

But what about those who were rejecting Christ, those who were refusing to see Him as the Messiah? The parables have a different purpose for them. Matthew gives us the second purpose of parables: **Jesus was concealing truth from those who were denying the obvious**. In spite of miracle after miracle, teaching after teaching, the crowds and religious leaders refused to believe in Jesus as the Christ. Jesus said that it "has not been given to them" to understand these stories (v. 11), and that even the understanding they had would be taken away (v. 12). Then in verse 13 Jesus tells us why He is doing things this way: "For this reason

I speak to them in parables, because looking they do not see, and hearing they do not listen or understand." Jesus follows this statement by quoting from Isaiah 6 where, right after the prophet's commissioning, God told Isaiah that he would preach but the people would not listen, for their hearts were dull, their ears were shut, and their eyes were closed (Isa 6:9-10).

Many people in Jesus' day saw His miracles outwardly, but they refused to see what those miracles said about Him. They heard what He had to say about being the Lord of the Sabbath, but they didn't understand the ramifications of such a pronouncement. Jesus knew that these parables would not be rightly understood, and according to Isaiah 6:9-10, **this was evidence of God's judgment**. Even though many had the person of Christ and the words of Christ right in front of them, they were rebelling against Him.

What is the kingdom of heaven?

All of these parables in Matthew 13 are about the kingdom of heaven, which leads to the fourth and final question.[27] Matthew uses the phrase "kingdom of heaven" 32 times, and it plays an important part in His overall message. Much could be said here because this is a subject that spans all of Scripture. In short, the kingdom of heaven is **the redemptive rule or reign of God in Christ**. The fundamental word is "rule" or "reign" because when we talk about the kingdom, we are talking about the authority and sovereignty of God as King. Notice also that God's reign is "redemptive." In one sense, we could say that God has authority and sovereignty over everything in the universe. The kingdom of heaven, then, could refer to everything in the world, because God has rule and reign over everything in the world. However, even though Scripture clearly teaches that God rules over all things, this kind of comprehensive rule is not the primary way that the phrase "kingdom of heaven" is used in Matthew's Gospel. Instead, the kingdom of heaven is used to describe how God is asserting His authority in the redemption of sinners through Christ, the promised Messiah. A few examples may help clarify this point.

---

[27] For more on Matthew's use of the phrase "kingdom of heaven," see Pennington, *Heaven and Earth in the Gospel of Matthew*. For a brief summary of Pennington's work, see Schreiner, *New Testament Theology*, 46–47.

In Matthew 6:9-10 Jesus says, "Therefore, you should pray like this: Our Father in heaven, Your name be honored as holy. Your kingdom come. Your will be done on earth as it is in heaven." Jesus is telling the disciples to pray that God would assert His redemptive rule and reign across the earth in Christ. Matthew 6:33 communicates a similar idea: "But seek first the kingdom of God and His righteousness, and all these things will be provided for you." Jesus was instructing His disciples not to worry about their basic needs, but rather to seek and submit to the redemptive rule and reign of God in every facet of their life. The things that seem to be so worrisome—food, clothing, etc.—will be provided for them by God. Finally, in Mark 10:15 Jesus says, "I assure you: Whoever does not welcome the kingdom of God like a little child will never enter it." The point is that followers of Christ must, like a child, receive and embrace the rule or reign of God through Christ in their life. This perspective on the kingdom of heaven helps us understand why Jesus' teaching on the subject is so important.

Before leaving the topic of the kingdom of heaven, we should also note its timing. There's a sense in which the kingdom of heaven is **a present reality: The King is here, and His kingdom is advancing**. That's what we've been reading about in Matthew—God's rule and reign over disease and disasters and death is being asserted redemptively through Christ. So there is a very real sense in which the kingdom of heaven is at hand; it is present. At the same time, there's also a sense in which the kingdom of heaven is still **a future realization: The King is coming back, and His kingdom will one day be complete**. That particular theme of the future aspect of the kingdom is one of the main purposes of the parables in Matthew 13. The redemptive reign of God in Christ is infiltrating the world now, but His kingdom will not be consummated until later, when Jesus returns. We are, in a sense, living between the times.

After Jesus had died on the cross and risen from the grave, His disciples asked Him, "Lord, are You restoring the kingdom to Israel at this time?" (Acts 1:6). In reply, Jesus reoriented their perspective: "It is not for you to know times or periods that the Father has set by His own authority. But you will receive power when the Holy Spirit has come on you, and you will be My witnesses in Jerusalem, in all Judea and Samaria, and to the ends of the earth" (vv. 7-8). After saying this, Jesus ascended to the right hand of the Father, and two angels told the on-looking disciples that Jesus would return (v. 11). Then the rest of the New Testament involves these disciples bringing people into the kingdom by proclaiming the redemptive rule and reign of God in Christ all over the world.

Now, two thousand years later, we are still called to extoll God in Christ as King and to live our lives proclaiming His redemptive rule and reign to our neighbors and all over the nations. God is advancing His kingdom now, and one day He will fully and finally establish His kingdom over all things in Christ. On that day, followers of Christ will dwell in a new heaven and a new earth, where sin and suffering will be no more (Rev 21:1-4). We look to that day with great anticipation.

Eight Parables
MATTHEW 13:1-52

Once we understand our place in the outworking of God's purposes and the establishment of His kingdom, the parables of Matthew 13 should begin to make more sense. Matthew's organization of these eight parables is masterful, as He gives us a clear structure and a clear overlap in meaning concerning how these parables relate to one another. The end result is a picture of God's kingdom that defies human expectation.

The parable of the Sower (vv. 1-9, 18-23)

First, Jesus tells the parable of the Sower. In reality, this is not the parable of the *Sower* as much as it is the parable of the *Soil*, because the soil is the key variable in the story. The sower and the seed never change. Gratefully, we have Jesus' explanation for this parable in verses 18-23, so we don't have to wonder what point He's trying to get across. Here are the different elements of the parable with the benefit of Jesus' commentary.

The sower is the Son of Man and the seed is the message of salvation. Jesus is clearly the sower, either directly proclaiming the message while He was on earth or indirectly proclaiming the message through His disciples. That message is the message of salvation—the good news of the kingdom—that God will save and redeem sinners through Christ. Next, Jesus tells us that **the soil is the human heart**. This is an important part of the story in terms of understanding its importance in the context of Jesus' ministry. Jesus was teaching and preaching the good news of the kingdom, yet many people were either rebelling against what He was saying or else they were casually responding to Him. This kind of reception probably left the disciples puzzled.

Jesus' diagnosis of this situation is that the problem of rejection is not with the seed (the gospel of the kingdom) and not with the sower (Jesus); the problem is with the soil (the human heart). Jesus points to four different kinds of soil representing four different heart-responses to the message of salvation. The first kind of soil on which the seed fell was **the hard heart**. Verse 4 describes seed that had fallen "along the path" and had been eaten up by birds. This kind of soil represents those who hear the message of the kingdom but reject it, and thus the Devil comes and snatches the good news of the kingdom away.

The second kind of soil Jesus mentions is **the superficial heart**, and this is represented by the "rocky ground" (v. 5). This kind of heart receives the message and responds to it, but there's no root enabling it to grow and develop. When pressure and persecution come, the person falls away. You can't help but think about "easy-believism" that was rampant in the first century and is now rampant in the twenty-first century— "just pray this prayer, and you will be saved." But then a year or two (or maybe more) later, it becomes clear that that heart never truly received the message of the kingdom and that it failed to submit to the rule and reign of God in Christ. This scenario has continued to play out across church history.

George Whitfield, the passionate and powerful preacher of the First Great Awakening, used to preach to massive crowds numbering in the thousands, and people were greatly affected by his evangelistic message. When Whitfield was asked how many people were saved, he would say, "We'll see in a few years." The point is not that people needed to earn their salvation, but rather that it would take time for true salvation to be demonstrated. This is a very different approach than we hear of today, where the number of decisions is often touted boldly. We need to be careful in light of Jesus' clear teaching on the superficial heart.

Third, Jesus alerts us to **the divided heart**. The divided heart hears the Word, but there is no room for it because the cares and wealth of this world are too consuming. This is a clear warning for Christians today, especially those who live in prosperity, which is to say a majority of people in the Western world. We must watch out for the cares of this world lest they choke our hearts, for Jesus speaks of "the seduction of wealth" (v. 22). There's a subtle danger implied in the imagery here: a thorn does not choke suddenly, but gradually, almost unknowingly. The desire for and consumption of money and things divides and eventually destroys the heart.

Finally, there is a fourth kind of soil that Jesus refers to as "good ground" (vv. 8, 23). This is **the fruitful heart** that hears the word and understands it and then bears fruit. The measure of that fruit may be different from person to person—notice the 30-, 60-, and 100-fold increases in verse 23—but there is fruit nonetheless. The fruit of the Word will be evident in people's life in the world.

The question then becomes, What kind of heart do *you* have? Are you rejecting the message of the kingdom? Did you make a decision or pray a prayer years ago that has no real meaning in your life today? If so, I urge you to receive the good news of the kingdom today. By the mercy of God, soften your heart toward Christ.

There is also an application here for those who have already received the good news of the kingdom. One of the ways we bear the fruit of the kingdom is by sowing the seed of the gospel in the lives of others. Jesus' disciples had already been sent in Matthew 10 to sow seeds of the kingdom by spreading the message of salvation, and undoubtedly, just as Jesus had promised, they had faced resistance. It's encouraging to hear Jesus tell us to keep sowing the seed. This is also a good word for parents with rebellious children, for those with spouses who are hard-hearted toward the gospel, and for those with friends and coworkers who seem apathetic to the gospel. And finally, for missionaries around the world who serve in extremely difficult areas where there seems to be no receptivity to the gospel, Jesus' message is this: Don't stop sowing the seed. Yes, there is an adversary who is at work to rip that seed from hearts; and yes, there are pressures, persecutions, worries, and wealth to keep people from receiving this message. Nevertheless, keep sowing the seed. Then hope and pray and trust that the Lord of the harvest will indeed bring about the fruit of the gospel.

The parables of the Weeds and the Net (vv. 24-30, 36-43, 47-50)

Next we turn to the parables of the Weeds and the Net. The parable of the Weeds comes in verses 24-30 and the parable of the Net comes in verses 47-50. Since the point of these parables is almost identical, we'll consider them together. In a sense, they both build off of the parable of the Sower. In **the parable of the Weeds**, fruit-bearing plants are sitting side by side with weeds in a field, which leads workers to ask the question, "So, do you want us to go and gather them up?" (v. 28). In other words, "Do you want us to remove the bad (weeds) from the good (wheat)?" This is an understandable question, particularly when applied to the kingdom of God.

Jesus had come into a setting where most people in Israel saw themselves as part of the kingdom. However, Jesus had made clear that some Jews were part of the kingdom, while others were clearly not. Many thought that when the Messiah came, He would bring judgment on the wicked and unrighteous, which was in part why John the Baptist had wondered in Matthew 11 if Jesus were, in fact, the Messiah. John probably thought that the process of separating the wicked from the righteous would be well under way by that time; however, judgment had not yet come, and it's almost as if Jesus were saying in this parable, "Just wait."

Jesus explains the parable of the Weeds in verses 36-43. **The good seed represents believers**, "the sons of the kingdom" (v. 38). These are people who submit to the reign of God in Christ, the fruit-bearing plants from the parable of the Sower. On the other hand, **the weeds represent unbelievers**. There is some debate about whether "weeds" here refers to all unbelievers, or if Jesus was only speaking of people who were not true believers but who would have identified themselves either as a part of the people of Israel or even as a part of the church. This reality of false professors can be found throughout Matthew (7:21-23) and the entire New Testament (1 John 2:19). In contemporary terms, we might think of the scores of people today who outwardly identify with Christ or the church but who haven't been genuinely converted. While Jesus may be referring specifically to such false professors here, at the very least He is referring simply to unbelievers who live side by side with other believers in the world but whose hearts are far from Jesus.

At the end of verse 39, Jesus explains that **the harvest represents future judgment**, the time when the weeds will be separated from the wheat. The picture is grim, for this will be **a day of terrifying condemnation for the wicked**. In verse 40 Jesus says that the weeds are "gathered and burned in the fire," and in verses 41-42 His warning is even more sobering:

> *The Son of Man will send out His angels, and they will gather from His kingdom everything that causes sin and those guilty of lawlessness. They will throw them into the blazing furnace where there will be weeping and gnashing of teeth.*

This day of judgment that will be so terrifying for the wicked will be **a day of triumphant celebration for the righteous**: "Then the righteous will shine like the sun in their Father's kingdom" (v. 43). Those who have believed on Christ as King, Lord, and Savior will radiate His glory forever and ever. Instead of dread, this day evokes great joy for the righteous.

The parable of the Net reiterates the same truth as the parable of the Weeds. Clearly this is a point worth emphasizing. Jesus is driving home the point that **coming judgment is inevitable**. MacArthur puts it somberly: "The dragnet of God's judgment moves silently through the sea of mankind and draws all men to the shores of eternity for final separation to their ultimate destiny . . . believers to eternal life and unbelievers to eternal damnation" (MacArthur, *Matthew 8–15*, 395). On the day of God's final judgment, all mankind will be divided into two categories according to how we respond to Jesus. For the hard, superficial, and divided hearts who did not embrace Christ as King, **coming wrath is unimaginable**. God's angels will throw them into the "blazing furnace" (v. 42), a metaphor Jesus uses for hell. Here's how John Bunyan described that awful place:

> [In hell] thou shalt have none but a company of damned souls with an innumerable company of devils to keep company with thee. While thou art in this world, the very thought of the devil's appearing to thee makes thy flesh to tremble and thine hair ready to stand upright on thy head. But oh, what wilt thou do when not only the supposition of the devil's appearing but the real society of all the devils of hell will be with thee— howling, roaring and screeching in such a hideous manner that thou wilt be even at thy wit's end and ready to run stark mad again for anguish and torment. If after ten thousand years, an end should come, there would be comfort. But here is thy misery: here thou must be forever. When thou seest what an innumerable company of howling devils thou art amongst, thou shalt think this again—this is my portion forever. When thou hast been in hell so many thousand years as there are stars in the firmament or drops in the sea or sands on the seashore, yet thou hast to lie there forever. Oh, this one word—ever— how will it torment thy soul. (Bunyan, "Hell," 450)

The parable of the Weeds and the parable of the Net remind us that coming judgment is inevitable. What about you? Are you among the wheat or the weeds?

The parables of the Mustard Seed and Yeast (vv. 31-33)

These parables make similar points, though in slightly different ways. Jesus tells the parable of the Mustard Seed to illustrate how **outwardly, the kingdom expands from an insignificant beginning to an extravagant end**. The Messiah was supposed to usher in the kingdom of God, yet the kingdom seemed to be so small during Jesus' ministry, so relatively insignificant, particularly compared with what people were expecting. So Jesus chooses the smallest seed possible to say that yes, these are seemingly small beginnings, but the fruit that is born in the kingdom will lead to an extravagant end.

This idea of small beginnings leading to unimaginable expansion fits what we've already seen in Matthew's Gospel. The story began with a baby in a manger amid sheep and cattle. Then Jesus, Mary, and Joseph were virtually exiled to Egypt before arriving in tiny Nazareth, of all places. Now, in Matthew 13, Jesus is gathered with a small handful of disciples sitting around Him, a weak and inept group. However, in the days to come this unimpressive collection of men would begin to turn the world virtually upside down (Acts 17:6), so much so that we are impacted by their witness two thousand years later and thousands of miles away. We are part of this same kingdom they proclaimed, a kingdom that God is continuing to expand. This will continue until one day a throng from every nation and tribe and people and language will shout the praises of Christ the King. On that day the kingdom that began as a mustard seed will be in full bloom. It's the realization of Revelation 11:15: "The kingdom of the world has become the kingdom of our Lord and of His Messiah, and He will reign forever and ever."

There is another side to the advance of God's kingdom: it not only expands outwardly, but **inwardly, the kingdom permeates every facet of our lives and every corner of the earth**. In verse 33 Jesus tells the parable of the Yeast, or leaven, which transforms bread from the inside out. Just a little bit of yeast can spread into every part of the dough. This is the picture of the kingdom of heaven. On a personal level, the kingdom starts off as a seed in your heart, and slowly it works its way through your thoughts, beliefs, affections, motives, and actions. It then works through you into others' lives and through them into still others' lives. In this way, just as we have seen in the other parables, the point Jesus makes here is that the kingdom of heaven slowly advances throughout the world.

The parables of the Treasure and the Pearl (vv. 44-46)

Jesus shifts from talking about the eventual worldwide impact of the kingdom to talking about the parables of the Treasure and the Pearl. The story of the man who finds a treasure in a field may sound strange to our ears, but remember that Jesus is telling this parable in a day when treasure could not be stored in safety deposit boxes or well-protected banks. Instead, people would simply bury their greatest possessions in a remote place. This particular treasure had apparently been completely forgotten, even by the owner of the field. The man who found the treasure went and sold everything he had to buy that field, knowing that it was worth more than everything else he owned put together. People may have thought that he was crazy, but he wasn't. He was wise and happy, for he knew he had found something worth losing everything for.

The parable of the Priceless Pearl communicates a similar truth to the parable of the Treasure, though the man who found the pearl was actually *searching* for these fine jewels (Blomberg, *Matthew*, 224). Still, the pearl that he finds far exceeds his expectations. Both for those who are searching and those who are surprised, **the kingdom of heaven is something worth losing everything for**. There is great reward in submitting to the redemptive rule and reign of God in Christ, and this reward is greater than everything this world offers. As Paul says in Philippians 3:8, "I also consider everything to be a loss in view of the surpassing value of knowing Christ Jesus my Lord. Because of Him I have suffered the loss of all things and consider them filth, so that I may gain Christ." Jesus and the kingdom that He calls us to are better than money, health, strength, and even our own families. Christ is supremely satisfying in such a way that if you lose everything on this earth, but you get the kingdom of heaven, you have a happy trade-off. And nothing in eternity can ever take away this great treasure.

Because the kingdom of heaven is something worth losing everything for, **we joyfully let go of all things in order to passionately take hold of one thing**. Jesus is speaking to disciples who, like the merchant seeking for pearls, would lose much for following Christ; in fact, most of them would lose their lives. But they were following a King who promised, "And everyone who has left houses, brothers or sisters, father or mother, children, or fields because of My name will receive 100 times more and will inherit eternal life" (Matt 19:29). We come to Christ because He offers great reward; He *is* great reward.

The parable of the Homeowner (v. 52)

Finally, Jesus tells the parable of the Homeowner. Jesus talks about the master of a house who brings out of his treasure-vault things both old and new. This is a description of a scribe—a student or teacher of the law—who has been trained for the kingdom of heaven and understands it. Jesus then makes two primary points of comparison between the scribe and this homeowner in order to teach His disciples. First, **the disciple's treasure: We have seen the secrets of the old covenant revealed in the new covenant!** Just as a homeowner has valuables from the past and the present in his home, so the disciple of the kingdom knows that there is value in both the old and the new. He does not reject the revelation of God in the past; he values it and treasures it. At the same time, he understands God's past revelation in light of God's present revelation, particularly the present revelation of Christ as the supreme fulfillment of all that God has promised.

Stop and consider the privilege followers of Christ have today in terms of what we know of God's Word. We have the Old Testament in its entirety, and we can see how all of it points forward so magnificently, so brilliantly, so powerfully to Christ. Charles Spurgeon once said, "Don't you know, young man, that from every town and every village and every hamlet in England, wherever it may be, there is a road that leads to London? . . . So from every text in scripture there is a road towards the great metropolis, Christ."

Keep in mind that a disciple's prerogative is not merely to learn and understand for his or her own benefit. Like scribes, disciples are teachers of the Word, not students only. Bringing forth treasure both new and old was not merely for personal gain. There is more to **the disciple's task: We now proclaim the good news of the kingdom to every person and every people group on the planet!** We announce that Jesus is King, and we tell people that He has died on the cross for our sins in order to reconcile us to God. And we call people to submit to His rule in their lives, telling them of the glorious hope of the consummation of His kingdom.

Two Primary Applications

In light of Matthew 13, I invite you, if you have not already, to **humbly and joyfully receive the message of the kingdom**. Let go of the guilt and shame of sin. Leave behind the pleasures and pursuits and possessions of this world, and find in Christ a King worth losing everything for. Receive His mercy, and submit to His good and gracious mastery of your life. Do not harden your heart toward Him, do not toy superficially with Him, and do not give Him token affection in the midst of your riches in this world. I invite you to yield your heart and mind and life to Him.

And when you do, and for all who have humbly and joyfully received the message of the kingdom, I invite you to **confidently and urgently spread the message of the kingdom**. The dragnet of God's judgment is moving silently through the sea of mankind, and one day soon He will draw all men to the shores of eternity for final separation to their ultimate destiny in either everlasting life or eternal death. We know His judgment is coming, so warn and plead and pray and work—sow the seed of the gospel—so that the people around you and people groups around the world know the good news of the kingdom of God.

There's an ancient hymn called "How Sweet and Awful Is the Place" (it's been renamed "How Sweet and Awesome Is the Place"), and I was reflecting on its lyrics as I studied this text. In light of the mercy of God by which we hear and understand this good news of the kingdom, and in view of His coming judgment, consider these words:

> How sweet and awesome is the place
> With Christ within the doors,
> While everlasting love displays
> The choicest of her stores!
>
> While all our hearts and all our songs
> Join to admire the feast,
> Each of us cry, with thankful tongues,
> "Lord, why was I a guest?
>
> "Why was I made to hear Thy voice,
> And enter while there's room,
> When thousands make a wretched choice,
> And rather starve than come?"
>
> 'Twas the same love that spread the feast
> That sweetly drew us in;
> Else we had still refused to taste,
> And perished in our sin.
>
> Pity the nations, O our God!
> Constrain the earth to come;

Send Thy victorious Word abroad,
And bring the strangers home.

We long to see Thy churches full,
That all the chosen race
May with one voice, and heart and soul,
Sing Thy redeeming grace.

Reflect and Discuss

1. How did Jesus' parables both reveal *and* conceal truth?
2. Explain how the kingdom can be both present and future.
3. How would you sum up the parable of the Sower in one or two sentences? How might the parable of the Sower help us avoid being manipulative in our preaching, teaching, and evangelizing?
4. What are some signs that the cares and riches of the world are choking out saving faith as the Bible describes it?
5. How is persevering faith different from works-righteousness?
6. What would you say to someone whose only evidence of salvation was a momentary decision?
7. What encouragement might come to persecuted believers from the parables of the Mustard Seed and Yeast?
8. What do the parables of the Weeds and the Net have to teach us about the final judgment? Why is it sometimes difficult to discern who is and who is not part of the kingdom?
9. How could you use the parables of the Treasure and the Pearl of Great Price to respond to someone who said, "I want to follow Jesus, but I don't want to make drastic changes in my life"?
10. What wrong conceptions of the kingdom has Matthew 13 corrected for you?

Worship the King

MATTHEW 13:53–14:36

Main Idea: What we believe about Jesus will determine everything about how we worship Him.

I. **Two Pictures of Unbelief**
   A. Jesus' hometown
      1. They heard His words.
      2. They saw His works.
      3. They denied Him worship.
   B. Herod the tetrarch
      1. A flashback to John the Baptist's beheading
      2. A foreshadowing of Jesus' crucifixion
II. **Two Pictures of Belief**
   A. Faith in the face of need
      1. Reflect Jesus' compassion.
      2. Rely on Jesus' resources.
      3. Receive Jesus' blessing.
   B. Faith in the face of fear
      1. Jesus is sovereign over you.
      2. Jesus is interceding for you.
      3. Jesus is present with you.
      4. Jesus is strength in you.
      5. Jesus is peace around you.
III. **The Picture of Worship**
   A. Fall at the feet of the One who saves the perishing.
   B. Feast at the table with the One who satisfies the hungry.

There are many things we can glean from Matthew 14, but there is one over-arching truth that springs off the page, and it is this: Our worship of Christ is a reflection of our belief in Christ. We could also put it this way: What we believe about Jesus will determine everything about how we worship Jesus.

If we believe Jesus is a good man who did good things for us, then we will honor Him as we honor good men who do things for us. But if we believe Jesus is the majestic, glorious, universal King over all creation, then that belief will be evident in the way we sing to Him, the way we pray to Him, and the way we worship Him. Pastor and theologian Sinclair Ferguson has said,

> It is God who gives us the spirit of worship (Psalm 133:3), and it is what we know of God that produces this spirit of worship. We might say that worship is simply . . . what we think about God going into top gear! Instead of merely thinking about Him, we tell Him, in prayer and praise and song, how great and glorious we believe Him to be! (Ferguson, *A Heart for God*, 111)

Our goal, then, in reading Matthew 14 is to believe in Jesus more deeply, and as a result, to grow in our worship of Him.

In chapter 13, Jesus told eight different parables to describe what the kingdom of heaven is like. The first parable was about a sower and the four kinds of soil representing the human heart in response to the message of salvation. This parable is especially relevant for Matthew 13:53–14:36, for here we see examples of the various heart conditions that Jesus spoke of. The hard heart that rejects the gospel is evident in the people of Nazareth (13:53-58) and in Herod (14:1-12). The superficial heart that believes in Jesus as long as He provides food can be found among the large crowds who ate the loaves and fish (14:13-21). There is no real root to the faith of such people, as is evidenced by their later abandoning of Jesus (John 6:22-71). Though we don't specifically see the divided heart, we know that lurking in the midst of the disciples is Judas, a man who saw everything Jesus did yet still rejected Him. Underneath the surface, the ways and wealth of this world choked out the faith of this imposter. Finally, the receptive heart represented by the good soil was evident in the disciples as they rose to new heights in their faith (14:33).

As we consider those four kinds of heart responses to Jesus, I want to hone in on two general categories of people—those who were believing in Jesus and those who were not believing in Jesus. We'll consider the two pictures of unbelief in the first part of the text and then the two pictures of belief in the second part of the text. Our worship will be determined by which category we fit into.

Two Pictures of Unbelief
MATTHEW 13:53–14:12

Jesus' hometown (13:53-58)

The first picture of unbelief comes from the reaction of Jesus' hometown. Jesus' ministry in Galilee up to this point in Matthew's Gospel had lasted approximately two years, beginning around the time of Matthew 4:12. Christ's death on the cross was about a year away, and during this last year of His earthly ministry Jesus made a decided turn toward His inner group of disciples. Even when He spoke to the crowds, He focused on His relationship with His disciples. In Matthew 13:53 Jesus left Galilee and came to Nazareth, His hometown, and He began teaching. The people were "astonished," asking, "How did this wisdom and these miracles come to Him?" (13:54). Yet just like the crowds at Capernaum (11:23-24), they refused to believe in Jesus (13:58). They questioned where His authority came from, doubting that it came from God. Verse 57 says that they were "offended" by Jesus.

The picture we get of the crowds in Jesus' hometown is this: **they heard His words, they saw His works**, and yet **they denied Him worship**. The text says they were "offended," a term indicating their strong negative reaction,[28] so that they failed to honor Him (v. 57). And so it goes today: many people hear about Jesus and even see evidence of Jesus at work, yet they deny Him the worship He is due.

Herod the tetrarch (14:1-12)

The second picture of unbelief can be seen in Herod the tetrarch, a man whose story reads like a twisted soap opera. Herod was also known as Herod Antipas, with Antipas being a reference to the region he ruled over. This is the region where much of Jesus' ministry took place, and Herod heard all about Christ's fame. Herod got scared because he thought that Jesus was John the Baptist come back to life. Matthew is prompted at this point to pause and look back at how John the Baptist had died. Chronologically, verses 3-12 are **a flashback to John the Baptist's beheading**. Salome, Herod's daughter, did a seductive dance

---

[28] The word translated "offended" in verse 57 comes from the verb *skandalizo* and could also be translated as "be repelled by someone." BDAG, s.v. "*skandilizo*," 926.

before what was likely a group consisting of her drunken father and his friends. This prompted Herod to offer her whatever she wanted. It's at this point that Herodias (Salome's mother) told her daughter behind the scenes to ask for "John the Baptist's head on a platter!" (v. 8). At great risk to his own life, John had called out Herod on the king's adulterous, incestuous actions with Herodias. In response, Herod imprisoned John in a dungeon, though Herod didn't want to kill John because he knew John's righteous reputation (Mark 6:20) and he feared the reaction of the people.

Recall that John the Baptist was previously described as the prophet Elijah (Matt 11:14; cf. Matt 3:4 and 2 Kgs 1:8). One of the parallels between these two prophets can be seen in their confrontation of the sins of ungodly leadership. Just as Elijah confronted King Ahab in 1 Kings 18, John confronted the sin of Herod. There's an application here for anyone who speaks the truth of God's Word: as long as you and I call sin for what it is in our culture, it will be costly. However, regardless of the cost, speaking the truth is worth it. As one writer has put it, "It cost [John] his head; but it is better to have a head like John the Baptist and lose it than to have an ordinary head and keep it" (A. T. Robertson, as cited in MacArthur, *Matthew 8–15*, 420). Let us stand for Christ with conviction no matter the cost, and let us pray for our brothers and sisters around the world who are doing so at this moment at the risk of their lives.

John the Baptist's beheading was not only a flashback in Matthew's narrative, but it was also **a foreshadowing of Jesus' crucifixion** (France, *The Gospel of Matthew*, 522). Matthew is linking John the Baptist and Jesus together, particularly in terms of their place under Herod's rule. Herod had charge over the region where John the Baptist was preaching, and his leadership (or lack of leadership) led to John's beheading. Likewise, when we fast forward to Jesus' trial, we see that Pilate sent Jesus to this same Herod, and there Herod the tetrarch played another passive role that set the stage for Jesus' death (Luke 23:6-12). Herod's unbelief led to both John the Baptist's beheading and Jesus' crucifixion.

Two Pictures of Belief
MATTHEW 14:13-36

There is a clear shift in the next two stories concerning the disciples and Jesus' relationship with them. Jesus was moving on from those who

would not believe to those who did believe, and it is here that we begin
to see the disciples' faith grow.

Faith in the face of need (14:13-21)

Jesus' feeding of the five thousand is the only miracle recorded in all
four Gospels. It's a story that is familiar to most Christians, as Jesus took
five loaves and two fish and fed more than five thousand people. Each
Gospel writer tells the story from a different angle to emphasize different points. Matthew is telling this story in a way that emphasizes its
effect, not so much on the large crowd that ate that day, but more specifically on the disciples. As the disciples observed Jesus in this story,
their faith began to grow in several ways.

First, the disciples learned to **reflect Jesus' compassion**. Jesus withdrew into a boat for rest, as He was almost certainly weary from dealing
with the thronging crowds as well as the gathering opposition. Yet in
His few moments of quiet, and despite His attempts to withdraw, the
crowds found Him. As soon as Jesus arrived on land, He was swarmed
with people who were hurting, sick, and in need of healing (vv. 13-14;
cf. vv. 34-36). Notice what Jesus didn't do at this point: He didn't order
the crowd to go home and come back the next day. Instead, Matthew
tells us that Jesus was (once again) moved with compassion for them
(v. 14), even for those who were superficially attached to Him. These
individuals were like the second type of soil in the parable of the Sower,
people who received Jesus gladly one moment, and then rejected Him
completely the next (13:20-21). Even in the face of such shallowness,
Jesus was compassionate.

Second, the disciples also learned to **rely on Jesus' resources**. As evening approached and the sun was beginning to set, the disciples suggested
sending the crowds home to get something to eat (14:15). They were out
in the middle of nowhere and they felt completely inadequate for the
task; however, these men had no idea just how much they had for meeting
the people's needs. It was like standing in front of Niagara Falls and still
not being able to find anything to drink. Jesus looked at them and said
emphatically, "They don't need to go away. . . . You give them something
to eat" (v. 16).[29] The disciples responded by pointing out that they only

---

[29] Osborne notes that the redundant use of "you" in the Greek emphasizes the
responsibility of the disciples. Osborne, *Matthew*, 566.

had five loaves and two fish, which was precisely Jesus' point. He was calling them to do something that they could not do in their own power and with their own resources. He wanted them to recognize their insufficiency and at the same time to realize His sufficiency in at least two ways.

First, **Jesus meets needs *in* us**. His sufficiency to meet the deepest needs in our lives is undoubtedly a key aspect of this story. In John's account of the story this point becomes even more clear, as Jesus used this miracle to teach the crowds that He is the bread of life (John 6:35). He isn't simply the One who *gives* what satisfies; He *is* the One who satisfies. To put it another way, He came not merely to *give* us bread, but rather to *be* our bread—to be the sustaining Satisfier of our souls. This truth is illustrated through several uses of Old Testament imagery and history that point to Jesus. **He is the new Moses**, a point made clear in John 6:32-33: "I assure you: Moses didn't give you the bread from heaven, but My Father gives you the real bread from heaven. For the bread of God is the One who comes down from heaven and gives life to the world." Here we have a reference to Exodus 16 and God's provision of bread to the children of Israel through Moses. Jesus is now the One who meets this need for God's people, the church.

In addition to Jesus' role as the new Moses, we also see that **He is the greater prophet**. The prophet Elijah had caused a widow's jar of flour and a jug of oil to last throughout a drought (1 Kgs 17:8-16), while Elisha had fed a hundred men with twenty loaves of barley and fresh ears of grain (2 Kgs 4:42-43). However, Jesus took these prophetic miracles to new heights by feeding over five thousand people with a very small amount of food.

Finally, Jesus meets needs in us in that **He is the Messianic host**. Many scholars believe that Jesus' feeding of the crowds was a foretaste of what He talked about earlier (Matt 8:11) concerning those who would recline with Him in the kingdom of heaven to enjoy a feast (Osborne, *Matthew*, 566). For every soul that is hungry to be satisfied, and for those who have tried to fill their stomachs with the things of this world only to come up empty every time, Jesus invites you to taste and see that the Lord is good (Ps 34:8). He alone is able to meet the needs of our souls.

Jesus not only meets needs in us, as if that weren't enough, but **Jesus meets needs *through* us**. If the point of this story was only to show us Jesus' sufficiency, He could have called down bread from heaven right into people's laps. The people would have seen and maybe even recognized Him as the new Moses. However, Jesus not only prays for the

Father's blessing, but He also calls His disciples to do the serving. Jesus did not give out a single piece of bread; instead, He gave the bread to the disciples, and they distributed it. We're not told exactly how this miracle took place, so we can only imagine how five loaves suddenly, or maybe slowly, began to multiply from Jesus' hands into the hands of the disciples and eventually into the hands of the crowd. So yes, Jesus alone is sufficient to meet needs in us, but He is also gracious to use us to meet needs in others. Disciples of Jesus are an extension of Christ's mercy and His miraculous power.

How might this miracle impact you where you live? Are you surrounded by needs among the people you live with and work around—in your own city and across the world? Are you aware of urgent spiritual and physical needs? If so, do not think, "Well, what can I do about it? I have so little." Follower of Christ, you are standing at Niagara Falls! Don't you see that there is plenty of water? Jesus stands ready to meet the deepest needs of our souls *and* to use our lives, with all of His resources at our disposal, to meet others' needs. Oh, let us be the most generous, giving, serving, sacrificing, proclaiming people on the planet as an extension of the mercy and miraculous power of Christ. May He use us for the good of others and the glory of His name.

As Jesus' disciples learned to reflect His compassion and rely on His resources, they also learned to **receive His blessing**. Can you even imagine the blessing of being involved in this miracle? You initially saw five loaves and two fish, but then you passed out loaf after loaf and fish after fish to thousands of people without knowing where it was coming from. It's hard to fathom the joy and elation associated with this scene. And as if that's not enough, Jesus made sure to take care of the disciples as well. It's no coincidence that when the disciples picked up leftovers, there were *12* basketfuls. When you serve with the resources of Christ and the compassion of Christ, you will be blessed in the process. As you serve others, Jesus will always show Himself to be enough for you.

Faith in the face of fear (14:22-32)

In verses 13-21 we saw faith in the face of need. Now in the second picture of faith, we see faith in the face of fear. We know from John's account of these stories that after this miraculous feeding the people were ready to crown Jesus as king right there on the spot (John 6:14-15). Of course, Jesus knew that that was not the Father's plan, and therefore He and the disciples needed to get away as quickly as possible.

The story of Jesus walking on water reveals a number of truths about His character and His sustaining power on behalf of His people. These are glorious truths for all disciples in all times, particularly in difficult times. Even if you're not facing difficult trials right now, these truths are crucial to remember for the time when the circumstances of your life begin to toss you back and forth across the waves of this world. There are at least five truths illustrated in this story.

First, **Jesus is sovereign over you**. Jesus is the One who sent the disciples off into the boat, probably sometime around seven to nine o'clock at night. Later, the text tells us that Jesus came out to them on the sea in the fourth watch of the night, which is anywhere between three and six o'clock in the morning. This means that the disciples were in the boat by themselves for at least six hours, if not more, while Jesus was over on the mountainside. During this time a windstorm arose, and we know from Matthew 8:23-27 that Jesus had control over such things. This entire episode was His design. During the time that these disciples were battling this wind, Jesus was holding both the disciples and the wind in His hands.

We too need to remember these truths as we walk through difficult circumstances. Jesus is not unaware of what we're going through. He is familiar with our weaknesses (Heb 4:15; 2 Cor 12:9), and He is working for our good in all things (Rom 8:28). He is sovereign over our lives and our trials.

The second way to have faith in the face of fear is to realize that **Jesus is interceding for you**. While the disciples were being tossed around in the middle of the sea, there on the mountainside Jesus was on His knees in prayer. Imagine that scene in light of Romans 8:31-39:

> *What then are we to say about these things?*
> *If God is for us, who is against us?*
> *He did not even spare His own Son*
> *but offered Him up for us all;*
> *how will He not also with Him grant us everything?*
> *Who can bring an accusation against God's elect?*
> *God is the One who justifies.*
> *Who is the one who condemns?*
> *Christ Jesus is the One who died,*
> *but even more, has been raised;*
> *He also is at the right hand of God*
> *and intercedes for us.*

Who can separate us from the love of Christ?
Can affliction or anguish or persecution
or famine or nakedness or danger or sword?
As it is written:
Because of You we are being put to death all day long;
we are counted as sheep to be slaughtered.
No, in all these things we are more than victorious
through Him who loved us.
For I am persuaded that not even death or life,
angels or rulers,
things present or things to come, hostile powers,
height or depth, or any other created thing
will have the power to separate us
from the love of God that is in Christ Jesus our Lord!

You can look at your trials differently when you know that the very Son of God is at the right hand of the Father, at this moment, interceding for you. He is ready to give you strength and sustenance through His Spirit at every single moment you need it. You are not alone, which leads to the third truth: **Jesus is present with you**. When Jesus came out to His disciples walking on the water, they were understandably frightened, thinking He was a ghost. Jesus responded by saying, "Have courage! It is I. Don't be afraid" (v. 27). The language Jesus uses directly echoes God's revelation of Himself to Moses in Exodus 3:14, when God revealed Himself as the Lord, as "I AM."[30] Jesus not only stills storms, but He also uses storms as a pathway to a greater revelation of Himself.

According to the Bible, there is no question that God sovereignly ordains trials in our lives at various points in order to reveal His character and nature to us in ways that we would never know apart from the storm. And it is in the middle of the storm that the presence of Christ becomes all the more real. This is a truth that Jesus will reiterate at the end of Matthew's Gospel, as He promises to be with His disciples as they go to the ends of the earth with an unpopular gospel message (28:20). He is with us; therefore we have no reason to fear.

Fourth, you can face fear confidently because **Jesus is strength in you**. When Peter saw Jesus walking on the water, he decided he wanted

---

[30] The phrase "I AM" in the Greek version of the Old Testament—the Septuagint (LXX)—is *ego eimi*. This is precisely the wording Jesus uses in Matt 14:27 when He says, "It is I."

to be with the Lord. Rather than reading Peter's request as an "if" (Lord, if it's You . . .), this request might be better translated, "Since it's You, command me to come to You on the water" (Osborne, *Matthew*, 575). Recognizing that it was Jesus, Peter trusted that he could join Jesus on the water in light of the Lord's power and authority. How comforting to know that when you face trials, you may not have strength, but Jesus does, and as you trust in Him, you experience His strength in you. The key is that we must trust Him, something Peter found out the hard way. When he stepped out of the boat and saw the wind (or more appropriately, the effects of the wind on the waves all around him), he began to sink. He cried out, "Lord, save me!" (v. 30). Jesus then reached out His hand and saved Peter, exclaiming, "You of little faith, why did you doubt?" (v. 31).

There is a pastoral caution when it comes to faith. If we are not careful, we will hear Jesus' criticism of "little faith" here and miss the point of this story. We will begin to think that we need to muster up more faith, and if we do, the result will be healing or some other immediate benefit. But that is not the point of what Jesus was saying. That kind of thinking skews faith because it makes faith entirely dependent on what man can manufacture or muster up. Scripture, however, gives us different guidelines for understanding faith. We'll consider three of them.

First, **what matters most is not the measure of your faith**. Even when Jesus referred Peter's faith as "little" (v. 31), He was not primarily referring to faith as something subjective that we must create. **Instead, what matters most is always the object of your faith**. Peter's faith was little because he took his eyes off of Jesus, the object of his faith. This is what caused Peter to sink. The point, then, is clear: **your faith is strong only when the object of your faith is strong**. As long as your faith is in your circumstances, or as long as your faith is focused on anyone or anything apart from Christ, then it won't matter how much faith you have. You will fall sooner or later.

On the other hand, when your eyes are on Christ, the all-sovereign, gracious, loving, and merciful Savior and King of creation, you can always rest secure. Your faith will be constant, because Christ is constant. Hebrews 12:2 tells us to be "keeping our eyes on Jesus, the source and perfecter of our faith, who for the joy that lay before Him endured a cross and despised the shame and has sat down at the right hand of God's throne." Instead of trying to be stronger, trust in Jesus' strength. When you are weak, He is strong.

The final reason we can have faith in the midst of fear is that **Jesus is peace around you**. Almost as a passing note at the end of the story in verse 32, we read that the wind immediately ceased when Jesus got into the boat. He is the only One able to bring peace in the middle of the storm, and there is coming a day when He will bring total and complete peace to His people. This gives us encouragement to persevere amid trials and temptations.

The Picture of Worship
MATTHEW 14:33

The climax of the chapter occurs in verse 33. Following Jesus' miracle of walking on the water, the disciples in the boat responded to Jesus by saying, "Truly you are the Son of God." This is the first time that the disciples addressed Jesus in this way. We've seen the Father call Jesus the Son (3:17), and we've even seen demons call Jesus the Son of God (8:29), but this is the first time the disciples identify and worship Him in this way. We see once again the relationship between belief and worship: Once you recognize who Jesus is, you realize how He is to be worshiped. The same principle holds true for us as well. As we come to know Jesus through His Word, we too should respond in adoration. Let us fall at the feet of the One who saves the perishing, and feast at the table with the One who satisfies the hungry.

Reflect and Discuss

1. How can the rejection of Jesus by His own hometown serve as a warning for you?
2. Why is costly faith better than convenient unbelief? What means of grace does God use to strengthen our faith?
3. Explain the difference in merely being amazed at Jesus' miracles and responding in faith.
4. List two truths to be gleaned from Jesus' feeding of the five thousand.
5. What people around you most need the compassion of Christ? What are some practical ways you might serve them?
6. What evidence is there in your life that you are not relying on God to meet your needs? What anxieties and habits are indications of unbelief?

7. How does this passage present Jesus as greater than Moses? What does this teach us about the purpose of the Old Testament?
8. Explain the following statement: The most important thing is not the measure of our faith, but the object of our faith.
9. Make a list of Jesus' attributes that are on display in Matthew 14.
10. In what ways does Matthew 14 demonstrate Jesus' deity?

Truth in the Church for the Nations

MATTHEW 15

Main Idea: Rather than superficial religion, we need supernatural regeneration based on the authority of God's Word, for this work of God produces holiness of heart and it reaches all peoples.

I. **Exalt the Authority of God's Word.**
   A. Minimize the thoughts of man.
      1. They promote self-centeredness.
      2. They fuel self-righteousness.
      3. They serve self-interest.
   B. Magnify the truth of God.
      1. Let the Word consume your teaching and preaching.
      2. Let the Word drive your decisions and practices.

II. **Promote Authenticity in God's Worship.**
   A. Worship is more than physical action.
   B. Worship is all about spiritual affection.

III. **Cultivate Hearts of Holiness.**
   A. The truth
      1. Our greatest need is not cleaner hands.
      2. Our greatest need is changed hearts.
   B. The implication
      1. What the world doesn't need is the spread of superficial religion.
      2. What the world does need is the spread of supernatural regeneration.

IV. **Nurture Passion for the Nations.**
   A. The harvest field is ripe.
   B. The divine plan is global.
   C. Spend yourselves for the glory of God's name.
   D. Give your lives to the accomplishment of God's mission.

It may surprise you to find out that some of the biggest threats to faithful discipleship come from highly esteemed religious traditions. The road we're on may be marked "narrow," but looks can be deceiving. We often fail to identify evil because we associate it with a pitchfork, but Satan is usually more subtle than that. Our adversary disguises himself as an angel of light, Paul tells us (2 Cor 11:14). And while some of our practices and traditions have a "reputation of wisdom," being a scrupulous rule-keeper in religion doesn't necessarily equate with godliness (Col 2:23). If Satan can't trip us up with outright immorality, he is more than happy to use seemingly good things to direct our attention away from Christ and the gospel. The Pharisees in Jesus' day presented just such a danger. They put on a good show, but Jesus' piercing gaze saw right through their flesh-fueled holiness. As we look at Matthew 15, we should be reminded that Jesus sees right through ours as well.

Exalt the Authority of God's Word
MATTHEW 15:1-7

At this point in Matthew's narrative, a group of Pharisees and scribes came from Jerusalem (v. 1), likely an official contingency. Their goal was to find out what Jesus was teaching and how they could stop Him. They asked Jesus in verse 2 why His disciples broke the traditions of the elders by not washing their hands when they ate. In His response, Jesus teaches us to exalt the authority of God's Word. This is the antidote to accepting man-made authority.

Washing your hands in the context of Jesus' day was not a hygiene issue for the Pharisees, like a mother telling her children to "wash up" before dinner. This was a ritual-cleansing issue established by tradition. The "tradition of the elders" (v. 2) goes all the way back to the books of Ezra and Nehemiah, when the book of the law was rediscovered. Scribes began to study it, and teachers began to explore all the ways that the law should be applied to specific situations in people's lives. The end result was something akin to two authorities: (1) the law of God and (2) the teaching of the elders. The teaching of the elders was mainly oral and it was passed down from generation to generation. By AD 200, these traditions were compiled in a book called the Mishnah.

As the scribes and Pharisees added all kinds of rules and regulations to the law, their traditions were eventually seen as authoritative and began to trump the law itself. Some considered it to be worse to disobey the teaching of the elders than it was to disobey the commands of the law. Part of the tradition of the elders dealt with ceremonially washing your hands a certain way before a meal. This background helps us understand Jesus' response. When these religious leaders questioned him about keeping their traditions, He turned the tables on them and asked them why *they* were breaking the commandments of God for the sake of their traditions (v. 3), as if to say, "You're one to talk!"

Jesus illustrates His point in verses 4-6 using the example of God's command for children to honor their father and mother (Exod 20:12; Deut 5:16). The Pharisees and scribes had come up with traditions that actually allowed children *not* to provide for their parents. If a parent needed something but a child didn't want to give it, the child could simply claim that what was needed was dedicated to the Lord.[31] This tradition could be used to avoid honoring one's father and mother. In this and a number of other ways, the elders' traditions were trumping the Word of God.

Minimize the thoughts of man.

Although most believers today don't have to address the issue of ritual washings or inheritance laws from the Mishnah, there are still some massively important takeaways for us in this passage. In order to be faithful to God's Word in our lives and in our preaching and teaching, we must minimize the thoughts of man. Men have no authority to shepherd Christ's church based on their own teachings. This danger is rampant across the church today, just as it was in Jesus' day. Consider some of the dangers of falling prey to the doctrines of men.

First, the thoughts and teachings of man are dangerous because **they promote self-centeredness**. We see this with the Pharisees in that children who didn't want to part with their resources could hold onto them instead of supporting their parents. However, when God's Word says to do something that is not easy, we shouldn't look for a way out; we should submit. Rather than being self-centered, disciples of Jesus ought to be God-centered.

Second, the thoughts of man should be avoided because **they fuel self-righteousness**. When we follow man's way of thinking we stop trusting in God and instead develop a prideful self-righteousness that has no

---

[31] In Mark 7:11 this practice is called by its name—Corban. Blomberg explains, "The *Corban* practice in view was that of pledging money or other material resources to the temple to be paid upon one's death. These funds could therefore not be transferred to anyone else but could still be used for one's own benefit while one was still alive (v. 5)." Blomberg, *Matthew*, 238.

need of Him. We stand on our own soapboxes instead of the timeless truths of Scripture.

A third danger of adopting man's thoughts is that **they serve self-interest**. Jesus was undercutting the role that the Pharisees and scribes played in Jewish religion. If the Word of God was held supreme, and not the teaching of the elders, then these scribes and Pharisees would be out of a job. Their thoughts fueled their own interests.

If we're not careful, the dangers of man-made teachings and the scruples of the Pharisees can sound somewhat distant. Their particular practices may not seem relevant today, so we miss the many ways in which the thoughts of man are exalted today. Here are just a few specific examples to watch out for:

Cultic teachers. Jehovah's Witnesses and Mormons are examples of cults that are alive and well today. These religious groups are not part of biblical Christianity. For example, in addition to the Bible, The Church of Jesus Christ of Latter-Day Saints (or the Mormon church) has three other books of teachings that it holds to be authoritative alongside the Bible: *Book of Mormon*, *Doctrine and Covenants*, and *Pearl of Great Price*. Joseph Smith, the founder of this movement, declared the *Book of Mormon* to be "the most correct of any book on earth, and the keystone of our religion, and a man would get nearer to God by abiding by its precepts, than by any other book" (as cited in McKeever and Johnson, *Mormonism 101*, 118). Mormons also embrace a number of other errant doctrines. Wayne Grudem claims that they do not hold to "any major Christian doctrines concerning salvation or the person of God or the person and work of Christ" (Grudem, *Systematic Theology*, 865). A number of other groups can be labeled as cults because of the way they deny or twist one or more biblical doctrines: Christian Scientists, International Churches of Christ, Scientologists, Unitarian Universalists, etc. Error has a variety of manifestations.

Catholic teaching. The Catholic Church acknowledges three sources of authority: the Bible (including the Apocrypha[32]), tradition, and the Magesterium, or teaching ministry of the church. Bishops, in communion with the pope, interpret the Bible and tradition. All three of these

---

[32] The Apocrypha is a collection of Jewish books that Roman Catholic and Eastern Orthodox Christians include as part of the Old Testament canon. Protestants rightly reject these books as a part of divinely inspired Scripture. For more on the Apocrypha, see Clayton Harrop, "Apocrypha, Old Testament," in *Holman Illustrated Bible Dictionary*, ed. Chad Brand, Charles Draper, and Archie England (Nashville: Holman Reference, 2003), 81–83.

sources are equally authoritative. In fact, the Catechism of the Catholic Church says that they (the three sources of authority) "are so connected and associated that one of them cannot stand without the others."

Cultural traditions. The temptation to elevate man's thoughts above God's is not just a problem for established religions. We do things as Christians in the twenty-first century that are nowhere prescribed in the Bible. We only think certain things are biblical because they're a part of the tradition that's been passed down to us. This is why we constantly have to look at the authority of God's Word and ask God to reveal our blind spots. We must be on guard against areas where we have put our thoughts, preferences, and traditions above Scripture.

Contemporary trends. The truth of God's Word is also pushed to the side by the pressure we feel to adopt things and ideas that are new. We are bombarded with new ways to do church and new teachings to trumpet. Unfortunately, many of the conferences, books, and teachings that are spread all across contemporary Christianity virtually ignore what the Word of God says. To be sure, not all trends and traditions are bad; some are quite good and helpful, but only if they promote the authority of God's Word.

Magnify the truth of God.

As we minimize the thoughts of man, we must at the same time magnify the truth of God. The primary way for pastors and churches to do this is to **let the Word consume our teaching and preaching**. If the pastor stops preaching the Word, the congregation should stop following him as pastor. Authority in the church doesn't come from any man's opinions or ideas, but only from Christ, the Head of the church (Col 1:18), who leads us by means of Spirit-inspired Scripture (2 Tim 3:16). This also means that we must **let the Word drive our decisions and practices**. Some of my favorite moments as a pastor happen when the other pastors and I are in a room with the Word before us, praying and seeking the Lord about a certain issue. It's like seeing the Word come alive, and I'm reminded again that this is how Christ leads His church.

Promote Authenticity in God's Worship
MATTHEW 15:8-9

Jesus addresses another element of faithful discipleship that is closely tied to exalting the authority of God's Word: we must promote authenticity in God's worship. Jesus quotes from Isaiah where the prophet called out the people of God for worshiping God in vain (Isa 29:13). Their hearts were far from Him, and in part this was fueled by the commandments of men. See, then, how the logic builds from the previous point: as long as the *thoughts of man* are central in the church, the *worship of man* will be central in the church. Alternatively, as long as the *truth of God* is central in the church, the *worship of God* will be central in the church. A Word-saturated church leads to God-glorifying worship.

Though Jesus' comments about worship are brief in this passage, there are a number of important implications. First, **worship is more than physical action**. The scribes and Pharisees were honoring God with their lips but not with their hearts or their lives. This is a danger for us today as well. You can stand, preach, pray, take the Lord's Supper, and any number of other things in worship, yet your heart can still be far from God. We must guard against this tendency in our churches and in our individual lives. One way to guard against false worship is not to be overly **concerned with form**, that is, what we do physically. This kind of preoccupation bypasses the heart. More important than what we do outwardly in worship is who we are; the heart is the real issue.

Second, as we think about authentic worship, we need to remember that **worship is all about spiritual affection**. It's about our hearts lifted high to God. Though some may go to unhealthy excesses, worship involves emotion and affection for God. This comes out in a number of ways: brokenness and contrition over sin, grief over our circumstances, fear and awe before God's greatness, gratitude for His grace, hope in His promises, and celebration of His salvation. All of these responses to God represent true worship. Isaiah 66:2 says, "I will look favorably on this kind of person: one who is humble, submissive in spirit, and trembles at My word." That is genuine spiritual affection.

Our spiritual affection is not simply about raw emotions but is **compelled by faith**. That is, our response toward God, including our emotions, ought to be quickened by our trust in Him. J. C. Ryle said,

> Let it be a settled resolution with us that in all our religion the
> state of our hearts shall be the main thing. Let it not content
> us to go to church and observe the forms of religion. Let us
> look far deeper than this and desire to have a heart right in
> the sight of the Lord. (Ryle, *Matthew*, 129)

Authentic worship and true spiritual affection come about as our hearts honestly listen to and engage our great God.

Cultivate Hearts of Holiness
MATTHEW 15:10-20

A third admonition comes in verse 11: "It's not what goes into the mouth that defiles a man, but what comes out of the mouth, this defiles a man." Though the disciples were stunned by what Jesus was saying, Jesus Himself was under no illusions that His message would be well received. He was throwing down the gauntlet with the scribes and Pharisees, men whom these disciples revered. Jesus was totally transforming their thinking.

The truth that Jesus goes on to communicate in verses 13-20 is foundational for how we ought to think about holiness. **Our greatest need is not cleaner hands**, that is, for physical cleansing. What goes into the body eventually comes out of the body, Jesus very candidly points out (v. 17). Therefore, dirty hands are not the real spiritual danger. These scribes and Pharisees were so focused on the externals that they had completely bypassed the internal. They needed to see that **our greatest need is changed hearts**. This is why Jesus said speech, which comes out of the mouth, defiles a person, for it proceeds from the heart. Jesus lists all kinds of sins in verse 19—murder, adultery, sexual immorality, stealing, lying, slandering—and all these are issues of the heart. Man's greatest need, then, is not to try to clean his hands or fix his life on the outside; man's greatest need is a changed heart on the inside. Holiness begins in the heart, and only Jesus can produce this kind of change.

Consider how heart change is actually brought about in our lives. It begins as **Jesus forgives us of all our sin**. The prophet Ezekiel had spoken of a day when God would cleanse the hearts of His people (Ezek 36:25), and this happened as a result of Christ's sin-bearing death. In connection with this forgiveness, heart change also happens as **Jesus fills us with His Holy Spirit**. Ezekiel's prophecy of a new covenant included the following promise from God: "I will place My Spirit within you" (Ezek 36:27). Only the Holy Spirit can change us from the inside out. This is the only way we can obey the exhortation in 2 Corinthians 6:17 (quoting Isa 52:11) to "come out from among them and be separate." We cannot be casual about holiness, but rather we must by the power of the Holy Spirit pursue purity. We must be holy as God is holy

(1 Pet 1:16; Lev 11:44) by cultivating our hearts. Once again, J. C. Ryle's comments are helpful here:

> What is the first thing we need in order to be Christians? A new heart. What is the sacrifice God asks us to bring to him? A broken and a contrite heart (Psalm 51:17). What is the true circumcision? The circumcision of the heart (Romans 2:29). What is genuine obedience? To obey from the heart. What is saving faith? To believe with the heart. Where ought Christ to dwell? To dwell in our hearts through faith (Ephesians 3:17). (Ryle, *Matthew*, 126)

Everything revolves around the heart.

If our need is to cultivate holy hearts that have been changed by God's Holy Spirit, then **the implication** for our witness in the world is clear. **What the world doesn't need is the spread of superficial religion**, which is precisely what many false teachers offer. A lost world doesn't need more people monotonously carrying out religious rules and regulations under the banner of Christianity. The Pharisees may have been well respected, but Jesus told His disciples that **false teachers are destined for judgment**. They weren't planted by God (v. 13), which implies that they were planted by the evil one. However, they would be uprooted in due time. In addition to facing judgment themselves, **false teachers are dangerous to others**. They are the blind leading the blind, bringing their own followers into a pit with them (v. 14). This is why the church must guard against false teachings.

Don't think that you are immune to the attacks of the evil one, particularly his attacks through wolves in sheep's clothing (Matt 7:15). The world doesn't need the spread of superficial religion, but **what the world does need is the spread of supernatural regeneration**. We must never be satisfied with superficial holiness. Instead, we want hearts that produce holy lives, and this is the work of God.

Nurture Passion for the Nations
MATTHEW 15:21-39

The fourth and final challenge from Matthew 15 comes from a very interesting story in verses 21-28. Many people have been puzzled concerning Jesus' interaction with this Canaanite woman in these verses. Perhaps we will better understand this dialogue by noting two things about this encounter. First, geography is significant here. Verse 21 tells us that Jesus withdrew from Galilee, a predominantly Jewish territory, and went to the district of Tyre and Sidon, a predominantly Gentile territory. This is the only time in Matthew's Gospel that Jesus journeyed into Gentile lands, and the first person who comes up to Him is a Canaanite. The Canaanites were ancient enemies of the people of Israel throughout the Old Testament, making this woman's identity all the more significant.

Second, this dialogue makes more sense when we consider how the narrative is playing out from the perspective of the disciples. The disciples' world had just been rocked when Jesus turned their thinking upside down about what makes someone clean. Now He takes them into Gentile territory, a place filled with unclean people according to the standard Jewish view. Many Jews would have felt compelled to send this Canaanite woman away; yet this whole story, and the story that comes after this, is intended to be a reflection of the reality that Jesus' plan involved much more than Israel. His salvation would spread far beyond Israel to the ends of the earth, an idea that may have been shocking to these 12 Jewish disciples. Through His words and demeanor, Jesus was subverting the standard Jewish view of the Gentiles. According to Jews, the Gentiles had no right to the children's bread, for they were "dogs." Jesus aimed to change this mind-set.

In the midst of Jesus' encounter with the Canaanite woman in Tyre and Sidon, He was teaching these disciples an invaluable lesson. Even in Gentile territory **the harvest field is ripe**. Clearly Jesus did not ultimately ignore her or send her away. After all, He refused when the disciples pled for Him to do that (v. 23). Instead, He used this encounter as a teaching opportunity. He highlighted the persistence of this Canaanite woman's faith, a woman who cried out, "Have mercy on me, Lord, Son of David!" (v. 22). This Gentile actually recognized Jesus as the Jewish Messiah!

When Jesus responded in verse 26 that it wouldn't be right to throw the children's bread to dogs—i.e., take that which belongs to Jews and give it to Gentiles—the woman responded, "Yet even the dogs eat the crumbs that fall from their masters' table!" (v. 27). This drew Jesus' commendation: "Woman, your faith is great. Let it be done for you as you want" (v. 28). She is one of only two people praised for their faith by Jesus in the book of Matthew, and the other one is the *Gentile* centurion in Matthew 8:5-13.

The fact that the harvest fields are ripe is closely connected to the truth that **the divine plan is global**. Yes, Jesus has come to save God's people, Israel, from their sins, but that's not all. He has come to save all nations, and this has been the plan from the beginning (Gen 12:1-3). God blesses His people for the sake of His praise among all the peoples of the world, even the Canaanites.

Jesus continued His journey into Gentile territory in verses 29-31. He healed many—"the lame, the blind, the deformed, those unable to speak, and many others"—and the text says, "they gave glory to the God of Israel" (vv. 30-31). Jesus was doing the same things in Gentile territory that He did among the Jews, and the disciples were taking it all in. Their perspective was challenged, and ours should be as well. God's worldwide mission ought to affect everything we do.

If we are to nurture a passion for the nations and be a part of God's global purposes, we must **spend ourselves for the glory of God's name**. We work and preach and serve among the nations so that they will give glory to God. Even today, there are many people groups who have never heard the gospel and are not giving God glory. Our churches don't exist for our immediate neighborhoods only; they exist to go and give and send people to the nations. Our task is to make disciples and multiply churches among the peoples of the world. This mind-set should be in our spiritual DNA, for we want the peoples to praise our God (Ps 67).

If you've been reading through Matthew's Gospel, when you reach 15:32-39 you may wonder whether you've already seen a miracle of a miraculous feeding. The answer is "yes"—see 14:13-21—but that's the point. The feeding of a multitude has reappeared, only now there are a few differences: the number of people, the amount of food, and other miscellaneous details. Notice that it wasn't the disciples who were concerned about the people's hunger; it was Jesus. You can almost picture the disciples asking, "Would Jesus perform the same miracle among a Gentile crowd that He performed among the Jewish people?" This mind-set was evident after Jesus' resurrection in Peter's vision in Acts 10:9-15. Peter received a vision from the Lord on his rooftop, where the Lord commanded him, "What God has made clean, you must not call common" (v. 15). God was referring to Gentiles and Peter's prejudice against them. This prejudice was keeping Peter from spreading the gospel outside of His own people. The Lord commanded Peter to go to the house of Cornelius, a Gentile centurion, to eat with him. Though this would have previously been unthinkable, the Lord had welcomed Cornelius into His kingdom. I imagine that on that day in Acts 10 Peter remembered this day in Matthew 15.

Jesus made clear in this last section of Matthew 15 that He came to serve, satisfy, and save people from all nations. Part of the point of the feeding of the 5,000 in Matthew 14 was to depict Jesus as the messianic host. That was a foretaste of the day when all of God's people, Jews and Gentiles, would gather around Christ for a banquet in the kingdom to come (Rev 19:6-10; Isa 25:6-12). One day all peoples will be represented around that table (Rev 5:9). This is what the disciples would later give their lives to. As followers of Christ today, our desire should be the same. We **give our lives to the accomplishment of God's mission** until we die or until Jesus returns.

Reflect and Discuss

1. What sources of authority and traditions compete with God's Word in the context in which you live?
2. If not everyone who quotes Scripture speaks the truth, then how can you prepare yourself to discern truth from error?
3. Answer the following question: "The Bible was written by men, so how can it be true in everything it says?" What passages might you appeal to in your answer?
4. What contemporary trends are putting pressure on believers to compromise faithfulness to God? How can our response involve courage *and* humility?
5. What is the danger of emphasizing emotions in our corporate worship without being driven by God's Word? What kind of spiritual affections should our corporate worship encourage?
6. In your own words, explain the difference between superficial religion and supernatural regeneration.
7. Jesus teaches that holiness proceeds from the heart. Practically, then, how do you cultivate such holiness?
8. How do you identify false teachers? Is it unloving to reject their teaching? If not, why not?
9. Like this Gentile Canaanite woman, what unlikely converts has God placed around you? How have you doubted God's power and mercy in relation to such people?
10. How does Jesus' interaction with this Canaanite woman and His feeding of the Gentile crowd help forecast the Great Commission in Matthew 28:18-20?

The Institution and Confession of the Church

MATTHEW 16

Main Idea: The church is the community of people who know Jesus intimately, proclaim Jesus confidently, and obey Jesus sacrificially.

I. **The Characters in Matthew 16**
   A. The Pharisees were marked by self-righteousness: asserting themselves in the face of God.
   B. The Sadducees were marked by self-indulgence: pleasing themselves apart from God.
      1. They were all focused on temporal matters.
      2. They were all blind to eternal realities.
   C. The disciples were marked by self-denial: crucifying themselves for the glory of God.
      1. They would leave behind temporal pursuits.
      2. They would live for eternal pleasure.

II. **The Church in Matthew 16**
   A. The community of people who know Jesus intimately
      1. A true understanding of Christ comes not from human invention.
      2. A true understanding of Christ comes only from divine revelation.
      3. Who you say Jesus is will determine everything about how you follow Him.
   B. The community of people who proclaim Jesus confidently
      1. The rock of the church: the people of God proclaiming the gospel of Christ
      2. Death cannot stop this Messiah.
      3. Christ gives His authority to the church.
      4. Is Peter the first pope?
   C. The community of people who obey Jesus sacrificially
      1. Jesus would suffer necessarily.
      2. We now suffer willingly.

In Matthew 16 Jesus instituted what we know as the New Testament church. This is one of only two times in all the Gospels when Jesus explicitly referred to the "church" (see also Matt 18:17). We are, in a sense, going back to our roots as followers of Christ. One writer has called Matthew 16 "*the* central or critical chapter in Matthew's account of [Jesus'] life, death and resurrection. . . . It is *the* high point in Jesus' teaching and the disciples' growth in spiritual understanding" (Boice, *The Gospel of Matthew*, 279, 301). Needless to say, this initial institution and confession of the church has huge implications for understanding who we are and what we are to do as members of our own local churches today.

Matthew 16 begins on the western shore of the Sea of Galilee in the region of Magadan, a Jewish territory (15:39). Jesus was returning from His journey into explicitly Gentile territory, having healed a Canaanite woman as well as many others with various needs (15:21-31). He then fed more than four thousand Gentiles with seven loaves of bread and a few small fish (15:32-38). At the end of chapter 15, Jesus got into a boat with His disciples and came back into Jewish territory, and as soon as He did, He was greeted by a group of Pharisees and Sadducees (16:1). It's as if they were waiting to pounce on Him again. In order to understand Jesus' exchange with these leaders, as well as His interaction with His own disciples, it will be helpful to identify this cast of characters.

The Characters in Matthew 16
MATTHEW 16:1-12

The first two groups on the scene in Matthew 16 were **the Pharisees and the Sadducees**. These groups represented the Sanhedrin, a Jewish council that essentially ruled over various spheres of Jewish life.[33] They had likely been sent as an official delegation to confront and question Jesus. Even though the Pharisees and Sadducees differed from one another in terms of their beliefs and practices, they were united in their opposition to Jesus.

The Pharisees were a conservative body of leaders who held to strict observance of the law *and* tradition. In chapter 15, we saw that the Pharisees had taken their traditions and teachings and elevated them to the place of God's Word (even trumping God's Word in some

---

[33] For more on the Sanhedrin, see Twelftree, "Sanhedrin," in *Dictionary of Jesus and the Gospels*, 728–32.

instances). The very name "Pharisees" means "separated ones," and they had basically set themselves apart by their rigid devotion to God's law and their own teachings, and in the process, they were guilty of basing their status before God on their own rigid obedience to the law and tradition. They were **marked by self-righteousness: asserting themselves in the face of God**.

The Sadducees, on the other hand, were a bit different. They were **marked by self-indulgence: pleasing themselves apart from God**. The Sadducees were predominantly from the wealthy class of Jewish people. Though they were more strict than the Pharisees in some ways, they were known for pursuing both political and social approval and power. They didn't believe in the resurrection of the dead, so they took the mind-set, "Hey, this life is all there is, so let's make the most of it," and they had the means to do so. Many of them made fortunes on temple concessions, money-changing, and ritual sacrifices.

While there's a lot to criticize about the Pharisees and Sadducees, we should be able to see in them a reflection of tendencies in our own hearts. On the one hand, the Sadducees loved to adjust the rules to fit their own preferences, priorities, and pursuits in this world. On the other hand, the Pharisees loved to keep the rules, and they were taking great pains to do everything right according to the law and their tradition. If we're honest, we can see ourselves in these two extremes. Some of us love to adjust (or even break) the rules in order to prioritize our own pursuits in this world, while others of us try our best to live nice, decent, moral, and even religious lives. Part of the point of this story in Matthew 16 is that both of these approaches—self-righteousness and self-indulgence—entirely miss who Jesus is. They both oppose Him.

Despite the fact that the Pharisees and Sadducees were at odds with one another, often being antagonists of one another in Jewish leadership, here in the face of Jesus they stand **together**. A common opponent always transforms enemies into friends. So they tested Jesus by asking Him to show them a sign from heaven (v. 1), as if Jesus had not already given enough demonstrations of His divinity. At this point in the story, Jesus looked back at them and started talking about the weather. These men could discern the weather based on the color of the sky—a red sky in the evening meant fair weather, while a red sky in the morning meant bad weather (vv. 2-3)—but they couldn't interpret the signs of the times.

Jesus criticized these religious leaders because **they were all focused on temporal matters**. They could discern weather patterns, yet **they were**

all blind to eternal realities. Amid their supposed knowledge of God and His ways, they were missing the signs God was performing right in front of them in the promised Christ, the Messiah. They paid so much attention to things like changing weather conditions that they were missing epoch-making changes in the history of redemption. Could they not see? God had broken into the world, coming as a man to heal the sick, raise the dead, cast out demons, quiet storms, and bring salvation. Christ's entire earthly ministry was evidence of the victory of God over sin, suffering, the Devil, and demons. Those who saw Jesus got a foretaste of a kingdom that will never be destroyed. All of this was being done right before their eyes, and the Pharisees and Sadducees were missing it.

The Pharisees and Sadducees began by asking Jesus for a sign in verse 1, and Jesus responded in verse 4 by saying that "no sign will be given to it [this evil and adulterous generation] except the sign of Jonah." Matthew 12:28 sheds some light on the sign of Jonah, a reference to Jesus' resurrection. Just as Jonah was three days in a fish, so Jesus would be three days in the grave, and then He would rise again. But even this miraculous sign would not be enough for Jesus' opponents. His decisive victory in the resurrection would not be enough to convince these hard-hearted leaders who, in their self-righteousness and self-indulgence, were so focused on temporal matters that they had become blind to eternal realities.

Don't miss the strong word of warning here. Self-indulgence and self-righteousness will blind you from seeing and knowing Jesus. Like a little bit of yeast that inevitably spreads, these heart-attitudes will slowly ruin your soul. So guard against a focus on this world—what you can obtain and achieve in the here and now—that blinds you to the world to come. Focus on what matters for all of eternity by fixing your eyes on Jesus Christ.

The focus shifts from the Pharisees and Sadducees to **the disciples** in verse 5. Clearly the disciples were slow to grasp Jesus' teaching, as evidenced in this exchange in verses 5-12. When they forgot to bring bread with them on their journey, Jesus told them to beware of the "yeast of the Pharisees and Sadducees" (v. 6). They missed His point entirely, thinking He was speaking of literal yeast. "You of little faith!" was Jesus' reply (v. 8). The yeast He was referring to was the "teaching of the Pharisees and Sadducees" (v. 12). Then Jesus asked them a series of questions concerning their failure to grasp what they had seen in His ministry (vv. 8-11). The two miraculous feedings had apparently made little difference for the faith of these hapless disciples.

When I read about the disciples, I am tempted to get a bit frustrated with them. They seem to be so clueless at times, particularly with all that Jesus was saying and doing in their presence. You would think they would eventually get it! But then I see myself, and I think, "How many times has the Lord in His mercy taught me the same truths again and again and again?" He has shown Himself so faithful to me in everything, and yet I sometimes doubt Him. Oh, how we should praise God for His mercy and patience with us, for His *faithfulness* when we are *faithless*! This contrast plays out in the next section in Jesus' interaction with Peter.

In verses 13-28 we read of Peter's confession of Christ, and we learn the implications of what it means to be a disciple. Unlike Pharisees and Sadducees, disciples of Jesus are not marked by self-righteousness or self-indulgence; they are **marked by self-denial: crucifying themselves for the glory of God**. And **the lesson** they would learn was that in following Jesus, **they would leave behind temporal pursuits**. Quite literally for most of these disciples, they would lose their lives in this world. But in the process, **they would live for eternal pleasure**. In losing their lives, they would actually find their lives. Indulging yourself or trying to earn the favor of God by following all the rules is a sure recipe for losing your life in this world. But if you want to know the favor of God and you want to experience the eternal pleasure of God, then deny yourself, take up your cross, and follow Jesus. For *this* is what it means to be a disciple. This is what it means to be a part of the church.

The Church in Matthew 16
MATTHEW 16:13-28

In verses 13-20 we see the first mention of the "church," and it comes from the mouth of Jesus, the Head of the church: "You are Peter, and on this rock I will build My church." Notice the word "church" in verse 18—*ekklesia* in the original language. Jesus uses this word to refer to an assembly of Christ-followers. Based on these verses, we can identify three characteristics of the people who make up the church.

First, the church is **the community of people who know Jesus intimately**. The contrast in this text is clear, not only between the disciples and the Jewish leaders but between the disciples and just about everyone else. Jesus asked His disciples in verse 13, "Who do people say that the Son of Man is?" The disciples listed several common answers: John the Baptist, Elijah, Jeremiah, or one of the prophets come back from the dead (or at the very least a new prophet *like* one of these prophets from old). No one, however, thought Jesus was the Messiah. He was a good man, or even a godly man, but certainly not God Himself.

Jesus then turned the same question on His disciples in verse 15: "Who do you say that I am?" The "you" here is plural and emphatic (Carson, *Matthew*, 365), so Jesus was basically confronting all of His disciples with this central question. In response, Peter, representing the other disciples, says in verse 16, "You are the Messiah, the Son of the living God!" Peter's language is loaded with theological meaning, and this is the first time we see the disciples truly confess who Jesus is. Jesus responded by saying, "Simon son of Jonah,[34] you are blessed because flesh and blood did not reveal this to you, but My Father in heaven" (v. 17). Not even Peter could have grasped the full significance of what he had uttered.

If everyone else had missed the fact that Jesus was the Messiah, how did Peter come to this realization? Not by "flesh and blood," Jesus said (v. 17), for **a true understanding of Christ comes not from human invention**. Instead, **a true understanding of Christ comes only from divine revelation**. Jesus tells Peter that this insight has been revealed by Jesus' Father (v. 17).

We must never forget that the grace of God is the only way that anyone can behold the beauty of Christ. Jesus says in John 6:44, "No one can come to Me unless the Father who sent Me draws him." In and of ourselves, we are blind, just like the Pharisees and Sadducees. We love the darkness (John 3:19). But God, in His mercy, has opened our eyes to see Jesus, to know who He is, to believe in Him, and to confess Him as the Christ, the Son of the living God. This is the testimony of every Christian.

There were a lot of people in the first century who would have said they believed in Jesus. Some, for instance, believed He was Elijah, and others Jeremiah. Likewise there are a lot of people in the twenty-first century who would say they believe in Jesus. Approximately 85 percent

---

[34] This is the only time Peter's full name "Simon son of Jonah" occurs in Scripture. In John 1:42 Jesus gave to Simon the name "Cephas," which means "Peter," the word for "rock" in the Greek.

of Americans say they believe Jesus was a true historical figure, and among that 85 percent, almost all of them (more than 9 out of 10 of them) believe that Jesus actually rose from the dead. But the more important question is, "Who exactly is the Jesus that you believe in?" *This* is the crux of the issue.

Who you say Jesus is will determine everything about how you follow Him. If you think Jesus was a good teacher, then you will follow Him like you would a good teacher. If you think Jesus merely had some good ideas, then you will listen to what He says every once in while. If you think Jesus was a good example, then you will try to follow His example.

However, if you believe that Jesus was and is the promised Messiah who came to the earth to save us from our sins, to conquer sin and death, and to reign and rule over all as Lord, then that changes everything about how you live. The church is made up of people who believe in *that* Jesus and know Him intimately. Do *you* know Jesus intimately?

As those who know Jesus intimately, the church is also **the community of people who proclaim Jesus confidently**. Based on Peter's identification of Jesus as the Messiah and Son of God, Jesus responds, "And I also say to you that you are Peter, and on this rock I will build My church, and the forces of Hades will not overpower it" (Matt 16:18). This one verse has caused all kinds of questions and controversies in the history of the church. Everyone wants to understand the church's foundation. So what is the rock that the church is built on? Is it Peter? Jesus? The apostles? The gospel? Yes. Let me explain.

Sometimes this issue is confusing because different metaphors are used in other parts of the New Testament to describe the church. For example, Paul calls Jesus "the foundation" (1 Cor 3:11), the "rock" (1 Cor 10:4), and the "cornerstone" (Eph 2:20). However, in Ephesians 2:19-20 the apostles and prophets are referred to as the foundation of the church, and in 1 Corinthians 3:10 Paul describes himself as a "skilled master builder" in relationship to the church. These various metaphors are used to make different points. Given this variety, we need to understand Matthew 16 in light of its context, knowing that other New Testament writers are using different metaphors to make different points. So what's the point that Jesus is making here?

The name Peter means "rock," so there's a bit of a play on words here. In essence, Jesus is saying, "I tell you, you are *rock* and on this *rock* I will build my church." Jesus acknowledges, then, some kind of foundation in Peter. By God's grace alone, Peter has just confessed that Jesus is the Christ, the Son of the living God. It's immediately after this confession that Jesus spoke of the church that He is building upon Peter and his confession of faith. Therefore, based on the immediate context, this is how we should understand **the rock of the church: the people of God proclaiming the gospel of Christ**.

Peter is the first apostle who makes this declaration of Christ's identity, and he is the apostle upon whom much of the church's foundation would be built beginning in Acts 2. As a result of Peter's initial proclamation of the gospel in Jerusalem on the day of Pentecost, around three thousand people were saved (Acts 2:41). Right after this, the early church devoted themselves to the apostles' teaching of the Word and thousands more came to Christ in the days ahead (Acts 2:42-47). Jesus was building His church, and Peter continued to play a central role in this mission throughout the first 12 chapters of Acts. But Peter was not alone, for Paul says in Ephesians 2:20 that the church is built on the foundation of all the apostles. (By the way, Peter was not perfect, either; see how he is called "Satan" just a few verses later!) And beyond Peter, Martin Luther declared, "All who agree with the confession of Peter (in Matt 16:16) are Peters themselves setting a sure foundation" (as cited in MacArthur, *Matthew 16–23*, 29). This is not to take away from the uniqueness of Peter, but it is to remind us that as we proclaim the gospel, we too are building upon the foundational confession made by Peter approximately two thousand years ago.

As the church proclaims the gospel of Christ, Jesus says that the "forces of Hades will not overpower it" (v. 18). The "forces of Hades," also translated as the "gates of hell" (ESV), is a Jewish idiom for the powers of death. **Death cannot stop this Messiah**, for like Jonah, Jesus would rise from the dead in victory over the grave. And it's not only Jesus who won't be stopped; **death will not stop His messengers**. J. C. Ryle said,

> Nothing can altogether overthrow and destroy [the church]. Its members may be persecuted, oppressed, imprisoned, beaten, beheaded, burned. But the true Church is never altogether extinguished: it rises again from its afflictions; it lives on through fire and water. When crushed in one land, it springs up in another. The Pharaohs, the Herods, the Neros . . . have laboured in vain to put down this Church. They slay their thousands, and then pass away and go to their own place. The true Church outlives them all, and sees them buried each in his turn. [The Church] is an anvil that has broken many

a hammer in this world, and will break many a hammer still.
[The Church] is a bush which is often burning, and yet is not
consumed. (Ryle, *Principles for Churchmen*, 118)

Death cannot stop this Messiah or His messengers, and we know
this because **Christ gives His authority to the church**. Matthew 16:19 is
another verse that has sparked debate and discussion: "I will give you
the keys of the kingdom of heaven, and whatever you bind on earth is
already bound in heaven, and whatever you loose on earth is already
loosed in heaven." Based on these verses, all kinds of errant ideas and
practices have come about. People walk around claiming to bind this or
that object or demon, all the while claiming the authority of Jesus. Once
again we must consider the context of Jesus' instructions.

When Peter or the other apostles, or any follower of Christ for that
matter, proclaims the gospel, it is done under Jesus' authority—His
authority to save sinners and to judge sinners. Jesus' authority to save
means that we can say to any person in the world, "If you turn from your
sin and trust in Jesus as Savior and Lord, you will be free from sin forever."
That's a guarantee based on the authority of Christ and His Word. At the
same time, we can also say to any person in this world, "If you do not turn
from your sin and trust in Jesus as Savior and Lord, you are bound to your
sin and its payment for all eternity in hell." Authority has been entrusted
to us as the church to proclaim this message. We tell people whether or
not they are going to heaven or to hell, whether or not they are in the
kingdom of heaven or not, all based on the authority of God's Word.

This truth is directly related to Jesus' upcoming discussion on
church discipline (Matt 18:15-20). Being a part of the church is not
simply like joining a club; it is an extremely important confession with
eternal ramifications. And these ramifications are not only for being a
part of the church, but also for what we do as a church—**we speak with
the authority of Christ**. The urgency and priority of evangelism is one
important implication that flows from these truths.

Unfortunately, this passage has been used and abused throughout
church history, particularly in its exaltation of Peter and a supposed
succession of leaders after him. Given this history, people are naturally
led to wonder, **Is Peter the first pope?** The Catholic Church teaches the
following:

The Lord made Simon alone, whom he named Peter, the
"rock" of his Church. He gave him the keys of his Church,

and instituted him shepherd of the whole flock. The office of
binding and loosing which was given to Peter was also assigned
to the college of apostles united to its head. This pastoral
office of Peter and the other apostles belongs to the Church's
very foundation and is continued by the bishops under the
primacy of the Pope. (*Catechism of the Catholic Church*, 881)

Catholicism claims that Peter was given a special authority that is now
passed down to a succession of church leaders, specifically bishops,
under the primacy of the Pope. While this text absolutely acknowledges
Peter's instrumental role in his initial confession and foundation of the
church, we must disagree here with the Catholic church's teaching. **This
text is not about a supreme pope; it's about a sovereign Savior**. Jesus
said, "*I* will build *My* church" (v. 18). Jesus is the architect of the church.
Peter's authority is completely tied to Jesus' authority as the Christ, the
Son of the living God. Jesus alone is pre-eminent in this text, and His
Word alone is supreme.

A second error flowing from these verses needs to be addressed: **this
text is not about a necessary pope; it's about a non-negotiable declaration**. It's the church's proclamation of Christ that is primary. Wherever
the gospel of Christ is proclaimed, the church will be built, and the
gates of hell will not prevail against it.

Finally, **this text is not about an infallible pope; it's about an invincible mission**. The pope does not speak new revelation that carries with it
the weight of Christ's authority, as the Catholic church teaches. Rather,
the church proclaims *old* revelation, the revelation of God saving sinners
through Christ. Only with this message do we have Christ's authority to
call people to be saved. This is why we referred to the church earlier as
a community that proclaims Jesus confidently.

Following this controversial and foundational passage in verses
13-20, the tone in the narrative shifts dramatically in verses 21-23. The
disciples learn that **Jesus would suffer necessarily**. The Lord Jesus gave
these men a detailed prediction of His sufferings, death, and resurrection, things that "must" happen (v. 21). And just when we begin to think
that Peter is getting it, he steps up and rebukes Jesus. Clearly, Peter was
not infallible! He goes from rock to stumbling block, which is the literal meaning of that word "offense" in verse 23 (Carson, *Matthew*, 377).
"Get behind Me, Satan!" may seem like strong language, but recall from
Matthew 4 that a similar temptation was aimed at Jesus in the desert.
Satan tried to seduce God's Son to gain His rightful rule and authority

apart from God's plan of suffering and death. However, Jesus knew in Matthew 4 and He knows here in this passage that He must go to the cross to fulfill the Father's will.

In light of the path that Jesus took, the path of obedience that accomplished for us our salvation, the question becomes, "Will we follow Him?" He suffered once for all necessarily; **we now suffer willingly** (vv. 24-28). This is what it means to follow Jesus and be a part of His church. You **die to yourself** by putting aside self-righteousness, self-indulgence, and everything that belongs to you—your desires, your ambitions, your thoughts, your dreams, and your possessions.

At the same time, **you take up your cross** (v. 24). For the early disciples, the language of taking up your cross would have immediately brought to mind images of crucifixion. Anyone carrying his cross was a dead man walking. Your life as you once knew it was over.

As we die to ourselves and take up our cross, we cannot forget the end of verse 24. We are not simply leaving behind sin and self, we are committing to **follow Jesus**. This echoes Jesus initial invitation in Matthew 4:19 to "Follow Me." Pursue Me, Jesus says. Walk in My footsteps, according to My Word, adhering to My ways, trusting in My power, living for My praise. You hear echoes of this in Paul's language: "I have been crucified with Christ and I no longer live, but Christ lives in me" (Gal 2:19-20). Though it may sound foolish to the world, this is how we **find life:** "For whoever wants to save his life will lose it, but whoever loses his life because of Me will find it" (v. 25).

Oh, the great reversal! Live for yourself and you will die. Die to yourself and you will live. And as you live, **eagerly expect the King to come**. Verse 27 tells us that the Son of Man is going to come and reward people according to what they have done, and since this coming is imminent, we must be prepared for it. The last verse in Matthew 16 is yet one more controversial point in this passage. Jesus said that some of those who were there with Him would live to see the Son of Man coming in His kingdom. Though more could be said on this difficult verse, the coming of Christ's kingdom could refer to a number of different aspects of that kingdom. The context here, however, seems to refer to the spread of the gospel in the early church through the power of the Son of Man. Some of these disciples, after Jesus' death and resurrection, would be a part of the manifestation of Christ's kingly reign expanding throughout the Roman empire, as hosts of people were ushered into the kingdom.

Disciples of Jesus not only expect the King, but in this sense they also **eternally experience the kingdom to come**.

Matthew 16 should cause each of us to ask the following questions: Have you died to yourself? Have you taken up your cross? Are you following Jesus? Have you found your life in Him? Are you eagerly proclaiming the good news of the kingdom as you eagerly await the return of the King? This is what it means to be a disciple. This is what it means to be a part of Christ's church.

Reflect and Discuss

1. How does self-righteousness blind us to Christ?
2. If Jesus performed signs in His ministry, why was it wrong for the Pharisees and Sadducees to request signs?
3. How is self-denial different from works-righteousness?
4. Define the church.
5. If a true understanding of Christ is God's work, how should that affect our evangelism? How should it affect your pride in receiving the gospel?
6. Explain why Christ's identity is foundational for the church.
7. How do you think your unbelieving neighbors and coworkers would answer Jesus' question, "Who do you say that I am?" How could you work a similar question into an evangelistic conversation?
8. How would you respond to a Catholic neighbor who asked, "Why don't you recognize the Pope as legitimate?"
9. What does Jesus' rebuke to Peter in verse 23 say about the place of the cross in God's plan?
10. What does it mean for someone to "take up his cross" (v. 24)?

Behold Our God!

MATTHEW 17

Main Idea: As we behold the glories of Jesus Christ, we will become more like Him.

I. **We Will Become Like What We Behold.**
    A. Behold the divine glory of the Son.
        1. Moses (the Law) had reflected divine glory.
        2. Elijah (the Prophets) had proclaimed divine glory.
        3. Jesus (the fulfillment of the Law and the Prophets) now reveals divine glory.
    B. Behold the patient power of the Son.
        1. Jesus endures our unbelief.
        2. Jesus meets our need.
        3. Jesus enables our ministry.
    C. Behold the willing sacrifice of the Son.
    D. Behold the certain victory of the Son.
    E. Behold the humble authority of the Son.
        1. Jesus is greater than the temple, yet He still pays the tax.
        2. Jesus is sovereign over the sea, yet He graciously stoops for our salvation.

II. **How Shall We Respond?**
    A. Let us look to His worth.
    B. Let us listen to His Word.
    C. Let us live for His renown.
        1. Let's proclaim the One we praise.
        2. Let's embrace suffering as we follow our Savior.
        3. Let's live as responsible citizens of this kingdom for the eventual coming of His kingdom.
    D. Let us long for His return.

I recently had the privilege of coaching my son's T-ball team. After one of the games, my son told me that he too wanted to be a baseball coach. When I asked why, he said, "Because you are, and it looks like it's a lot of fun." As we drove on, I was reminded that my kids continually watch me, and the more they watch me, the more they will imitate me, for better or for worse. As they learn to talk, their words will mirror mine. As they learn to make decisions, they will begin to process things like me. As they behold my life, they will, in many ways, begin to look like me. This is a humbling reality for a dad.

We Will Become Like What We Behold

The idea that we become like what we behold is not only true in terms of parenting, but in many different areas of life. The more we study someone, the more we listen to someone, the more we watch someone—whether it's in sports or entertainment or politics or work—the more we begin to emulate them.

Nathaniel Hawthorne wrote a short story in the nineteenth century titled "The Great Stone Face." The story is about a mountain overlooking a village, and on this mountain was etched in the stone the face of a man. The legend was that one day, a man with that face would come and visit the village, and he would be a blessing to all the villagers. A boy named Ernest heard that legend and longed for that man to come. Ernest would gaze continually on that "great stone face," studying its contours and contemplating all the ways that the man could bring blessing to that village. Every once in a while, rumors would circulate about someone with a resemblance to the "great stone face" coming to the village, and Ernest would rush in his excitement to see if it were he, only to recognize quickly that this was not the one. As Ernest grew older, he loved the village he was a part of, and he became known for his wisdom and care for the villagers. One day, a man was walking with Ernest, and Ernest turned to look at the man as they were talking. As the man gazed at Ernest, he could see the "great stone face" in the background, and suddenly, the man threw his arms around Ernest and shouted, "Behold! Behold! Ernest is himself the likeness of the Great Stone Face!" Ernest had become like the one he beheld.

The truth that Hawthorne communicates is not just a reality in short stories; it's true in Scripture too. Listen to Paul in 2 Corinthians 3:18:

> *We all, with unveiled faces, are looking as in a mirror at the glory of the Lord and are being transformed into the same image from glory to glory; this is from the Lord who is the Spirit.*

The more we behold Christ, the more we become like Him. The more we fix our attention and our affection on Him, the more our lives begin to resemble His. Our goal, therefore, as we read Matthew's Gospel (and the rest of Scripture) is that we would behold the Lord Jesus Christ. Matthew 17, in particular, gives us one of the most exhilarating, awe-inspiring, and worship-evoking portraits of Jesus in this Gospel. And as we see Him, we want to become like Him. Of course, we don't become divine like Jesus, but we do become like Him in the sense of being conformed to His character, His love, and His life. This beholding of Christ leads us to long for the day when He will come back for His people. This is the process of sanctification; this is the Christian life.

Behold the Divine Glory of the Son (17:1-13)

We're going to see five different portraits of Jesus in this chapter. Unpacking the first portrait will require the most space, and then we'll move through the remaining four more quickly. First, we need to behold the divine glory of the Son. The word "transformed" in verse 2 is from the same word that Paul uses in 2 Corinthians 3:18 to describe how we are "transformed" into the image of Christ. In both instances, this word refers to a change of form. As we are transformed into the image of Christ, we begin to take on a new form, that is, the life of Christ begins to transform the way we think, feel, believe, act, and worship. Paul uses the same word in Romans 12:2 to talk about how we must not be conformed to the pattern of this world, but "*transformed* by the renewing of your mind" (emphasis added). If that's what being transformed means for us, what then does it mean for Jesus to be transformed?[35]

The picture we have in Matthew 17 is nothing short of glorious. Jesus was on a mountain alongside two men of God from the Old Testament: Moses and Elijah. Recognizing the significance of Moses and Elijah helps us understand this passage. Moses represented the law of God, for God had met with His people in the book of Exodus to give them His law. Significantly, this giving of the law took place on a mountain, Mount Sinai. While everyone else among the Israelites had to stand back from the mountain in fear, it was Moses who met with God. Here is what Moses asked for and God's response in Exodus 33:18-23:

---

[35] Some Bible versions use the translation "transfigured" to speak of what happened to Jesus in Matthew 17.

Then Moses said, "Please, let me see Your glory."
*He said, "I will cause all My goodness to pass in front of you,
and I will proclaim the name Yahweh before you. I will be gracious to
whom I will be gracious, and I will have compassion on whom I will
have compassion." But He answered, "You cannot see My face, for no
one can see Me and live." The LORD said, "Here is a place near Me.
You are to stand on the rock, and when My glory passes by, I will put
you in the crevice of the rock and cover you with My hand until I have
passed by. Then I will take My hand away, and you will see My back,
but My face will not be seen."*

God kept His word, and in Exodus 34:6-7 Moses was given an unprecedented glimpse of Yahweh (the name by which God called Himself in the Old Testament). Here was the Lord's proclamation:

*Yahweh—Yahweh is a compassionate and gracious God, slow to anger
and rich in faithful love and truth, maintaining faithful love to a
thousand generations, forgiving wrongdoing, rebellion, and sin. But
He will not leave the guilty unpunished, bringing the consequences of
the fathers' wrongdoing on the children and grandchildren to the third
and fourth generation.*

After seeing Yahweh and receiving the two tablets of stone containing the Ten Commandments, even Moses' physical appearance was affected. The text describes the scene as follows:

*As Moses descended from Mount Sinai—with the two tablets of the
testimony in his hands as he descended the mountain—he did not
realize that the skin of his face shone as a result of his speaking with
the LORD. When Aaron and all the Israelites saw Moses, the skin of his
face shone! They were afraid to come near him. But Moses called out to
them, so Aaron and all the leaders of the community returned to him,
and Moses spoke to them. Afterward all the Israelites came near, and
he commanded them to do everything the LORD had told him on Mount
Sinai. When Moses had finished speaking with them, he put a veil
over his face.* (Exod 34:29-33)

As the one God used to reveal His law, **Moses had reflected divine glory**. He literally beheld God, albeit in a veiled depiction (since, according to Exod 33:20, no one can see God and live). Elijah, the person on the other side of Jesus on the mountain, played a different role. While Moses had reflected divine glory, **Elijah had proclaimed divine glory**.

The prophet's confrontation of the prophets of Baal in 1 Kings 19 is perhaps the clearest example of this truth.

In 1 Kings 18 Elijah challenged the prophets of Baal on another mountain—Mount Carmel. He proclaimed the glory of the one true God over Baal and other gods that were being worshiped by God's people. Elijah proclaimed God's glory, and God brought fire down from heaven. Then, in 1 Kings 19, Elijah fled for his life in fear of Jezebel. The story of his hiding out and of God's revelation to Him on Mount Horeb is given in verses 9-13. Elijah learned that God's glory is not only revealed in impressive displays of power, but also in less spectacular ways, even in a "soft whisper" (1 Kgs 19:12). More could be said about this passage, but suffice to say at this point that God had taken two men—Moses representing the law of God and Elijah representing the prophets—at strategic points to a mountain where He had shown them His glory. Their lives were changed in visible ways as a result. All this helps form the backdrop for Matthew 17.

As the fulfillment of the Law and the Prophets, **Jesus now reveals divine glory**. For our purposes, that word "reveals" is key. Jesus was not merely reflecting or proclaiming divine glory; Jesus was the revelation of divine glory. To put it another way, Jesus doesn't just mirror or imitate the glory of God; Jesus *is* the glory of God. John, who was on that mountain with Jesus in Matthew 17, would later write, "The Word became flesh and took up residence among us. We observed His glory" (John 1:14). John also said of Jesus that He has "revealed" the Father (John 1:18). We can, therefore, better understand why Peter's comment missed the mark in Matthew 17:4—he was putting Moses and Elijah on par with Jesus. God essentially told Peter to be quiet, for Jesus alone was to be the center of attention.

Jesus' appearance on the mountain to Peter, James, and John reveals God in a number of ways. **He radiates the splendor of God**. The text says that "His face shone like the sun" and "His clothes became as white as the light" (v. 2). It's as if a curtain were pulled back so that the disciples could see Christ's glory in a greater way. Jesus spoke of the glory He had with the Father before the world existed (John 17:5), yet when He came to earth, the full manifestation of Christ's glory was veiled. Philippians 2 says that He "emptied Himself by assuming the form of a slave, taking on the likeness of men" (Phil 2:7a). We see Jesus' weakness and humiliation played out in the Gospel accounts, but during these couple of moments here on this mountainside in Matthew 17, we see His glory unveiled. To quote the author of Hebrews, the disciples saw the One who is "the radiance of God's glory and the exact expression of His nature" (Heb 1:3).

In Jesus' transfiguration, we also see that **He unveils the presence of God**. A bright cloud overshadowed the scene (Matt 17:5), which reminds us of the Old Testament imagery of God leading His people by His presence in a cloud. On a number of occasions, this was God's way of manifesting His presence: a cloud protected God's people as they left Egypt (Exod 13:21-22), a cloud descended on Mount Sinai when Moses met with God to receive the law (Exod 19:9, 16), the cloud of glory enveloped the tabernacle when it was completed (Exod 40:34), and the cloud appeared at the dedication of the temple (1 Kgs 8:10-11).

Jesus' unique glory is also on display in this passage in that **He embodies the pleasure of God**. The Father's voice came from the cloud saying, "This is My beloved Son. I take delight in Him" (v. 5). These are the same words we saw in Matthew 3:17 when Jesus was baptized, and they are probably also an allusion to Psalm 2:7 and Isaiah 42:1 (Carson, *Matthew*, 386). The Father looks at the Son and cherishes what He sees. When the Spirit descends on the Son and the Father speaks, we touch on the mystery of the Godhead: three persons existing together in glorious harmony and love.

Jesus also reflects God's glory in that **He speaks the Word of God**. The Father adds one thing here to the words He had already declared in Matthew 3. He says, "Listen to Him!" (17:5). When you hear that, you can't help but think about Peter, the one who showed himself so quick to speak in the previous chapter and now again in this passage. It's as if God the Father were saying to Peter, "Be quiet. Listen to My Son. And when He speaks about the coming cross, listen to Him; do not rebuke Him." God's command to Peter picks up on Moses' prophecy of a coming prophet: "The LORD your God will raise up for you a prophet like me from among your own brothers. *You must listen to him*" (Deut 18:15; emphasis added). Matthew is pointing to Jesus as the One who fulfills this prophecy. **He is the prophet promised by Moses**.

Notice in verse 3 that Jesus had a conversation with Moses and Elijah, which naturally causes us to wonder, "What were they talking about?" Matthew doesn't tell us, but Luke's Gospel gives us a little more information: "Suddenly, two men were talking with Him—Moses and Elijah. They appeared in glory and were speaking of His death, which He was to accomplish in Jerusalem" (Luke 9:30-31). The conversation was about Jesus' departure in death—the word translated "death" is the Greek word from which we get the word "exodus." **In the great exodus of the Old Testament, the Father used Moses to deliver His people from slavery**. Now, as the culmination of His saving actions, **the Father sent Jesus to deliver His people from sin**. The greater and final exodus happened as the Son of God went to the cross to liberate His people from the slavery of sin.

Jesus is not only the prophet promised by Moses to speak God's word and deliver His people, but also **He is the messenger preceded by Elijah**. When Jesus and His disciples came down from the mountain, He commanded them, "Don't tell anyone about the vision until the Son of Man is raised from the dead" (v. 9). The disciples were confused in light of the prophecy that Elijah must come before the great Day of the Lord. But Jesus had already referred to John as "the Elijah who is to come" (Matt 11:14), and here in verse 12 He reiterates that truth. John the Baptist fulfilled the following prophecies of Malachi:

> "See, I am going to send My messenger, and he will clear the way before Me. Then the Lord you seek will suddenly come to His temple, the Messenger of the covenant you desire—see, He is coming," says the LORD of Hosts. (Mal 3:1)

> Remember the instruction of Moses My servant, the statutes and ordinances I commanded him at Horeb for all Israel. Look, I am going to send you Elijah the prophet before the great and awesome Day of the LORD comes. And he will turn the hearts of fathers to their children and the hearts of children to their fathers. Otherwise, I will come and strike the land with a curse. (Mal 4:4-6)

According to Malachi, Elijah the prophet would come and prepare the way of the Lord. On one level, then, the disciples' question to Jesus could be chronological, i.e., "We just now saw Elijah; how come He didn't come before you?" Jesus answers that question in Matthew 17:12 by pointing out that John the Baptist, the Elijah to come, had already come. But that simply leads to a deeper theological question: How is John the Elijah who would restore all things if John had been beheaded?[36] John didn't usher in a great restoration, or so the disciples thought. Jesus had to help the disciples understand that the kingdom of God was not being ushered in the way they thought it would be.

---

[36] See Carson's discussion on the disciples' question in Carson, *Matthew*, 388–89.

They expected a messianic forerunner and then a Messiah who would together usher in a kingdom on this earth marked by triumph and power. However, God's kingdom was coming in a very different way.

The promised Elijah, John the Baptist, did in fact have a ministry of restoration. He announced that the kingdom of heaven was near and he called people to repent (Matt 3:2). However, **in the end, John the Baptist's ministry of restoration resulted in his suffering and death**. John's death is what Jesus referred to when He said, "They did whatever they pleased to him" (v. 12). Such treatment was not only true of John; Jesus was also preparing the disciples for His own death. Jesus closes verse 12 by saying, "In the same way the Son of Man is going to suffer at their hands." The disciples were being prepared for the reality that **Jesus' ministry of redemption would be accomplished through His suffering and death**. This is a key truth that keeps reappearing in Matthew's Gospel.

The disciples (along with many other Jews) wanted an immediate and glorious kingdom set up on this earth by the Messiah. That's one of the reasons Peter suggested putting up three tabernacles, for he saw that in Jesus the kingdom was dawning.[37] But Jesus refused, for **the cross of Christ must come before the crown of Christ**. He instructed the disciples in verse 9 not to tell anyone about what they had seen. They were to wait until after Jesus' death (and resurrection), since there is no true glory apart from the cross. Suffering must precede splendor. This truth doesn't make sense to the world, but it is crucial if we are to see the divine glory of the Son.

Behold the Patient Power of the Son (17:14-21)

So far we've seen the divine glory of the Son from a number of different angles. As we turn to verses 14-21, let us behold the patient power of the Son. Once Jesus and the three disciples come down from the mountain, the scene in Matthew's Gospel shifts from one extreme to the other. It turns from the glory of God in Christ on a mountain to the pain and suffering of the world. We are seeing the God who stooped to become a man, the One who identified with us in our suffering in order to bring us salvation from sin.

---

[37] Carson notes that the Festival of Booths or Tabernacles may be in the background here (Lev 23:42-43), a feast that had eschatological overtones. Carson, *Matthew*, 385–86; see also Osborne's comments, *Matthew*, 647.

In verse 14 Jesus was approached by a man whose son had epilepsy as a result of demon possession. The boy had seizures and would often fall into fire and water (v. 15). I'm reminded of being in a Sudanese hospital and seeing a child with sleeping sickness, a disease that caused him to go into a trance at any moment, which meant falling over unconscious. This happened one time as the boy was sitting next to a fire, and he tragically had half of his body charred. Suffering can be violent, and it reminds us of the tragic pain of living in a sinful world.

Jesus' disciples lacked the faith to do what Jesus had given them authority to do, namely, to deliver this epileptic boy from a destructive demon. In this portrait, we see that **Jesus endures our unbelief**. Keep in mind that this is the same Jesus whom we just saw in His unveiled glory in the previous verse. The One who was with the Father in glory and who commanded myriads of angels is now confronted yet again with the unbelief of men, even His own disciples. In verse 17 we see Jesus' frustration with this failure of faith: "How long must I put up with you?" The fact that He didn't immediately reject His disciples reminds us that God is patient. Christ was forbearing with people He encountered, and gratefully He treats us the same way.

Not only does He endure our unbelief, but also **Jesus meets our need**. In verse 18 He healed this demon-possessed boy, instantly bringing him out of his misery. Jesus alone has the power to heal, to save, to deliver, and to meet the deepest needs of our lives.

Following this healing, Jesus' disciples came to Him privately and asked why they couldn't drive the demon out (v. 19). This is where we learn that **Jesus enables our ministry**. We don't know all that was going on in the minds, hearts, and motives of these disciples as they failed to cast out this demon, something they had previously succeeded at by Christ's authority. But we do know from Mark's account of this story that Jesus told them, "This kind can come out by nothing but prayer" (Mark 9:29). The disciples had likely begun to look at their ministry as mechanical, being dependent on their own ability instead of on God. Jesus pointed them in a different direction: the way of trusting in His power. By telling them that their faith need only be the size of a mustard seed, Jesus was urging them to focus on the object of their faith. A little bit of faith in a great God can accomplish great things. Even mountains, Jesus says, will move. Nothing is impossible for the man or woman who trusts in the power of God to accomplish the will of God (v. 20).

Behold the Willing Sacrifice of the Son (17:22-23a)

This is Jesus' second major prediction in Matthew's Gospel of His suffering and death (cf. 16:21-23), and there will be more to come. John Calvin said, "The nearer the time of His death, the more often Christ warned His disciples, lest that particular sorrow should undermine their faith." Jesus was preparing these 12 men for His certain and willing death. We may be accustomed to hearing of the cross, but consider Christ's death in light of the portrait we have just seen earlier in this chapter. No one can overpower this man! He is God in the flesh. Who can take Him on? If Jesus died at the hands of men, which He did, it is clearly because He chose to die. This was no accident. Sinful men killed Him, but only because He walked into their hands at the Father's bidding.

Behold the Certain Victory of the Son (17:23b)

Christ's willing sacrifice leads us next to behold the certain victory of the Son. The disciples were having a hard enough time trying to grasp the fact that the Messiah would be killed by the Jewish leaders of the day; they had no concept at all of the reality of Jesus' impending resurrection. The same Jesus who was nailed to a cross would be raised in power and triumphant victory.

Behold the Humble Authority of the Son (17:24-27)

So far we've seen the divine glory of the Son, the patient power of the Son, the willing sacrifice of the Son, and the certain victory of the Son. Finally, we behold the humble authority of the Son. This story sets the stage for Matthew 18, where humility is a major theme. Interestingly, Matthew is the only Gospel writer who tells us this story, and it seems fitting given his former profession—a tax collector. Unlike most of the mentions of taxes and tax collectors elsewhere in the Gospels, the temple tax described in verse 24 was not a tax collected by the Roman government. Instead, the temple tax was collected by Jewish leaders for the service of the temple in Jerusalem. Based loosely on Exodus 30:11-16, the people of God were expected to help provide for the place that housed the glory of God. However, we've already seen Jesus claim to be greater than the temple (Matt 12:6). He was the literal dwelling place of God, and we know that He had come to usher in an altogether new and glorious way of access to God, namely, through Himself.

When Jesus died on the cross, the curtain of the temple was torn in two (27:51). So why should He and His followers pay for the upkeep of the temple? In His conversation with Peter, Jesus used the analogy of kings who raise money from taxes, and He asked Peter whether such taxes came from the king's sons, or from strangers (17:25). Peter gave the obvious answer, "From strangers" (v. 26). The point of the analogy is clear: Since God is King, Jesus (His Son) is free from the obligation to pay the temple tax, along with all who are with Jesus in the family of faith. However, in order not to give offense, Jesus says to pay the tax. In other words, **Jesus is greater than the temple, yet He still pays the tax**. But why? Not because He is under obligation, but because He is working for others' salvation.

Verse 27 records one of the more striking miracles in Jesus' ministry. He commanded Peter to go to the sea and pull up the first fish he caught, wherein he would find a coin to pay the tax. Consider what had to take place for this miracle to occur: Jesus ordained that somebody would drop a shekel into the water, that a fish would scoop it up in its mouth but not swallow it all the way, that that fish would swim over to the shore at the moment when Peter walked up, and as Peter cast out a hook, that he would catch *that* fish. All of that happened so that a temple tax could be paid in order not to bring unnecessary offense to people whom God desires to save from sin. **Jesus is sovereign over the sea, yet He graciously stoops for our salvation**.

How Shall We Respond?

There are a number of ways we can respond to the truths in Matthew 17. We'll note four of those ways. First, as we consider Christ in this passage (and in the entire Gospel of Matthew), **let us look to His worth**. See His divine glory, His patient power, His willing sacrifice, His certain victory, and His humble authority. Then fall on your face in worship, just like the disciples (v. 6). Fix your attention and your affection on the Lord Jesus Christ and stop spending your life on the trivial and temporal. Let those things grow strangely dim in the light of God's glory and grace.

Second, **let us listen to His Word**. This point is made powerfully in 2 Peter 1:16-21, a passage where we get Peter's reflection on the events of Matthew 17:

> For we did not follow cleverly contrived myths when we made known to you the power and coming of our Lord Jesus Christ; instead, we were

*eyewitnesses of His majesty. For when He received honor and glory
from God the Father, a voice came to Him from the Majestic Glory:
        This is My beloved Son.
    I take delight in Him!
    And we heard this voice when it came from heaven while we
were with Him on the holy mountain. So we have the prophetic word
strongly confirmed. You will do well to pay attention to it, as to a lamp
shining in a dismal place, until the day dawns and the morning star
rises in your hearts. First of all, you should know this: No prophecy
of Scripture comes from one's own interpretation, because no prophecy
ever came by the will of man; instead, men spoke from God as they were
moved by the Holy Spirit.*

After reading of Jesus' transfiguration, we might be tempted to think
that our lives would be dramatically different if only we could witness
that kind of event or hear God's Word with that kind of certainty.
However, we now have the New Testament, which contains the authoritative record of the transfiguration along with an explanation of its significance. We don't need any further confirmation, for we have all we
need in Scripture. If you want to behold the glory of God in Christ on
a daily basis, then read, study, meditate on, and memorize the Word of
God. Then you will see His glory, and you will love it.

Third, we ought to respond to this text by having a new motivation
for living: **let us live for His renown**. When you see the glory of God,
you want to spread the gospel of God. Therefore, **let's proclaim the
One we praise**. Let's not see His glory and then be silent. Let's speak
to people about the Christ we cherish. Also, **let's embrace suffering as
we follow our Savior**. Just as the cross preceded the crown for Jesus, so
suffering in this life will precede our final reward in the next. After all,
if Jesus suffered in the spread of God's kingdom, do we think that we
will have it easy? Remember, no one can follow Jesus without taking up
his or her cross (Matt 16:24). We give away our possessions, we risk our
reputations, and we go to the hard places knowing that our sufferings
"are not worth comparing with the glory that is going to be revealed to
us" (Rom 8:18). We don't seek suffering, but we do seek Christ, and this
will ensure at least some level of opposition in this world (2 Tim 3:12;
John 16:33).

In His teaching related to the temple tax, Jesus reminds us that
although our reward is still future, we have responsibilities in the here
and now. Therefore, **let's live as responsible citizens of this kingdom**

for the eventual coming of His kingdom. We must be mindful of the salvation of others and our witness in the world. We pay our taxes, not because we agree with everything our government supports, but because we are under law (Rom 13:5), and we want to live as responsible citizens in this earthly kingdom for the spread of Christ's heavenly kingdom.

Fourth and finally, **let us long for His return**. We should eagerly anticipate the day when our faith will be sight, when we will see Jesus as the Father sees Jesus, revealing the glory of God and radiating the splendor of God. Revelation 22:4 says of those who will enter God's eternal kingdom, "They will see His face." First John 3:2-3 talks about the transforming effect of such a vision:

> *Dear friends, we are God's children now, and what we will be has not yet been revealed. We know that when He appears, we will be like Him because we will see Him as He is. And everyone who has this hope in Him purifies himself just as He is pure.*

This is the Christian's hope. And as we behold Jesus, we will become like Him.

Reflect and Discuss

1. What hobbies, activities, and people do you spend most of your time with? How do these things affect your thinking and your behavior?
2. If we become like what we behold, then what does it look like to behold Christ today while He is not physically present?
3. List five attributes of Jesus Christ in Matthew 17.
4. How does this passage speak to the superiority of Jesus Christ over well-known Old Testament figures?
5. Describe the relationship between Elijah and John the Baptist in verses 9-13.
6. Does this passage speak to Jesus' divinity? Explain.
7. How is Jesus' patience different from our culture's idea of tolerance?
8. What about Jesus' prediction in verses 22-23 tells us that He wasn't a victim of circumstances?
9. Does Jesus' promise that nothing will be impossible for the one who believes (v. 21) mean that God is obligated to give us what we want if we believe sincerely enough? Why not?
10. What was Jesus' attitude toward the political powers of His day?

Kingdom Community

MATTHEW 18

Main Idea: We come to Christ initially with child-like humility and then continue to follow Him under the loving discipline of a local church.

I.   **Becoming a Christian**
  A. To be a citizen of the kingdom, you must become a child of the King.
  B. Jesus calls His disciples to humility of heart, not childishness of thought.

II. **Loving the Church**
  A. We protect one another.
    1. We are selflessly concerned about each other's holiness.
    2. We are radically committed to our own holiness.
  B. We love one another.
    1. In light of the Father's angelic provision for His children
    2. In light of the Father's individual pursuit of His children
  C. We restore one another.
    1. The process of church discipline and restoration
    2. God's promises amid church discipline and restoration
  D. We forgive one another.
    1. In Christ, we have received extravagant grace.
    2. As Christians, we now extend extravagant grace.

III. **How Shall We Respond?**
  A. As a part of a local church, we must care for every individual member.
    1. Elevating church membership
    2. Ensuring pastoral leadership
    3. Equipping small groups
  B. As Christians
    1. Are you causing, leading, or enabling a brother or sister to sin?
    2. Are you guarding, protecting, and nurturing your own personal holiness?
    3. How can you more clearly express the love of the Father to the church around you?

    4.   Is there anyone you need to humbly confront concerning sin for their good and for the Father's glory?

    5.   Are you harboring any bitterness or unforgiveness toward someone else?

  C. May the love of the Father through Christ compel the love of His children in the church.

In Matthew 18 we come to the fourth major teaching section in this Gospel.[38] One commentator has referred to this as "the single greatest discourse our Lord ever gave on life among the redeemed people in His church" (MacArthur, *Matthew 16–23*, 94). These instructions from Jesus span an entire chapter and they are very important, but they've also been severely misunderstood. Because many of these verses have been abused in a number of ways, we need to recover the riches that are contained here, particularly as they apply to the local church. For the second time in Matthew's Gospel, Jesus explicitly refers to the church (see also 16:18), and this time it comes in the context of church discipline and restoration. Nothing short of our commitment to one another as fellow members of God's family is at stake, as well as our witness to a watching world.

Becoming a Christian
MATTHEW 18:1-4

The first four verses of Matthew 18 set the stage for the rest of the chapter. Jesus uses an analogy to illustrate what it means to be a Christian. The rest of the chapter then unpacks how we as Christians should relate to one another in the church. Jesus is clearly concerned that His followers be marked by humility, love, and a willingness to grant lavish forgiveness to one another.

Matthew begins in verse 1 by saying, "At that time," cluing us in to the place in the narrative where this chapter starts and the previous chapter left off. In the previous two chapters, we've seen Peter's confession of Jesus as the Christ (16:16) as well as Jesus' transfiguration before

---

[38] The three previous major teaching sections were as follows: (1) Matt 5–7 (the Sermon on the Mount), (2) Matt 10 (the sending out of the disciples), and (3) Matt 13 (the parables of the kingdom).

Peter, James, and John on the mountain (17:1-2). These significant events seem to be at least a part of the reason for the disciples' question to Jesus in verse 1: "Who is greatest in the kingdom of heaven?" Perhaps some thought that the greatest was Peter, the disciple who was singled out by Jesus in the institution of the church (16:18) and who was also permitted to see Jesus' glory on the mountain. However, Peter was also rebuked for standing in the way of Jesus' path to the cross (16:22-23), not to mention the fact that James and John were also allowed to accompany Jesus on the mountain. So who, after all, is the greatest disciple?

Amid the discussion of greatness in the kingdom of heaven, Jesus called a child and put him in the middle of the disciples. He told His disciples that they must be "converted and become like children" (v. 3). That is, **to be a citizen of the kingdom, you must become a child of the King**. This is the essence of what it means to be a Christian. Jesus is pointing to **the necessity of conversion**. The language of turning and becoming like a child means that Jesus is calling His disciples to a fundamental change. In order to become a citizen of the kingdom, you must **turn from yourself** and **trust in the Father**. Like a child, you thrust yourself upon God and confess your need for Him. I'm reminded of my own children wanting and needing to be held, fed, read to, loved, and provided for. I know that when they run up to me with their arms in the air and a smile on their face, that's a picture of conversion. We too must humble ourselves like that before God.

A necessary clarification may be helpful at this point. We can take this imagery further than Jesus intends, equating all kinds of characteristics of children with what it means to be a Christian. But remember that **Jesus calls His disciples to humility of heart, not childishness of thought**. Children have many characteristics that the people of God are not to copy: they don't know a lot, they can't focus very well on things for a long period of time, and they make all kinds of poor decisions out of ignorance. We are not to be childish in these senses. The emphasis in this passage is on humility, so that the smartest, most intelligent, most successful, most noble, or most gifted person might come to Jesus with humility of heart, turning from themselves and trusting completely in the Father.

In light of these truths in verses 1-4, each of us is faced with the question, Are *you* a child of the King? Have you come to the point where you've realized that God is holy, you are sinful, and therefore you desperately need a Savior? Have you, like a child, left behind all you were holding on to, and have you run to God the Father through Jesus as the only One whom you can trust with your life, both now and forever? This is the essence of what it means to be a Christian, to be a child of the King. And it sets the stage for the rest of this chapter, where Jesus talks about the Father's love for His children and how this love affects the way we love one another in the church.

Loving the Church
MATTHEW 18:5-35

Continuing to talk about children, Jesus shifts the conversation to talk about receiving children in His name. Many people have misunderstood what He says here in verses 5-6. Some people interpret these verses to mean that we should not cause children to sin, and that because Jesus loved children, we should too. Obviously there's some truth to that interpretation—we should love children and we should never lead them into sin—but that's not the point of this passage. Remember that Jesus has just equated all of His followers with children, sons and daughters of His heavenly Father (vv. 3-4). He did this by using an actual child to illustrate a spiritual reality. Therefore, whenever we see "child" or "little one" in the rest of this passage, the reference is not to physical children but to the spiritual children of God the Father. Child refers to Christian in Matthew 18. Therefore, when Jesus says in verse 5, "And whoever welcomes one child like this in My name welcomes Me," He's not equating Himself with children. He's equating Himself with Christians (with children of the Father), as in, "When you receive a Christian (a child of the Father), you are receiving Me." When someone causes a spiritual child of the King to sin, on the other hand, this is a serious offense. It would be better for such a person if a "heavy millstone were hung around his neck and he were drowned in the depths of the sea!" (v. 6).

Most of the remainder of chapter 18 deals with how God's children (i.e., Christians) are to be cared for. Realizing the focus of the chapter makes the imagery of children in this text very powerful. For example, if you're a parent or if you've had a loving parent in your life, you know that it's one thing for someone to offend or hurt you, but it's even harder to deal with when someone hurts your child. You can offend me all day long, but if you hurt my daughter, things will not go well for you! That is the kind of zealous affection that our heavenly Father has for His children, and it speaks to the concern we should have for our fellow believers.

We Protect One Another (18:7-9)

As children of God who are part of the same spiritual family, we protect one another from sin and temptation. Jesus speaks solemnly here of the danger of temptations to sin. As followers of Christ committed to one another, **we are selflessly concerned about each other's holiness.** We don't want to cause another brother or sister to sin. There will continue to be temptations in the world as long as there is sin in the world; this is expected. However, we must not add to the world's temptations by leading one another to sin in the church. For instance, don't gossip to me when I am already fighting off that tendency in my own heart. Don't lead me astray in the name of your supposed Christian liberties when I'm fighting every day not to turn those liberties into license to sin. Both materialism and sexual temptations also come to mind in our culture, as it is all too easy to lead others astray in these areas without even realizing it. It would be better for you, Jesus says, if you would put a stone around your neck and throw yourself down into a watery grave (v. 6).

Christians are not only committed to the holiness of other believers; **we are radically committed to our own holiness.** Jesus speaks of cutting off our hands and feet and tearing out our eyes if necessary in order to fight sin (vv. 8-9). This is obviously strong figurative language aimed at making us realize that drastic action is necessary to overcome temptation. Jesus isn't literally calling us to get rid of body parts, since that would fail to deal with the root of sin in the heart. He's emphasizing the seriousness and violence that should characterize our battle with sin. Instead of flirting with sin, we should destroy it. If something is leading us to sin, we should get rid of it. See, then, how this point fits with the previous point: when we are zealous about holiness in our own lives, we will be zealous about protecting one another from sin. In turn, when we are zealous about protecting one another from sin, we will be all the more careful about sin in our own lives. If we're casual about our own sin, on the other hand, we will lead others to be casual about their sin. This is why we must be intentional about protecting one another.

We Love One Another (18:10-14)

Jesus teaches us that as His followers we love one another. He uses a parable about lost sheep to make the point. We shouldn't despise, look down on, or treat other believers with contempt. Instead, we should treat one another with love and care. This command may not sound new, but Jesus' reasoning for it may surprise us. He says that we should love one another **in light of the Father's angelic provision for His children**. The angels "continually view the face of My Father in heaven," Jesus says (v. 10). People have taken this passage to mean that each child in the world, or even each Christian in the world, has a guardian angel assigned to him or her. While the Bible has much to say about angels and the roles they play in God's purposes, it never says that the number of angels corresponds to the number of Christians in such a way that each one of us has a guardian angel assigned to protect us. Angels certainly protect God's children in Scripture: an angel rescued Peter out of prison in Acts 12, and angels shut the mouths of lions in order to protect Daniel (Dan 6:22). A number of other examples could be cited,[39] as angels carry out God's work in a variety of ways. In fact, it's likely that God is using angels to do the same sorts of things in the lives of His people today. Nevertheless, we are never told of a guardian angel assigned to each believer. Instead, the Bible speaks in more general terms about angels, as in Hebrews 1:14, where they are referred to as "ministering spirits sent out to serve" God's people. To use a basketball analogy, we might think of angels as providing "zone coverage" rather than "man-to-man" marking.

You may wonder why the Bible's teaching on angels is important. Consider: if the Father has angelic attendants that He sends out to serve and protect His children, then how much more should we love His children? That is, if God cares enough about His children to command angels to attend to their needs, how can we remain indifferent to our fellow believers? Jesus' parable of the lost sheep in verses 12-14 drives home a similar point. We are to love one another **in light of the Father's individual pursuit of His children**. When even one out of a hundred sheep goes astray, God pursues that one. Jesus says that the Father is not willing that "*one* of these little ones perish" (v. 14; emphasis added). If you're a child of God, take a minute and let that truth soak in. The Father cares for *you*. And He is committed to pursuing you as His child. We're reminded of Jesus' words in John's Gospel:

> *I am the good shepherd. I know My own sheep, and they know Me. . . .*
> *My sheep hear My voice, I know them, and they follow Me. I give them*

---

[39] For example, see also the promise of angelic protection in Ps 91:11-12, an angel's provision for Elijah in 1 Kgs 19:4-8, and the ministry of angels to Jesus in Mark 1:13 following His temptation in the wilderness.

*eternal life, and they will never perish—ever! No one will snatch them
out of My hand. My Father, who has given them to Me, is greater than
all. No one is able to snatch them out of the Father's hand. The Father
and I are one.* (John 10:14, 27-30)

These are rock-solid promises for the child of God. And if this is
how the Father loves His children, then this is how we must love one
another. We must pursue one another, particularly when one among us
wanders, because this is what God does.

We Restore One Another (18:15-20)

So far we've seen that those in God's family protect and love one
another. In verses 15-20 we're told that we restore one another. This
passage is foundational for understanding church discipline and restoration, something that is essential to the health of a church. Church
discipline sounds legalistic and unloving to many people in our day, but
the Bible has a different perspective. Of course, we want to show each
other grace, but this must be a grace defined by Scripture. Pastor Mark
Dever writes,

> Imagine this church: It is huge and is still growing numerically.
> People like it. The music is good. The people are welcoming.
> There are many exciting programs, and people are quickly
> enlisted into their support. And yet, the church, in trying to look
> like the world in order to win the world, has done a better job
> than it may have intended. It does not display the distinctively
> holy characteristics taught in the New Testament. Imagine such
> an apparently vigorous church being truly spiritually sick, with
> no remaining immune system to check and guard against wrong
> teaching or wrong living. Imagine Christians, knee-deep in
> recovery groups and sermons on brokenness and grace, being
> comforted in their sin but never confronted. Imagine those
> people, made in the image of God, being lost to sin because no
> one corrects them. Can you imagine such a church? Apart from
> the size, have I not described many of our American churches?
> (Dever, *9 Marks of a Healthy Church*, 186)

Similarly, J. Carl Laney writes,

> The church today is suffering from an infection which has
> been allowed to fester. . . . As an infection weakens the body

by destroying its defense mechanisms, so the church has been weakened by this ugly sore. The church has lost its power and effectiveness in serving as a vehicle for social, moral, and spiritual change. This illness is due, at least in part, to a neglect of church discipline. (Laney, *A Guide to Church Discipline*, 12)

This passage lays out four steps in **the process of church discipline and restoration**, and we'll consider each of them below.

STEP 1: PRIVATE CORRECTION

Verse 15 begins, "If your brother sins against you." Scholars are not sure whether the words "against you" are original, as there are variants in the early manuscripts. Jesus is either referring to confronting a brother who sins in general, or to a brother (or sister) who sins specifically against you. As always, the difference is very minor, for even if the words "against you" are included in this passage, Galatians 6:1 gives us the following general admonition: "Brothers, if someone is caught in any wrongdoing, you who are spiritual should restore such a person." Paul makes no specific reference to whether or not you as an individual are directly affected by that sin, but he still commands you and other believers to address it. So whether Jesus is referring to a brother caught in sin or a brother who sins "against you," a follower of Christ should address that sin with the person. Jesus says, "Go and rebuke him in private" (Matt 18:15). The goal is to keep the circle as small as possible as long as possible, rather than talking about the sin with someone else, which is often our first tendency.

As a word of warning, we will find *ourselves* in sin if we talk about a brother or sister in a way that doesn't build them up in Christ Jesus (see Eph 4:29-32). We must zealously guard and protect the character of fellow believers, both for their good and for the glory of Christ. The more a person's sin is known and discussed by others, no matter how well-meaning they may be, the easier it is for the one who is in sin to become resentful, and the harder it may be for repentance and restoration to take place. So don't fish around with hints to try to find out who knows what. Go directly to your brother or sister.

Remember, as we talk about confronting people in their sin in the context of church discipline and restoration, the implication is that a brother or sister is continuing in that sin and refusing to turn from it, i.e., they are unrepentant. That's the key. We're not talking about bringing the hammer down on someone for each and every sin. This passage is speaking of a situation where a brother sins directly against you and doesn't come to you for forgiveness, or he is caught in sin and is refusing to turn from it; in such situations, love him (or her) enough to privately address the sin. Love him enough not to talk to everyone in the world about it. Love him enough not to sit back and watch him wander deeper and deeper into sin. If the person responds rightly, Jesus says, "you have won your brother" (v. 15). Your communion in Christ may even be that much deeper as a result.

One final reminder for this first step in the process of church discipline: This step doesn't involve any kind of official organization or any leaders in the church. It begins between you and the other person, which is where most church discipline is intended to happen. This kind of interaction is supposed to happen all the time in the context of our relationships with one another. If we would only get this first step right, we might find that about 95 percent of the work of church discipline and restoration has been taken care of before anyone else becomes involved.

STEP 2: SMALL GROUP CLARIFICATION

Next, Jesus addresses the second step in the church discipline and restoration process, the step that becomes necessary for a brother "if he won't listen" (v. 16). If a brother refuses to listen to loving confrontation, Jesus says to "take one or two more with you" (v. 16). He cites the Old Testament requirement for two or three witnesses to establish a fact (Deut 19:15). In the context of the church, this step of discipline involves one or two others—the circle remains really small here—and these should be believers who are gentle, humble, loving, and willing to go with you to speak to an unrepentant brother or sister. The point of this step is to broaden the circle slightly so that one or two others get involved in the situation, but not to begin ganging up on that brother or sister with people whom you can build a case with. Instead, these other believers can help you think through the situation better. A church leader does not necessarily need to be involved at this point, though he could be. Oftentimes it's best to involve someone else who knows and cares for that particular brother or sister. This increases the chances that the confrontation will be humble and gracious.

STEP 3: CHURCH ADMONITION

In verse 17 the word "church" (*ekklesia*) appears for the second time in Matthew's Gospel. At this third step, the circle of involvement in church discipline grows to include the gathering of believers in a local church, as they are made aware of the brother or sister's unrepentant sin. This step may sound unloving or even embarrassing, but we need to feel the tone behind what Jesus is saying here. We're tempted to think, "Why tell a whole group of people about this brother and his sin?" In reality, however, the entire church is saying together, "We love you, and we want you to come back to Christ." God loves us so much that if we are caught in sin, He will send an entire army of believers to us as a demonstration of His love and mercy.

STEP 4: CHURCH EXCOMMUNICATION

In the remainder of verse 17, Jesus lays out the consequences for a person who refuses to repent after being confronted by the entire church body. He says to consider the person "like an unbeliever and a tax collector." In other words, treat him like he is no longer your brother in Christ or part of the church body. He must be excommunicated, or expelled, from the church.

While this fourth step may sound extreme in our day, keep in mind that it is not optional. This is a command from Jesus, so that a failure to do this in the church is sin. If we're honest, excommunication is a difficult step for everyone involved. Some people struggle to understand why we do it at all. Isn't the church supposed to be welcoming? Though it may be difficult, church discipline is what Jesus calls us to do, a point we see played out in the early church. For example, in 1 Corinthians 5 Paul instructed the Corinthians to remove a man from the assembly for gross sexual immorality. Again, the goal in church discipline and restoration is that people will see their sin and return to Christ and that sin will not spread further like leaven (1 Cor 5:5-6). This is for the good of that individual and the protection and purity of the church. Ultimately, it's for the glory of God in the body of Christ.

Because church discipline can be difficult, we must trust Jesus in this process and obey what He says. It is good, therefore, to reflect on **God's promises amid church discipline and restoration**.

First, **He has given us His authority**. In verse 18 Jesus says, "I assure you: Whatever you bind on earth is already bound in heaven, and whatever you loose on earth is already loosed in heaven." This language is very similar to Matthew 16:19. Again, Jesus is not giving some special authority to us outside of Himself, but rather it is attached to Him and His Word. He is saying that what we do as a church in His name, with His authority, is a reflection of what He does in heaven. So, if someone comes to the church and says, "I am living in sin and I am unrepentant— I will not turn to Christ," then we can say to that person with authority, "You are living bound in sin and your sin is not forgiven." To be clear, their sin is not unforgiven because we said so; their sin is unforgiven because Christ has said so in His Word. Similarly, if someone says that they are willing to turn from their sin, then we can say to them with full confidence that their sin is forgiven and they are now free from it. Jesus has given us the privilege of proclaiming what He has said to be true.

The fact that Christ has given us His authority is important to remember as we carry out the work of excommunication. Someone might ask, "By whose authority are you doing this?" According to Matthew 18:18, we are doing this by Jesus' authority. One writer said, "Never is the church more in harmony with heaven and operating in perfect accord with her Lord than when dealing with sin to maintain purity" (MacArthur, *1 Corinthians*, 126). There is a humble confidence that comes with knowing that Christ has given us His authority to speak against sin in the church.

A second promise we can take comfort from in this passage appears in verse 19. Jesus says that if we "agree about any matter you pray for," the Father will do it. **He has granted us His support**. This is another verse that has often been abused. Jesus is not giving us a blank check whereby we simply find someone else who agrees with us, and then God automatically responds by giving us whatever we want. Remember the context: Jesus has just finished talking about the scenario when two or three believers confront a brother in sin (vv. 15-16). He's saying that we have the full support of the Father in heaven when we gather together in unison to confront sin in the church. Jesus knows that church discipline is not easy, and that we will be tempted to shy away from it and not carry it out. He's encouraging us with the resources of heaven.

Related to God's promised support is a third promise in this passage: **He has guaranteed us His presence**. This is probably the most abused verse in this passage. If you've been a Christian for any length of time, you've likely heard the idea that where two or three believers are gathered, Jesus is there. But what about when you were in your prayer

closet alone today—does that mean Jesus was waiting for someone else
to show up before He came into the picture? No, definitely not (Matt
6:6). Jesus is not saying, "Once you've got two or three together, count
Me in." Instead, in this context He's talking about the difficult work of
church discipline when two or three believers are gathered to address
a brother or sister living in unrepentant sin. When we do the tough
work of gentle, loving confrontation, we can be assured that Christ's
presence, which is always with us (Matt 28:20), will be especially real
and strong in the middle of that situation. This should give us great
confidence.

We Forgive One Another (18:21-35)

This is the last exhortation for the church in Matthew 18. The point of
the parable of the Unforgiving Servant is fairly self-explanatory, and it
relates to Jesus' discussion in the previous section. Although the conversation has moved on from church discipline, the way in which we treat
one another's sin is still the issue at hand.

In those days, it was common among rabbis to encourage people to
forgive a brother for repeated sin up to three times, after which there
would be no more forgiveness. So Peter, thinking he had a really big
heart, asked Jesus how often he should forgive his brother, possibly even
seven times. Jesus responds by saying, "70 times seven" (v. 22). Then, in
what can only be labeled an extreme illustration, Jesus tells the story of
a man who owed upwards of what today could be labeled millions if not
more than a billion dollars, clearly an amount of money that this servant
could never repay to the king. And yet the king, out of sheer compassion for the servant, forgave the entire debt.

There are a number of takeaways from this parable. **In Christ, we
have received extravagant grace**. To use the analogy of the debt this
servant owed, there is no price-tag that you or I could ever put on our
sinfulness before an infinitely holy God. When you and I think, "Well, I
haven't sinned as much as this person or that person," we show that
we have no clue as to the extent of our own sin. Our debt is deep—
infinitely deep. But Christ has paid it. Out of sheer compassion, the
Father sent His Son to endure the wrath you and I deserve, and now
we are free from sin's penalty—free not only as a servant, but as a son!

Because we have received extravagant grace in Christ, **as Christians,
we now extend extravagant grace**. How harsh for this servant who was
forgiven a large fortune to go to a man who owed him a tiny fraction

of that amount and put him in prison for failure to pay. That's outlandish! Yet for a Christian not to forgive is to do the exact same thing. The Bible is not saying that it's *easy* to forgive or that it's *natural* to forgive; however, it's *Christian* to forgive. In fact, the Christian has no other option. We forgive not because we have to, but because in love we are compelled to.

Only Jesus can enable the kind of forgiving heart this passage calls for. Gratefully, He reminds us of the extravagant compassion He has shown to us as the least deserving sinners, and by His grace, He enables us to extend that same extravagant compassion to those whom we would label as the least deserving. This kind of forgiveness should characterize the church.

How Shall We Respond?

There are a number of ways to respond to a text like Matthew 18. **As a part of a local church, we must care for every individual member**. This is a challenge for all churches, and larger churches face some especially thorny questions in this regard; nevertheless, this is a challenge we must take up. One way to begin is by **elevating church membership**. Being a member of a local church is not very important to most professing Christians today. Church hopping and shopping are common in much of evangelicalism, as people are wary of committing themselves to a church. If this passage teaches us anything, it teaches us that it's important for every Christian to be committed to a church. By doing so, we say to the church body, "If you wander from the Lord, I'm coming after you, and if I wander from the Lord, I want you to come after me." This is the kind of care Jesus calls us to.

Matthew 18 should also lead us to respond on a more personal level. Here are some helpful questions for application. **As Christians**:

- Are you causing, leading, or enabling a brother or sister to sin?
- Are you guarding, protecting, and nurturing your own personal holiness?
- How can you more clearly express the love of the Father to the church around you?
- Is there anyone you need to humbly confront concerning sin for their good and for the Father's glory?
- Are you harboring any bitterness or unforgiveness toward someone else?

These are not easy questions to deal with in our lives, and these are not easy issues to deal with in the church. It would be easier, or so we think, just to sit back and ignore these questions. That's the tack that many churches have taken today. But as followers of Christ, we don't have the option of ignoring these issues. Why not? Because of how we have been loved: the Father has protected us, pursued us, restored us, and forgiven us. How, then, can we not pursue others as individuals and as churches with this kind of love? Obedience is not an option when it comes to church discipline, and we shouldn't want it to be. **May the love of the Father through Christ compel the love of His children in the church.**

Reflect and Discuss

1. What does it mean to become like children in verse 3? What is the difference between having childlike faith and being immature in your faith?
2. How does the requirement of humility in verses 1-4 compare with our culture's view of greatness?
3. Explain how a biblical view of the church goes against a culture that prizes independence?
4. How should the parable of the Lost Sheep in verses 10-14 inform our view of church discipline?
5. Respond to the following objection to church discipline: If our church disciplines members, then unbelievers will be turned off and discouraged from coming.
6. What is the ultimate goal of church discipline?
7. What does Matthew 18 have to add to our view of church membership?
8. List things that should and should not be matters of church discipline.
9. What is the main point of the parable of the Unforgiving Servant (vv. 23-35)?
10. If you aren't showing mercy to others, how might that be an indication that you are not being shaped by the gospel?

The Gospel and Divorce

MATTHEW 19:1-12

Main Idea: God created and defined the covenant of marriage, and therefore He alone sets the grounds for divorce, which He hates; nevertheless, God continues to hold out hope in the gospel for all who have disobeyed Him in this area.

I. **God Created Marriage.**
   A. Marriage is defined by God; only God can make marriage and only God can break marriage.
   B. Marriage is a covenant under God, a demonstration to the world of Christ's covenant with His people.

II. **God Hates Divorce.**
   A. Divorce is always a result of sin.
   B. Divorce is almost always sinful.

III. **God Regulates Divorce.**
   A. One ground for divorce in Matthew 19: adultery
   B. One ground for divorce in 1 Corinthians 7: abandonment
   C. Remarriage is biblically permissible only for the offended spouse after a biblical divorce.

IV. **God Redeems Divorce.**
   A. He is always forgiving and He is always faithful.
   B. He will never commit adultery against you and He will never abandon you.

V. **Practical Application**
   A. If you are single, maximize your singleness to advance the gospel.
   B. If you are married, love your spouse in a way that portrays the gospel.
   C. If you are considering divorce, remember the preciousness and power of the gospel.
   D. If you are divorced for a biblical reason and single, rest in the gospel in your singleness or possibly in a future marriage.
   E. If you are divorced for an unbiblical reason and single, repent and rely on the gospel to glorify God in your singleness.

F.   If you are divorced for an unbiblical reason and remarried,
     repent and reflect the gospel in your current marriage.

I t's probably not a stretch to say that every member of your church has
been affected in some way by divorce. Whether it's someone in the
family, a friend, or another church member, this issue likely hits close
to home. Few things are more painful than divorce, and its impact on
our culture cannot be overestimated. This is the very issue Jesus is asked
about at the beginning of chapter 19. His reply certainly doesn't fit with
our current cultural expectations, and many people today consider it
outdated. However, God's design for marriage hasn't changed, and His
Word is still *the* authority in this matter. For the good of our marriages
and the glory of His name, we desperately need to hear the voice of the
One who created marriage in the first place.

This first section of Matthew 19 centers on Jesus' dialogue with
the Pharisees about divorce (vv. 3-9). He has just come to Judea from
Galilee, and His ministry of healing continues. The dialogue began as
the Pharisees posed the following question: "Is it lawful for a man to
divorce his wife on any grounds?"

As we think about the Pharisees' question and Jesus' reply in this
passage, we can't help but think of the issue of divorce in our own context. We must consider this issue with care in the church, and at the
same time we must have confidence in God's design as we engage our
culture. Few times in history has it been so easy to break one's commitment to marriage. All you need is a statement of irreconcilable differences. In fact, you can even get divorced online—cheaply, quickly, and
without leaving your computer. Far too often, we practically ignore this
issue in the church. We insulate ourselves and isolate one another as
we struggle to know how to walk alongside brothers and sisters who are
considering divorce or have been divorced. The result is that Christians
oftentimes go running to court to address marital conflict when we
should be running to the church.

If a Christian is contemplating divorce today, the first person he
or she often contacts is sadly a divorce lawyer. Now to be clear, I'm
not advocating disobedience to civil law, but based on Scripture, God
has a different way of dealing with these issues among His people.
Paul says to the Corinthians, "If any of you has a legal dispute against
another, do you dare go to court before the unrighteous, and not
before the saints?" (1 Cor 6:1). In Matthew 18, Jesus laid out how

disputes between Christian husbands and wives are intended to be addressed, namely, through church discipline and restoration (Matt 18:15-20). As believers, we share life with each other, and among married couples, this inevitably involves sharing marital struggles with one another. Authentic biblical community is intended to provide a nurturing environment for all sorts of conflict in our lives, including marital conflict. In my own church, this happens primarily in small groups, where members walk together honestly and lovingly through conflict and struggle.

Far too often, we as the church have sat back, abdicated our biblical responsibilities, and watched the state take over the institution of marriage in such a way that the church is hardly involved at all. While I have great respect for men and women who work in the legal profession, we should not let lawyers or judges determine the fate of our families. Taking a Christian brother or sister to court for divorce discredits the testimony of the church and it disgraces the name of Christ (1 Cor 6:1-8). What are we saying to an increasingly secular court system when half of the divorce cases they are dealing with involve two supposed Christians? In the same way, lawyers who are professing Christians should not be building their careers on making divorce cheap and easy. Such individuals should repent and seek the forgiveness of God for scorning His design for the glory of Christ in marriage.

So how should all of this affect the way we approach divorce in the church? The church, I believe, has a two-fold responsibility in addressing divorce. First, God calls us to **comfort one another with love**. We come alongside divorced persons, including children of divorce, in order to help them find joy, forgiveness, and strength in Christ. Instead of isolating them or ignoring their situation, we weep with them, serve them, and point them to the ever-constant presence of God and the ever-faithful Word of God.

The second responsibility of the church is to **confront one another with truth**. We want to comfort others, but we don't want to comfort with falsehood; that would be no comfort at all. We want to avoid saying what "feels" best in divorce situations, or possibly even twisting what Scripture says to make it fit what a struggling husband or wife wants to hear. That is unloving and deceptive, and though it may seem to have benefits in the short-term, it has disastrous consequences. In the long-term, we trust that communicating scriptural truths will produce countless blessings for future generations.

God Created Marriage
MATTHEW 19:1-6

Based on Matthew 19, four truths emerge related to divorce from the mouth of Jesus. First, in an appeal to God's original design, Jesus points out that God created marriage. He quotes Genesis 2:24 to make the point that a man is to be "joined to his wife" and that the "two will become one flesh" (Matt 19:5). Jesus very clearly says that **marriage is defined by God**. God authored it and designed it; therefore He defines it.

We cannot redefine what only God has the prerogative to define. Marriage is the one-flesh union of a man and a woman in a whole-hearted, mutual, and lifelong relationship. This is Jesus' point in verse 6: "Therefore, what *God* has joined together, man must not separate" (emphasis added). **Only God can make marriage and only God can break marriage**. One author has put it this way:

> If marriage were of human origin, then human beings would
> have a right to set it aside. But since God instituted marriage,
> only He has the right to do so. . . . Marriage as an institution
> (which includes individual marriages, of course) is subject to
> the rules and regulations set down by God. . . . Individuals may
> marry, be divorced and be remarried only if, when and how
> He says they may without sinning. . . . The state has been given
> the task of keeping orderly records, etc., but it has no right
> (or competence) to determine the rules for marriage and for
> divorce; that prerogative is God's. (Adams, *Marriage, Divorce,
> and Remarriage in the Bible*, 4)

It's not only the state that lacks the right and competence to define marriage; we *all* lack this authority. God's Word must be *the* starting point for any discussion of divorce. We must be willing to submit our lives and our churches to His authority.

Once we've established that marriage is defined by God, we also need to see that **marriage is a covenant under God**. This covenant between a man and a woman is a reflection of God's covenant-keeping nature, for **marriage is a demonstration to the world of Christ's covenant with His people**. In Ephesians 5:22-33 Paul says that God created marriage to be a depiction of Christ's love for His church. As long as Christ is faithful to His bride, husbands must be faithful to their brides; on the day that Christ discards His church, then a man can divorce his wife. But that won't happen, and marriage is designed to show that it won't happen.

God Hates Divorce
MATTHEW 19:7-8

Given that marriage was created by God, and given the implications that flow from that, it makes sense that God hates divorce. Divorce is fundamentally at odds with His purpose in creation. This helps us understand Jesus' response to the Pharisees when they asked Him about Moses' teaching on divorce. In verse 7 the Pharisees pointed to allowances for divorce in the Old Testament, and Jesus tells them that these allowances were made to address the hardness of the hearts of God's people. These permissions of divorce were definitively not God's original design. **Divorce is always a result of sin**. Remember that marriage is the uniting of two dreadful sinners, so that in any marital conflict, no matter how complex, sin is always involved. Furthermore, **divorce is almost always sinful**. The cases where divorce is allowed in Scripture, which we'll see more about below, are few.

God Regulates Divorce
MATTHEW 19:9

As we consider the possible scenarios in which Scripture allows for divorce, we need to keep in mind that God regulates divorce. Although divorce was not a part of God's original plan for marriage, passages like Deuteronomy 24, Matthew 19, and 1 Corinthians 7 all address this issue. God isn't giving us truths that are open to be added to or taken away from by pastors, counselors, lawyers, or anyone else in the twenty-first century. He is giving us non-negotiable commands to be obeyed. Pastors and scholars whom I respect deeply have disagreed over the meaning of these passages, but none of us has the right to alter God's regulations.

After Jesus quoted from Genesis 2:24 and spoke of the permanence of the marital union, the Pharisees gave a follow-up question based on the permission for divorce in the Old Testament law in Deuteronomy 24:1-4. They were essentially trying to pin Jesus down, as there were different schools of thought in first-century Judaism about what might allow for divorce. One school of thought believed that a man could divorce his wife if she had committed any type of immodest behavior or sexual

immorality (the school of Shammai). The other school of thought
(Hillel, the more dominant point of view) interpreted Deuteronomy
24 much more broadly, saying that divorce was possible whenever a wife
did anything displeasing to her husband. This latter interpretation of
the law basically led to men divorcing their wives for just about any reason. This is the background for the question posed to Jesus (Blomberg,
Matthew, 289–90).

Scripture arguably gives two biblical grounds for divorce, and one of
them is given in Matthew 19:9. Jesus replied to the Pharisees, "Whoever
divorces his wife, except for sexual immorality, and marries another,
commits adultery." In that one sweeping statement, Jesus clearly nar-
rowed the parameters in this discussion by allowing for **one ground for
divorce in Matthew 19: adultery**. There's some debate about the word
for sexual immorality here—*porneia*—which is a word used to refer to all
kinds of sexual sin in the Bible. Yet in the context of this passage where
Jesus has just referred to the one-flesh union of marriage, the picture
seems to be one of a spouse who violates that one-flesh union. That is a
serious violation, not only against a spouse, but also against God.

Adultery in the Old Testament was punishable by stoning.
Deuteronomy 22:22 says, "If a man is discovered having sexual relations
with another man's wife, both the man who had sex with the woman and
the woman must die" (see also Lev 20:10). No wonder Proverbs 6:32 says
that the one who commits adultery "lacks sense" and "destroys himself."
Anyone even flirting with the idea of adultery ought to consider the
warning in Proverbs 7 about the seductive adulteress. Here's a sample:

> She seduces him with her persistent pleading;
> she lures with her flattering talk.
> He follows her impulsively like an ox going to the slaughter,
> like a deer bounding toward a trap
> until an arrow pierces its liver,
> like a bird darting into a snare—
> he doesn't know it will cost him his life.
>
> Now, my sons, listen to me,
> and pay attention to the words of my mouth.
> Don't let your heart turn aside to her ways;
> don't stray onto her paths.
> For she has brought many down to death;

her victims are countless.
Her house is the road to Sheol,
descending to the chambers of death. (Prov 7:21-27)

To further underscore the seriousness of adultery, consider the following warnings in the New Testament:

Do not be deceived: No sexually immoral people . . . adulterers . . . will
inherit God's kingdom. (1 Cor 6:9-10)

Marriage must be respected by all, and the marriage bed kept
undefiled, because God will judge immoral people and adulterers.
(Heb 13:4)

[The] sexually immoral . . . their share will be in the lake that burns
with fire and sulfur. (Rev 21:8)

In light of these and other verses, adultery is an extremely serious offense against God. But notice that Jesus did not say that divorce is certain or required in such situations. Instead, He says that **divorce is possible in this situation**. Initially, it may sound as if Jesus were lining up with the first school of thought among first-century Jews (those who allowed for divorce in cases of sexual immorality), but these Jews would have seen divorce as more certain in cases of sexual immorality. In Jesus' view we begin to see the radical implications of the gospel for divorce in Scripture. He is approaching the possibility of divorce in a redemptive manner, which was a totally different perspective from these Pharisees.

The Pharisees were searching for circumstances in which it would be possible to end a marriage relationship, but Jesus says that **we are not looking for reasons to divorce**. The goal is not to look for a loophole in the law; instead, **we are longing for reconciliation to occur**. Remember that this teaching in Matthew 19 comes right on the heels of the parable of the unforgiving servant in Matthew 18, where Jesus taught His disciples to forgive extravagantly (Matt 18:21-35). The implication is that we are to work and pray toward reconciliation and restoration, not because it's easy, but because Christ is in you. Divorce is possible, but because of the gospel, it's not inevitable.

In addition to this passage in Matthew 19, Scripture does seem to point to **one ground for divorce in 1 Corinthians 7: abandonment**. Paul is talking about marriage between a believer and an unbeliever, and he says the following in verses 12-14:

> *If any brother has an unbelieving wife and she is willing to live with him, he must not leave her. Also, if any woman has an unbelieving husband and he is willing to live with her, she must not leave her husband. For the unbelieving husband is set apart for God by the wife, and the unbelieving wife is set apart for God by the husband.*

Paul teaches that a believing spouse should not initiate divorce with an unbelieving spouse, but should stay married and work toward that unbelieving spouse's salvation. However, in the case that the unbelieving spouse wants to leave, he says that the Christian spouse is "not bound in such cases" (v. 15). In other words, if an unbelieving spouse chooses to abandon a believing spouse despite that believing spouse's love for them, then **divorce is preferable in this situation**. We don't initiate this kind of divorce, but we don't have to fight it if someone insists on leaving.

The fact that the Bible mentions adultery and abandonment as the only proper grounds for divorce has caused some people to conclude that the Bible's teaching is impractical or unrealistically narrow. But God is wise. He has not been caught unaware by the challenges of the twenty-first century, for even though there are all sorts of new challenges and struggles that marriages encounter, God doesn't leave us to fend for ourselves. He has given us the church, including its discipline and restoration, to be the means by which we walk through pain, hurt, neglect, and marital strife together. When a brother or sister continues in sin against his or her spouse, we address that in a serious manner with the gospel. This is yet another reason church membership, the sharing of life with one another, is so crucial as we follow Christ.

Outside of adultery and abandonment, divorce leads to adultery in remarriage. **Remarriage is biblically permissible only for the offended spouse after a biblical divorce**. Again, there are biblical scholars and Bible-believing pastors who would say that remarriage is not even permissible then; however, it seems that Scripture is at least implying that remarriage is permissible when divorce is permissible. Practically speaking, then, the non-adulterous spouse in the first exception (adultery) and the Christian spouse in the second exception (abandonment) can remarry according to these passages. Outside of these parameters, if a man or woman divorces his or her spouse, then he or she is not free to remarry (widows and widowers being the only exceptions). Such remarriage would be adulterous.

God Redeems Divorce

So far we've looked at the following truths: God created marriage, God hates divorce, and God regulates divorce as a result of sin in our hearts. All of that may sound like very bad news if you've been a part of a divorce; however, that's not the whole story. God redeems divorce, and those who have been involved in a divorce still have reason to hope.

Undoubtedly this subject brings old and new wounds to the surface, as these are tough words in Scripture for some people to hear, but there's a reason divorce is addressed like this. **The reason God is so serious in His Word about our marriage covenants with each other is because He is so serious about His marriage covenant with us**. Christians who have been a part of a divorce are still part of the bride of Christ. Jesus is worthy of our praise because **He is always forgiving and He is always faithful**.

Even if the marriage covenant in your life was broken in the past, know that the ultimate marriage covenant is still firmly intact. God picks you up daily where you are, and He carries on His covenant of love with you. Unlike an earthly spouse, **He will never commit adultery against you and He will never abandon you**. No matter what happens in this world, Jesus never forsakes His bride—never! This is the gospel.

There's a risk in emphasizing God's grace like this, and it might lead some who are thinking of getting a divorce to think, "Even if this is not biblical, God will forgive me." This thought process completely misses the gospel and deliberately dishonors God. Nevertheless, this is a risk we must take for the sake of divorced brothers and sisters who are sincerely looking to the grace of Jesus Christ. He is an Eternal Savior who is gracious and merciful, and He is committed to sustaining and satisfying you forever.

Practical Application
MATTHEW 19:10-12

There are a number of ways these truths play out practically. In verse 10 the disciples responded to Jesus' teaching on divorce by saying, "If the relationship of a man with his wife is like this, it's better not to marry!" Jesus told them that people were eunuchs—that is, single and pure—for different reasons, but that some were eunuchs for the sake of the kingdom of heaven (v. 12). That is, there are individuals who, for the sake of usefulness in the Lord's work, feel as if God has given them an ability to stay single and pure. Even for singles who desire to marry someday, there is still a secondary application: **if you are single, maximize your singleness to advance the gospel**. More of your time and attention can be given to the Lord.

In Matthew 19 and 1 Corinthians 7, we see Jesus and Paul commending singleness for the spread of God's kingdom. It's not that marriage is bad, but it is not best for all people. Many people think that you have to be married in order to live a complete life, but that is simply not true. Jesus was the most complete man, the most fully human person who ever lived, yet He was not married. In fact, many of the heroes of the New Testament and church history were not married. God has used and continues to use single people for His purposes.

Whatever your situation, there are biblical applications that can be drawn from this passage. Consider where you fit it in among these possibilities.

If you are married, love your spouse in a way that portrays the gospel. Husbands, love your wives with sacrificial love and take responsibility for the glory of Christ in your marriage. Wives, respect your husbands and honor Christ through building your husband up as the spiritual leader of your home.

If you are considering divorce, remember the preciousness and power of the gospel. I encourage you to ask, first, if you have biblical grounds for divorce. If you do not, I want to urge you to consider how in the context of your marriage, and possibly with the help of the church, you can resolve the conflict, which is undeniably real and damaging. This is only possible through the preciousness and power of the gospel, but any other route is sinfully disobedient to God. On the other hand, if you do have biblical grounds for divorce, I want to likewise encourage you to consider the preciousness and power of the gospel with a view toward reconciliation in your marriage, possibly with the help of others in the church. The gospel can change even the hardest and darkest of hearts, so keep restoration and reconciliation at the forefront of your desires even if you begin the process of divorce.

If you are divorced for a biblical reason and single, rest in the gospel in your singleness or possibly in a future marriage. If you were divorced on biblical grounds, i.e., in cases of adultery or abandonment, then I encourage you to rest in the singleness God has given to you at this time. If He grants you continued singleness, I pray that by the power of the gospel He will enable you to rejoice in it. If He doesn't and He leads you to remarry, I pray that by the power of the gospel you will display the love of Christ for His church in your remarriage.

If you are divorced for an unbiblical reason and single, repent and rely on the gospel to glorify God in your singleness. Repent of your sin both to God and to your former spouse. Then let the gospel of Christ give you great hope for a life that thrives in the advancement of the gospel as a single while you await the next wedding where we will join Jesus together for all of eternity.

If you are divorced for an unbiblical reason and married, repent and reflect the gospel in your current marriage. If you divorced for unbiblical reasons, Scripture encourages you to repent genuinely before God and your former spouse. However, Scripture nowhere indicates that you should break another covenant marriage by divorcing again. Instead, Scripture encourages you to focus on magnifying Christ in the marriage you have now by the power of the gospel.

Based on Jesus' teaching in Matthew 19 and the whole of God's Word, let's pray that the grace and glory of Christ will be displayed in the church through the way we obey the Word and apply the gospel to marriage, divorce, and singleness in our day.

Reflect and Discuss

1. List some ways that our culture's view of marriage is unbiblical (think TV, radio, advertising, etc.).
2. Why is it crucial to begin our discussion on marriage with God's design in Genesis? Discuss the idea that divorce is fundamentally an offense against God.
3. What wrong messages about Christ and His redemption are communicated to the world when Christians don't obey God's Word concerning marriage and divorce?
4. How can churches show both tenderness and courage in confronting the issue of divorce?
5. Why was the Pharisees' questioning misguided and wrongly motivated?
6. If a friend asked, "When is it OK to get a divorce?" how would you answer?
7. Why is it so crucial for Christians to take the approach that we ought to be looking for every opportunity to reconcile?

8. What are practical steps to strengthen an existing marriage?
9. What does it mean practically for a single person to maximize his singleness?
10. What counsel would you give to someone who had been divorced and who thought their usefulness in God's kingdom had ended? How would you counsel someone who had abandoned a spouse?
11. How might a wrong view of marriage and divorce be a precursor to other issues in society such as homosexuality, abortion, etc.?

Miraculous Mercy

MATTHEW 19:13–20:34

Main Idea: Salvation is a free gift of divine mercy totally devoid of human merit.

I. **One Overarching Truth**
II. **The Little Children and the Rich Man**
    A. One primary truth from this correlation:
        1. Jesus receives the humble.
        2. Jesus rejects the proud.
    B. Many secondary truths in these illustrations:
        1. Children are important to the heart of Jesus.
        2. Children are safe in the arms of Jesus.
        3. Jesus' call to salvation demands radical surrender.
        4. We must realize the dangerous, deadly nature of desire for possessions.
        5. We must understand our use of money and possessions in the context of redemptive history.
        6. Jesus' call to salvation guarantees radical reward.
III. **The First and the Last**
    A. God's grace is surprising.
    B. God's grace is sovereign.
IV. **Twelve Proud Disciples**
    A. Why Jesus came
        1. He came to suffer.
        2. He came to save.
        3. He came to be our substitute.
        4. He came to show us how to live.
        5. He came to serve us.
    B. What this means
        1. Jesus is our servant.
        2. We are Jesus' servants.
    C. How we respond
        1. We trust Jesus to serve us.
        2. We exalt Jesus by serving others.

V. Two Blind Men
   A. Boldly confess your need for His mercy.
   B. Humbly believe in His power to do the miraculous.

This section of Matthew's Gospel contains several stories that at first seem completely unrelated, at least on the surface. After all, what do children (19:13-15), rich people (19:16-30), workers in a vineyard (20:1-16), Jesus' prediction of His own death and resurrection (20:17-19), a mother's request for her sons' future reward (20:1-28), and the healing of two blind men (20:29-34) have to do with one another? You might be surprised. Among the various truths we can glean from these stories, there stands one overarching truth, a truth that is foundational throughout Scripture and that is crucial for the entire Christian life.

One Overarching Truth

The one overarching truth running through Matthew 19:13–20:24 is that **salvation is a free gift of divine mercy totally devoid of human merit**. Quite simply, salvation is impossible without the mercy of God. This is good news for unbelievers *and* believers, for all of us should live our lives by relying on God's mercy and not our own works and efforts. We'll see how this plays out first with little children and a rich man.

The Little Children and the Rich Man
MATTHEW 19:13-30

Each of the first three Gospels tells the story of the rich young man preceded by the story of Jesus gathering children around Himself (Mark 19:13-31; Luke 18:15-30). There's clearly a reason why these stories appear back-to-back, though the correlation may not be immediately obvious. In one story Jesus *received* people—children—and then in the next story, to our surprise, Jesus *rejected* someone—a rich man. Or consider this from the perspective of the disciples: Jesus received those whom the disciples thought He should reject, and He rejected a man the disciples thought He should receive. There is, then, **one primary truth from this correlation**, and it has two sides.

First, **Jesus receives the humble**. We saw this truth in the previous chapter when Jesus said, "Therefore, whoever humbles himself like this child—this one is the greatest in the kingdom of heaven" (Matt 18:4).

Children are a living illustration of the humility that should characterize Christ's followers. In verse 14 Jesus warns the disciples that the children must not be prevented from coming to Him. The kingdom belongs to the humble, not the haughty.

Second, if you are arrogant before God, you will miss the kingdom of heaven, for **Jesus rejects the proud**. This rich man[40] thought that he could gain eternal life. In verse 16 he asked Jesus, "Teacher, what good must I do to have eternal life?" Jesus told the man that he needed to keep God's commandments (v. 17). When the man claimed to have kept the commandments, Jesus put His finger on the real issue, saying, "Go, sell your belongings and give to the poor, and you will have treasure in heaven. Then come, follow Me" (v. 21). The point to take away is not that this man would have earned eternal life if he had only been willing to give up his riches. We need to look deeper than that, to the condition of this man's heart. This rich man did not come to Jesus humbly, willing to do and give whatever Jesus asked. If he had trusted Jesus, he would have gladly sold his possessions and given them to the poor. But his heart was proud and he clung to his possessions, so he walked away, and frighteningly, Jesus let him go.

Following His encounter with this rich man, Jesus turned to address His disciples on this matter. He says in verse 24 that it is "easier for a camel to go through the eye of a needle than for a rich person to enter the kingdom of God." The "eye of a needle" is not a reference to a tiny side gate leading to the city of Jerusalem, though that has been a popular interpretation of this verse. There is no evidence that this gate existed in Jesus' day (Keener, *A Commentary on the Gospel of Matthew*, 477). Moreover, this explanation misses the point of the passage. It's not merely *hard* for a rich man to enter the kingdom of heaven; it's impossible! Wealth was and continues to be a huge stumbling block for those who want to enter God's kingdom. In our sin, we are naturally drawn to trust our own resources rather than the One who is all sufficient. This truth applies to more than just rich people, though. It's impossible for any man to do anything to enter the kingdom of heaven. So the disciples ask, "Then who can be saved?" (v. 25). Jesus says that it's only possible with God, for we need Him to do the impossible. This brings us back to the one overarching truth in this section: Salvation has

---

[40] This man is referred to as a "ruler" in Luke's Gospel (Luke 18:18), which is why he is often referred to as the "rich young ruler."

absolutely nothing to do with human merit and absolutely everything to do with divine mercy.

In addition to this one overarching truth concerning God's mercy, there are **many secondary truths in these illustrations**, truths taught throughout Scripture. For example, we know that **children are important to the heart of Jesus**. In Matthew 18 Jesus referred to physical children as an illustration of His spiritual children, but here children are not merely an illustration. Jesus quite literally laid His hands on children and received them; they were (and are) important to Him. His example beckons us to do the same. We are to care for children, nurturing them in every way, particularly in regard to spiritual things. J. C. Ryle said,

> Let us draw encouragement from these verses to attempt great
> things in the religious instruction of children. Let us begin
> from their very earliest years to deal with them as having souls
> to be lost or saved, and let us strive to bring them to Christ;
> let us make them acquainted with the Bible as soon as they
> can understand anything; let us pray with them, and pray for
> them, and teach them to pray for themselves. The seed sown
> in infancy is often found after many days. (Ryle, *Matthew*, 170)

Moms and dads should strive to teach their children to know God and His ways. They should pray *for* them and pray *over* them. Family worship is one way to put these things into practice,[41] in addition to daily instructions and being an example of godly living. While moms and dads should (ideally) be the ones who see to the spiritual formation of children, this calling should also be important to the church. Churches should think through how they can most effectively pass the gospel on to the next generation. And it's not just *our* children; we are to care for *other* children, both in our neighborhood and around the world. Through our sacrificial giving, we can see children in poverty escape physical death and begin to thrive. Even better, we can see the gospel made available to children who would not otherwise hear of Jesus Christ. Every child is important to Him.

Pastorally, the topic of Jesus' care for children can be applied in a number of ways. One important question has to do with the heart-wrenching issue of whether or not children who die in infancy go to

---

[41] For help thinking through family worship, see Donald S. Whitney, *Family Worship: In the Bible, in History and in Your Home*, 2006.

heaven. We might also include within this question children who die in a miscarriage, or children who die at a young age before they are able to grasp the gospel.[42] Scripture does not address this issue directly; however, it does give us good reason to trust that **children are safe in the arms of Jesus**. I think we can point to three primary reasons for this position.

First, God is gracious and merciful and good (Exod 34:6). As the Judge of all the earth, He always does what is right (Gen 18:25). God desires all people to be saved (1 Tim 2:4; 2 Pet 3:9), and He cares particularly about children according to Matthew 19:13-15. Yet these truths are insufficient in and of themselves to prove that children go to heaven, for otherwise *all* unbelievers would be safe due to God's free grace. Nevertheless, our thinking on this question must begin with the reality of God's character. This God whom we meet in Scripture cares particularly for children, and He is good.

Second, the Bible seems to express confidence that believers will see young children after death. After losing his own young son, David worships God and says, "But now that he is dead, why should I fast? Can I bring him back again? I'll go to him, but he will never return to me" (2 Sam 12:23). David comforts his wife with this hope. In this example, Scripture expresses confidence and a comfort that all who trust in God's salvation will be with such children again.

The third reason that supports the idea that children who die in infancy are safe in the arms of Jesus has to do with the level of accountability God holds these little ones to. The Bible seems to indicate that young children are held to a different measure of accountability than those who are older and more capable of grasping truth. This is not what some have referred to as an "age of accountability," a certain age when a child becomes accountable before God for his or her sin. Instead, this is the idea that, according to Scripture, God holds us accountable before Him based on a couple of criteria.

First, we are liable to God's judgment because we have an understanding of right and wrong. Romans 2:14-16 says that we have God's moral law written on our hearts, so that all people everywhere know good and evil, right and wrong. This is not the same case in the same

---

[42] Along with infants, we could also include in this category those persons with physical and mental impairments that prevent them from understanding foundational truths about God and His revelation as per Rom 1:19-20.

way with young children. Speaking to disobedient Israel, Deuteronomy 1:39 refers to the children as "your little children . . . who don't know good from evil." In this context, the children were not held accountable for the disobedience of the Israelites in their day. Even though God had cursed the Israelites, the children were allowed to enter the Promised Land.

The second criterion that affects our accountability before God in judgment is found in Romans 1:18-21:

> *For God's wrath is revealed from heaven against all godlessness and unrighteousness of people who by their unrighteousness suppress the truth, since what can be known about God is evident among them, because God has shown it to them. For His invisible attributes, that is, His eternal power and divine nature, have been clearly seen since the creation of the world, being understood through what He has made. As a result, people are without excuse. For though they knew God, they did not glorify Him as God or show gratitude. Instead, their thinking became nonsense, and their senseless minds were darkened.*

This passage teaches that God has revealed His glory to all people, and this revelation leaves them without excuse for rejecting His glory. However, if a child is unable to know or perceive God's glory, then that child does not have the same level of moral culpability before God. Unlike everyone else, this child is *not* "without excuse" (Rom 1:20). Therefore, the child will not be judged in the same way everyone else is judged.

To be clear, having a different standard of accountability doesn't mean that young children stand innocent before God. The Bible is clear that we all have a sinful nature at the core of who we are; no one is innocent (Eph 2:3; Rom 3:9-20). A child does not learn to sin, but rather expresses the sinful nature that is inherent in all of us. Therefore, anyone who is saved from God's judgment is saved because of God's grace in Christ. Colossians 1:19-23 indicates that Christ is the only way we are reconciled to God. Therefore, young children still need the grace and righteousness of Christ attributed to them in some way. So how does God do this? Admittedly, there is mystery here; God does this in accordance with His infinite wisdom. Yet, given the way God saves people throughout Scripture, we should not be surprised to find out that the salvation of young children comes as a gift. It is not of human merit, but completely of divine mercy.

There are also a few secondary truths we can glean from Jesus' interaction with the rich man in this passage. Since we are among the wealthiest people ever to walk the planet, the story of a man whose riches kept him from the kingdom of heaven certainly hits close to home. We need to be reminded that **Jesus' call to salvation demands radical surrender**. Despite our current practices and our best intentions, salvation is not an invitation to pray a prayer. Salvation is a summons to lose your life, to let go of everything you have and everything you are in submission to Jesus. *This* is what it means to be a Christian.

It's worth noting two common errors in handling this passage. On one hand, some people universalize it, saying that every follower of Jesus should sell everything they have and give the proceeds to the poor. But we know this is not true based on what we see in the rest of the New Testament. Not every disciple of Jesus is divested of possessions, for Scripture indicates that some of Jesus' disciples still had homes (John 19:27; 20:10) and fishing boats (John 21:3), while a number of women provided for Jesus and His 12 disciples out of their own means (Luke 8:1-3). So this passage clearly isn't saying that a Christian can't own private property or possessions.

On the other hand, our usual tendency is to minimize this passage. Jesus does call some of His followers to sell everything they have and give it to the poor, and the reality is that He could call any of us to do the same. One commentator has said, "That Jesus did not command all his followers to sell all their possessions gives comfort only to the kind of people to whom he would issue that command" (Gundry, *Matthew*, 388). Some have suggested that the rich man in this passage just needed to be *willing* to sell all of his possessions, but that's not what Jesus meant, or else that's what He would have said. He didn't tell the man merely to be *willing* to sell everything he possessed, but to "go, sell your belongings and give to the poor" (v. 21). These were not options for this man to consider; these were commands for this man to obey. We must not dilute the call of Christ, for His call to salvation demands radical surrender.

Another secondary truth illustrated in this story is that **we must realize the dangerous, deadly nature of desire for possessions**. We are accustomed to thinking of wealth only as a blessing, but it is often a barrier in our relationship to God. Paul warns about this fatal temptation:

> *But those who want to be rich fall into temptation, a trap, and many*
> *foolish and harmful desires, which plunge people into ruin and*

> destruction. *For the love of money is a root of all kinds of evil, and*
> *by craving it, some have wandered away from the faith and pierced*
> *themselves with many pains.* (1 Tim 6:9-10)

If even the desire for riches plunges people into ruin and destruction, then consider the danger for people (like us!) whose lives are filled with riches. We can easily slip into a mind-set where our security and our ultimate hope are grounded in our bank account, and not in God. We must run from the desire for riches and the love of money as fast as God's mercy will enable us.

For the follower of Christ, every topic should be considered within a biblical framework, which means that **we must understand our use of money and possessions in the context of redemptive history.** Notice that the disciples were shocked at Jesus' teaching on wealth (v. 25), and their assumptions remind us that we cannot base a theology of wealth on the Old Testament alone. Frequently in the Old Testament, God promised material blessings for spiritual obedience. We see this play out with the patriarchs, with the people of God entering the Promised Land, and with Israel's kings;[43] however, when you get to the pages of the New Testament, material reward is never promised for spiritual obedience. Craig Blomberg makes this very observation:

> The NT carried forward the major principles of the OT and intertestamental Judaism with one conspicuous omission: never was material wealth promised as a guaranteed reward for either spiritual obedience or simple hard work. . . . Material reward for piety never reappears in Jesus' teaching, and [in fact it] is explicitly contradicted throughout. (Blomberg, *Neither Poverty Nor Riches*, 145)

The idea that there is no material reward from God based on obedience was revolutionary in Jesus' day, and it is still revolutionary in our day. God's plan is not to display His glory through Christians who have higher standards of living than the rest of the world; rather, God's plan is to spread His glory through the radical sacrifice of our lives for the

---

[43] Although wealth and possessions were often a part of God's blessing in the Old Testament, the love of money in its various forms was condemned, particularly when the poor were mistreated. See for example: Exod 22:25; Deut 17:14-17; Prov 30:7-9; Jer 9:23.

rest of the world. At this point in redemptive history, this is the mind-set that should shape our view of money.

In light of everything this passage teaches us about money and discipleship, someone might come away thinking that following Jesus is solely about what we give up. A person with this perspective will be surprised to hear that **Jesus' call to salvation guarantees radical reward.** Jesus tells the rich ruler to go and sell his possessions, but He follows it up by saying, "and you will have treasure in heaven" (v. 21). Jesus was not calling the rich man *away from* treasure but *to* treasure. There's actually a tinge of self-serving motivation here, as in, sell everything you have in order to get something better! The question for us is whether we will live for short-term pleasures we cannot keep or for long-term treasure we cannot lose. We don't want to miss the reward in Christ because we want more stuff in this world. Jesus is infinitely better, and His reward is eternal. In verse 29 we see what a wise investment our radical surrender is, for Jesus says that our return will be a hundredfold, both now and in the age to come. That's radical reward.

Jesus closes in verse 30 by saying, "But many who are first will be last, and the last first." This truth serves not only to conclude verses 13-30—where children are received by Jesus, while a respected and wealthy man was turned away—but it also sets the stage for chapter 20.

The First and the Last
MATTHEW 20:1-28

Jesus illustrates the truth that the last will be first and the first will be last by telling the disciples a parable of workers in a vineyard. This parable is not difficult to follow: The workers who were first hired, and thus worked longer than the rest, complained about those who had been hired last. Those workers hired at the eleventh hour only had to work one hour, yet they were equally compensated. We learn from this that **God's grace is surprising**, for it surpasses our normal expectations. We tend to recoil at a story that's all about people *not* getting what they deserve. It's not fair; and that's the point. God's grace in salvation is, by definition, not fair. D. A. Carson has put it rather candidly: "Do you really want nothing but totally effective, instantaneous justice? Then go to hell" (Carson, *How Long, O Lord*, 161). Gratefully, God surprises us with His mercy. **He does what we would never expect according to what we could never earn.** Once again, we see this underlying truth emerge:

God doesn't owe us salvation for something we have done; He gives us salvation *despite* everything we have done. Salvation is a free gift of divine mercy totally devoid of human merit. God owes us nothing, yet He gives us everything in Christ.

Not only is God's grace surprising, but also **God's grace is sovereign**. God is under no obligation to extend forgiveness to sinners like us. **He has the right to dispense His mercy as He pleases**. This is Paul's point in Romans 9, where he answers the objection that God's mercy is not fair: "But who are you, a mere man, to talk back to God?" (Rom 9:20). Mercy is dispensed as God sees fit. This is actually good news for sinners who are unable to save themselves. We have small minds and small ways, but God's grace is wonderfully surprising and gloriously sovereign.

In verses 17-19 we see God's surprising and glorious grace expressed in the sacrifice of His Son. In His mercy, God ordained that His Son would be murdered by sinful men for the sake of our salvation. Jesus told His disciples of His own impending death, a death that would include being "mocked, flogged, and crucified" before being raised again (v. 19).

But the disciples didn't understand Him, a point that becomes evident in verses 20-28. In this passage we have a mom representing the prideful hearts of her sons. James and John wanted a prominent place in Jesus' kingdom, and we know this request ultimately came from them, because when Jesus responds, He addresses them directly (v. 22). In fact, in Mark's account of this story, the mom is not even mentioned (Mark 10:35). Jesus addressed the pride of these two disciples, but they weren't the only ones who needed more humility, as the other ten disciples were indignant when they heard this (v. 24). Their anger likely came from their own pride, so that in the end, the Lord had to address 12 proud disciples.

Twelve Proud Disciples
MATTHEW 20:28

In a statement loaded with theological meaning, Jesus says to His proud disciples, "The Son of Man did not come to be served, but to serve, and to give His life—a ransom for many." Verse 28 gets to the heart of **why Jesus came**, and this truth can be broken down into several related components.

First, **He came to suffer**. The title Jesus used for Himself, "the Son of Man," highlights in a significant way His identification with us as men. As a man, He was able to sympathize with us in our suffering (Heb 4:15), and He was qualified as a sacrificial substitute for sinners (Rom 8:3). When He spoke of the cup that He would drink (Matt 20:22), He was speaking of drinking down the wrath of God in the place of sinners. Jesus willingly walked into the jaws of suffering and death on our behalf.

Verse 28 speaks of a second component to Jesus' coming: **He came to save**. That's what He means when He speaks of giving His life as "a ransom for many." The word Matthew uses for "ransom" is *lutron*, a word that can refer to a payment made to release someone from slavery. Today we might associate this word with a hostage situation, which is fitting given sin's control over us. We are slaves to sin, self, and death, but Jesus gave His life so that we might be free from these things (Rom 6:17; Heb 2:15).

You may be wondering how this is possible, that is, how does Christ's death save us from sin and death? The key lies in that little word "for" in verse 28. In this instance the word carries the sense of "in place of" (Osborne, *Matthew*, 742–43), and it speaks to the fact that **He came to be our substitute**. Jesus gave His life in the place of those He would save. We stand under the weight of our sin and the wrath of God, fully deserving death, but Jesus took our place; He became our substitute. This is the glory of the gospel: not just that Jesus died for you in order to express a loving sentiment, but that He died *instead of* you.[44]

Jesus came to suffer, to save, to be our substitute, and based on this context in Matthew 20, **He came to show us how to live**. Unlike worldly rulers who lorded their authority over people (vv. 25-26), Jesus' disciples were to manifest a different kind of leadership. Like their Master, they were to live selflessly for the good of others. God's glory, and not their own reputation, was to be their goal. The disciples were to love people by serving them. When Jesus tells James and John, "You will drink my cup," He is telling them that they too will lose their lives serving others. To be sure, these disciples didn't experience the cup of suffering that Jesus experienced on the cross in an atoning sense, but their lives would be lived in sacrificial service to others based on what Jesus had done. James was beheaded (Acts 12:2), and John was exiled as a prisoner on

---

[44] For an excellent resource dealing with what Christ's death accomplished, see Leon Morris, *The Apostolic Preaching of the Cross*, 3rd ed. (Grand Rapids: William B. Eerdman Publishing Co., 1965).

the island of Patmos (Rev 1:9). This kind of sacrificial service is what defines kingdom greatness.

Jesus' desire to show us how to live leads to the final purpose for His coming in this context, and this purpose is really at the center of all the others: **He came to serve us**. This truth may seem simple, but it's worth pondering for a moment. The reality here completely reverses our expectations. Consider:

- Jesus did not come to be served by you; He came to serve you.
- Jesus did not come to be helped by you; He came to help you.
- Jesus did not come to be waited on by you; He came to wait on you.

For a religious teacher to talk like this sounds like lunacy. However, unlike earthly rulers, Jesus did not come as some potentate whose personal whims were to be catered to by lowly servants. He came to *be* our lowly servant by becoming a man and providing salvation for us. The One who deserves to *be* served came *to* serve, and this service was ultimately demonstrated on the cross. Matthew may very well be alluding to the "Servant" prophesied by Isaiah, the One who "bore the sin of many" (Isa 53:11-12). We need Him in the profoundest sense of the word; He doesn't need us. We need to consider, then, **what this means**.

Jesus is our servant, but in order to understand what Jesus *does* mean here, we need to make sure we also understand what Jesus *does not* mean. **This does not mean we tell Jesus what to do**; He's not our servant in that way. Mark's Gospel records this kind of misguided approach by James and John, as they told Jesus, "Teacher, we want You to do something for us if we ask You" (Mark 10:35). That's not the way to approach Jesus, as if He is there to do all our bidding. That's a classic example of what this text does not mean.

This text does not mean we tell Jesus what to do, but **this does mean Jesus gives us what we need**. This point is absolutely key to understanding Christianity. Jesus had just told James and John that they were going to suffer and that following Him would involve the radical sacrifice of their lives in service to others. But this radical call to service from Jesus was accompanied by a radical promise from Jesus. To renounce the ways of this world and to give their lives as slaves in this world was not possible, humanly speaking; but Jesus could empower James and John by His service to them.

The one overarching point in this section of Matthew's Gospel surfaces once again: salvation is all of divine mercy, and not by human merit.

That we are utterly and completely dependent on God's mercy is not only true at the point of conversion. Even after we're saved, we are dependent on divine mercy in every part of our lives. Jesus promises to give us what we need on a daily, moment-by-moment basis. When He leads His children into difficult places or calls us to do difficult things, He enables us to do these things because He is our servant.

Some people wonder whether Jesus' teaching in this passage contradicts what Paul and other New Testament authors say about being a "slave," or "servant," of Jesus Christ (Rom 1:1; Jas 1:1; 2 Pet 1:1). The Bible does talk about our service to Him: "Do not lack diligence; be fervent in spirit; *serve* the Lord" (Rom 12:11). So which is it—is Jesus our servant? Or are we supposed to serve Him? Yes . . . and no.

We are Jesus' servants. The Bible is clear on this point. But **this does not mean that Jesus needs our aid**. When some people hear this servant language, they assume that Jesus needs our help. Acts 17:25 is a good corrective here: "Neither is He [God] served by human hands, as though He needed anything, since He Himself gives everyone life and breath and all things." God is Almighty, and He needs no support. We cannot supply His needs, since He has none. He never gets tired, hungry, or lonely. He does not need us; we need Him. So, then, what does the Bible mean when it says we are servants of Jesus? **This does mean that we submit to Jesus' authority**. He reigns over us as Lord and King, and we now gladly live for His glory and His purposes on earth.

How we respond to Jesus says a lot about our view of Him. **We trust Jesus to serve us** because **Jesus' service to us enables our obedience to Him**. Every time Jesus calls us to do something, it is His way of telling us how He wants to serve us. When He calls us to give up everything we have, for example, or when He calls spouses to love each other even when times are tough, in all these situations Jesus aims to serve us and sustain us. Everything Jesus commands us to do is a call to trust Him, and only with such trust is obedience possible.

We are being served at every moment, and as we realize this, **we exalt Jesus by serving others**. As we are strengthened by His power and love, **our service to others demonstrates His sacrifice for us**. This was Jesus' point to His disciples in John 13:35: "By this all people will know that you are My disciples, if you have love for one another."

Two Blind Men

MATTHEW 20:29-34

So far we've had a story of children who in their humility *could* see Jesus and a rich man who in his riches *could not* see Jesus. We've also observed disciples who in their pride were struggling to see the love of Christ. These stories are capped off at the end of chapter 20 with a story of two blind men who, based upon confession of faith in Jesus, the Son of David, were brought from darkness to light.

For those in need of Jesus' help (which is all of us), the application of this story is simple: **boldly confess your need for His mercy**. Throw aside your pride and say, maybe for the first time in your life, "Lord Jesus, have mercy on me." That was the cry of these blind men, for they knew that they could not open their own eyes. They were fully dependent on Jesus' power and kindness. Even if you're already a Christian, the same truth applies: Daily confess your need for Christ's mercy. Trust Him to serve you.

As we boldly confess our need for God's mercy, we also need to **humbly believe in His power to do the miraculous**. We must trust God to do what only He can do. When Jesus asked these two men what they wanted done for them, they responded in verse 33 by saying, "Open our eyes!" They were trusting in the sovereign power of Jesus to cure their blindness. We are reminded one last time in this section that the entirety of the Christian life is based on divine mercy, not human merit.

Reflect and Discuss

1. Why are people so resistant to receiving salvation as a free gift? How does our sinful nature play into this?
2. Explain the difference between Christianity and the false religions of the world with regard to human merit.
3. In your own words, describe what it means to come to Christ like a child.
4. What is the difference between childlike faith and simply being immature in your faith? How can childlike faith exist alongside a diligent and disciplined pursuit of God and His Word?
5. What might Matthew be showing us by contrasting whom Jesus accepted with the rich ruler?

6. In Matthew 19:16-22, was Jesus calling the rich man to earn his salvation by obedience and sacrificial giving? Explain your answer.

7. What does the parable of the workers in a vineyard teach us about God's grace?

8. How does the misguided approach of the disciples beginning in Matthew 20:20 parallel your own approach to God and the Christian life?

9. How does Jesus' healing of the blind men in Matthew 20:29-34 contrast with the request for privilege by James and John in the previous paragraph?

10. Why can't grace and pride coexist? Can you think of other Scriptural passages that speak to this truth?

The King Is Coming
MATTHEW 21:1-22

Main Idea: The glorious attributes of King Jesus are on display during and following His triumphal entry into Jerusalem, the beginning of the climactic ending to His first coming.

I. **Attributes of the King**
   A. He is the divine King.
   B. He is the prophesied King.
   C. He is the righteous King.
   D. He is the Savior King.
   E. He is the gentle King.
   F. He is the peaceful King.
   G. He is the global King.
   H. He is the Messianic King.
   I. He is the compassionate King.
   J. He is the prophetic King.
   K. He is the holy King.
   L. He is the authoritative King.
   M. He is the coming King.
      1. He came the first time humbly riding on a colt
         a. to rescue sinners.
         b. to be crucified as King.
      2. He will come the second time sovereignly reigning on a horse
         a. to rule sinners.
         b. to be crowned as King.

II. **Application to Our Lives**
   A. Let us give Him praise: Gladly surrender to this King today.
   B. Let us prioritize prayer: Continually seek this King every day.
   C. Let us bear fruit in our lives: This King desires—and deserves—more than hollow worship and hypocritical religion.
   D. Let us have faith as His church: This King can—and will—do the impossible when we ask.

The beginning of the end.

That's the best way to describe Matthew 21. For 20 chapters we have journeyed with Jesus from Bethlehem to Egypt to Nazareth, throughout Galilee, into Capernaum and Gennesaret, into the Gentile areas of Tyre and Sidon, to Magadan and Caesarea Philippi, and into Jericho and Judea. Now, for the first time in Matthew's Gospel, Jesus enters Jerusalem.

Matthew 21 records the last week of Jesus' life. For three years Jesus had preached, taught, and healed, and now, during Passover week, He was entering the holy city. It would be difficult to exaggerate the significance of the events that transpire in the remainder of this Gospel. Over a period of eight days, Jesus entered Jerusalem, cleansed the temple, challenged the religious leaders, instituted the Lord's Supper, got arrested, was tried, was crucified, and then was raised from the dead. This was the week all of creation had been waiting for. Back in the garden, God had promised the serpent, "I will put hostility between you and the woman, and between your seed and her seed. He will strike your head, and you will strike his heel" (Gen 3:15). The Son of God ultimately fulfilled that promise, crushing the head of the snake by His death and resurrection. The events of this week, planned before the foundation of the world, were not just climactic for Jesus' life; this was the climactic week for all of history!

Over a quarter of Matthew's Gospel—eight chapters—is devoted to these last eight days. Up to this point, Jesus has told those who were healed not to tell others, since it was not the time for His full identity and purpose to be more fully revealed. For example, when He healed two blind men in Matthew 9:27-31, Matthew writes, "Jesus warned them sternly, 'Be sure that no one finds out!'" (v. 30). However, at the end of Matthew 20, Jesus again healed two blind men, but this time He gave them no such warning (20:29-34).

In Matthew 21 Jesus asserts Himself as the Messiah, the promised King who would save His people from their sins (cf. 1:21). But He was not a King for the Jews only, for His saving rule would extend to the nations. You and I are also part of this purpose, for we are called to submit every part of our lives to His rule and reign. Christ is worthy of our adoration and the abandonment of our lives. In this chapter and the ones to follow, Matthew gives us a breathtaking, awe-inspiring, life-transforming picture of this King who will one day return. His attributes are on display, and the picture is stunning.

Attributes of the King
MATTHEW 21:1-22

In this chapter alone we see (at least) 13 important and glorious attributes of King Jesus. We'll consider each of them below.

God designed every detail of the scene of Jesus' entry to show us the kind of King Jesus is. In the first three verses we see that **He is the divine King**. The glory of the incarnation is evident as Jesus, a man, divinely ordains where a donkey and a colt will be at a certain time for a certain purpose. If the disciples are asked why they are taking the animals, they are to respond, "The Lord needs them" (v. 3). To say that the "Lord" needs these animals in this context means that Jesus is more than one's personal master, teacher, or rabbi, as we might use these terms to show respect. This was a claim to be *the* Lord *of all*.

Next, Matthew points to yet another way in which Jesus fulfills the Old Testament. In verses 4-5 **He is the prophesied King**. The quotation in verse 5 comes from Zechariah 9:9, and "Daughter Zion" is a reference to the inhabitants of Jerusalem.

> *Rejoice greatly, Daughter Zion! Shout in triumph, Daughter Jerusalem! Look, your King is coming to you; He is righteous and victorious, humble and riding on a donkey, on a colt, the foal of a donkey.*

Jerusalem is often referred to in the Bible as Zion, because Mount Zion is the highest, most prominent hill there. Zechariah prophesied to God's people after they had come back from the exile. This remnant of Israelites had come back to Jerusalem to rebuild the temple and re-establish the city. It was a time of joy and of struggle. God's people had repeatedly seen the tragedy of failed kings, but Zechariah held out hope, promising a day when God would send His King. Zechariah 9:9 begins with a note of joy in light of the coming King. It specifies the way He would arrive, and the fulfillment we see here is truly amazing: 500 years before Jesus came, God promised that a donkey and a colt would be available the week before Passover for Jesus to ride into Jerusalem. You don't write a script like that unless you are God!

Jesus not only stands forth as the prophesied King in Zechariah's prophecy, but also **He is the righteous King**. Unlike Israel's other kings, Jesus would be "righteous." Moreover, this righteous King would be "victorious" on behalf of His people, for **He is the Savior King**. This is why the crowds were crying "Hosanna" (Matt 21:9), which literally means, "Save now" (Osborne, *Matthew*, 756). This cry of "Hosanna" is itself a quotation from Psalm 118:25-26, where the psalmist cries, "LORD, save us! LORD, please grant us success! He who comes in the name of the LORD is blessed" (Osborne, *Matthew*, 756).

The timing of these events is also crucial for understanding the significance of these quotations. This was Passover week, a time when the population of Jerusalem would swell up to five or six times its usual size. People were coming to celebrate this feast of remembrance, a feast that reminded them of the time when God rescued their fathers from slavery in Egypt and brought salvation through the blood of a lamb. Now Jesus, the Lamb of God (John 1:29, 36) and the One who was inaugurating a new and greater exodus (Matt 2:13-15), was coming into Jerusalem during Passover week. This was no coincidence.

Despite Jesus' greatness and the significance of His coming, Matthew also tells us that **He is the gentle King**. Jesus did not come arrogantly, but humbly. Unlike other earthly rulers, He was meek (see also Isa 11:4; Matt 5:5). Most people in the West today don't understand the concept of a king. Many of the examples we see of monarchies are monarchies in symbol only. But in most places throughout history, a king would be honored with reverence and fear at his coronation. He would be dressed in ornamental, regal attire, surrounded by splendor and pageantry. Jesus, on the other hand, was surrounded by lowly Galileans as he came into the city not with riches, but in poverty; not in majesty, but in meekness. He came humbly and mounted on a donkey.

Zechariah's prophecy about Jesus also tells us that **He is the peaceful King**. Verse 10 of chapter 9 says that God's king would "proclaim peace to the nations." It was not uncommon for a king to ride on a donkey; the key is *when* a king would ride on a donkey. If a king was going to war, he would ride on a warhorse as a picture of power. When he was not at war, the king would ride on a donkey as a picture of peace. The fact that Jesus came riding on a donkey speaks to His mission as the One who came to make it possible for us to have peace with God. When Luke records this account he notes how the crowds cried out, "*Peace* in heaven and glory in the highest heaven!" (Luke 19:38; emphasis added). Then as Jesus drew near the city and wept, He said, "If you knew this day what would bring peace . . ." (Luke 19:42). This message of peace is good news for those who are by nature enemies of God (Rom 5:10).

Jesus brought a message of peace: peace between God and man, and peace between men. We are reconciled to God through Christ, and we are reconciled to one another in Christ. This message was very different from what many people would have expected. They were looking for a ruler to come wielding his power and to overthrow Israel's oppressors. God's King, however, did not come wielding political power, but bringing spiritual peace. He is the "Prince of Peace" (Isa 9:6).

The peace that Jesus came to bring was not just for Israel. Zechariah had predicted that the coming King would "proclaim peace *to the nations*," and that "His dominion will extend from sea to sea . . . to the ends of the earth" (Zech 9:10; emphasis added). **He is the global King.** Jesus rules over every leader, king, prime minister, and president in the world, and the salvation that He accomplished is good news for all peoples.

Related to Jesus' global reign is another important theme that has surfaced throughout Matthew's Gospel: **He is the Messianic King.** When Jesus entered Jerusalem, the city was "shaken," asking, "Who is this?" (Matt 21:10). Both those who were following Jesus and those ahead of Him were shouting, "Hosanna to the Son of David! . . . This is the prophet Jesus from Nazareth in Galilee!" (vv. 9, 11). The phrase "Son of David" continues to be used in Matthew's Gospel, appearing as early as the first verse in the opening genealogy (1:1). Jesus has been portrayed as the promised Messiah, the King who would come from the line of David. In essence, then, the crowds in verse 9 were shouting, "Messiah, save us!" These crowds may not have known *how* Jesus would save them, since presumably no one, not even the disciples, had connected the dots between Zechariah 9 and Isaiah 53. It was not clear that the conquering King would be the Suffering Servant, that the Messiah would save His people from their sins by shedding His blood during Passover week. The significance of all that was happening in these final chapters of Matthew's Gospel would only be truly realized after Jesus' death and resurrection. Only then would these events and their significance come into focus, through the illumination of the Holy Spirit (John 14:26).

When Jesus arrived in Jerusalem, some people wanted to kill Him (Matt 20:18), but He didn't respond in the way we might expect an earthly king to respond. **He is the compassionate King**, and Luke tells us that Jesus wept over Jerusalem as He approached it (Luke 19:41). The heart of the Messiah was gripped for the sinners He came to save. Even though the crowds who asked, "Who is this?" would soon cry out,

"Crucify Him!" (Mark 15:13), Jesus continued His journey to the cross to suffer and die. This was the ultimate act of compassion.

Amid the questions and the chaos swirling around Jesus, the crowds were partially right in their assessment of His identity. In verse 11 they referred to Him as the "prophet Jesus," which reminds us that **He is the prophetic King**. This statement may not seem noteworthy, but in the context of Matthew's Gospel it is incredibly significant. Matthew 21 gives us a glimpse of Jesus as the fulfillment of the Old Testament, as the perfect prophet, priest, and king. We've already seen Him depicted as King (Matt 21:5), and soon Matthew will portray Jesus in a priestly role in the temple (vv. 12-16), foreshadowing the new way to God He will make for sinners. Likewise, Jesus is a prophet, for He is God's Word revealed to men in the flesh (John 1:1, 14).

In addition to His various roles, Jesus is also unique in terms of His character. There are many things we could say about Jesus' character, but first and foremost **He is the holy King**. Another prophecy made around 500 years before Jesus came witnesses to Christ's holiness and purity. Based on the prophecy in Mal 3:1-4, the Jewish people expected the Messiah to come and purify the temple and the people of Jerusalem. Here is what we read:

> "See, I am going to send My messenger, and he will clear the way before Me. Then the Lord you seek will suddenly come to His temple, the Messenger of the covenant you desire—see, He is coming," says the LORD of Hosts. But who can endure the day of His coming? And who will be able to stand when He appears? For He will be like a refiner's fire and like cleansing lye. He will be like a refiner and purifier of silver; He will purify the sons of Levi and refine them like gold and silver. Then they will present offerings to the LORD in righteousness. And the offerings of Judah and Jerusalem will please the LORD as in days of old and years gone by.

Malachi speaks of God's messenger restoring the worship life of the people of God and purifying the priests. But once again, Jesus fulfills these expectations in a way the people never could have expected. He walked into a scene where people were bustling in the outer court of the temple, known also as the court of the Gentiles, a place for the nations to meet with God in worship, praise, and prayer. Instead of such worship, however, Jesus found a commercial business filled with scores of people selling sacrifices and exchanging money. People were profiting off of one another and even taking advantage of one another, all while ignoring the purpose of the temple. So Jesus, in righteous anger, drove them all out, overturning their tables and their seats (Matt 21:12). He said to them, "It is written, 'My house will be called a house of prayer.' But you are making it a den of thieves!" In Isaiah 56:7, God says that His house will be called a "house of prayer for all nations." Yet here in Matthew 21, the people of God were *preventing* the nations from praying.

In the second part of verse 13, Jesus says that God's house has been made into a "den of thieves." This is likely a reference to Jeremiah 7:10, a temple address in which God disciplined His people for offering ritual sacrifices while living in total disobedience to Him. Jeremiah's wider context is worth quoting here:

> "Do you steal, murder, commit adultery, swear falsely, burn incense to Baal, and follow other gods that you have not known? Then do you come and stand before Me in this house called by My name and say, 'We are delivered, so we can continue doing all these detestable acts'? Has this house, which is called by My name, become a den of robbers in your view? Yes, I too have seen it." This is the LORD's declaration.
> (Jer 7:9-11)

God's people were offering worship in Jeremiah's day, yet they did not behave in obedience to God. Jesus walked into a similar situation in Matthew 21, and as a holy King, He came to cleanse and to purify God's temple. This hideout for criminals *against* God needed to be restored to a house of prayer *for* God. Jesus does not deal with sin lightly, but in righteous anger. This leads to the next attribute of Jesus.

Jesus has the right to cleanse the temple because **He is the authoritative King**. In this chapter and the chapters that follow, Jesus' authority is put on display. This section of Matthew's Gospel has been referred to as Jesus' final break with Judaism, for He takes the religious leaders of Jerusalem head-on, making claims that they considered blasphemous—claims that would lead them to crucify Him. Consider four different aspects of the authority Jesus demonstrates in this text.

First, **He has authority over the temple**. Jesus had made clear in Matthew 12:6 that He is greater than the temple. Indeed, He is Lord of the temple, and He has the right to do in it whatever He desires, including throwing it into disarray. It must have been quite shocking for Jewish leaders who prided themselves in religious practices at the temple to have Jesus come in and turn it upside down. Who does He think He is? Is He in charge of this place? Yes, as a matter of fact, He is.

Second, **He has authority over disease**. This is not only a scene of righteous anger, but of divine compassion. Some were welcomed into the temple, including the blind and the lame, individuals who would often sit at the temple and beg for help. These individuals were restricted from going into the actual temple area, being confined to the outer courts (Carson, *Matthew*, 442). But Jesus did not cast them out; He cared for them and healed them (v. 14). This is the only miracle of healing in Matthew's Gospel that Jesus performs in Jerusalem. He is King, not only over kings, nations, and religious leaders, but also over disease. It's no coincidence that when heaven is described in the book of Revelation, the picture is very temple-like, and there, in the presence of Jesus and the worship of God, there is no sickness, disease, hurt, or pain (Rev 21).

Third, in addition to Christ's authority over the temple and over disease, **He has authority over all people**. Children in the temple cried out, "Hosanna to the Son of David!" (v. 15). It's a real problem for these religious leaders when children all over the temple begin shouting, "Save us, Messiah!" Indignantly, the chief priests and scribes asked Jesus, "Do You hear what these children are saying?" (v. 16). How could Jesus stand there and accept such blasphemous praise? Jesus responded to them by quoting Psalm 8:2: "You have prepared praise from the mouths of children and nursing infants" (Matt 21:16). Psalm 8 is all about praising God, and it begins, "Yahweh, our Lord, how magnificent is Your name throughout the earth!" (Ps 8:1). Jesus is deliberately accepting praise that God alone is due.

Fourth, in Jesus' cursing of the fig tree we see that **He has authority over all creation**. Though Mark tells us this wasn't the season for figs (Mark 11:13), this fig tree had leaves, which usually indicates that fruit is there. But Jesus found no fruit on this tree, so He cursed it, not because He was angry at it, but in order to make a point.

The cleansing of the temple and the cursing of the fig tree are closely related; in fact, Mark brackets the story of the temple cleansing with references to the fig tree (Mark 11:12-25) to make the same point. Jesus was commenting on the religious life and worship of God's people, particularly Israel's leadership. They had leaves, so to speak, on the outside, but on the inside there was no real fruit. There was a lot of man-centered religious activity completely devoid of God-centered spiritual productivity. These spiritually dead individuals claimed to worship God in the temple, all the while rejecting Jesus, who was God in the flesh (John 1:1, 14), the new and greater temple (John 2:19). Jesus had no tolerance for such hollow worship and hypocritical religion.

To summarize what we've seen so far, Matthew is presenting Jesus as a royal figure. **He is the coming King**, and this is presented in two stages. **He came the first time humbly riding on a colt**, bringing peace through His shed blood. That was His purpose for coming to Jerusalem—**to rescue sinners**. He came **to be crucified as King**, not to deliver Israel from the power of Rome, as so many thought the Messiah would do. He came to deliver all people everywhere from the power of sin.

In Revelation 19 Jesus is no longer pictured coming on a donkey, but on a warhorse. Here is John's vision of the coming King:

> *Then I saw heaven opened, and there was a white horse. Its rider is called Faithful and True, and He judges and makes war in righteousness. His eyes were like a fiery flame, and many crowns were on His head. He had a name written that no one knows except Himself. He wore a robe stained with blood, and His name is the Word of God. The armies that were in heaven followed Him on white horses, wearing pure white linen. A sharp sword came from His mouth, so that He might strike the nations with it. He will shepherd them with an iron scepter. He will also trample the winepress of the fierce anger of God, the Almighty. And He has a name written on His robe and on His thigh:*
> *KING OF KINGS*
> *AND LORD OF LORDS.* (19:11-16)

King Jesus came the first time humbly riding on a colt, but **He will come the second time sovereignly reigning on a horse**. That final day will be very different from the one we see in Matthew 21. If you have not already given your allegiance to this King on that last day, it will be too late. He will come not to rescue sinners but **to rule sinners**. He will not come to be crucified as King; He will come **to be crowned as King**.

Application to Our Lives
MATTHEW 21:20-22

There are a number of exhortations for us based on what we've seen so far in Matthew 21. First, **let us give Jesus praise**. That praise begins as you **gladly surrender to this King today**. Second, **let us prioritize prayer**. Praying to God was one of the purposes of God's house, the temple, in the Old Testament, and though God doesn't dwell in a physical building today, He inhabits His people. We need to **continually seek this King every day** through prayer. In a day when we are bombarded with Christian commercialism, consumerism, and materialism, when our religion is filled with so much stuff and so much activity, let us not neglect to commune with God through Jesus the King. Third, **let us bear fruit in our lives**. We don't want to be like Israel of old, having all the signs of outward religion, but lacking real spiritual fruit. Jesus curses superficial religion throughout the Gospel of Matthew and throughout Scripture. He hates profession without practice. We shouldn't have songs on our lips without surrender in our lives, for we cannot separate outward acts from inward affection. **This King desires—and deserves—more than hollow worship and hypocritical religion**. Let us be on guard as a result of this text, and let us bear fruit in keeping with faith.

After all of these things, Jesus uses the cursing of the fig tree (based on the cleansing of the temple) to bring the discussion back to prayer in verses 20-22. Jesus speaks of telling a mountain to be lifted up and thrown into the sea. This is obviously a figurative expression to illustrate a spiritual reality. The point is not that we must muster up enough faith; rather, the point is that if we have faith in God, then we will receive what we ask, even when something seems too difficult, humanly speaking. What seems impossible to us is possible with God in prayer.

In these verses the verbs are all plural, so while these truths certainly apply to individuals, Jesus is specifically giving this promise to the community of disciples. So what is your church asking God for that can only be accomplished by His power? Have you asked Him to give you an impact on nations, such that He alone gets the glory? These are prayers that God will answer. If we ask and believe, we will receive these things, so **let us have faith as His church**. We have every reason to be confident in Jesus, no matter what lies ahead. **This King can—and will—do the impossible when we ask**.

Reflect and Discuss

1. What attributes do you think your unbelieving neighbors and co-workers would use to describe Jesus?
2. In your opinion, which attributes of Christ mentioned in this chapter seem to be lacking in the church's picture of Christ today? What is the danger of having a distorted view of Christ's character?

3. How does the rich variety of Christ's attributes speak to His uniqueness?
4. In what sense is this section of Matthew "the beginning of the end"?
5. List the ways in which Jesus' authority is displayed in this chapter.
6. Which attributes mentioned in this chapter have been missing in your own view of Christ? Are there other Scriptures that speak to these attributes?
7. Respond to the following statement: "The Jesus of the New Testament is different from the angry God of the Old Testament."
8. Was it inconsistent with His compassion for Jesus to cleanse the temple the way He did? Why not?
9. How would you summarize Jesus' point in verses 20-22?
10. How will Christ's first and second comings be different?

The Rejection of the King and His Authority*

MATTHEW 21:23–22:46

Main Idea: Jesus' authority has been and continues to be questioned and rejected by some people due to sin and unbelief, but His vindication can be seen in His death, resurrection, and final restoration.

I. **Some Question Jesus' Authority.**
  A. These questions often come from unbelief.
  B. These questions often come from misplaced fear.
II. **Some Reject God the Father and His Authority.**
  A. The rejection of one of His sons.
  B. The rejection of some of His servants.
  C. The rejection of some of His invited guests.
III. **Jesus' Rejecters Often Have Underlying Motives.**
  A. Some are power hungry and prideful.
  B. Some are worldly and wannabes.
  C. Some are secularist and materialist.
  D. Some are deceived "experts" and cold-hearted "scholars."
IV. **Jesus Questions the Questioners and Rejecters.**
  A. Am I the Christ?
  B. Am I the Son of God?
  C. Am I the King of your heart?
V. **Some Reject God the Holy Spirit and His Authority.**
  A. His words through the prophets are rejected by some.
  B. His words in the Bible are rejected by some.
VI. **His Authority Will Be Rejected by Some, but Finally Proven.**
  A. God the Son's Final Authority Will Always Be Rejected by Some.
  B. King Jesus' Deity and Authority Was and Will Be Finally Proven.
    1. Through divine rejection
    2. Through divine resurrection
    3. Through glorious restoration

---

*This section is based on a sermon by Deric Thomas.

287

The one true and living God—Father, Son, and Holy Spirit—is perfect. He alone deserves our full submission, allegiance, and trust as our good and perfect authority. Scripture is absolutely clear on this point, and the child of God should take great comfort in this truth. However, the idea of authority isn't a pleasant thought for everyone.

As we think about the concept of authority, we need to remember how many people have been deeply wounded and even abused by authority figures. Many people have been taken advantage of or mistreated by a person they trusted and submitted to, whether it's a parent, a sibling, a friend, a spouse, a teacher, a boss, a government official, or a religious leader. Great suffering results from this kind of mistreatment. We gratefully recognize that God's grace is sufficient to meet this kind of hurt; He is a refuge for those who suffer (Ps 46:1). In contrast to the abusive authority we're all too accustomed to on earth, God uses His authority for the ultimate good of His children. Therefore, we can trust Him and submit fully to Him without any reservations. And when we do, we will find the joy and the peace that comes from submission to such a glorious heavenly Father.

Matthew has made clear up to this point in his Gospel that Jesus of Nazareth is the Messiah, the Christ, the Promised One that the entire Old Testament pointed forward to. He is the King of kings and Lord of lords, and His kingdom is eternal. Yet, even in light of these glorious truths, not everyone responded to such authority with submission.

Some Question Jesus' Authority
MATTHEW 21:23-27

We see this recalcitrance in the case of the chief priests and elders. Jesus knew that God the Father had given Him the authority to do everything He had done up to this point in His life and ministry (John 5:19-29). Matthew 21 has already presented several aspects of this authority: Christ came to Jerusalem and received praise and worship from the people, cleansed the temple, and taught in the temple courts. These actions led the religious leaders to ask, "By what authority are You doing these things? Who gave You this authority?" (v. 23).

At root, the religious leaders were questioning Jesus' authorization or prerogative to do what He did. They essentially asked, "**Is it from God or from man?**" Today people still wonder whether Christianity is from God or whether it is just another man-made religion. Lest we think these were just innocent questions by the religious leaders, remember that they had already rejected John the Baptist's message (v. 32); **these questions often come from unbelief.** They had already rejected earlier revelation from God, so their rejection of Jesus was not altogether unexpected.

Unbelief isn't the only reason people question Jesus' authority. **These questions often come from misplaced fear,** which is what we see in verse 26. Instead of fearing God, which the Bible says is the beginning of knowledge (Prov 1:7), these leaders had an unhealthy fear of man. This misplaced fear is what led them to question Jesus, and it leads many people to question Jesus' authority today. The question for us is, Will we let unbelief and the opinions of others control us, or will we submit to God and His Son Jesus Christ?

Jesus responded to the questions of the chief priests and the elders by posing a question of His own. To force their hand, He asked them whether John's baptism was from heaven or from man (v. 25). John had made Jesus' identity as the Messiah clear, and the people respected John as a prophet. Therefore, the religious leaders couldn't reject John, or the people would turn against them. However, if they claimed that John's authority was from heaven, then they would be guilty of rejecting God, since they denied that Jesus was the Messiah. Jesus knew that His question would uncover their hearts. Their professed agnosticism—"We don't know"—in verse 27 was simply a smoke screen.

Some Reject God the Father and His Authority
MATTHEW 21:28–22:14

After seeing Jesus' authority challenged in verses 23-27, Matthew gives us three parables: the parable of the Two Sons (21:28-32), the parable of the Tenants (21:33-44), and the parable of the Wedding Feast (22:1-14). In these parables we see that some reject God the Father and His authority.

The Rejection of One of His Sons

In the parable of the two sons in verses 28-32, a father gave the same command to his two sons, but their reactions were completely different. We see the rejection of one of his sons, in this case the second son, which becomes a picture of the Jewish religious leaders. Jesus essentially asks the same question that He posed earlier in 21:25 concerning John's baptism, though now He draws their hearts out through a story. As the master teacher, Jesus exposed these hypocrites. Again Jesus refers to

John the Baptist in His response, pointing out their rejection of John's ministry. The tax collectors and prostitutes were represented by the first son, the one who eventually repented in this parable.

It's quite astonishing to consider who is identified in this parable as being obedient to the father. Women who were slaves to sex (prostitutes) had experienced a radical transformation by submitting to God through John's ministry. They were previously trying to find thirst-quenching satisfaction in people, but now they found it in the living water that only comes from the King's cup. Men like Matthew, the author of this Gospel, were changed from greedy tax-collectors to lavish givers. Yet the religious leaders, who had seen great changes in people through God's grace, still refused to believe. Sure, with their lips they said they loved God, but their hearts were far from Him. They ultimately failed to follow His will. They were like the second son who said "yes," but their lives said "no." **This is a story of dead faith without works**, a topic James' epistle speaks to (Jas 2:14-26). To put it another way, **this is a story of confession without repentance and submission**. While some people genuinely turned from their sin and trusted in God, the chief priests and elders merely gave verbal affirmation to Him; there was no real repentance or submission.

The Rejection of Some of His Servants

In verses 33-45 we read the parable of the Tenants. Jesus also told this parable to draw out what was in the hearts of the religious leaders. In this parable, a master, symbolizing God the Father, came looking for fruit from his servants in the vineyard. He sent his slaves to get this fruit, but they were beaten, killed, and stoned (vv. 35-36). He then sent his son, but they killed him too, supposing that they could take his inheritance. Jesus follows this story up by asking in verse 40, "Therefore, when the owner of the vineyard comes, what will he do to those farmers?" The religious leaders answered emphatically: "He will completely destroy those terrible men . . . and lease his vineyard to other farmers who will give him his produce at the harvest" (v. 41). Once again, Jesus has gotten these leaders to admit their own guilt, though they didn't initially recognize it. These Jewish leaders in Jesus' day were doing the same thing many in Israel had done throughout the Old Testament. God's spokesmen were persecuted and even killed throughout Israel's history; three days later, they would kill God's Son.[45]

---

[45] This was Tuesday of that last week of Jesus' life, sometimes referred to as "Holy week." Jesus' crucifixion would occur on Friday of this same week.

To the emphatic response of the religious leaders, Jesus replies by quoting Psalm 118:22-23: "The stone that the builders rejected has become the cornerstone. This came from the Lord and is wonderful in our eyes." The implication from this quotation is that God had planned the rejection of His Son, the "cornerstone." The kingdom would be given to "a nation producing its fruit" (v. 43). This "nation" would be the church, the body of believing Jews and Gentiles. For those who rejected the Lord's cornerstone, Jesus warns of judgment: "Whoever falls on this stone will be broken to pieces; but on whoever it falls, it will grind him to powder!" (v. 44). Matthew tells us in verse 45 that the religious leaders realized that Jesus was talking about them, and that they wanted to arrest Him; nevertheless, because of their fear of man—"they feared the crowds" (v. 46)—they waited.

Israel's leadership was supposed to be caring for God's vineyard (Isa 5:2), but instead they had rejected God and the prophets He sent. Most significantly, they had rejected God's Messiah. And this rejection was not only because of the fear of man; **this is a story of selfish anger and greed**. These leaders loved themselves more than they loved God and others. Their hearts were filled with greed, and they wanted the vineyard and everything that came with it. Verse 38 pictures them as grasping after the inheritance, for they lusted after power, control, and authority in God's kingdom. They wanted it so badly that they were willing to kill the Master's Son in the process. This parable would be played out vividly in just three short days when they crucified the Son of God, the very Son the Father had sent to save Israel.

The Rejection of Some of His Invited Guests

At the beginning of chapter 22 Jesus tells another parable. This parable pictures a wedding feast, but the theme is still rejection. It pictures the patience of God the Father as the king continually calls on people to enjoy the feast he has prepared for his son. When the king's servants were rejected by the invited guests, the king sent other servants, and these servants were also rejected, and eventually killed (v. 6). In his anger, the king "destroyed those murderers" and went and burned their city down (v. 7).[46] Afterward, the king sent out others who gathered "both evil and good" until the wedding hall was filled (v. 10). However,

---

[46] Some commentators think that the reference to burning the city in Matt 22:7 may have in view (at least as a partial fulfillment) the burning of Jerusalem when the Romans destroyed the city in AD 70.

the king found one man who had no wedding garment (v. 11), so he ordered the man to be thrown into the "outer darkness, where there will be weeping and gnashing of teeth" (v. 13). We need to hear in this parable the call of God the Father. He wants us to be with Him forever in His kingdom, to enjoy Him and all His good and perfect gifts. But apart from His grace, we refuse, just like this unprepared wedding guest. **This is a story of ingratitude, rebellion, obstinacy, complacency, and anger**.

We also need to see that **this is a story of nominal Christianity**. This wedding guest did what many people do today: they profess Christ while their lives show no evidence of saving faith. Such people are ungrateful to God, and their obstinacy when confronted reveals a deep-seated rebellion against God's authority. They have no joy in God, no real desire to read or hear His Word. They continue to pursue the fleeting and empty false joys that this world has to offer, but they end up miserable and angry at God. In the end, **this is a story of eternal rejection**. This wedding guest, and nominal Christians in general, reject God, until He finally rejects them. They are rightly punished and cast into darkness forever. The Bible speaks of excruciating pain in a place where there will be "weeping and gnashing of teeth" (v. 13). This horrifying judgment is the direct result of rejecting God. Oh, how we need to hear the King's gracious invitation and come to Him in repentance!

In the next two sections of Matthew 22 it becomes obvious that

Jesus' Rejecters Often Have Underlying Motives
MATTHEW 22:15-40

In verse 16 those sent by the Pharisees were trying to flatter Jesus. Meanwhile, they waited for the opportune time to trap Him in His words, which was precisely the point in their question about paying taxes to Caesar. If Jesus told them to pay taxes, then they could either make Jesus out to be idolatrous, given that Caesar's image was on the coin, or they could portray Him as upholding a tax system that many Jews vehemently resented. However, if Jesus had refused to pay taxes, there would surely be consequences for such insubordination to the Roman Empire. Jesus responded by saying that they should pay taxes (even to a pagan government like Rome's in the first century). God's kingdom is not of this world, and though we have certain responsibilities as earthly citizens, our entire lives should be devoted to His service. Paying taxes doesn't have to indicate one's ultimate allegiance.

Of those who reject Jesus, **some are power hungry and prideful**, like the Pharisees in this account. The hypocrisy of the Pharisees is laid out in Matthew 23, as Jesus offers a blistering critique of these self-righteous rulers. They did not want to submit to Jesus because that would have meant losing power in the eyes of the people; their egos would have been crushed. This happens today as well, as some reject Jesus because they want to retain power over their lives and over the lives of others. They may claim to know God, but they are really two-faced hypocrites.

Not only are some who reject Jesus power hungry and prideful, but **some are worldly and wannabes**. Verse 16 says that it was the followers of the Pharisees who were sent to question Jesus—Pharisee wannabes, if you will. Along with these social climbers, the Herodians joined in to question Jesus (v. 16). In many ways, the Pharisees and Herodians would have been opposed to one another in economic and political matters, but they were united in their opposition to Jesus. These Jewish Herodians had a strong allegiance to Rome and the rule of Herod (hence the name Herodians). They too were wannabes—Herod wannabes. Love for the world and the things of this world led them to reject Jesus and His authority. This is a huge temptation for us as well today, as the American Dream is often chosen over Christ and biblical Christianity. We must guard against a love for anything that supersedes our love for God, His Son, and His kingdom.

In verses 23-33, we see of Jesus' rejecters that **some are secularist and materialist**. The Sadducees did not believe in the resurrection or the afterlife. They were the wealthiest members of the Jewish ruling body called the Sanhedrin. In a sense, we could say that they sought to have their "best life now" by living for the present. This background is important as we consider their question about a woman who had had seven husbands. This is a curious question from a group that didn't believe in the resurrection and the afterlife, a question clearly intended to trap Jesus. Jesus responds by telling them that earthly marriages are not eternal (v. 30). This may sound like bad news if you're in a good marriage, but we can be assured that the relationship we have with our Christian spouses now will be even better in the next life. In the resurrection we who know Christ will be joyful and fulfilled in the eternal presence of God. In that day there will be no sorrow or sadness (Rev 21:4), and all our relationships will be perfect.

In verse 31 Jesus continues His answer and proves the Sadducees wrong. He quotes from Exodus 3:6, which is significant since the

Sadducees only believed that the first five books of the Old Testament—known as the Torah or the Pentateuch—were authoritative. When Moses wrote these words, Abraham, Isaac, and Jacob had been long dead. But God was still their God, and He is the God of the living. Therefore, Jesus makes clear that God was still in relationship with these patriarchs, and that these men would one day be resurrected as God had promised. Yet the Sadducees' secular and materialistic mind-set had blinded them to the truth of the resurrection and the truth of who Jesus is.

Finally, we see in verses 34-40 that **some are deceived "experts" and cold-hearted "scholars."** The man who approached Jesus was a supposed "expert in the law," but he had actually missed the One to whom the entire Bible was pointing, since Jesus was standing right in front of him. This lawyer was deceived, and though his head was full, his heart was cold. He sought to test Jesus by asking Him about the greatest commandment. Jesus answered by quoting Deuteronomy 6:5, known to Jews as the *Shema*. Faithful Jews would have cited the *Shema* daily, and they also would have known the command in Leviticus 19:18 to love one's neighbor. Even though this lawyer knew these truths, he missed their application. Had he fully loved God with all his heart, he would have recognized Jesus and loved Him. Yet he was rejecting Jesus instead, attempting to trap Him with a question.

Jesus Questions the Questioners and Rejecters
MATTHEW 22:41-46

In the last section of Matthew 22, the tables are turned on the religious leaders. Jesus quoted Psalm 110:1 to show that the Messiah would not only be the son of David, which all good Jews would have recognized, but also the Son of God. He was forcing them to see that David himself spoke to this mysterious reality in Scripture. The Messiah would be both human (an heir of David) and divine (David's Lord). The Pharisees had no reply when Jesus put this truth before them. This Messiah who was both human and divine was standing before them, and His wisdom had confounded them. Three questions from Jesus arise here, questions that the Pharisees needed to answer, and questions that we need to answer:

Am I the Christ? Do we believe that Jesus is the promised Messiah?
Am I the Son of God? Do we believe that Jesus was more than just a
    prophet? Is He, in fact, divine?

Am I the King of your heart? Have you submitted to Jesus, not only with your head but with your heart?

Some Reject God the Holy Spirit and His Authority
MATTHEW 22:43-44

After seeing the rejection of the Father and the Son, we see that some reject God the Holy Spirit and His authority. In verse 43 Jesus said that David was "inspired by the Spirit," referring to the Spirit's inspiration of these prophetic words by David in Psalm 110. In addition, the Pharisees had previously rejected John the Baptist's message. So **His words through the prophets are rejected by some.** Similarly, **His words in the Bible are rejected by some** today, for people continue to disbelieve the Spirit-inspired words of the Old and New Testaments.

His Authority Will Be Rejected by Some, but Finally Proven
MATTHEW 27–28

In the end, we shouldn't be surprised by the rejection of the Jewish leadership in this passage. **God the Son's final authority will always be rejected by some,** a truth that will be played out through the end of Matthew's Gospel (see 27:1-2, 24-26). Jesus' authority will eventually be rejected both **by leaders and by followers,** including the chief priests, scribes, elders, experts in the law, Pharisees, Sadducees, Herodians, and even the Roman Governor Pilate. Those who followed these leaders, both Jews and Gentiles, also rejected Jesus and agreed to His crucifixion.

Despite the nearly universal rejection that we see in this passage, **King Jesus' deity and authority was and will be finally proven** (see 27:45–28:10). Though it may seem strange, Jesus' final vindication comes **through divine rejection** (27:45-50). All of us have experienced rejection before, whether by parents, siblings, friends, or certain groups of people. At a deeper level, we have all feared being rejected by God. Some are even haunted by that fear—a fear of dying and facing God, only to be rejected by Him. I sympathize with you, but even better, Jesus sympathizes with you. He knew what it was like to be rejected.

It may sound counter-intuitive, but Jesus' identity and His authority to forgive sins were proven when He was forsaken by God the Father on the cross. Jesus lived a perfect life and then died as a substitute for our sins. He was rejected on the cross, forsaken by God the Father (27:46), so that we don't have to be rejected by God the Father when we breathe our last breath. In Christ, we can be forgiven and received as children by God. We don't have to fear death, eternal darkness, eternal weeping, or the just judgment of God. Jesus was judged for us; He was rejected so that you and I could be accepted.

Jesus' deity and authority were decisively demonstrated **through divine resurrection** (28:1-10). Jesus is alive and He has defeated sin, death, the grave, Satan, and eternal judgment for you. Jesus' authority and deity will finally be proven **through glorious restoration**. Christ the King will return at some point in the future and make all things new (Rev 21:5). He will restore this broken creation.

In light of these truths, the question becomes, **How will you respond to King Jesus today, His work and His authority?** The one true and living God—Father, Son, and Holy Spirit—is perfect. And He alone rightly deserves our full and ultimate submission, allegiance, and trust. He is our rightful, good, and perfect authority. Will you surrender to Him today?

Reflect and Discuss

1. Define submission in your own words.
2. What current ideas or popular philosophies in our culture reject the idea of submission?
3. How would you counsel someone who rejected God's authority because of bad experiences with authority figures?
4. How does the fear of man result in rejecting Christ's authority? Describe how you've seen this play out in someone's life.
5. How might Matthew 21:28-32 be an indictment on nominal Christians, that is, those who profess Christ but do not truly know Him?
6. How would you summarize the warning in the parable of the Wedding Feast in Matthew 22:1-14?
7. What were the underlying motives of those who questioned Jesus in Matthew 22:16-40?
8. What is at the root of all rejection of Jesus? (Hint: Read John 3:19-21.)
9. Explain why Jesus' question in Matthew 22:41-46 would have been perplexing to these Jewish leaders.
10. How would you respond to someone who said they rejected the authority of God's Word but they loved Jesus?

The Danger of Damnation in Sincere Religion

MATTHEW 23

Main Idea: The danger of spiritual deception is real, even for those who are sincere in their religious convictions; therefore, we must submit to God's Word and look to the mercy of Christ in the gospel.

I. **A Serious Caution**
   A. It is possible for you and me to believe genuinely that we are doing God's work, obeying God's Word, and accomplishing God's will, yet to be deceived and to experience eternal damnation.
   B. May God expose our blind spots, uncover our hearts, and save us from ourselves.

II. **Key Questions**
   A. Do we fail to practice what we preach?
   B. Are we not content with the approval of God?
   C. Do we assert our superiority over others?
   D. Are we hypocritically centered on ourselves?
   E. Are we hindering people's salvation?
   F. Are we more concerned with biblical minutiae than we are with practical ministry?
   G. Are we focused on outward cleanliness instead of inward holiness?

III. **The Final Charge**
   A. They had murdered God's messengers.
   B. They would murder Christian missionaries.
   C. They were about to murder the promised Messiah.

IV. **The Frightening Conclusion**

V. **The Inevitable Certainty**
   A. The condemnation of sinners is imminent.
   B. The salvation of sinners is possible.
   C. The exaltation of Jesus is guaranteed.

VI. **How Shall We Respond?**
   A. Among our church leaders

1. Let us lead with integrity from God's Word as the only source of authority for what we believe and how we behave.
2. Let us lead by submission to God's Son as our Chief Shepherd and the Coming King.
B. In our own lives
1. Let us humbly hide under the shelter of Christ's mercy.
2. Let us wisely walk in surrender to Christ's authority.
3. Let us passionately proclaim the supremacy of Christ's glory.

By all accounts, Matthew 23 is a difficult text. It's not difficult to understand, as most people can grasp what Jesus is getting at in this passage. But this text *is* difficult in that its message is especially penetrating and convicting. Jesus exposes the hypocrisy of the Jewish leaders. And if we're listening rightly, we can feel our own hearts being operated on in the process. One writer said of Matthew 23,

> Jesus' words in this passage fly from His lips like claps of thunder and spears of lightning. Out of His mouth on this occasion came the most fearful and dreadful statements that Jesus uttered on earth. (MacArthur, *Matthew 16–23*, 374)

In this text, Jesus addresses the scribes and the Pharisees, and He calls them hypocrites, sons of hell, blind guides, fools, robbers, self-indulgent, whitewashed tombs, snakes, vipers, persecutors, and murderers. Many people read this passage and focus on how evil these men must have been to evoke such wrath and condemnation from Christ. However, the scribes and Pharisees were the most highly regarded religious leaders of their day, being very devout in the things of the law. And we shouldn't see them as being insincere; they believed fully in what they were doing, that it was right and good. And so did everyone else. For this very reason, this text offers us a serious caution.

A Serious Caution

The warnings in Matthew 23 apply not just to scribes and Pharisees but to anyone who professes Christ. One sobering reality stands before us in this passage: **It is possible for you and me to believe genuinely that we are doing God's work, obeying God's Word, and accomplishing God's will,**

yet to be deceived and to experience eternal damnation. The scribes and Pharisees genuinely believed that they were doing God's work, obeying God's Word, and accomplishing God's will; yet, despite their sincerity, they were deceived. As a result, they experienced the most severe pronouncements of damnation ever uttered by Christ. The phrase "Woe to you, scribes and Pharisees" appears seven times in this passage. This expression is a way of pronouncing condemnation, damnation, or judgment on someone, and Jesus said it to people who believed that what they were doing brought honor to God. That's sobering.

Jesus' condemnation could actually be leveled against major religions all around the world. Whether they are Muslims, Hindus, Mormons, or devout Jews, there are scores of people who believe they are pleasing God, but they will, apart from God's gracious intervention, experience eternal damnation. Of course, in our culture this is not politically correct to say, but it's what Scripture teaches. However, it's not only people in other religions who are in danger of being deceived; it's also possible for you and me to believe that we are doing God's work, obeying God's Word, and accomplishing God's will, all the while being deceived and headed for eternal damnation.

In light of these realities, we shouldn't read this text as if it were simply directed toward a couple of groups of people in Jesus' day 2,000 years ago. Instead, we need to ask, "Have we missed it?" and "Where are we deceived?" Below we'll look at a number of questions this text should cause us to ask ourselves based on what Jesus says to the scribes and Pharisees. Don't answer these questions too quickly, and don't think, in your pride, "That's definitely not me." Pause and consider the remaining sin in your own heart, and think on these questions honestly. In the process, **may God expose our blind spots, uncover our hearts, and save us from ourselves**. Personally, this text has led to much personal confession. But by God's mercy, this is a good thing.

Key Questions
MATTHEW 23:1-28

Based on what Jesus says in this chapter about the sin and hypocrisy of the scribes and Pharisees, we need to ask ourselves seven questions. Jesus begins His address of the crowds and His disciples with a description of the scribes and Pharisees (vv. 1-4). The first question we need to ask ourselves is, **Do we fail to practice what we preach?** In a statement of pure irony, Jesus says that the scribes and Pharisees sit on Moses' seat, that is, they have Moses' authority—the authority to teach God's Word—so people should practice and observe what they say. But we know that Jesus doesn't mean that we are supposed to do everything the scribes and Pharisees were teaching, since He says in verse 15 that their proselytes are children of hell. Jesus means that people should obey these leaders insofar as they teach the Word of God rightly. Their actions, on the other hand, are not to be imitated.

The Jewish religious leaders preached but they didn't practice, we might say. Therefore, their example is not to be followed. These individuals piled heavy burdens on others, but they weren't willing to carry any of those burdens themselves (v. 4). This is why Jesus calls them hypocrites throughout this chapter. Obviously no one is perfect or completely holy. I don't presume to carry out perfectly everything I call the church to do, but it is crucial that I seek to practice what I proclaim. What about you? Is there consistency between what you say and how you live—as a parent, in your profession, on your campus, in your marriage, or in your friendships? Leaders in the body of Christ must hear this instruction, especially since they teach the Word to others. Those who teach should be committed to do what they call others to do. We must beware of a hypocritical inconsistency.

The second question is based on verses 5-7: **Are we not content with the approval of God?** Do we desire the applause of men? Matthew had addressed this theme earlier in the Sermon on the Mount when Jesus talked about those who give, pray, and fast in order to be seen by men (6:1-18). That same accusation is directed toward the scribes and Pharisees in this passage. They "enlarge their phylacteries and lengthen their tassels" for this very purpose (23:5). Phylacteries were small boxes inscribed with texts from God's law that were worn on the arms or fastened to the forehead. Tassels were prescribed by Scripture and were worn on the outer corners of one's clothes (Deut 22:12). Instead of drawing attention to God and His Word, the scribes and Pharisees used these things to draw attention to themselves.

The question for us, then, is whether we are content with the approval of God. It is a deadly thing to desire the applause of men, for once you receive it your flesh enjoys it, and you want it more and more. As a result, you become less and less content with the approval of God. Scripture, on the other hand, calls us to be so content with God's gracious smile that we are dead to what men say to or about us. We need to pray for that kind of attitude for ourselves and for others in the church. I have asked my own church to pray this way for me.

The third question based on this passage is, **Do we assert our superiority over others** (and in the process usurp Christ's superiority over all)? Jesus ends verse 7 by talking about the delight the scribes and Pharisees take in being called "rabbi" by others. Then He says we should avoid that practice. At first, this passage can sound as if Jesus were forbidding any teachers in the church. However, we know that's not His point, since elders are prescribed throughout the New Testament to teach and to lead in the church.[47] Paul even calls himself a spiritual father to Timothy, his son in the faith (Phil 2:11).[48] Later in this passage, Jesus talks about sending "prophets, sages, and scribes," essentially as missionaries, so He is not denouncing every form of spiritual leadership among God's people. But His words are a clear rebuke to those who have used their leadership position to assert some sort of superiority over others, to the point where they usurp or subvert Christ's superiority over all. And that's exactly what these scribes and Pharisees were doing: they were calling themselves rabbis and teachers and spiritual fathers and instructors, and in doing this, they were drawing people to themselves and away from Christ.

Consider these diagnostic questions for the pride in your own heart:

- Does your heart delight in receiving honor over other people?
- Do you find comfort whenever you realize that you are in a better or a higher position than someone else?
- Are you prone to, even in your own mind, exalt yourself above others?
- Do you compare yourself with other people, subconsciously measuring yourself against them to discern your own level of spirituality?

In his well-known book *Mere Christianity*, C. S. Lewis devotes an entire chapter to pride. He calls pride, or self-conceit, "the great sin." Lewis says, "If you think you are not conceited, it means you are very conceited indeed" (Lewis, *Mere Christianity*, 114). He then provides the

---

[47] See for example: Acts 14:23; 1 Tim 5:17; Titus 1:5).
[48] Likewise in 1 Cor 4:15, Paul says that he became the "father" of the Corinthians "in Christ Jesus through the gospel."

remedy for pride: "If anyone would like to acquire humility, I can, I think, tell him the first step. The first step is to realise that one is proud" (Lewis, 114). Finally, it is relevant for our purposes to see how Lewis links pride with competition:

> Now what you want to get clear is that pride is essentially competitive—is competitive by its very nature. . . . Pride gets no pleasure out of having something, only out of having more of it than the next man. We say that people are proud of being rich, or clever, or good-looking, but they are not. They are proud of being richer, or cleverer, or better-looking than others. If every one else became equally rich, or clever, or good-looking there would be nothing to be proud about. It is the comparison that makes you proud: the pleasure of being above the rest. (Lewis, 110)

We are naturally prone to compete with one another, to measure ourselves against our neighbor, and this sinful habit cuts both ways. If I'm doing better than the person next to me, I feel good about myself spiritually. If I'm doing worse than the person next to me, I feel bad about myself spiritually. But this is the wrong perspective altogether; we are brothers and sisters in Christ, equal before God through Christ, and He alone is superior.

May God help us to live, lead, and relate to one another in ways that affirm equality as brothers and sisters in Christ.

This previous question above leads naturally into the fourth question: Do we humbly serve others or **are we hypocritically centered on ourselves?** Jesus addresses this question in verses 11-12. We've already seen humility discussed numerous times in the book of Matthew. Jesus goes against the grain of every worldly leadership principle by making clear that God humbles the self-exalted and exalts the self-humbled. This principle of humility is expressed most clearly in the way we serve others (or fail to). Are we consistently looking for ways and opportunities to serve others, or are our thoughts more along the lines of, "What would be best for me in this situation?" Humble service is the way of Christ. Is this *your* posture?

This fourth question leads us into the first of seven woes that Jesus pronounces upon the Pharisees in verse 13. Jesus transitions from talking *about* the Pharisees to talking *to* them. These seven woes have been grouped in different ways, but for our purposes we will group the first six woes into three sets of two. These six appear to overlap in certain ways, and they lead to three questions in this text, each of which has separate parts. All of this leads to the seventh and final woe.

The fifth question that arises in this text has to do with our effect on others, namely, **Are we hindering people's salvation?** This is the crux of what the scribes and Pharisees were doing—they were keeping people out of the kingdom of heaven. Yet don't miss their sincerity in doing it! In verse 15 Jesus says to them, "You travel over land and sea to make one proselyte." The scribes and Pharisees were giving their lives to spread a message they thought was right, but in the process, they were hindering people's salvation. So can this be true of us? Consider two ways this might play out.

First, we can hinder someone's salvation **through deceiving potential disciples of Jesus**. In their blindness to Jesus as the Messiah, the scribes and Pharisees were keeping others from seeing Jesus' true identity. False teachers abounded in the New Testament and throughout church history. Some had malicious motives, but others were sincere; nevertheless, all of them deceived people.

Being in Africa recently brought this truth home to me. There are prominent teachers and preachers in America who are wildly popular in some places in Africa, spreading teachings and thoughts that are devoid of the gospel. One of these teachers recently led a huge campaign in my own hometown, and the message was essentially this: Trust in Jesus, and things will go well for you. Simply believe in Him and you will have a better life—health, wealth, prosperity, and success in this world. People in the slums of Africa are eating this message up, but it's not the gospel. Instead of clinging to Jesus for mercy, it's a way of using Jesus to get what you want.

On the other end of the spectrum, I spoke with one woman in Africa who has come to faith in Christ, and this could very easily lead to her having her throat slit. Yet, she has turned from her sin and from herself and trusted in Christ because she believes He's worth it. To follow Christ, to enter into the kingdom of heaven, costs you everything you have in this world, and to preach anything less than that is to preach a false gospel. This is why we must clearly and boldly confront false teaching and easy-believism in all its forms, no matter how sincerely it is communicated. False gospels are deceptive, dangerous, and damning.

Second, even if we aren't deceiving potential disciples of Jesus, we have to ask whether we are deceiving others **through creating virtual disciples** of ourselves? The scribes and Pharisees were leading others down a road of legalistic self-exaltation. Their converts were "twice as fit for hell as you are!" (v. 15). May God help us never to create disciples of ourselves, since following the thoughts and teachings of men will always lead down a road of condemnation. Only Christ can draw people into the kingdom of heaven, so let us constantly and consistently call people to Him.

Two more woes appear in verses 16-24. The fifth question, based on this text, is, **Are we more concerned with biblical minutiae than we are with practical ministry?** This question is liable to be misunderstood, as if there were anything unimportant in the Bible. To be clear, everything in the Bible is important because it is God's Word. But there are "more important matters," Jesus reminds us (v. 23). We need to avoid the danger of focusing on lighter things while ignoring weightier things. We can unpack this question in two ways.

First, **do we justify sin according to our traditions or do we flee sin according to God's truth?** Jesus refers to taking oaths by the sanctuary, the gold of the sanctuary, the altar, etc. He's referring to rules that had been concocted to allow people to swear by certain things and not be bound or swear by other items and be bound. In essence, people only had to keep a promise under certain circumstances. However, Jesus made it clear that any oath makes one accountable to God, for God owns everything anyway, including the temple. These man-made rules about oaths were, quite simply, an attempt to justify sin. The same thing can happen in our lives when we think, "I suppose that's technically a sin, but everyone does it, and it doesn't seem like a big deal, so it's okay." Sins like gossip, gluttony, small "white" lies, and materialism might fit in that category for us. We adjust to sin because it's common to us, instead of fleeing sin because it's repulsive to God.

This issue of justifying sin leads to what is perhaps one of the most convicting questions, namely, **Do we pride ourselves on following convenient laws or do we spend ourselves expressing costly love?** Jesus mentions the law of the tithe in verse 23, and He talks about the scrupulous, careful ways the scribes and Pharisees had sought to obey that law; however, in the process they ignored "justice, mercy, and faith." This is an allusion to Micah 6:8, where God calls His people "to act justly, to love faithfulness, and to walk humbly with your God." God's people had failed to give justice to the poor and express kindness to the needy. These things are the overflow of walking humbly with God, but they weren't characteristic of Israel's leadership in Jesus' day.

In a world where nearly half of the population lives on less than two dollars a day, and approximately a billion people live in desperate poverty, it doesn't make sense to spend our lives priding ourselves on obeying convenient laws that are easy for us to do or debating minute truths that are easy for us to get hung up on, when there is such great need to show justice and mercy in our own city and across the globe. Again, it's not that those convenient laws (like tithing) are unimportant; Jesus says they are important: "These things should have been done" (v. 23). But even weightier is the need to express the mercy and justice of God to the poor and needy, and that is costly love. The question for us is whether or not we are willing to go out of our comfort zones and to get our hands dirty in practical ministry. Or are we content to spend our lives mining through biblical details and doing that which we find relatively easy? Far too many professing Christians seem to have settled into this latter option.

There's a sixth question we need to address based on the last pair of woes in verses 25-28. Jesus' indictment of the hypocrisy of the scribes and Pharisees forces us to ask the question, **Are we focused on outward cleanliness instead of inward holiness?**

Throughout the book of Matthew, the tendency of the scribes and Pharisees has been to observe principles and practices on the outside, while neglecting humility and purity on the inside. And Jesus reminds them through this fierce denunciation that **purity always begins in the heart**. You don't merely clean the outside of a cup; you clean the inside first, and then the outside will become clean. When you only focus on the outside and your religion is all about external improvement, you become like "whitewashed tombs" (v. 27).

All followers of Christ need to be reminded that **religion is a subtly dangerous cover-up for spiritual deadness**. We go to church, we attend small group, we read the Bible, we go through the motions, we check off the boxes, but if we're not careful, we can miss the point altogether. In all our efforts at moral renewal, we only cover up the curse of sin that lies at the core of who we are. That's why we must ask ourselves some probing questions: Is there life inside me? Is there inner transformation? Is my heart being changed so that I desire Christ more than I desire the things of this world? Is there love and affection for Christ at the root of my obedience? Is Christianity a matter of duty for me or is it a matter of delight? Is holiness being joyfully cultivated in my heart? The answer to these questions was a clear "no" in the case of the scribes and Pharisees.

The Final Charge
MATTHEW 23:29-36

In this last section of Matthew 23, Jesus pronounces His seventh and final woe. In verse 29 Jesus refers to the "tombs of the prophets." Monuments were often erected to Israel's prophets, as if to imply that the present generation would have never done what the previous generation did to these prophets, that is, persecute them and put them to death (v. 30). But Jesus told the current Jewish leadership that they were doing the very same thing that their disobedient fathers did. In essence, **the scribes and Pharisees had murdered God's messengers**. They were the sons of murderers in the Old Testament, and they would show this in the days ahead when **they would murder Christian missionaries**. Jesus said that He would send "prophets, sages, and scribes," and that the scribes and Pharisees would "crucify . . . flog . . . and hound" them (v. 34). This is exactly what we see unfold in the lives of disciples and missionaries of Christ who spread the gospel in the book of Acts.

The Jewish religious leaders in the book of Acts were always at the heels of Christians who were proclaiming the gospel.[49] Then in Matthew 23:35, Jesus gives a climactic overview of how, from the blood of Abel to the blood of Zechariah, God's people had murdered the messengers He sent. The time period from Abel to Zechariah covers the span from the first to the last recorded murders of righteous people in the Old Testament.[50] The blood of all these prophets and messengers would be on the hands of the scribes and Pharisees (v. 35), for **they were about to murder the promised Messiah**. The culmination of Israel's opposition to God and His Word was evident in the Jewish generation of Jesus' day.

In a matter of days, the Jewish leaders would incite the crowds to cry out for the crucifixion of the Messiah, leading them to shout, "His blood be on us and on our children" (Matt 27:25). Those who called for Jesus' crucifixion filled up the full measure of their fathers' sin (v. 32), and God would tolerate it no more. We've seen this kind of language in Scripture before: in Genesis 15:12-16 God said He would delay His

---

[49] For example, see Acts 13 at Pisidian Antioch; Acts 14 at Iconium, Lystra, and Thessalonica; Acts 17 at Thessalonica and Berea; Acts 18 and 20 at Corinth; Acts 20–23 at Jerusalem.

[50] Abel was the first person murdered in the Old Testament (Gen 4:1-16), while Zechariah was the last man murdered according to the Hebrew arrangement of the OT Scriptures (2 Chr 24:20-22).

wrath for 400 years—four generations—until the sins of the Amorites were complete. When the iniquity of the Amorites had reached its full measure, God brought His wrath on them. That same principle was applied at different points to different nations in Scripture, but until now it had not been applied to the people of Israel. Jesus was now pronouncing "woe" (condemnation) on these *Jewish* leaders.

The Frightening Conclusion

It's easy to read these condemnations from Jesus and shake our heads at the scribes and Pharisees. However, the questions that we've raised in this chapter are, as you may have already gathered, not as foreign to us as we would like to think. As we come to the climax of these condemnations of the scribes and Pharisees, as well as of the crowds who called for the crucifixion of the Messiah, we come face to face with a frightening conclusion: **We are they**.

We too have hearts that would murder the Messiah, and to think anything different is to flatter ourselves in the same way these scribes and Pharisees did.

The old Negro spiritual asks, "Were you there when they crucified my Lord?" And the answer is, "Yes, I was there." Not as a spectator, but as a participant, a guilty participant—plotting, scheming, betraying, bargaining, and handing Jesus over to be crucified. John Stott said, "Before we can begin to see the cross as something done for us (leading us to faith and worship), we have to see it as something done by us (leading to repentance)" (Stott, *The Cross of Christ*, 59–60). Along the same lines, the great Scottish hymn-writer Horatius Bonar wrote the following:

> Twas I that shed the sacred blood; I nailed him to the tree;
> I crucified the Christ of God; I joined the mockery.

> Of all that shouting multitude, I feel that I am one;
> And in that din of voices rude I recognize my own.

> Around the cross the throng I see, Mocking the Sufferer's groan;
> Yet still my voice it seems to be, As if I mocked alone.
> (Bonar, "I See the Crowd in Pilate's Hall")

We have all rebelled against God, turning from Him and from His Word. This is the same God who has been supremely revealed in His

One and Only Son, Jesus Christ, and we have rejected Him outright. Therefore, no matter how sincere we are, no matter how hard we try, no matter what we do, we have hearts that warrant the wrath and condemnation of God. These final verses of Matthew 23, while applicable to the people of Israel in Jesus' day, also have particular application to each of us.

The Inevitable Certainty
MATTHEW 23:37-39

Jesus announced to Jerusalem that their rejection of Him would lead to the inevitable certainty of judgment. This sobering judgment is certain for us too if we persist in our rebellion against God's Messiah. Regardless of how things seem and the consensus of those around us, **the condemnation of sinners is imminent**. This was true for most of the people in Jerusalem in Jesus' day, for in these verses the audience has broadened from the scribes and the Pharisees to the people who followed their lead. *All* of them would experience the wrath of God. The temple, which is the "house" Jesus referred to in verse 38, would be utterly desolated within a matter of years.[51] The Jews in that day experienced divine judgment, and while we are in a different context at a different time in history, the condemnation of sinners is still imminent today.

With God's just and righteous judgment as the backdrop, we need to be reminded of the good news of the gospel. **The salvation of sinners is possible**. Jesus called out to those who rejected Him, saying, "Jerusalem, Jerusalem! . . . How often I wanted to gather your children together, as a hen gathers her chicks under her wings, yet you were not willing!" (v. 37). Hear, then, the patient and merciful pleas of the Son of God. Salvation is possible for all who come to Him, so do not resist Him. Come to Jesus today in repentance and faith, and you will, by the grace of God, be a citizen of the kingdom of heaven.

So far we've seen that while the condemnation of sinners is imminent, the salvation of sinners is possible. We can also be assured that **the exaltation of Jesus is guaranteed**. His people would not see Him again until they said, "He who comes in the name of the Lord is the blessed One!" (v. 39). Jesus *will* come back as the reigning Lord, and every knee

---

[51] The Romans completely destroyed the temple in Jerusalem in AD 70.

will bow (Phil 2:9-11). The question is, when Jesus returns, will you see Him coming as your consuming Judge or your welcomed King?

How Shall We Respond?

In light of the truths in this passage, I believe it is appropriate to apply this text to two groups of people. The first group is **church leaders**, or more specifically, pastors. Such individuals receive the severest of warnings from Jesus, just as Israel's leaders had received the sternest warnings from God in the Old Testament. God's most furious wrath is reserved for those who claim to be His servants, that is, those in positions of leadership, who deceive and mislead God's people away from God's glory (Matt 18:6; see also 2 Pet 2).

In our churches there is a special need for right doctrine and godly living among our elders.[52] Therefore, let us lead with integrity from God's Word as the only source of authority for what we believe and how we behave. Hypocrisy is to be avoided at all costs; God's Word should be clear from our lips and clear in our lives. The church must be guided by the truth and not our traditions. Scripture is to be the bright sun around which everything in our lives and everything in our churches revolves.

Elders also need to be aware that they do not rule the church, but rather they are ruled by Christ. Therefore, **let us lead by submission to God's Son as our chief Shepherd and the coming King**. Christ is our "chief Shepherd" (1 Pet 5:4), and this is His church, not ours. We are accountable to Him for how we shepherd His body (Heb 13:17). So let us love Christ and let us lead His church to be ready for the day when He returns to claim His people fully and finally.

This passage can also be applied **in our own lives** as members of the church who are not in leadership. There are three takeaways in this regard. First and foremost, **let us humbly hide under the shelter of Christ's mercy**. We need the mercy of Christ, and this is the primary thing the scribes and Pharisees failed to grasp. The recognition of our need for mercy is what separates true religion that brings glory to God from sincere religion that warrants wrath from God.

---

[52] The term *elder* (1 Tim 3:1) refers to the same role as an overseer (1 Tim 5:19) or a pastor.

Second, **let us wisely walk in surrender to Christ's authority**. This involves **understanding His Word rightly**. At root, the woes Jesus pronounced revealed a fundamental failure to discern the meaning of God's Word. However, God has not left us alone to figure out how to honor and obey Him. We are not wandering in the dark. He has revealed Himself to us in His Word, and He has provided His Spirit to guide us, so we must read and study the Word, not in attempts to twist it according to our tastes, but in surrender to it as His truth. We also walk in surrender to Christ by **desiring His worship wholeheartedly**. Let us refuse to live for anything else but the glory of Christ in our own lives.

Third, **let us passionately proclaim the supremacy of Christ's glory**. In this chapter we not only see Christ's *condemnation* pronounced *on* sinners, but also His *compassion* expressed *for* sinners. Jesus longed for Jerusalem's salvation, and Luke's Gospel even records that Jesus wept over the beloved city (19:41). We too should feel compelled to reach out to sinners in need.

Today there are literally billions of people in various places in the world who are giving themselves to sincere religion, and they genuinely believe they are honoring God (or whatever gods they worship). But they are deceived and they are headed to eternal damnation. From the wealthiest of the wealthy to the poorest of the poor, to every tribe, tongue, and clan in Africa, and to every other people group on the planet, let's give our lives and our churches to passionately proclaiming the supremacy of Christ's glory. Such a King deserves so much more than outward religion.

Reflect and Discuss

1. Even for unbelievers, hypocrisy is despised. Why do you think this is? Define hypocrisy.
2. Why is it not enough simply to be sincere in what you believe? How does this passage serve as a warning in this regard?
3. Compare Matthew 23 to the teaching about faith and works in James 2:14-26 and the necessity of righteousness in 1 John 3:4-10.
4. What is the difference between strong, biblical leadership and leadership that is self-promoting? How might these principles apply to Christians who aren't spiritual leaders?
5. What other sins does pride lead to? How can you fight against a proud heart? Can you think of any relevant biblical passages?

6. What does it mean to neglect the "more important matters of the law" (v. 23)?

7. If purity begins in the heart, then what should our fight against sin look like?

8. In what ways do you see yourself in Jesus' indictment of the Pharisees? Be specific.

9. What counsel would you offer to someone who is not sure whether his faith is genuine?

10. How can we be diligent about holiness without being overly introspective and without expecting perfection?

Return of the King (Part 1)

MATTHEW 24:1-36

Main Idea: Jesus' prophecies concerning the destruction of Jerusalem and His second coming are a call for His disciples to trust in His authority, persevere in His power, and long for His return.

I. **Trust in the Authority of Christ.**
   A. Understanding the text
      1. Prophecy concerning the destruction of Jerusalem
      2. Prophecy concerning the return of Jesus
   B. Applying the text
      1. The things of this world are passing.
      2. The truth of His Word is permanent.
II. **Persevere in the Power of Christ.**
   A. Followers of Jesus will face deception.
   B. Followers of Jesus will face tribulation.
      1. Christians are not saved from trials.
      2. Christians are saved through trials.
   C. Followers of Jesus will face temptation.
   D. Followers of Jesus will face persecution.
      1. Persecution inevitably follows kingdom proclamation.
      2. Proclamation ultimately results in kingdom consummation.
III. **Long for the Coming of Christ.**
   A. He came the first time lying in a manger; He will come the second time riding on the clouds.
   B. He came the first time in humility to provide salvation; He will come the second time in glory to execute judgment.
   C. Christians confidently watch: His timing will confound our wisdom.
   D. Christians patiently wait: His return will exceed our expectations.
   E. Christians urgently work: His church (our lives!) will accomplish His mission.

It seems that everyone wants to know the future. I still recall the first time I went to Jackson Square in the French Quarter of New Orleans. This area was littered with fortune-tellers and tarot card readers, as well as tourists who seemed eager to find out their futures from these street vendors. As first-semester seminary students, it didn't take long for my friends and me to seize upon this opportunity for very different purposes, as we had a different view of the future that people desperately needed to hear about. We decided that we wanted in on the action, so we plopped down right beside the Voodoo Queen of New Orleans.

We told people (free of charge!) that their future didn't look good, but that it could change based on who Christ is and what He had done for them. It didn't take long to realize that that's not what people were looking for when they sat down in front of us. Most people were looking for *details* about their lives: Were they going to be married? Were they going to stay married? Would they have children? Would they get rich? Would they get sick? Would they experience some sort of tragedy? How successful would they be? Strangely, most people wanted to talk about some specifics of their more immediate future, but they had no interest in talking about their eternal destinies. They didn't want to hear about what mattered most.

Missing what matters most is not only a danger for tourists looking to fortune-tellers in Jackson Square; it's also a reality for followers of Christ who know and love God's Word. As we approach one of the most controversial chapters in the New Testament, a chapter where Jesus foretells the future and talks about the end of the world, there's a danger that we will miss truths that affect our eternity because we are caught up in trying to discern details that may or may not be answered in the text. Christians continue to mine Matthew 24, sometimes referred to as The Olivet Discourse,[53] for various details about the future, including the timing of certain events. Some have even predicted the exact date of Jesus' return and the end of the world, only to look ridiculous later when these things didn't come to pass. But it's not just lunatics who debate these issues, for these are important realities that Scripture addresses. Solid, Bible-believing Christians and scholars debate the various details of Matthew 24, including whether or not this text supports

---

[53] This title comes from the fact that Jesus spoke these words while seated with His disciples on the Mount of Olives (Matt 24:3).

premillennialism, postmillennialism, or amillennialism.[54] In addition, there's the issue of the rapture: does Matthew 24 support a pre-, post-, or mid-tribulation rapture?[55] Or is there a rapture at all? Again, these are critical questions that deserve our serious study and attention. However, if we're not careful, we will miss what is most important in this text.

Amid all the minor questions that arise in Matthew 24, there are major questions that must be answered in the lives of every one of us. So regardless of the details about when or how or where this or that thing is going to happen in the future, ask yourself the following questions: Are you ready for whatever may happen in your life this week or in the next year? Are you prepared for what may happen in the world in the next ten years? And are *you* absolutely certain of where your life will be in eternity? There are no more important questions than these. Jesus' primary goal in Matthew 24 is not to answer our questions about every single detail of the end times, but rather to prepare us for whatever the future may hold—this week, this month, this year, the next ten years, and even the next ten *billion* years from now. Followers of Christ have something, or rather Someone, to bank their future on.

Based on this controversial, oftentimes confusing text, there are three *clear* words of encouragement for your life and your future: trust in the authority of Christ, persevere in the power of Christ, and long for the coming of Christ.

Trust in the Authority of Christ

Seeing the big picture of this passage and understanding how this text is arranged should give us a greater appreciation for Christ's sovereign

---

[54] The term "millennium" comes from the references in Revelation 20 to the period of 1,000 years during which Satan will be bound. There are three main schools of thought, with variations in each position: *Premillennialists* believe Christ's return will precede the millennium, *Postmillennialists* believe that Jesus' return will happen after the millennium, and *Amillennialists* believe that the millennium is a reference to the present age, which began following Christ's resurrection and ascension. There is also considerable debate about whether the millennium is a reference to a literal 1,000 years.

[55] The term "rapture" refers to Christ's coming in the air to rescue His church prior to the millennium and the final judgment mentioned in Rev 20:11-15. Only believers will meet the Lord in the air and be raptured. In support of this view, commentators point to passages such as 1 Thess 4:13-18. Pre-tribulationists believe this rapture will occur prior to a period of "great tribulation" mentioned in Matt 24:21-31 and elsewhere, while post-tribulationists believe the rapture will occur after the tribulation. Mid-tribulationists believe the rapture will occur at the midpoint of the tribulation (after 3½ years).

control of the future. There are two main prophecies that Jesus is addressing here, and these prophecies deal with two main events. It's important, therefore, in **understanding the text** to distinguish *when* Jesus is talking about *what*. Admittedly, not all scholars agree on the distinctions made below, but the majority of scholars do see a clear distinction in this chapter between two primary events being prophesied.

The first prophecy in this passage is a **prophecy concerning the destruction of Jerusalem**. This is what Jesus begins talking about in verse 15; however, to set the scene, we need to go back to verse 2, where Jesus foretells the destruction of the temple in Jerusalem. While seated on the Mount of Olives, His disciples asked Jesus two questions privately, the first of which was, "Tell us, when will these things happen?" (v. 3). In reply, Jesus begins talking about true and false signs pointing to Jerusalem's destruction in verses 4-14. Then in verse 15 He says, "So when you see the abomination that causes desolation, spoken of by the prophet Daniel, standing in the holy place (let the reader understand), then those in Judea must flee to the mountains!" This "abomination that causes desolation" is a sign that Jerusalem is right on the verge of being destroyed. And then in verse 21 Jesus says of that time period, "For at that time there will be great tribulation, the kind that hasn't taken place from the beginning of the world until now and never will again!" This reference in verse 21 is still to the destruction of the city of Jerusalem, and the temple in the middle of it.

When Matthew talks about "the abomination that causes desolation" in Daniel's prophecy, he is likely referring to several texts, including Daniel 8:13; 9:27; 11:31; and 12:11. Centuries prior to Christ's coming, the prophet Daniel foretold a time when a foreign ruler would come into the temple and profane it. Most Jewish people linked that prophecy with something that happened around 168 BC, when a ruler named Antiochus Epiphanes came into the temple and erected a pagan altar. He even sacrificed pigs on it, thus defiling the house of God (France, *The Gospel of Matthew*, 911). But Jesus seems to be saying that that event, which would have been blasphemous and detestable in the eyes of the Jews, was only a foretaste of what will happen when Jerusalem is destroyed.

Approximately 40 years after Jesus spoke these words, around AD 70, Roman armies began surrounding the city of Jerusalem to overtake it. And when they did take the city, the Roman army destroyed the temple and made sacrifices to false gods, declaring Titus, the Roman emperor, to be supreme. Daniel 12:1 refers to a time like this: "There will be a time of distress such as never has occurred since nations came into being until that time." This is the same language that's used in Matthew 24:21.

The time of Jerusalem's destruction in AD 70 was a horrifying, ghastly time. It was a virtual bloodbath of Jewish men and women who were pummeled by the Roman army. The Jewish historian Josephus described the savagery, slaughter, disease, and famine that marked the Jewish people during those years. Parents resorted to cannibalism with their own children and many Jews were taken into slavery. The death toll was in the millions. And all of this took place about 40 years after Jesus said these words to His disciples. It's little wonder that He tells them in verse 15 to flee when these things start taking place. They were told not even to go to their homes to get their clothes when the Roman army invaded. We begin to understand why Jesus spoke of "woe" to "pregnant women and nursing mothers," for if their flight were on the Sabbath, they couldn't take the necessary precautions, or if their flight were in winter, the frequent rains would cause the waters to rise, making it difficult to escape (v. 19).

The first prophecy in this chapter, then, concerns the destruction of Jerusalem. The temple would be obliterated, so that, as Jesus predicted, "Not one stone will be left here on another that will not be thrown down!" (v. 2). This happened in AD 70, and we'll see in the rest of this chapter how this figured in to Christ's second coming and the end of the age.

The second prophecy in this passage is described in verses 29-31, and this is a **prophecy concerning the return of Jesus**. Verse 29 speaks of the moon becoming dark and the "celestial powers," or the heavens, being shaken. Based on this language, it seems that verses 29-31 are about more than simply the destruction of Jerusalem. Jesus will come back in splendor and glory with a trumpet call from heaven. He will come to fully and finally assert His reign and His rule over the world as the sovereign Son of Man who deserves the praise of all peoples.

The difficulty then comes with understanding the rest of the passage, namely, how does it relate to the two prophecies mentioned above? There are two main schools of thought on how to interpret the remainder of this passage in verses 29-51, and both of these interpretations are possible (to be honest, I have gone back and forth between them).

The first option, the one that represents most scholars today, is that these two events—the destruction of Jerusalem and the return of

Jesus—are intended to be seen like two progressive mountain peaks, one of which sets the stage for the other. The destruction of Jerusalem, according to this interpretation, foreshadows the coming of the Son of Man.

The second interpretive option is to see verses 4-28 as one prolonged description of distress and tribulation that will happen in the world before Christ's return. With this interpretation, verses 29-51 focus on Christ's climactic return, while the destruction of Jerusalem serves as one (albeit potent) example of the coming time of tribulation, an example that was especially pertinent for these Jewish disciples.

Regardless of which of these two interpretations you choose, two things are clear: (1) Jerusalem is going to be destroyed, and (2) Jesus is going to return. To the disciples, these were earth-shaking realities. But why are these truths so critical for those of us in the twenty-first century? In **applying the text**, there are a couple of extremely important realities that we must grasp.

First, **the things of this world are passing**. These country boys from Galilee came to the big city of Jerusalem, and they were stunned by its splendor, particularly the splendor of the temple (v. 1). Of course, the disciples had reason to be impressed, as the temple was a massive and awe-inspiring edifice. It was built with large stones, some of which measured 40 feet long, 12 feet wide, and 12 feet deep. These stones could weigh more than 200,000 pounds each and they were stacked on top of one another—quite impressive for a day in which there was no advanced construction equipment! The massive, stacked stones led up to a roof bathed in a sea of gold. The white marble on the top of the temple would virtually blind you when you looked at it in the reflection of the sun. You can understand the shock of the disciples, therefore, when Jesus told them that not one stone would be left upon another (v. 2). The things of this world—even the best, most incredible things of this world—are passing. Jesus says as much in the first part of verse 35: "Heaven and earth will pass away."

The second reality that springs from this text has to do with the last part of verse 35. Although heaven and earth will pass away, Jesus says, "My words will never pass away." **The truth of His Word is permanent**. Regardless of how we interpret some of the details in this text, there's no denying that Jesus accurately predicted the destruction of Jerusalem approximately 40 years before it happened. He is not some sham fortune-teller offering His opinion; He is the Lord of history, and He speaks with authority about the future. Jesus not only knows the future, but He ordains it. Jesus spoke about the destruction of Jerusalem, and it happened. He also spoke about His return one day, and that too will happen. The question is, "Will *you* be ready for that day?" You may be wondering what it means to be ready. This question leads to the second exhortation based on this text.

Persevere in the Power of Christ

This prophetic text leads us not only to trust in the authority of Christ, but also to persevere in the power of Christ. Jesus was preparing His disciples at that time for Jerusalem's destruction, and simultaneously He is preparing disciples in all times for His return. Though different challenges have come about throughout history, Jesus calls all of His followers to persevere. This is one reason the emphasis on date-setting is misguided in interpreting this chapter. After all, Jesus said in verse 36, "Now concerning that day and hour no one knows—neither the angels in heaven, nor the Son—except the Father only." That's a pretty remarkable statement from the lips of the Son of God. If this text leads us only to speculation, then we have missed the point.

Jesus intends His followers to walk away from this text prepared for what is sure to come before His return. In this chapter there are at least four things that we will face as we wait for Jesus' coming. First, **followers of Jesus will face deception**. Jesus says in verses 4-5, "Watch out that no one deceives you. For many will come in My name, saying, 'I am the Messiah,' and they will deceive many." He says essentially the same thing in verses 23-26, warning of those who will say, "Look, here is the Messiah!" (v. 23). This is what Jesus' followers are to expect: "False messiahs and false prophets will arise and perform great signs and wonders to lead astray, if possible, even the elect" (v. 24). When we see and hear such things, our instructions are clear: "do not believe it" (v. 26). Individuals like Jim Jones, David Koresh, and other blatantly false teachers typically come to mind when we hear such warnings, but deception can be much more subtle. Many people promote a picture or a version of Jesus that is not found in the Bible, and they continue to deceive scores of Christians.

Second, as we wait for Christ's return, **followers of Jesus will face tribulation**. Whether in the first century or in the twenty-first century, life will not be easy for those who bear witness to the Lord Jesus Christ. In verses 6-8 Jesus speaks of the "beginning of birth pains" (v. 8), which will include "wars and rumors of wars," as well as "famines and earthquakes in various places" (vv. 6-7). These things were familiar to first-century Christians, and they are certainly familiar to us today. We hear of wars and rumors of wars across the Middle East, escalating tensions between Israel and Iran, and nuclear threats from North Korea. The daily news is also littered with reports of famine in parts of Africa, where hundreds of thousands of men, women, and children have starved and are starving. Earthquakes, cyclones, flooding, and tsunamis have taken countless lives in a matter of minutes. Needless to say, we are not immune to tribulation in this world, not one of us. And Jesus tells us to *expect* these things, not so that we can pinpoint a date for His coming based on one particular event, but so that we will be reminded about how to live and what to prepare for in this fallen world before He returns.

Astoundingly, in light of the terrifying events mentioned in this chapter, Jesus tells us not to fear: "See that you are not alarmed, because these things must take place, but the end is not yet" (v. 6). Your hope as a follower of Christ should not come and go based on political trends or potential disasters; these things are not to alarm you. We're reminded of Paul's reference to the "labor pains" of creation, for even creation is waiting to be "set free from the bondage of corruption into the glorious freedom of God's children" (Rom 8:21). Remember, **Christians are not saved from trials**; Scripture is very clear on this. Rather, **Christians are saved through trials**.[56] Jesus is saying, in effect, "Trust in Me. Even when it seems that everything is out of control, I am in control." With such confidence in Christ and by the power of the Holy Spirit, we can persevere through tribulation and deception.

Third, **followers of Jesus will face temptation**. In verse 10 Jesus says that many will "take offense, betray one another and hate one another." The increase in lawlessness will cause "the love of many to grow cold" (v. 12). Followers of Christ will be tempted not to trust in God, but instead to trust in themselves. Those who we thought were believers—people who were identified with the church—will turn away, and we will be tempted to do the same.

Fourth and finally, **followers of Jesus will face persecution**. Jesus warns us in verse 9, "They will hand you over for persecution, and they will kill you. You will be hated by all nations because of My name." You

---

[56] For just a few scriptural examples, see: Matt 5:11-12; John 16:33; Rom 8:17; 2 Tim 3:12; Jas 1:2; 1 Pet 4:12-14.

will experience suffering because you bear the name of Christ, so don't be surprised at the world's opposition. Persevere, for "the one who endures to the end will be delivered" (v. 13). As we persevere, we do so with the promise of Christ's power and presence, for He tells us at the end of Matthew's Gospel, "I am with you always, to the end of the age" (28:20).

As we persevere, we do so proclaiming this gospel of the kingdom. Matthew 24:14—a verse George Ladd once called "perhaps the most important single verse in the Word of God for God's people today" (Ladd, *The Gospel of the Kingdom*, 123)—says the following: "This good news of the kingdom will be proclaimed in all the world as a testimony to all nations. And then the end will come." Jesus has just given us a long list of things that will happen that are *not* necessarily signs of the end; they're just birth pains leading to the end. The end will come when the gospel has been proclaimed as a testimony to all nations. This is why we long to make the gospel known to every people group in the world. These truths about worldwide proclamation set the stage for the Great Commission in Matthew 28:18-20, where Jesus gives that foundational command to the church to "make disciples of all nations" (v. 19). But this glorious task will not be easy.

While the gospel of the kingdom will be proclaimed to all nations, **persecution inevitably follows kingdom proclamation**. If you give your life to proclaiming the gospel of the kingdom in your workplace or somewhere across the world, life will get harder for you, not easier. If you want to live a nice, comfortable, safe Christian life, then don't share the gospel. Of course, that's not an option if we love Jesus and want to be faithful to Him! We make Him known, regardless of the cost, because His reward is worth it.

One of the reasons we can rejoice in making the gospel known is because **proclamation ultimately results in kingdom consummation**. Jesus will return and consummate His kingdom when this mission is accomplished. The accomplishment of this mission will happen when every nation, that is, every group of people on the planet, has been reached with the gospel. This is what we give our lives and resources to. Christians often ask, "How will you know when all the nations have been reached with the gospel of the kingdom?" I can't improve on Ladd's response:

> God alone knows the definition of terms [here]. I cannot
> precisely define who all the nations are, but I do not need
> to know. I know only one thing: Christ has not yet returned;

therefore, the task is not yet done. When it is done, Christ will come. Our responsibility is not to insist on defining the terms; our responsibility is to complete the task. So long as Christ does not return, our work is undone. Let us get busy and complete our mission. (Ladd, *The Gospel of the Kingdom*, 137)

May God help us to proclaim the gospel of the kingdom throughout the world as we persevere in this world in the power of the King.

Long for the Coming of Christ

We've already seen in Matthew 24 that we are to trust in the authority of Christ and persevere in the power of Christ. Now, based on what we see in this chapter and the portrait of Christ we see throughout Matthew's Gospel, we should **long for the coming of Christ**. The realities of tribulation, deception, temptation, and persecution create anticipation. The more we live *in* this world, the more we will long for Christ to come back *to* this world.

This text leaves no doubt that the day of Christ's return will be evident to all. His coming will be no secret: the angels of heaven will let out a trumpet blast, and every eye will behold the Son of Man in the sky (vv. 29-31). How different this will be from His first coming! The first time He came to a remote, obscure town just outside Jerusalem, where He went largely unnoticed, save for a few shepherds and some farm animals. **He came the first time lying in a manger**; however, **He will come the second time riding on the clouds**. This is what Daniel prophesied centuries before:

And I saw One like a son of man
coming with the clouds of heaven.
He approached the Ancient of Days
and was escorted before Him.

He was given authority to rule,
and glory, and a kingdom;
so that those of every people,
nation, and language
should serve Him.

His dominion is an everlasting dominion
that will not pass away,

and His kingdom is one
that will not be destroyed. (Dan 7:13-14)

Just as surely as **He came the first time in humility to provide salvation**, so **He will come the second time in glory to execute judgment**. Matthew's reference to "the clouds of heaven" in verse 30 is not just an allusion to Daniel 7. Throughout the Old Testament, God reveals His glory in the image of a cloud. It was a pillar of cloud that led God's people in the exodus from Egypt (Exod 13:21). Then, at the end of the book of Exodus, God's glory was revealed in a cloud that covered the tabernacle (Exod 40:34-38). Psalm 104:3 says that God makes the clouds "His chariot," and Isaiah 19:1 depicts the Lord riding on a "swift cloud." The picture we get in Matthew 24 is of the glory of God revealed in the glorious Son of God, who will come on the clouds in power to execute judgment.

In verse 30 Jesus says that the tribes of the earth will "mourn" when they see Him coming. That day will be a day of judgment, and all who are not ready for that day—that is, those who have refused to turn from their sin and to trust in Christ as Savior and King—will come face to face with the Holy One whom they have rejected.

This text should cause us to ask ourselves, "What if this happened today? Would *I* be ready?" If not, then repent and believe in Christ today.

If you are a genuine follower of Christ, are there things in your life that you still need to repent of, sins that you're holding on to and toying with? What are you doing today that would cause you to be ashamed before Jesus if He were to come this moment? If so, let go of these things. Confess your sin and find mercy in Your Savior, so that you will be ready for His coming.

Following Jesus' description of His second coming in verses 29-31, He tells the parable of the fig tree in verses 32-33. The lesson of this parable is that **Christians confidently watch**, for they see the leaves on the tree (the signs Jesus has spoken of) indicating that the Lord's return is near. In a very real sense, we keep our eyes on the sky and our hearts prepared, even though we don't know the exact timing of His coming. Yet we know that **His timing will confound our wisdom**. When the Son returns, we will see that the Father's timing makes perfect sense, so we watch with confidence in the sovereign control of God.

While we watch, **Christians patiently wait**. In verse 34, Jesus says, "I assure you: This generation will certainly not pass away until all these things take place." This verse has been particularly confusing, because it seems that Jesus is saying that the generation He was speaking to would see His second coming. There's much discussion over what is meant by terms like "generation," "pass away," and "all these things." Good scholars have reached different conclusions. It seems clear, however, that Jesus did not mean that He would return before His disciples died. After all, He explicitly told Peter in John 21:18-19 that Peter would be put to death. Matthew 24:34 seems to teach that all of the things that Jesus has talked about—tribulation, deception, temptation, and persecution—would come upon His disciples, and that others in that generation would see the destruction of Jerusalem as a foretaste of the return of Jesus. But those things would not be the end. In the midst of these signs, from generation to generation, followers of Christ are called to wait patiently.

As we wait for the coming of our glorious King, we know for certain that He is coming back and that today we are closer to His return than we were yesterday. And when He comes, **His return will exceed our expectations**. We've all been hopeful for some thing or some anticipated event, waiting eagerly to experience it, only to be deeply disappointed when it didn't meet our expectations. It will not be so with the second coming of Christ. Our words are inadequate to describe the glory of what that scene will be like, as well as all that will unfold in the days to come after that. In *The Chronicles of Narnia*, C. S. Lewis gives us a rich, imaginative picture of what that eternal state will be like. He ends the last book in the series like this:

> As Aslan spoke, he no longer looked to them like a lion; but the things that began to happen after that were so great and beautiful that I cannot write them. And for us this is the end of all the stories, and we can most truly say that they all lived happily ever after. But for them it was only the beginning of the real story. All their life in this world and all their adventures in Narnia had only been the cover and the title page: now at last they were beginning Chapter One of the Great Story which no one on earth has read: which goes on forever: in which every chapter is better than the one before.

For believers, the return of Christ and the end of this world will be the beginning of a new heaven and a new earth (Rev 21–22). While waiting and watching confidently, **Christians urgently work**. We fight deception and temptation, we persevere through tribulation, and we endure persecution as we proclaim the gospel of the kingdom throughout the whole world. We do this in full dependence on God, as we pray, "Your kingdom come" (Matt 6:10). This is what we give our time and resources to. We spend our lives, even lose them, if necessary, knowing Christ's power will ensure that **His church (our lives!) will accomplish His mission**.

Reflect and Discuss

1. What differentiates unhelpful speculation from a sincere desire to understand our future hope?
2. Summarize the overarching point of Matthew 24:1-36 in one or two sentences.
3. What factors make it difficult to determine the timing and the relationship between the destruction of Jerusalem and Jesus' second coming?
4. How should we respond to those who take a different view of prophecies such as those we read in Matthew 24?
5. Explain how this passage points us away from sinful, short-term pleasures.
6. How does this text speak to the authority and divinity of Jesus Christ?
7. What kind of treatment should believers expect as they await Christ's return?
8. What does it look like for followers of Christ to be eagerly watching for Jesus and urgently working for His kingdom purposes?
9. As it concerns Jesus' return, which truths in this passage should discourage us from date-setting or from making rash judgments based on current events?
10. How should the second coming of Christ inform our witness in the world?

Return of the King (Part 2)

MATTHEW 24:36–25:46

Main Idea: Although Christ's delay may be long, His return in judgment will be sudden and irreversible, so we must be prepared by trusting Him now with a persevering faith that bears fruit.

I. **The Sobering Setup That We Need to Feel**
   A. His delay will be long.
   B. His return will be sudden.
   C. His judgment will be irreversible.
   D. Our hearts will be exposed.
   E. Our sentence may be surprising.
   F. Our lives will stand alone.
   G. We must be prepared.

II. **The Penetrating Questions That You and I Must Ask**
   A. Am I keeping watch for Christ?
   B. Am I faithfully following Christ?
   C. Am I trusting Christ?
   D. Am I serving Christ with what He has given me?
   E. Am I serving Christians whom God has put around me?

III. **Two Eternal Destinations That Await Us All**
   A. Either heaven
      1. Unhindered enjoyment of the Father's love
      2. A kingdom filled with delight
      3. Limitless joy
      4. Everlasting satisfaction
   B. Or hell
      1. Total separation from the Father's love
      2. A place prepared for demons
      3. Unquenchable agony
      4. Never-ending suffering

In the previous section, Matthew 24:1-35, Jesus told his disciples that He would come back, and that His second coming would be visible for all to see. He, the Son of Man, would come on "the clouds of heaven with power and great glory" (v. 30). On that day—it could be today, tomorrow, or a thousand years from now—the angels will gather Christ's elect from the ends of the earth (v. 31). These are grand and glorious truths to bank our futures on; but what do they mean for our lives now, at this moment? How does the reality of Christ's return affect the way we should think and feel right now? The answer to these questions begins in Matthew 24:36, and it runs all the way through the end of Matthew 25. Jesus tells parables and stories to help us understand how we should live in light of His coming. The second coming, we learn, is an intensely practical doctrine. It's a sobering one, too.

The Sobering Setup That We Need to Feel

In this next section of Matthew's Olivet Discourse, as it is sometimes called, it's helpful to remember the context of Jesus' words. Jesus is in the middle of a conversation with His disciples just days before He would be crucified for the sins of men and women throughout history. And before He died and rose from the grave, He prepared His disciples for His departure, promising them that He would return. How His disciples, both then and now, live in light of this reality is the subject Jesus picks up on beginning in verses 36-42.

Looking and waiting for Christ's return should not lead us to be impatient, though Jesus tells us that **His delay will be long**. Remarkably, Jesus says in verse 36 that even He doesn't know the day and hour when this will happen; no one knows this, except the Father in heaven. Here we see the genuine humanity of Christ, for He humbly chose to take on the limitations of knowledge that other men have, though He Himself (simultaneously) remained omniscient and fully divine. Jesus' statement is a reminder that no man, regardless of what he claims, knows the timing of the second coming.

This theme of delay shows up several times in chapters 24–25. In Matthew 25:5 Jesus describes a bridegroom who was "delayed" in coming. Likewise in 25:19 He tells of a master who waited "a long time" to settle accounts with his servants. Jesus began this discourse by speaking of tribulation, persecution, and opposition that would come to His disciples, and in the same breath He promised that the gospel would be proclaimed to all nations (vv. 3-14). All of these realities imply a long delay.

The fact that Jesus' return may involve a long delay should not lead to presumption on our part. After all, the delay may seem particularly long to us, but we need to consider these things from the Lord's perspective: "With the Lord one day is like a thousand years, and a thousand years like one day" (2 Pet 3:8). Christ's delay may feel like it's long in coming, but **His return will be sudden**. To make His point, Jesus refers to the days of Noah prior to the flood, when people were eating and drinking and marrying; in other words, everything was normal—that is, until all of a sudden a flood came and swept them away (Gen 6–8). That's how it's going to be at Christ's second coming: people will be eating lunch, enjoying company, going through their routine, and to their surprise, Christ will return in judgment. Beware of thinking that the day-to-day "stuff" of your life in this world will last. One day it's all going to be turned upside down—instantaneously.

Once Jesus returns, it will be too late to rethink your life and your priorities. **His judgment will be irreversible**, and there will be no second chance to repent. The stories Jesus tells in the remainder of chapters 24–25 illustrate this point. There are servants who are not ready when their master returns, so they are cast out into darkness, where there is weeping and gnashing of teeth (24:45-51). Bridesmaids (called "virgins") are locked out of a marriage feast, and the door is shut, never to open for them (25:1-13). Notice that punishment for such individuals is described as everlasting, as there is absolutely no hint here or anywhere else in the Bible that there will be a second chance for anyone to be saved on the day of Christ's return.

On the day that Jesus returns, **our hearts will be exposed**. The true nature of who we are before God will come to light. Nothing will be hidden; everything will be revealed (Matt 10:26). All the things we like and presume to cover up will be made known. There will be things that, in our pride, we didn't even realize were wrong; these too will be exposed. This heart-penetrating truth leads to the sobering conclusion that **our sentence may be surprising**. In each case, people are surprised when the master casts them out or turns aside from them. This fits what Jesus said near the conclusion of His most famous sermon, when many called Him "Lord" and recounted the things they had done in His name (Matt 7:22). Jesus' response surely came as a terrible surprise: "Then I will announce to them, 'I never knew you! Depart from Me, you lawbreakers!'" (v. 23). Many people will be shocked on the last day to find out that the road they have been on, a road they thought was the narrow road leading to heaven, was actually the broad road that leads to hell (7:13-14).

Matthew 7:21-23 is one of the most frightening passages in all of Scripture for me as a pastor, and the truths it contains fit with what we see here in chapters 24–25. There may be *many* people, even in my own church, who think that they are eternally safe when in fact they do not know Jesus. I think of one brother in our faith family, Tom, who came to us having spent his entire life in church. He had served on just about every committee that any church had ever created, and he had served well. One of the pastors from Tom's former church called one of our pastors to tell us what a great man Tom was and how helpful Tom would be as a member of our church. The only problem is that Tom did not know Jesus. He had checked off every box—he had prayed the prayer, been baptized, signed up, served, taught, and led—yet he had never come to saving faith in Christ. When he was baptized, he shared, "For all those years, I sat in the seats of a church thinking I knew Christ when I did not."

Jordan, a college student in our church, shared a similar story during her baptism testimony:

> I prayed to ask Jesus into my heart when I was younger, yet as
> I grew older, I knew that I had done that—and was doing all
> kinds of other activities in the church—in order to earn the
> favor of God. Until one day, I was finally confronted with the
> extreme tension that exists between my sinful self and God's
> holy nature. I realized that only Christ's work was sufficient for
> the favor of God, and I fell on my knees in fear and trembling
> and adoration and confessed my need for Jesus. Now I know
> that I am crucified with Christ, and I no longer live, but Christ
> lives in me.

Sadly, I don't think the stories of Tom and Jordan are unique. They represent a pandemic problem across contemporary Christianity. Many people have made decisions, prayed prayers, signed cards, been baptized, but they don't truly know Christ. It is little wonder that Jesus speaks in this passage of the surprising sentence that will be passed over the lives of many who profess to be His followers.

In the end, He's saying that **our lives will stand alone**. In verse 40 of chapter 24 He speaks of two men in the field: one is taken and one left. Verse 41 refers to two women grinding at the mill: one taken, one left. It doesn't matter who you're around on that day, as homes, neighborhoods, communities, and nations will be divided among two groups: those who truly know Christ and those who do not know Christ. On that final day, it won't matter what home you're in, whom you're married to, or what your parents believed; your life will stand alone.

So far we've considered the following realities in Matthew 24–25: Jesus' delay will be long, His return will be sudden, His judgment will be irreversible, our hearts will be exposed, our sentence may be surprising, and our lives will stand alone. There is only one way to respond to these truths: **We must be prepared**. That's the point of Matthew 24:36–25:46 in a nutshell. We must be prepared because our lives and our eternities are at stake. As strange as it may sound, this text prepares you for your future ten billion years from now. What could be more important than that?

Based on these five different stories told by Jesus, I want to offer five questions aimed at helping you discern whether or not you are prepared for Christ's coming.

The Penetrating Questions That You And I Must Ask

For the first question, **Am I keeping watch for Christ?** we need to consider the unexpected nature of Jesus' return. In a rather startling illustration in verses 42-44, Jesus describes His coming as being like a thief in the night. The rest of the New Testament uses this same imagery as a description of Christ's coming, also referred to as the Day of the Lord[57] (1 Thess 5:2; 2 Pet 3:10; Rev 3:3; 16:15). The point of this imagery is clear: if you know a thief is coming to your house, then you stay awake and keep watch. Likewise followers of Christ are to keep watch for their Lord, and their lives should be evidence of this reality. So what does this look like practically? What does it mean to watch for Christ? A real-life illustration may help.

When my wife was pregnant with our last child, the doctors gave us the usual expected due date. They expected my son to come around December 7, which meant for us that right around mid-November we would be on "high alert." From that point, through the waning days of the month, and right up to the due date, we were watching and waiting. I

---

[57] The Day of the Lord is an expression used in both the Old and New Testaments that often refers to the time when God's judgment is finally poured out on unbelievers. This expression can also be used in reference to God's previous judgments in history, which often prefigure His final day of reckoning. For the righteous (those in Christ), the Day of the Lord will be a day of salvation and vindication. See for example: Isa 13:6; Jer 46:10; Joel 1:15; 1 Cor 5:5; 2 Thess 2:2.

repeatedly asked Heather, "Babe, how do you feel?" Every moment I was at the office, I had my phone with me, looking and waiting for her to call.

Periodically, I would check in just to make sure I hadn't missed anything. It affected when and where I went, how I traveled, and what I did. I didn't necessarily put my whole life on hold, but I did live with a constant expectation that that particular day could be the day when my child arrived. I couldn't wait to see this person that I already had so much love and affection for. I was watching for him. This kind of anticipation captures something of the essence of what it means to watch for Christ. So do you think about the coming of Christ like *that?*

Christ's second coming should be on our minds and in our hearts, not in such a way that we stop everything we're doing and sit still, but in such a way that it affects everything we're doing. Our thinking about Him is not forced; it's a result of love. When Christ is on your mind, you can't wait to see Him. If this is not the case, consider what this might say about your heart and what this might mean about where your priorities and passions lie. These are questions we need to ask.

The second question comes from Matthew 24:45-51 and Jesus' description of the faithful and wicked slaves. The contrasting descriptions of the faithful slave and the wicked slave should lead you to ask, **"Am I faithfully following Christ?"** There are some details in these stories that we don't need to press too far, but we should be compelled to ask who the "faithful" slave is. One slave faithfully honors his master until he comes, while the other virtually forgets that his master is coming back. This latter, "wicked" slave dishonors his master and is thus surprised by His return. I'm reminded at this point of Jonathan Edwards' resolutions, particularly those relating to time management. His goal was to rehearse these resolutions to himself once a week for his entire life:

- Resolved, never to do anything, which I should be afraid to do, if it were the last hour of my life.
- Resolved, never to do anything, which I should be afraid to do, if I expected it would not be above an hour, before I should hear the last trump.
- Resolved, to inquire every night, as I am going to bed, wherein I have been negligent, what sin I have committed, and wherein I have denied myself: also at the end of every week, month and year.
- Resolved, to ask myself at the end of every day, week, month and year, wherein I could possibly in any respect have done better.

- Resolved, I will act so as I think I shall judge would have been best, and most prudent, when I come into the future world.
- Resolved, to endeavor to my utmost to act as I can think I should do, if I had already seen the happiness of heaven, and hell torments. (Edwards, "Resolutions," xx–xxii)

How about you? How would you live differently today if you knew Jesus was coming back tonight? Will you be found walking in obedience to Him when He returns, or will you be found wandering in disobedience? Will you be found loving your neighbor or ignoring your neighbor? Will you be found passionately devoted to your spouse or practically negligent of your spouse? Will you be found hating sin or holding on to sin? Are you involved in actions, thoughts, and attitudes that would not make sense if it were the last hour of your life?

The consequences of our unfaithfulness are deadly serious. We need to see the horror of Jesus' words in verse 51: "He will cut him to pieces and assign him a place with the hypocrites. In that place there will be weeping and gnashing of teeth." The stakes are high, which leads us to the next question: **Am I trusting Christ?**

Again, we shouldn't get caught up in some of the details of this story of foolish and wise virgins (25:1-13). The virgins are essentially bridesmaids in a wedding. We don't know all the details behind this wedding ritual, but clearly there was a party awaiting the coming of the groom. The bride isn't even mentioned, only bridesmaids who were waiting for the groom in order to go with him into the wedding feast. The only thing that separates one group of bridesmaids from the other is that five of them were prepared with oil in their lamps when the groom came, while the other five were unprepared. The five who were not prepared were left out of the wedding feast altogether. The groom denied them entrance, saying, "I assure you: I do not know you!" (v. 12).

This parable speaks poignantly to people who are not prepared to persevere until Jesus comes back. They have enough oil to burn lights for a bit, but they do not have enough to persevere through the night until the coming of the groom. We can't help but think of Jesus' earlier teaching about the seed that fell on the rocky ground in the parable of the Sower in Matthew 13:5-6, 20-21 (Blomberg, *Matthew*, 371). The seed immediately sprang up, but since it had no depth of soil, it was scorched when the sun came up. In a similar way, these bridesmaids were not prepared to persevere until the groom came back.

It's clear, then, that **the kingdom of heaven is not for those who simply respond to an invitation**. All of these bridesmaids had done that, so to speak. Similarly, **the kingdom of heaven is not for those who simply make a confession**. Each of these bridesmaids would have said they were a part of the bridal party. Their cry in verse 11 as they stand outside the wedding feast sounds eerily similar to the cry of the damned in Matthew 7: "Lord, Lord!" We also need to keep in mind that these bridesmaids were not indifferent to the bridegroom. This was a happy occasion that they were glad to be a part of, but **the kingdom of heaven is not for those who merely express some affection**. Positive sentiments toward Jesus won't be enough on the last day.

At this point, you may be left wondering who *is* fit for the kingdom of heaven. These chapters speak to this as well. **The kingdom of heaven is only for those who endure in salvation.** Earlier, in Matthew 24, Jesus warned the disciples about the danger of falling away. Speaking of those who looked like and claimed to be disciples, Jesus says,

> *Then they will hand you over for persecution, and they will kill you. You will be hated by all nations because of My name. Then many will take offense, betray one another and hate one another. Many false prophets will rise up and deceive many. Because lawlessness will multiply, the love of many will grow cold. But the one who endures to the end will be delivered.* (Matt 24:9-13)

Some people will look like followers of Jesus—they may have responded to an invitation, made a confession, and expressed some affection toward Christ—but they will not endure to the end. This is prevalent in our day, as many would call themselves Christians because of something that happened in the past, but their hearts are now far from God. They aren't trusting in Christ *today*. The issue is not what you did a long time ago, but right now, in your heart, amid the difficulties and inevitable trials that are sure to test you, are you trusting Christ in the present? Ligon Duncan has said of the foolish virgins,

> They have a form of piety, but they deny its power. And unprepared, they travel on to meet the judge. None of us, none of us may presume to be prepared. All of us must be watchful of our hearts. We must examine ourselves to see if we are trusting in Him, lest we unprepared travel on. (Duncan, "The Ten Virgins")

So are you trusting in Christ today? The question is not whether we've responded to an invitation to Christ or expressed some affection toward Him in the past, but whether we are trusting in Christ *at this moment* for our salvation. This is how we prepare for Jesus' coming, by persevering in faith and trusting Him at all times.

The fourth major question in this section comes in verses 14-30 of Matthew 25. The parable of the Talents should prompt the question, **Am I serving Christ with what He has given me?** This story is unique because it goes beyond simply watching and waiting for Jesus to return and focuses primarily on working until Jesus comes back. D. A. Carson has put it this way:

> It is not enough for Jesus' followers to "hang in there" and
> wait for the end. They must see themselves [as] servants . . .
> who improve what [their Master] entrusts to them. Failure to
> do so proves they cannot really be valued [as] disciples at all.
> (Carson, *God with Us*, 149)

Jesus speaks of servants entrusted with varying amounts of talents. To feel the force of the illustration, realize that a talent could be, according to some, worth several hundred thousand dollars in terms of today's money. And the overall parallel is clear: **Jesus is our Master** who has given us much. **We are His stewards**, responsible for that which has been entrusted to us. We are to work diligently, and so honor our Master by maximizing His resources.

Key to understanding Jesus' point in this parable is the realization that this is not simply about an employee-employer relationship that is cold, hard, and focused on the bottom line. See, for example, the joy in the relationship between these first two servants and their master. Hear the excitement in the first servant's voice: "Look, I've earned five more talents" (v. 20). One commentator imagined the scene this way, "The man's eyes are sparkling. He is bubbling over with enthusiasm, is thoroughly thrilled, and, as it were, invites his master to start counting" (Hendriksen, *Exposition of the Gospel According to Matthew*, 881). And then his master says to him, "Well done, good and faithful slave! . . . Share your master's joy!" (v. 23). There is intimacy between the master and the servant, and this is God's design for us as well. The question becomes, **Will you be commended for your love?** Do you keep watch for Christ in such a way that love is the overflow of your waiting for Him?

When my wife goes out of town, I don't become so preoccupied with other things that I forget about her. I can't wait for her to come back! I love her so much that I talk to her about when she's coming back. This is the kind of anticipation we ought to have for Christ, our Master. This is what Jesus is getting at in John 15:10-11: "If you keep My commands you will remain in my love, just as I have kept my Father's commands and remain in His love. I have spoken these things to you so that My joy may be in you and your joy may be complete." Are you trusting in and serving Him because you love Him? Or is your service mere routine and loveless duty?

Unlike the first two slaves, the third slave was not commended by the master. This slave was not condemned for what he did, but for what he didn't do; he was lazy. When we apply this part of the parable, the question becomes, **Will you be condemned in your laziness?** Don't miss the reason the third slave gives for his inaction. In verse 24 he refers to the master as a "difficult man" who unjustly expects to gather where he hasn't sown. Do you see the lack of joy and intimacy? He blamed the master for his own lack of responsibility. In the end, he was condemned, and his relationship with the master was severed. As a steward, a failure to serve and honor the master with the mercy he has entrusted to you indicates a lack of love and desire for the master. This truth is at the heart of what it means to be Jesus' disciple.

So, what are you doing with what God has entrusted to you? To be sure, this is not an attempt to "earn your keep" before Jesus returns; rather, this is a demonstration of your love for Christ and your gratitude for what He has given you. Will you be commended for your love, or condemned for your laziness?

The fifth and final question from Jesus' discourse in chapters 24–25 is this: **Am I serving Christians whom God has put around me?** Many people are confused about this passage (25:31-46), taking the point to be that whenever we do something good for someone, it's the same as doing it for Jesus. That line of thinking misses part of Jesus' point. Verse 40 helps us to understand this passage rightly, as Jesus says, "Whatever you did for one of the least of these *brothers* of Mine, you did for Me" (emphasis added). The point is that Jesus is identifying Himself with His followers, His brothers, those who have trusted in Him. There are other examples in the New Testament where we see Jesus identify Himself in the closest possible terms with Christians. For instance, when Paul was blinded on the road to Damascus in Acts 9, Jesus appeared to this persecutor of Christians and said, "Saul, Saul, why are you persecuting *Me*?" (v. 4; emphasis added). In other words, Jesus says, "You mess with them, and you're messing with Me." Similarly, in Matthew 25:40 Jesus counts service to His followers as service to Him.

It would be wrong to think that Jesus' close identification with His followers means that we should not help people who aren't Christians. Throughout Scripture we're encouraged to love and serve non-Christians;[58] Jesus has even told us to love our enemies (Matt 5:43-48). However, that's not the specific point of *this* passage. This passage calls us to examine whether we are serving Christians in need whom God has put around us.

There's another misunderstanding of this passage that we need to avoid. You serve Christians God has put around you **not because you want to get to heaven**, as if you could earn your right standing before God. These saints who are welcomed into heaven in this passage are surprised at what Jesus says: "Lord, when did we see You hungry and feed You, or thirsty and give You something to drink?" (v. 37). Clearly, their acts of service—giving away food and clothes, welcoming strangers, visiting the sick and the imprisoned—were not done in order to get to heaven, for they were shocked to hear that these works had been noticed. You serve Christians whom God has put around you not because you want to get to heaven, **but because Jesus has changed your heart**.

Our love for other believers is constantly held out in Scripture as a mark that God has made us His own. In John 15:12, Jesus told His disciples, "Love one another as I have loved you." Likewise, the book of 1 John is all about love—love for God and love for the children of God. Consider several passages in John's epistle that speak to the love Jesus calls for in Matthew 25:

> *Dear friends, let us love one another, because love is from God, and everyone who loves has been born of God and knows God. The one who does not love does not know God, because God is love.* (1 John 4:7-8)

> *We love because He first loved us. If anyone says, "I love God," yet hates his brother, he is a liar. For the person who does not love his brother he has seen cannot love the God he has not seen. And we have this command from Him: The one who loves God must also love his brother.* (1 John 4:19-21)

---

[58] See for example the parable of the Good Samaritan in Luke 10:25-37.

This is how we have come to know love: He laid down His life for us.
We should also lay down our lives for our brothers. If anyone has this
world's goods and sees his brother in need but closes his eyes to his
need—how can God's love reside in him? (1 John 3:16-18)

These are much-needed reminders for people (like us) who have so
much of the world's goods. We are surrounded by brothers and sisters in
Christ who are in need, so let us not close our hearts to them. Rather, let
us give extravagantly to *them*, and in the process, show extravagant love
to *Him*! We should make sacrifices in ministries and comforts *here* in our
church culture so that our brothers and sisters who are starving can live
over *there*. This is the fruit of a heart that's been changed by Christ, and
it's a fundamental way we prepare for the coming of Christ. We serve
Christians that God has put around us. Again, we do this knowing that
sacrificial service is not a means of earning salvation. We don't serve
other people, specifically our brothers and sisters in Christ, in order
to gain enough favor from God so that we can enter heaven. Instead,
sacrificial service is necessary evidence of salvation. A heart that has
truly trusted in Christ and a life that is truly longing for Christ will be
consumed with serving men and women who are in Christ.

Two Eternal Destinations That Await Us All

What is obvious from every one of these stories in Matthew 24–25 is that
when we die, or when Jesus comes back (whichever comes first), all of us
will be divided between two destinations. Every individual ever created
will stand alone before God at the judgment.

For some of us, **heaven** will be our destination, a place where people
will experience **unhindered enjoyment of the Father's love**. This is what
we read about in Matthew 25:34: "Then the King will say to those on His
right, 'Come, you who are blessed by My Father, inherit the kingdom
prepared for you from the foundation of the world.'" These will enter
a kingdom filled with delight, limitless joy, and **everlasting satisfaction**.
That's the beautiful imagery we've seen all over these stories—a blessed
slave (24:45-46), a wedding feast (25:10), servants entering into the joy
of their master (25:21, 23), and now the righteous entering into eternal
life (25:46). Why would we not long for this day? Oh, how we should
keep watch for Christ, faithfully following Him until He returns! Let's
trust Him, serve Him, and serve those children of His who are in need

around us. It won't be long until we're together in the Father's kingdom enjoying the Son's reward.

Every person will either experience this glorious reward in heaven, or **hell** will be their destination. Hell is the polar opposite of the rewards mentioned in this passage. Those who have not trusted in Christ and are not prepared for His coming will hear the words, "Depart from Me, you who are cursed, into the eternal fire prepared for the Devil and his angels!" (25:41). Jesus speaks of **total separation from the Father's love**, and this will be in **a place prepared for demons**. Hell is not a place where the Devil torments sinners; hell is a place where he is tormented *alongside* sinners. One writer said, "What a destiny! To spend eternity shoulder to shoulder with an evil being whose one goal has been to defy God and bring others to share in suffering forever." Hell is a place of **unquenchable agony**. Consider the imagery Jesus uses for the fate of unbelievers: "cut him to pieces . . . weeping and gnashing of teeth" (24:51), "outer darkness" (25:30), and "eternal fire" (25:41).

People have wondered, based on these images, how hell can be darkness and have fire at the same time? But this misses the point: these are words and images to depict agony and misery that will mark all who are destined for this place. In one writer's words, "The purpose of imagery is to point beyond what literal language can convey. If a literal burning by fire is bad, the reality of hell's suffering must be immeasurably and inexpressibly worse." Worst of all, hell is a place of **never-ending suffering**. The same word—"eternal"—that is used to describe life with God in heaven is now used to describe the horror of punishment from God in hell (25:46).

If we're honest, these truths about heaven and hell are a little overwhelming. Thinking about such weighty topics goes against the grain of what we're used to. We wonder, "Is this really true?" Of course, if Jesus did not rise from the dead, then we don't have to worry about believing such difficult truths. However, if Jesus was who He said He was, and if He did conquer death, then we must embrace everything He said. He is our Lord and we gladly submit.

In light of the authority of Jesus and the truth of His Word, we need to ask ourselves, "Am I ready for His return?" Even if Jesus doesn't return today, we may take our last breath in the coming hours. We must, therefore, be prepared to meet God. And how do we do that? By clinging to Christ today. By repenting of sin and trusting in the gospel. Jesus died on a cross to pay the price for your sins, and He has risen from the grave in victory over death. *All* who repent and believe in Him will be reconciled to God (John 3:16). The words of John Owen serve as a fitting conclusion:

> This is somewhat of the word which he now speaks unto you:
> Why will ye die? Why will ye perish? Why will ye not have
> compassion on your own souls? Can your hearts endure,
> or can your hands be strong, in the day of wrath that is
> approaching? . . . Look unto me, and be saved; come unto
> me, and I will ease you of all sins, sorrows, fears, burdens,
> and give rest to your souls. Come, I entreat you; lay aside
> all procrastinations, all delays; put me off no more; eternity
> lies at the door . . . do not so hate me as that you will rather
> perish than accept of deliverance by me. (As cited in Packer,
> *Evangelism and the Sovereignty of God*, 102)

Reflect and Discuss

1. Do you ever doubt that Christ's second coming will actually happen? What are some factors that lead you to question whether this promise will actually be fulfilled?
2. Discuss the parallels between Christ's second coming and the account of the flood in the days of Noah (Genesis 6–9).
3. How would you reply to the supposition that individuals will receive a chance to respond to the gospel either as Christ returns or after His return? How might this passage inform your reply?
4. Describe the difference between the faithful slave and the wicked slave in Matthew 24:45-51.
5. In your own words, what does it mean to keep watch for Christ, and how is this mind-set different from inactivity?
6. How are endurance and faithfulness—marks of true, saving faith—different from attempting to earn a right standing before God?
7. How would you reply to someone who asked the following questions? "What does the Bible say about the destiny of those who are genuinely followers of Christ? What is the fate of those who persist in unbelief?"
8. Practically speaking, how does the reality of eternal punishment affect how you live day to day?
9. How does this passage speak to the glory of Jesus Christ?
10. What are some evidences that we are true followers of Christ? Do you see these evidences (even if not perfectly) in your own life?

The Centerpiece of All History and the Determinant of Our Eternity

MATTHEW 26–27

Main Idea: As the centerpiece of all history and the determinant of our eternity, the cross reveals God's holiness, our wickedness, and the humility of Jesus Christ.

I. **Remember the Holiness of God.**
   A. He is sovereign over all.
   B. He is righteous above all.
   C. He is just in all His wrath.
   D. He is loving toward all His creation.
   E. How can a righteous God be loving to rebellious sinners who are due His wrath?

II. **Tremble at the Horror of Wickedness.**
   A. Jewish leaders: rejecting, arresting, accusing, and judging the Son of God
   B. Roman leaders: sentencing and crucifying the Son of God
   C. Soldiers: stripping, scourging, mocking, beating, and spitting on the Son of God
   D. Crowds: ridiculing, reviling, and shouting at the Son of God
   E. Disciples: betraying, denying, disobeying, scattering, and deserting the Son of God

III. **Behold the Humility of Christ.**
   A. Substitution: Jesus died our death.
      1. He is the Passover lamb (Exod 12) who saves us with His blood.
      2. He is the covenant keeper (Exod 24) who seals us with His blood.
      3. Before the cross, we were headed to eternal death; because of the cross, we now have eternal life.
   B. Propitiation: Jesus endured our condemnation.
      1. The cup of the cross is not primarily physical suffering; it is predominantly spiritual suffering.
      2. Jesus was not a coward about to face Roman soldiers; He was a Savior about to experience divine wrath.

3.   Before the cross, we were afraid of God; because of the
       cross, we are now friends of God.
 C. Reconciliation: Jesus suffered our separation.
  1.   The cry on the cross
  2.   The curse of the cross
  3.   Before the cross, we were cast out of God's presence;
       because of the cross, we are now invited into God's
       presence.
IV. Respond to the Cross.
 A. Surrender your heart to God.
 B. Proclaim the hope of the gospel.

As we turn to Matthew 26–27, we are treading on some of the most holy ground in all of Scripture. Christ's death on the cross is the climax of Matthew's Gospel, the point toward which everything has been moving, for Jesus is the One who would "save His people from their sins" (1:21). Here we approach the Mount Everest of the biblical landscape. Charles Spurgeon's words about the garden of Gethsemane could be applied to this entire text:

> Here we come to the Holy of Holies of our Lord's life on
> earth. This is a mystery like that which Moses saw when the
> bush burned with fire, and was not consumed. No man can
> rightly expound such a passage as this; it is a subject for
> prayerful, heart-broken meditation, more than for human
> language. (As cited in Boice, *The Gospel of Matthew*, vol. 2, 566)

In light of the gravity of this text, we should approach it with a sense of trembling. The cross is the centerpiece of history and the determinant of our eternity. E. Stanley Jones said, "The cross is the key. If I lose this key I fumble. The universe will not open to me. But with this key in my hand I know I hold its secret" (as cited in Miller, *The Book of Jesus*, 358). Most believers agree with Jones that the cross is important, but they haven't stopped to consider *why* it is that what happened 2,000 years ago is still so significant. In other words, why is the death of Jesus of Nazareth *the* key to understanding everything? The answers to such questions require that we take a step back and consider the biblical context of the cross. We must see how Christ's suffering and death in Matthew 26–27 relate to what we know about God and His plan for the world.

Remember the Holiness of God

An understanding of God and of man's relation to God is critical to understanding the cross. If we humans are essentially intact spiritually, only in need of some minor changes in our lives, then with a little bit of effort on our part salvation can happen. But if man is totally depraved apart from God, then something radical has to happen to span this divide. Once we see God for who He is and ourselves for who we are, we begin to see the cross for what it means. Its wonder and necessity become so obvious that we are astonished we never saw it before. Therefore, before we reflect on the events of Matthew 26–27, it will be helpful to pause first and consider the character of God.

Sovereignty

First, as we consider God's character, we must come to grips with His relation to the world—**He is sovereign over all**. To say that God is sovereign is to say that He has all authority. Psalm 24:1-2 says, "The earth and everything in it, the world and its inhabitants, belong to the LORD, for He laid its foundation on the seas and established it on the rivers." God created all things, knows all things, sustains all things, and owns all things. He has authority to govern the world and He has authority to govern our lives. He has *all* the rights, so we belong to Him.

Although we belong to God and He has absolute authority over our lives, **we have denounced His sovereignty** and rebelled against Him. This rebellion began back in Genesis 3, when God told Adam not to eat from the tree of the knowledge of good and evil (v. 17). We do the same thing today; even though God says "no" to something, we do it anyway. We don't want Him as Lord over us. This kind of rebellion is evident in the lives of every one of us.

Righteousness

Second, understanding God's character also means believing that **He is righteous above all**. Everything God does is right. In Genesis 18:25 Abraham asks, "Won't the Judge of all the earth do what is just?" And the psalmist declares, "The Lord is righteous in all His ways and gracious in all His acts" (Ps 145:17). God has never had a wrong thought, never done a wrong deed, never had a wrong motive, and never said a wrong thing. Yet, **we have despised His righteousness**. Romans 3:10-12 says,

There is no one righteous, not even one. There is no one who understands; there is no one who seeks God. All have turned away; all alike have become useless. There is no one who does what is good, not even one.

We are the complete opposite of God in terms of righteousness. We intentionally have wrong thoughts, do wrong deeds, possess wrong motives, and say wrong things. In short, we reject His righteousness.

Wrath

The third characteristic of God's character has to do with His judgment. Though this is an unpopular truth today, the Bible teaches that **He is just in all His wrath.** Because God is holy and righteous, He hates sin. And because His justice flows from His righteousness, God's wrathful response to sin and evil is not just a possibility, it is an inevitability. Scripture refers to God's wrath more than 580 times, using more than 20 different words to describe it. In the Old Testament God's wrath is real, personal, intense, and steady.[59] It is not mysterious or irrational; it is fully in line with God's character. Wrath is the consistent response of a holy and righteous God to sin. While this may be offensive to the world, God's wrath should be seen as pure and loving for those who know Him. It is, after all, good for God to hate that which destroys us.

And it's not only the Old Testament that teaches this. The New Testament only deepens our understanding of God's wrath. Recall Matthew 3 and John the Baptist's announcement that the King is coming with a "winnowing shovel" in His hand (v. 12). John the Baptist warned people to flee God's coming wrath. Likewise the Gospel of John speaks of Jesus' ministry in the context of God's wrath: "The one who believes in the Son has eternal life, but the one who refuses to believe in the Son will not see life; instead, the wrath of God remains on him" (John 3:36). Like the Old Testament, the New Testament portrays God's wrath as deserved, dreadful, final, and eternal.[60]

Some people complain that God's wrath is too severe, that is, the punishment doesn't fit the crime. But the reality is that because God is *infinitely* worthy and honorable, one sin against Him is an *infinite* offense

---

[59] For a description of God's holy wrath in the Old Testament, see Nah 1:1-14.

[60] See for example 2 Thess 1:5-10 and Rev 19:11-21.

and shows *infinite* dishonor, thus making it worthy of *infinite* punishment. Remember that one sin led to the curse of God (Gen 3:14-19), and remember too that this one act of disobedience continues to affect the entire world today. In Romans 5:18 Paul says that Adam's sin brought condemnation to all men. The effects on the natural order have also been catastrophic: world wars, the holocaust, cancer, disease, tsunamis, earthquakes, hurricanes, tornadoes, terrorism, pain, and suffering—all because of one sin.

In light of the dreadful effects of one sin, consider that you and I have committed thousands upon thousands of sins. This is why the Bible makes clear that God is just in bringing His wrath on us. Nevertheless, even though God is just in punishing sinners, **we have disregarded His wrath**. His judgment has been questioned, mocked, and ultimately ignored.

Love

The fourth characteristic we need to consider about God's character is His love. **He is loving toward all His creation**, and this too affects everything He does. First John 4:16 says, "And we have come to know and to believe the love that God has for us. God is love, and the one who remains in love remains in God, and God remains in him." Once again, even though we know this aspect of God's character, **we have denied His love**. In Romans 2:4 Paul says that we have despised the "riches of [God's] kindness, restraint, and patience." We have not believed that God loves us, and so we have turned aside to our own ways.

The Problem

With this brief summary of God's character in mind—the sovereignty, righteousness, wrath, and love of God—we come face to face with *the* question that is at the center of the entire Bible: **How can a righteous God be *loving* to rebellious sinners who are due His *wrath*?** To understand the cross, we must feel the weight of this question. This is the problem with which Scripture is ultimately concerned, and it is the ultimate question in the whole universe: How can sinful man be righteous before God? Proverbs 17:15 helps us feel this tension: "Acquitting the guilty and condemning the just—both are detestable to the LORD." When earthly judges pronounce the wicked to be innocent or the righteous to be condemned, it is an abomination. How much more is this true with God? As soon as God tells rebellious sinners that they are right before Him, God becomes an abomination to Himself. So how do sinners *not* receive a guilty verdict?

It's revealing that God's pardoning of the guilty is not the problem we normally identify. Not many people in our culture are losing sleep over how God can be just *and* kind to sinners at the same time. Instead, we are so warped in our thinking that we point the finger at God and say, "How can you punish sinners? How can you let people go to hell?" But the question of the Bible is just the opposite: "God, how can you be just and right and let rebels into heaven?"

If we are to grasp the wonder of the gospel, we must see that **God's forgiveness of our sin is a threat to His character**. John Stott even went so far as to say, "Forgiveness is for God the profoundest of problems" (Stott, *The Cross of Christ*, 110). Stott goes on to quote Bishop Westcott: "Nothing superficially seems simpler than forgiveness," whereas "nothing if we look deeply is more mysterious or more difficult" (Stott, 110). Romans 3:25 addresses this dilemma, where Paul says that the purpose of Christ's death was "to demonstrate [God's] righteousness, because in His restraint God passed over the sins previously committed." Passing over sins is what God did continually prior to Christ's coming. Consider, for example, the prophet Nathan's confrontation of David following the king's adultery, lying, and murder. David confessed, "I have sinned against the LORD" (2 Sam 12:13), to which Nathan replied, "The LORD has taken away your sin; you will not die." Did you catch that—adultery, lying, and murder passed over by God! We would immediately remove any earthly judge from the bench for that kind of decision. So how is that justice?

The seeming tension in God's character helps bring Christ's death into proper perspective. **Before the cross is for anyone else's sake, the cross is for God's sake**.

Ultimately, Christ did not die for you or me, or even for the nations; those answers are incomplete. Ultimately, Christ died for God. Watchman Nee said, "If I would appreciate the blood of Christ I must accept God's valuation of it, for the blood is not primarily for me but for God" (Miller, *The Book of Jesus*, 359). We have heard the gospel presented as God's answer to human problems, and it is that in many ways; but first and foremost, the cross is God's answer to a divine problem. Christ's death was for God's vindication and the declaration of His glory. God was demonstrating His justice and His righteousness.

In John 12:27-28, after His triumphal entry into Jerusalem and in preparation for His crucifixion, Jesus says explicitly that God's glory was at the heart of the purpose for His coming:

Now My soul is troubled. What should I say—Father, save Me from this hour? But that is why I came to this hour. Father, glorify Your name!

We talk about being on the Savior's mind when He went to the cross, but first and foremost, the Father was on the Savior's mind when He was on the cross. The cross vindicates God's character before it rescues us. As we think about the cross and the magnitude of what happened in Matthew 26–27, we need to keep this God-centered perspective in mind.

Tremble at the Horror of Wickedness

The realization of God's holiness and His perfect purity should immediately cause us to reflect on our own sinfulness. The horror of wickedness should cause us to tremble. One writer said,

[For thousands of] years wickedness had been growing. It had wrought deeds of impiety and crime that had wrung the ages with agony, and often roused the justice of the universe to roll her fiery thunderbolts of retribution through the world. But now it had grown to full maturity; it stands around this cross in such gigantic proportions as had never been seen before; it works an enormity before which the mightiest of its past exploits dwindle into insignificance, and pale into dimness. It crucifies the Lord of life and glory. (Thomas, *The Gospel of Matthew*, 536)

In Matthew 26–27, the wickedness of man is on display in different people at different times as they respond to the Son of God. The height of wickedness is reached as man seizes God in the flesh and crucifies Him. See first the **Jewish leaders: rejecting, arresting, accusing, and judging the Son of God**. This brazen response is evident in Matthew 26:63, where the high priest is sitting in judgment upon Jesus, and he says, "By the living God I place You under oath: tell us if You are the Messiah, the Son of God!" Jesus responded by saying, "You have said it. . . . But I tell you, in the future you will see the Son of Man seated at the right hand of the Power and coming on the clouds of heaven"

, referencing Old Testament prophecies concerning His own exaltation,[61] Jesus informed the high priest that He would one day sit in judgment of the high priest. This claim pushed the high priest over the edge, as he tore his robes and said, "He has blasphemed!" (v. 65) The Jewish leaders responded similarly, saying, "He deserves death!" (v. 66). Then they spit in His face and struck Him (v. 67).

After the Jewish authorities decided to put Jesus to death, they took Him to Pilate, the Roman governor. Here we see the response of the **Roman leaders: sentencing and crucifying the Son of God**. Pilate interrogated Jesus, and when he couldn't find any guilt in Him (v. 24), he gave the crowds the option of either releasing Barabbas, a murderous insurrectionist, or setting Jesus free. The crowds cried out to have Barabbas released and Jesus crucified (27:21-23). Pilate tried to absolve himself of responsibility, but there is no question that responsibility was on his hands, just as it was on the Jewish leaders' hands. Verse 26 indicates that Pilate was ultimately responsible for releasing Jesus to be scourged and crucified.

Pilate's guilt then leads us to the **soldiers: stripping, scourging, mocking, beating, and spitting on the Son of God.** They took the dreaded whip, which was full of bone or lead bound into leather thongs, and lashed Jesus' body to a bloody pulp. After that, they twisted a crown of thorns into His head, put a scepter in His hand and a robe around His naked body, and bowed down in mockery, saying, "Hail, King of the Jews." Then they spit in His face and led Him away to a cross (vv. 27-31). Crucifixion was the most degrading of all ways to die. One writer described it this way:

> Crucifixion was unspeakably painful and degrading. Whether tied or nailed to the cross, the victim endured countless paroxysms as he pulled with his arms and pushed with his legs to keep his chest cavity open for breathing and then collapsed in exhaustion until the demand for oxygen demanded renewed paroxysms. The scourging, the loss of blood, the shock from the pain, all produced agony that could go on for days, ending at last by suffocation, cardiac arrest, or loss of blood. When there was reason to hasten death the execution

---

[61] In Matt 26:64, Jesus references Dan 7:13 and Ps 110:1, prophecies that refer to the glorious exaltation of the Son of Man, God's chosen King. Blomberg, *Matthew*, 403.

squad would smash the victim's legs. Death followed almost immediately, either from shock or from collapse that cut off breathing. (Carson, *Matthew*, 574) ☞

The authorities dealt with Jesus cruelly, but we shouldn't get the impression that it was only the Roman and Jewish leadership, along with the Roman soldiers, who were responsible for Christ's crucifixion. See also the response of the **crowds: ridiculing, reviling, and shouting at the Son of God**. Those passing by shook their heads derisively, saying, "The One who would demolish the sanctuary and rebuild it in three days, save Yourself! If You are the Son of God, come down from the cross!" (27:40). We shouldn't comfort ourselves by thinking that we wouldn't respond like those in power, for no one responded to Jesus rightly. He was ridiculed by the average person on the street.

In the middle of all of the rejection, what was potentially most disheartening was the reaction of the **disciples: betraying, denying, disobeying, scattering, and deserting the Son of God**. Among Judas (26:47-50), Peter (26:69-75), and the other disciples (26:55-56), no one proved faithful. After three years of walking with Jesus, His closest companions deserted Him at His darkest hour.

Having seen the rejection of Jesus by different groups of people in Matthew's account, including Jesus' own disciples, we might be tempted to see the problem of sin and wickedness as being a problem in the lives of other people. However, we need to tremble at the horror of wickedness in our own lives as well. The characters in this story embody the same sin and rebellion that exists in our hearts, and like us, they need God's grace. Consider, then, which character you most identify with in the passion narrative. Would it be

- Peter, weeping as you realize the magnitude of your denial of Christ?
- Simon of Cyrene, carrying Jesus' cross for Him?
- the women who stood at a distance watching these things?
- Mary, standing near the cross of Jesus in gut-wrenching grief?
- the thief, asking Jesus to remember him in His kingdom?
- the centurion, who watched Jesus die and shouted out, "This man really was God's Son!"? (Mahaney, *Living the Cross Centered Life*, 86–87)

C. J. Mahaney's response is perhaps most appropriate:

I identify most with the angry mob screaming, "Crucify Him!" That's who we should all identify with. Because apart from God's grace, this is where we would all be standing, and we're only flattering ourselves to think otherwise. Unless you see yourself standing there with the shrieking crowd, full of hostility and hatred for the holy and innocent Lamb of God, you don't really understand the nature and depth of your sin or the necessity of the cross. (Mahaney, *Living the Cross Centered Life*, 87)

When you read Matthew 26–27, tremble at the horror of wickedness in your own heart.

Behold the Humility of Christ

On the surface, Matthew 26–27 is about the horror of wickedness in the crucifixion of Christ. We're taken aback by the sin of those who rejected Christ, and this is a reminder of the darkness of our own hearts. However, below the surface, another theme emerges: the humility of Jesus Christ. The cross is significant not ultimately because of all the physical suffering that comes to mind, though Christ's physical and bodily death are obviously essential to our salvation; the cross is ultimately significant because of the spiritual realities that converged in this one moment in history. There are depths of truth to be explored and uncovered in this scene, and I have highlighted three key words aimed at probing these depths. These three words are based on three significant events in these chapters: the Lord's Supper (26:26-29), the garden of Gethsemane (26:36-46), and Jesus' cry from the cross (27:45-50).

Substitution (26:17-29)

First, the humility of Christ is evident in His **substitution: Jesus died our death**. Scripture is clear that the payment for sin is death (Rom 6:23), but Jesus had no sin, so why are we reading a story about His death? Because He is our substitute. When we read of Christ's death in these chapters, we are seeing Him die in our place.

Beginning in verse 17, Jesus is celebrating the Passover meal with His disciples, a meal they ate every year to remember God's deliverance from Egypt (see Exod 12). For Passover, the Israelite homes were instructed to slaughter a spotless lamb and then put its blood above their doorposts. When God came in judgment on the homes of the Israelites and the Egyptians, He would put to death the firstborn son in any home that did not have blood over the doorpost. God provided the blood of a lamb, a substitute sacrifice, to save His people from the payment of sin. God's people would celebrate this meal every year, taking these lambs to be slaughtered. The Israelites would gather together in their homes and remember the original Passover night in Egypt. With that backdrop, Jesus refers to the cup in the Last Supper as signifying "*My* blood," which is "shed for many for the forgiveness of sins" (26:28; emphasis added). **He is the Passover lamb (Exod 12) who saves us with His blood**. When God's wrath and judgment come, we hide under the blood of a substitute sacrifice, Jesus the Lamb of God, and we are saved.

The account of the Last Supper also connects Jesus' death with the law God gave to His people. **He is the covenant keeper (Exod 24) who seals us with His blood**. Jesus refers to "My blood that establishes the covenant" in Matthew 26:28, and this is the only time the word "covenant" is used in Matthew's Gospel. Jesus is alluding to Exodus 24, when the law-covenant that God had given His people at Mount Sinai was confirmed. In Exodus 24:8 Moses sprinkled the blood of the sacrifice on the people, saying, "This is the blood of the covenant that the LORD has made with you concerning all these words." This was a picture not only of God's forgiveness, but also of His binding of the people to Himself in relationship. Now, with Jesus' death, we have a *new* covenant (Jer 31:31-34; Ezek 36:25-27) sealed not with the blood of an animal sacrifice, but with the blood of the Son of God Himself (Heb 10:1-18). He is our substitute sacrifice, and He has died the death we deserved to die.

The truth of Christ's substitutionary death is good news for sinners. **Before the cross, we were headed to eternal death; because of the cross, we now have eternal life**. At the Last Supper, Jesus promised His disciples that they would again drink of the fruit of the vine in His Father's kingdom (Matt 26:29). Those who trust in the substitute sacrifice of Jesus will live forever! We even see a foretaste of this promise of new life following Jesus' death and resurrection. Matthew tells us about the bodies of saints being raised (vv. 52-53), and while there is disagreement over how to understand this event, it is clear that Matthew portrays the death of Christ as that which makes resurrection to life possible for all who trust in Him.

Propitiation (26:36-46)

The second key word in this scene is **propitiation: Jesus endured our condemnation**. This word "propitiation" appears in Romans 3:25, where we read that God "presented [Christ] as a propitiation." A propitiation refers to something (in this case Someone) who turns aside wrath by taking away sin. This idea of propitiation only makes sense when we understand the character of God. It is because of God's holiness that His wrath must be satisfied. When Jesus went to the cross, He endured the wrath that we deserve; He is our propitiation. This point comes through clearly as Jesus cried out to God in prayer in Gethsemane. One commentator has called this a passage that we must "approach upon our knees" (Barclay, *The Gospel of Matthew*, 406). Similarly, D. A. Carson writes, "As Jesus' death was unique, so also was his anguish; and our best response to it is hushed worship" (Carson, *Matthew*, 543).

In Matthew 26:36-46, Jesus prayed to His Father in the garden of Gethsemane. He was preparing to be betrayed, arrested, and eventually crucified. In His anguish, He cried out, "My Father! If it is possible, let this cup pass from Me. Yet not as I will, but as You will" (v. 39). It's important to understand what Jesus means when He refers to this "cup." **The cup of the cross is not primarily physical suffering; it is predominantly spiritual suffering**. What is causing Jesus such anguish here is not the prospect of what is about to happen to Him physically, but the prospect of what is about to happen to Him spiritually. We know this because of the way Scripture talks about the cup:

> For there is a cup in the LORD's hand, full of wine blended with spices, and He pours from it. All the wicked of the earth will drink, draining it to the dregs. (Ps 75:8)

> Wake yourself, wake yourself up! Stand up, Jerusalem, you who have drunk the cup of His fury from the hand of the LORD; you who have drunk the goblet to the dregs—the cup that causes people to stagger. . . . They are full of the LORD's fury, the rebuke of your God. So listen to this, afflicted and drunken one—but not with wine. This is what your Lord says—Yahweh, even your God, who defends His people—"Look, I have removed the cup of staggering from your hand; that goblet, the cup of My fury. You will never drink it again." (Isa 51:17, 20-22)

> This is what the LORD, the God of Israel, said to me: "Take this cup of the wine of wrath from My hand and make all the nations I am

sending you to, drink from it. They will drink, stagger, and go out
of their minds because of the sword I am sending among them." (Jer
25:15-16)

In the Old Testament, the cup is a metaphor for God's wrath. This same imagery is picked up in the New Testament in Revelation 14:10, where John speaks of the judgment coming to those who have worshiped the beast, for they will "drink the wine of God's wrath, which is mixed full strength in the cup of His anger." Realize, then, that **Jesus was not a coward about to face Roman soldiers; He was a Savior about to experience divine wrath**. When Jesus went to the cross, the full cup of the wrath of God due our sin was poured out upon His Son. Jesus was enduring our condemnation. Behold the wonder and the beauty of the cross:

- At the cross, God expresses His full judgment upon sin.
- At the cross, God endures His full judgment against sin.
- At the cross, God enables free salvation for sinners.

Before the cross, we were afraid of God; because of the cross, we are now friends of God. And all of this is because of the propitiation of Christ's death. He endured the wrath of the Father that we might experience the love of the Father.

Reconciliation (27:45-46)

The third word that helps us explain the cross is **reconciliation: Jesus suffered our separation**. When Jesus cried out, "My God, my God, why have you forsaken Me?" in verse 46, He was suffering separation from God for our reconciliation. **The cry on the cross is *not* a cry of unbelief, confusion, or despair**. Jesus was not doubting the Father, and He wasn't confused about what was happening to Him. We shouldn't understand His cry from the cross as if He were saying to His Father, "Why are You doing this to Me?" He knew everything that was going on at that moment; in fact, He had foretold this moment (Matt 17:22-23; Mark 9:31), and He had willingly submitted Himself to it (John 10:17-18). He was confident in the Father even as He experienced abandonment.

Jesus' **cry on the cross was a cry of physical agony, spiritual anguish, and relational alienation**. He quoted from Psalm 22, and understanding that psalm is key to understanding this cry. Much could be said about the themes in this psalm and their relation to the crucifixion, but for now we should note that this was a cry of physical agony as Jesus physically hung on the cross. Psalm 22:14-16 captures this physical anguish:

> I am poured out like water, and all my bones are disjointed; my heart is like wax, melting within me. My strength is dried up like baked clay; my tongue sticks to the roof of my mouth. You put me into the dust of death. For dogs have surrounded me; a gang of evildoers has closed in on me; they pierced my hands and my feet.

Jesus' physical anguish was very real and His suffering was intense. However, as we noted earlier, Jesus' cry on the cross was also a cry of spiritual anguish. Jesus experienced the wrath of God, and not just for a moment, but for hours. Shrouded by darkness and seared with pain, He experienced the cup of God's wrath. In addition, this was also a cry of relational alienation. In a mysterious way, Christ was alienated not only from His friends, but also from the Father. This is **the curse of the cross** (see also Gal 3:13). As He came under the sentence of sin, **Jesus was cut off from the Father's favorable presence**. God's presence was real at the cross, but it was His presence in judgment and wrath toward sin.[62] **Jesus was given the full recompense of our disobedience**. This is what Paul speaks to in 2 Corinthians 5:21: "He made the One who did not know sin to be sin for us, so that we might become the righteousness of God in Him." Martin Luther spoke of this exchange:

> Our most merciful Father, seeing us to be oppressed and overwhelmed with the curse of the law [so that] we could never be delivered from it by our own power, sent his only Son in the world and laid upon him all the sins of all men, saying: Be thou Peter that denier; Paul that persecutor, blasphemer and cruel oppressor; David that adulterer; that sinner which did eat the apple in Paradise; that thief which hanged upon the cross; and briefly, be thou the person which hath committed the sins of all men; see therefore that thou pay and satisfy for them [all]. (As cited in Stott, *The Cross of Christ*, 345)

Jesus experienced the separation that we as sinners deserve, so that we might receive reconciliation. That is the effect of the cross for all

---

[62] In a similar way, God's presence is real in hell, but it is His presence in judgment and wrath toward sinners.

who trust in Jesus. **Before the cross, we were cast out of God's presence; because of the cross, we are now invited into God's presence**. This entrance into God's presence is why, right after Jesus died, the curtain of the temple was torn in two, from top to bottom (27:51). The barrier separating man from God was ripped away by God so that hell-deserving sinners could be welcomed safely into the presence of the infinitely holy God of the universe. Do you see now why the cross is so significant? What happened on the cross was so much more than a naked man dying on a wooden post on the side of the road in a non-descript part of the world. This was the holy God of the universe giving His Son to die our death, endure our condemnation, and suffer our separation so that we could be declared righteous and welcomed into His presence.

Respond to the Cross

All history revolves around this scene in Matthew 26–27, and all our lives are determined by what we do in response to this scene. At least two responses are appropriate as we think about the cross. First, **surrender your heart to God**. If you are an unbeliever, turn from sin and trust in Christ. Do not seek to add to His infinitely gracious and worthy sacrifice, but instead repent and embrace this free gift of salvation. If you are a believer, continue daily to trust in Christ, your substitute. Stop toying with sin and pursue the One who died to set you free from it.

Second, the cross ought to compel us to **proclaim the hope of the gospel**. The gospel is the greatest news in all the world. Many people know *that* Jesus died, but they don't know *why*. They don't know why the cross is the centerpiece of all history and the determinant of our eternity; but you do! So tell them, and pray for their salvation. Let everyone know that the Son of God has come to save sinners, and that He has given His life on the cross for those who deserve His wrath. This is the good news, and it is our great privilege to proclaim it.

Reflect and Discuss

1. Explain why Matthew 26–27 is so crucial to our understanding of God, the world, sin, salvation, etc.
2. What impact should the cross have on our reading of the previous chapters in Matthew's Gospel?

3. Discuss how the following attributes of God are displayed in the cross: sovereignty, righteousness, wrath, and love.
4. Explain what is meant by the idea that the cross is fundamentally for God's sake.
5. How does the cross expose our sin? What does it say about the seriousness of our sin?
6. How would you explain the terms *substitution* and *propitiation* to an unbeliever with little or no theological knowledge or vocabulary?
7. Why is it important to see Jesus as our substitute, propitiation, and reconciliation, and not just a loving example?
8. How does the truth of Christ's substitutionary death impact our daily pursuit of holiness?
9. Discuss several ways in which the cross fulfills Old Testament prophecies and expectations.
10. How does the cross rule out the possibility of a works-based righteousness?

The Ultimate Question

MATTHEW 28:1-15

Main Idea: Despite various attempts to explain away the resurrection, Scripture's account remains the most plausible, and it establishes Jesus' lordship over all things and all people, summoning us to trust in Him and surrender to Him.

Did Jesus Rise from the Dead?

I. **Possible Explanations**
    A. Jesus didn't die on the cross.
    B. Jesus' tomb was not empty.
    C. The disciples stole the body of Jesus.
    D. The disciples were delusional when they claimed to see Jesus.
    E. Jesus died on the cross and actually rose from the grave.

II. **Startling Implications**
    A. He has authority over life and death.
    B. He has authority over sin and Satan.
    C. He has authority over you and me.
        1. He reigns over us supremely.
        2. He loves us deeply.
        3. He will judge us eternally.

III. **Personal Questions**
    A. Do you believe in the historical resurrection of Jesus?
    B. Do you surrender to the universal authority of Jesus?

We live in a day when religion is looked at as a matter of preference or opinion. Many people believe that all religions are fundamentally the same; the differences are only superficial. Simply go about your life and choose what works best for you, and along the way, the question of truth can be completely avoided. Living that way is a huge and costly mistake.

Belief is irresponsible and empty if it's not based in truth. People say, "What is true for you may not be true for me," but no one *really* believes that. After all, what would you think if you went to withdraw money at the bank, and the teller said, "I don't *feel* like you have money in your account"? How the teller *felt* wouldn't matter to you if you needed money. Whatever is true for you had better be true for the teller as well: either you have money in your account or you don't. The last thing we want banks to do is to give out money based on how they feel!

In most areas of everyday life we know instinctively to operate on the basis of truth instead of feelings and preferences. Yet, when it comes to the most important questions in life, questions that deal with grand, eternal realities, why would we want to disregard the question of truth? Do we really think God governs the world based on what we prefer? Matthew 28:1-15 reports to us *the* event in all of history, and our response to it should be based on truth, not feelings. Our eternity hangs on whether the resurrection of Jesus Christ actually happened.

The Ultimate Question
MATTHEW 28:1-15

Below we'll consider some of the theories offered to explain the events narrated in Matthew 28:1-15. Matthew gives us a rather brief and straightforward account of the resurrection, though the events recorded in these verses are nothing short of supernatural and spectacular. Mary Magdalene and "the other Mary" (v. 1), likely the same Mary mentioned in 27:61, were the first eyewitnesses to the resurrection (Blomberg, *Matthew*, 426).[63] They came to the tomb after the Sabbath to anoint Jesus' body (Mark 16:1), when they unsuspectingly stumbled upon the truth that would change the course of history: the empty tomb. An angel whose appearance was "like lightning" had descended from heaven, causing a great earthquake (Matt 28:2-3). He rolled back the stone and sat on it, allowing the women to look inside. At the sight of the angel of the Lord, those guarding the tomb were "so shaken from fear of him that they became like dead men" (v. 4). The angel told the women to go and tell the disciples that Jesus had been raised. Leaving with "fear and great joy" (v. 8), these unlikely witnesses to the greatest event in history ran toward Galilee.

On their way to Galilee, the women were met by the risen Christ. They took hold of Jesus and worshiped Him (v. 9), to which He responded, "Do not be afraid. Go and tell My brothers to leave for

---

[63] These two Marys are also mentioned in Mark 15:40, 47.

Galilee, and they will see Me there" (v. 10). The women told the disciples (Luke 24:10; John 20:18), and Peter and John rushed to verify their story (John 20:3-10). Matthew also tells us that the guards reported these events to the chief priests of the Jews (v. 11). After assembling with the elders, the chief priests agreed to bribe the guards to give a different account of these events, namely, that Jesus' disciples had come and stolen the body (v. 13). This lie, Matthew tells us, continued to circulate among the Jews (v. 15).

At least two aspects of this account are worth noting before we look at alternative explanations to the resurrection. First, the women were unlikely witnesses to the resurrection because (in general) their testimonies weren't highly valued in that culture (Keener, *A Commentary on the Gospel of Matthew*, 698–99). If Matthew and the other Gospel writers were trying to persuade people of a hoax, then choosing two women as the first eyewitnesses to the empty tomb was a strange choice. If you were going to make up a story about the most significant miracle the world has ever known, would you put forward questionable witnesses as evidence?

Second, notice in verses 11-15 that the guards didn't deny that Jesus' body was missing from the tomb. Their main concern was coming up with an alternative explanation. Not even the Jewish leaders could produce the body of Jesus, something that would have put an end to the disciples' supposed charade. But no one actually denied that the tomb holding the crucified Jesus was now vacant. It would have been foolish to deny the truth because it would be easy to disprove such a denial. A better explanation was and is needed for the fact of an empty tomb.

To this day, the ultimate question for the Christian faith and for our individual lives is this: **Did Jesus rise from the dead?** We're not talking about resuscitation or reincarnation, but resurrection. In other words, was Jesus dead for three days, and did He afterwards rise up and physically walk out of the tomb? That is a question of truth, not preference. Jesus either did or did not rise, and the ramifications are eternal.

If Jesus didn't rise from the grave, then we as Christians are wasting our time. Our faith is a lie, and we are simply fools playing a religious game. In 1 Corinthians 15:19 Paul says that we are to be "pitied more than anyone" if we have hoped in Jesus in this life only. But if Jesus did rise from the grave, then the situation is drastically different. Most people think that the burden of proof lies exclusively on Christians to give evidence of the resurrection, but that's not entirely true. Yes, there's a burden of proof on those who believe in Christ, but there's also a burden of proof on unbelievers. Consider below what must be explained.

There's no question, even among the most secular of scholars, that around 2,000 years ago an entirely new religious movement and community were formed—almost overnight. And immediately, hundreds of people started claiming that Jesus rose from the grave, even when it meant they could die for such a claim. A fast-growing movement of people, which now makes up one-third of the world's population by some estimates, survives as a result. So how do you explain that? If you don't believe in the resurrection of Jesus, then there's a burden of proof to provide some other convincing explanation for how the church began. We need to consider several alternative explanations with the following question in mind: "Which is most *plausible*?"

Plausibility should be the criterion for "proving" the resurrection, because there's virtually nothing in history that can be established with 100-percent certainty. For instance, can we really know with 100-percent certainty that George Washington was the first president of the United States? Is it not possible that he was just a mythical figure that people wrote about and invented in order to encourage the citizens of a new country? Now we're *almost certain* this is not the case, but we can't say with 100-percent certainty that he was president. Someone once said, "We can't know with 100-percent certainty that all of us were not created five minutes ago, complete with built-in memories and food in our stomachs." You can see how much of a headache it is to establish perfect certainty for any past event! The question is "What is *most* plausible?" or "What can be established with the *most* certainty?" Several possible explanations have been given.

Possible Explanations[64]

Possible explanations for Jesus' resurrection have been proposed throughout history, with some dating back to the first century. Below we'll consider five different explanations that have been put forward by various individuals and groups. First, some say that **Jesus didn't die on the cross**, a claim that comes in different forms. Muslims, for example,

---

[64] For a more thorough discussion of the resurrection, see Keller, *The Reason for God*, 201–12.

say that Jesus didn't go to the cross, but rather the individual who died on the cross only *looked* like Jesus. According to the Quran, this is what Mohammed taught. This is a point where the two dominant religions in the world—Christianity and Islam—diverge, and notice that this is a point of truth, not of preference or ideology or opinion. Despite what Mohammed said six centuries after it happened, those much closer to the historical situation (Christian and non-Christian alike) reported that it was indeed Jesus who died on the cross.

Another version of this first explanation holds that Jesus didn't actually die on the cross. It was, in fact, Jesus of Nazareth who went to the cross, but instead of dying, He was only hurt (really, really badly). As the theory goes, Jesus fainted and became unconscious, at which time the soldiers thought He was dead. However, due to the time constraints with the Passover feast, they took Him down before He actually died and they quickly buried Him. Later, Jesus regained consciousness and escaped from the tomb. This explanation certainly explains away the supernatural element of overcoming death, but consider what it requires. It assumes that Jesus went through six trials, no sleep, a brutal scourging, thorns thrust into His head, nails thrust into His hands and feet, and after hours on a cross, He had a spear thrust into His side. Then, as if that weren't enough, He was wrapped in grave clothes and put in a tomb with a large stone rolled over the entrance. This tomb was guarded by armed Roman soldiers. In that situation and in that physical condition, are we really expected to believe that Jesus regained consciousness, stealthily nudged the stone out of the way, quietly hopped out of the tomb, tiptoed past the guards standing nearby, and coolly went about His way? This scenario seems highly unlikely, if not ridiculous. Needless to say, we can safely label this explanation as implausible.

A second explanation for the resurrection is the idea **Jesus' tomb was not empty**, often described as the "Wrong Tomb Theory." This theory states that the women went to a tomb that first Easter morning, but in their grief and shock over Jesus' death, they went to the wrong tomb and mistakenly thought Jesus had risen. Presumably, everyone else began going to the wrong tomb as well, leading them to believe that Jesus had risen from the dead. And since that time, everybody's been going to the wrong tomb. If they had only checked next door!

The idea that Jesus' tomb was not empty fails on multiple levels. The last thing Roman or Jewish authorities wanted was for a group of people to claim that their leader had risen from the dead, which is why guards were posted at the tomb according to Matthew 27:62-66. Is it really plausible that they guarded the wrong tomb? In reality, no one would have believed in Jesus' resurrection if the tomb was not actually empty. Someone could have identified the correct tomb, and the entire Christian movement would have been shut down from the start. We stand on pretty firm historical ground that the tomb was empty, though that in and of itself doesn't "prove" the resurrection of Jesus.

The third explanation is that **the disciples stole the body of Jesus**. That's exactly the conspiracy theory that the Jewish authorities (with the help of the guards) propagated from the very beginning according to Matthew 28:11-15. This explanation is unlikely, though, for at least two reasons. First, it is unlikely that these timid, scared Galilean disciples outmaneuvered a guard of highly skilled Roman soldiers in order to do that which all the Jewish and Roman authorities were trying to make sure would not happen. Second, the very idea of a resurrection was preposterous to many, so why would the disciples concoct such a risky plan in order to proclaim an event that no one had categories for? Many would-be Messiahs were executed in the first century, yet in no case do we find any of their followers claiming that their leader had risen from the dead. A resurrection like the one the disciples were proclaiming was not a part of the religious environment of Jesus' day. In much Greco-Roman thought, the goal in life was to be free, liberated from the body, so the last thing you would want was to come back into the body. For many Jews, the idea of individual resurrection back into a world of sickness, decay, and death was inconceivable. The kind of resurrection that Jesus experienced was not even an option. So why would the disciples steal Jesus' body and then tell people that His body had been resurrected?

When the facts of the empty tomb and the sightings of Jesus are taken together, the alternative theories for the resurrection become more implausible. If you only have an empty tomb but no sightings of Jesus, then you have something strange going on, but not a resurrection. It might be assumed that the body was stolen. On the other hand, if the disciples stole the body and then claimed that Jesus was alive, and yet nobody saw Him, then it would have been concluded that these men were fabricating a story. But if people actually saw Jesus after He had died on a cross, and if the tomb was demonstrably empty, then we have deeper questions that must be answered.

This leads to the next possible explanation for Jesus' resurrection. Some scholars have argued that **the disciples were delusional when they claimed to see Jesus**. The people of Jesus' day didn't have the scientific knowledge we have today, the theory goes, so they were more prone to believe in the supernatural. In their pain and grief over Jesus' death, the disciples still believed that Jesus was somehow guiding them and leading them. They even had visions in their minds of Jesus speaking to them. They may or may not have believed that Jesus was still physically alive, but they believed He was alive spiritually. This myth supposedly grew over the years, and it eventually morphed into the idea that Jesus rose from the grave physically. Some scholars have even argued that the disciples were hallucinating when they claimed to have seen these events. However, these and other theories concerning the mental state of the disciples don't account well for the shift in the disciples' worldview that occurred overnight. Think about it: there was no process, no development, no debate or discussion, yet in a relatively short time, thousands upon thousands of people believed that Jesus rose from the grave. It's one thing to claim that the disciples were delusional, but how do you explain their influence and the dramatic change in their behavior in the days after the resurrection?

In addition to the 12 disciples, hundreds of other people claimed to have seen the risen Christ. Unlike the reported miracles today, this was more than one individual who claimed to have seen a Christ-like image in the clouds. Jesus ate with people, drank with people, and talked with people. Hallucinations don't eat or drink! This was not just spiritual imagination, it was physical presence. Maybe a few people could have been deluded into thinking they had seen Jesus, but Paul tells us that Jesus appeared to "over 500 brothers at one time" (1 Cor 15:6). In other words, Paul says, "Go ask them what they saw. You can verify this!"

Suppose I told you the following story: In preparation for the Masters, the most prestigious golfing tournament of the year, professional golfer Phil Mickelson called me in order to get some tips and to play a practice round. I showed him how to drive the ball further, and in the middle of our round, I hit a hole-in-one on a par 3. Phil was so impressed that he asked me to be his caddy for the Masters. The only reason I couldn't do it was because I already had a busy schedule for that week, but rest assured, this actually happened. Would you believe me? If not, how would you discredit my story?

To discredit this ridiculous story, you could easily go to Phil Mickelson and say, "Do you have any clue who David Platt is or how terrible a golfer he is?" To which he would say, "I have no clue who David Platt is and I'm pretty sure he's a terrible golfer." (And *that* you could verify—on both counts!) You could also speak with people who have seen me play golf to either confirm or discredit my claims.

In a similar way, individuals in the first century were able to investigate the claims of the resurrection by speaking with the apostles and the hundreds of eyewitnesses who had physically seen Jesus. In fact, these eyewitnesses to the risen Christ were openly telling people about what they'd seen, and some were even losing their lives for it. Proclaiming the resurrection was not in their best interest. As Pascal said, "I believe the witnesses that get their throats cut" (Keller, *The Reason for God*, 210). It is, therefore, highly unlikely that the early Christians fabricated the idea of the resurrection. New Testament scholar N. T. Wright has said,

> The early Christians did not invent the empty tomb and the "meetings" or "sightings" of the risen Jesus. . . . Nobody was expecting this kind of thing . . . nobody would have invented it. . . . To suggest otherwise is to stop doing history and to enter into a fantasy world of our own. (Wright, *The Resurrection of the Son of God*, 707)

Given the implausibility of the explanations that we've seen so far, there's one explanation that remains: **Jesus died on the cross and actually rose from the grave**. If you claim that the physical resurrection of Christ did not necessarily cause this radical shift in history, then what did? The burden of proof is on you. There's evidence for this view outside of the Bible as well, evidence that is granted by virtually all historical scholars, even those skeptical of religion. For instance, few people would actually dispute the following facts:

- Jesus died by crucifixion.
- His followers believed that He rose from the grave and appeared to them.
- The lives of Christ's followers were radically changed as a result of seeing and following the risen Christ.

Concerning this last point, it is significant that even the most hardened advocates *against* Christianity (like Paul) became the strongest advocates *for* Christianity after seeing the resurrected Christ. Gary Habermas is probably the most renowned scholar on the resurrection of Jesus. He notes,

> In particular, when the early and eyewitness experience of the disciples, James, and Paul are considered, along with their corresponding transformations and their central message, the historical Resurrection [of Jesus] becomes the best explanation for the facts, especially because the alternative theories have failed. (As cited in Boa and Bowman, *Faith Has Its Reasons*, 196)

From the earliest days of the church, the Bible tells us that people have worked to cover up Jesus' resurrection. Yet, every proposed explanation has fallen short. If, on the other hand, the resurrection is true, if Jesus did indeed die on the cross and actually rise from the grave, then the implications of these truths are startling. We'll consider some of these implications below.

Startling Implications

Christianity stands or falls on the resurrection of Jesus Christ. That doesn't minimize anything else Jesus did, especially the cross; however, we can only see the significance of the cross and the rest of Christ's perfect work through the lens of the resurrection. When Matthew records for us the events of chapter 28, he is, through the inspiration of the Holy Spirit, making claims that change the world. We'll begin by looking at three implications concerning the authority of Christ based on the resurrection.

If Jesus didn't rise from the dead, then we don't have to worry about a thing He said, because it was a lie. But **if Jesus rose from the dead**, then we must accept everything He said, for His authority is absolute. Jesus closes this chapter and the Gospel as a whole by claiming, "All authority has been given to Me in heaven and on earth" (v. 18). Jesus' absolute authority based on the resurrection means that **He has authority over life and death**. Shortly before His own death, Jesus told His disciples the following:

> *No one takes it [My life] from Me, but I lay it down on My own. I have the right to lay it down, and I have the right to take it up again.* (John 10:18)

That's an astounding statement: Who among men determines when they live? None of us decides when we will come into this world, and when we die, none of us has the power to say, "I'm coming back to life." But that's precisely what Jesus did, and if He did rise from the dead, then He has absolute authority over life and death.

If Jesus rose from the dead, then we must also admit that **He has authority over sin and Satan**. All men die because they sin, for death is the payment for sin (Gen 2:17; Rom 6:23). However, Jesus is one man in all of history who died without sinning; so why did He die? Jesus died for our sins, in our place (1 Pet 2:24). After His death, Jesus rose from the grave, not only in victory over death, but in victory over sin. First Corinthians 15:55-57 teaches us that sin is the "sting of death":

> *Death, where is your victory? Death, where is your sting? Now the sting of death is sin, and the power of sin is the law. But thanks be to God, who gives us the victory through our Lord Jesus Christ!*

Sometimes it's easy to think of Jesus' authority in an abstract sense without making a personal application. However, the fact that Jesus has authority over life and death, as well as over sin and Satan, leads to one unavoidable conclusion: **He has authority over you and me**. That is, He is our rightful Lord and Master. Paul speaks to this reality in Romans 10:9-13, what we might refer to as the foundational confession of Christianity:

> *If you confess with your mouth, "Jesus is Lord," and believe in your heart that God raised Him from the dead, you will be saved. One believes with the heart, resulting in righteousness, and one confesses with the mouth, resulting in salvation. Now the Scripture says, Everyone who believes on Him will not be put to shame, for there is no distinction between Jew and Greek, since the same Lord of all is rich to all who call on Him. For everyone who calls on the name of the Lord will be saved.*

So what does it mean for Jesus to have absolute authority over you and me? First, it means **He reigns over us supremely**. Jesus is the sovereign Ruler over our lives. This is the case whether we believe it or not. Just as the grass is green, regardless of whether or not you believe it, so also Jesus is Lord over you regardless of your approval. Many times Christians say, "I've decided to make Jesus the Lord of my life." I hate to break it to you, but you didn't have a choice in the matter. Jesus *is* Lord over your life. Scripture says that one day every knee will bow and every tongue will confess that Jesus Christ is Lord (Phil 2:10-11). The question is not whether or not Jesus is Lord; the question is, "Will you submit to Him as Lord now or when it is too late?"

Second, not only does Jesus' authority mean that He reigns over us supremely, but also that **He loves us deeply**. Remember that the purpose of the resurrection is grounded in Christ's love for us. God sent His Son to pay the price for our sin, and the resurrection lets us know that our hope of salvation is not some made-up story, some fanciful myth. The resurrection of Jesus validates everything He said, taught, and told us He came to do. In Galatians 2:20 Paul speaks of the Son of God who "loved me and gave Himself for me." Believers should rejoice in Jesus' love demonstrated in both His cross *and* His resurrection.

Third, Christ's authority over us means that **He will judge us eternally**. Jesus speaks of His role as judge in John 5:21-23:

> And just as the Father raises the dead and gives them life, so the Son also gives life to anyone He wants to. The Father, in fact, judges no one but has given all judgment to the Son, so that all people will honor the Son just as they honor the Father. Anyone who does not honor the Son does not honor the Father who sent Him.

For all who believe in Christ, the truth of Christ's judgment is good news. It's good news because you can be saved from eternal judgment if you confess with your mouth that Jesus is Lord and believe in your heart that God raised Him from the dead (Rom 10:9). Christ's role as judge is also good news because the resurrection reminds us that this world is not all there is. If our only expectations are for this life, then we have no hope in the face of tragedy in this world. Furthermore, Christ's judgment means our efforts for justice in this world become meaningful. Pastor and author Tim Keller explains,

> Each year at Easter I get to preach on the Resurrection. In my sermon I always say to my skeptical, secular friends that, even if they can't believe in the resurrection, they should want it to be true. Most of them care deeply about justice for the poor, alleviating hunger and disease, and caring for the environment. Yet many of them believe that the material world was caused by accident and that the world and everything in it will eventually simply burn up. They find it discouraging that so few people care about justice without realizing that their

own worldview undermines any motivation to make the world a better place. Why sacrifice for the needs of others if in the end nothing we do will make any difference? However, if the resurrection of Jesus happened, that means there's infinite hope and reason to pour ourselves out for the needs of the world. (Keller, *The Reason for God*, 211–12)

All of us have built-in longings and desires for meaning and purpose, and this tells us that this world is not the entire picture. Neither disease nor natural disasters have the last word in this world; because of the resurrection, Jesus does. And He will have the last word in the lives of each of us for all of eternity.

Personal Questions

Based on everything we've seen about Jesus' authority, the ultimate question in the universe—Did Jesus rise from the dead?—becomes a very personal question. We can think of this personal application in two parts based on the truth we saw above in Romans 10:9. First, **do you believe in the historical resurrection of Jesus?** Romans 10:9 says that you must "believe in your heart that God raised Him from the dead" in order to be saved. This is a point where the message of Christianity is radically different from every other religion. Scripture doesn't give us a list of things to do, boxes to check off, or rituals to follow. There is only truth to be believed. If you don't believe the truth of the gospel, then the burden of proof is on you to disprove the resurrection.

The second part of this personal application also has to do with Romans 10:9, as there is more involved in salvation than believing in the resurrection. To be clear, there's no work involved on our part, but there is a confession to be made. In the area where I pastor, the overwhelming majority of people would say they believe in the resurrection of Jesus, but there are undoubtedly many of them who are *not* saved from their sins. We know that mere intellectual assent doesn't save, for even the Devil himself believes in the resurrection of Jesus, and he is not saved from his sin. I could ask the Devil, "Do you believe the Bible is the Word of God?"

He'd say, "Yes."

If I were to ask him, "Do you believe Jesus is the Son of God?"

He'd say, "Yes."

If I were to ask him, "Do you believe Jesus died on the cross and rose again?"

He'd say, "Yes."

If I were to ask him, "Do you believe Jesus is the only way to be saved?"

He'd say, "Yes."

If I were to ask him, "Will you commit to live a moral life and come to church and get involved in leadership?"

He could say, "Yes."

The crucial question is this: "Will you repent of your sin and surrender your life to Jesus as Lord?"

The Devil would clearly answer, "Absolutely not." We would do well to stress this aspect of submission in our own evangelism today.

In our day we urge people to assent intellectually to Jesus, pray a certain prayer, get involved in a particular church, live a relatively good life, etc., all with the promise (either explicitly or implicitly) that they will be saved. That's a lie. Scores of professing Christians have believed half of Romans 10:9, and they think they are saved from their sins, when in fact they are not. They give lip-service to Jesus, but their lives are not surrendered to His absolute authority. That's why we must ask the question, "**Do you surrender to the universal authority of Jesus?**" This is what it means to "confess with your mouth, 'Jesus is Lord'" (Rom 10:9). To confess with your mouth is not about saying some magic words; rather, it's about a heart condition that says, "Yes, I believe Jesus died on the cross for *my* sin and rose from the grave as *my* Savior, and my *life* belongs to Him as *Lord*." Eternity depends on our answer to that question.

Reflect and Discuss

1. What is the logical problem with the claim that truth is based on preference or opinion? How could you use such a discussion in an evangelistic encounter?

2. How would you respond to the following statement: "I'm a follower of Christ, but I don't believe Jesus rose from the dead"?

3. Is it enough to say that Jesus rose spiritually, but not bodily/physically? Why not?

4. Explain the contention that the Christian faith stands or falls based on Christ's resurrection.

5. Explain the connection between Jesus' resurrection and your own salvation.
6. How does the truth of the resurrection fit into a presentation of the gospel?
7. Why is it unlikely that Mary and Martha would have been included in Matthew's resurrection account if this were a fabrication? How does their appearance in this Gospel bolster the trustworthiness of Matthew's account?
8. Does affirmation of Jesus' resurrection necessarily imply that one is a follower of Christ? Explain your answer.
9. How does the resurrection speak to Jesus' lordship?
10. How should the resurrection inform your reading of the entirety of Matthew's Gospel and the ministry of Jesus?

Commissioned by the King

MATTHEW 28:16-20

Main Idea: Based on Christ's authority and His promised presence, His followers are to go and make disciples of all nations, baptizing them and teaching them to observe Jesus' commands.

I. **We Will Believe in the Authority of Christ.**
   A. Jesus is not just the personal Lord and Savior over us.
   B. Jesus is the universal Lord and Savior over all.
      1. He has authority over nature and nations.
      2. He has authority over disease and demons.
      3. He has authority over sin and death.
      4. He has authority over our lives.
      5. He has authority over every life.
   C. Jesus' authority compels us to go.
      1. His worth is the fuel of our mission.
      2. His worship is the goal of our mission.
   D. Jesus' authority gives us confidence as we go.
II. **We Will Obey the Command of Christ.**
   A. This is not a comfortable call inviting most Christians to come, be baptized, and sit in one location.
   B. This is a costly command directing every Christian to go, baptize, and make disciples of all nations.
   C. We share the Word.
   D. We show the Word.
   E. We teach the Word.
   F. We serve the world.
   G. May we make disciples and multiply churches in our neighborhoods and among all peoples.
III. **We Will Depend On the Presence of Christ.**
   A. This mission is not based on who we are or what we can do.
   B. This mission is based on who Jesus is and what He is able to do in and through our lives.
   C. Together, let's experience the power of His presence with us.
   D. Together, let's hope in the promise of His return for us.

In Matthew 28:16-20 we come to the conclusion of a journey with Jesus, a journey that began with His birth and has continued through His life, His teaching, His miracles, His death, and in the previous section of Matthew 28, His resurrection. Now in this final passage in Matthew's Gospel, we come to what has been called the Great Commission, a commission given by the Lord Jesus to those early disciples and to all His followers in subsequent generations. It's a call we need to hear afresh in our own day.

The Great Commission was not simply meant to be analyzed, though there is much here to think through. These few verses ought to, by the working of God's Spirit, awaken our hearts, both individually and collectively in our churches, with a renewed zeal to make disciples in our own communities and among all nations. For some followers of Christ, this might even result in going to an unreached people group to make known the glory of Christ.[65]

One commentator has referred to Matthew 28:16-20 as "the climax and major focal point not only of this gospel but of the entire New Testament. It is not an exaggeration to say that, in its broadest sense, it is the focal point of all Scripture, Old Testament as well as New" (MacArthur, *Matthew 24–28*, 329). Whether or not it can truly be said that this passage is "*the* focal point of all Scripture" is up for debate, but at the very least this is a reminder of the extreme significance of Jesus' final words in this Gospel. In verse 16 the 11 disciples[66] met Jesus in Galilee, just as He directed in verse 10. Matthew tells us that the disciples worshiped Jesus, though "some doubted" (v. 17). It was in this setting that the resurrected Lord Jesus gave us the Great Commission of verses 18-20.

Matthew's point in writing this book was not only to show us that Jesus is King; if that were the case, he would have stopped in the middle of chapter 28 after the resurrection. Instead, Matthew ends by telling us how Jesus sent out His disciples to proclaim Jesus as King to the ends of

---

[65] An unreached people group (UPG) is made up of less than a 2% evangelical presence. An unreached, unengaged people group (UUPG) is a subset of a UPG, having less than a 2% evangelical presence and no active church-planting methodology being implemented. This information is taken from the website of the International Mission Board (IMB) of the Southern Baptist Convention: http://imb.org/main/news/details.asp?StoryID=10652.

[66] Judas had already hanged himself according to Matt 27:5, and his place among the Twelve would not be filled until Acts 1:26, when Matthias was chosen.

the earth, and that's a story that continues even today. The beauty of this text is that you and I are a part of this story; we are disciples of Jesus the King, commissioned and sent out by Him to proclaim His life, death, and resurrection all over the planet. There are three implications for followers of Jesus based on this text and in light of all that we've seen so far in the Gospel of Matthew.

We Will Believe in the Authority of Christ
MATTHEW 28:18

As Jesus gathers His disciples on this mountain, He doesn't start with a command; He starts with a claim: "All authority has been given to Me in heaven and on earth" (v. 18). We have here the fulfillment of Daniel's prophecy centuries earlier, when the prophet spoke of a "son of man" (Dan 7:13) in this way:

> *He was given authority to rule,*
> *and glory, and a kingdom;*
> *so that those of every people,*
> *nation, and language*
> *should serve Him.*
> *His dominion is an everlasting dominion*
> *that will not pass away,*
> *and His kingdom is one*
> *that will not be destroyed.* (Dan 7:14)

Jesus' authority is *the* basis for everything else that follows in this text. His authority over heaven and earth means that **Jesus is not just the personal Lord and Savior over us**. We often speak of the moment of our conversion by saying, "I decided to make Jesus my personal Lord and Savior." While there is much truth to that statement, we need to be careful not to miss the point of Christ's lordship. As we've already seen, you and I don't *decide* to make Jesus Lord; He is Lord regardless of what we think of Him. Jesus died on the cross and rose from the grave, and now He is exalted at the Father's right hand as the Lord over all creation. All those things are true regardless of what you and I think or decide. Philippians 2:9-11 speaks to this truth in no uncertain terms:

> *For this reason God highly exalted Him and gave Him the name that is above every name, so that at the name of Jesus every knee will bow—of those who are in heaven and on earth and under the earth—and*

> *every tongue should confess that Jesus Christ is Lord, to the glory of*
> *God the Father.*

One day every knee is going to bow and every tongue is going to confess, "Jesus is Lord"—that's a guarantee. So will you confess Jesus as Lord now, or will you confess Him as Lord when it is too late?

Further, while Jesus saves us personally, loves us personally, and rules over us personally, He is not *only* the personal Lord and Savior over you, me, or any one people group. Instead, **Jesus is the universal Lord and Savior over all**. Christ died to save people from every nation and tongue and tribe (Rev 7:9). This worldwide purpose was life-changing for these Jewish disciples who were following a Jewish Messiah. From the beginning of Matthew's Gospel, Jesus' Jewish heritage has been highlighted, beginning with Abraham and then running through the line of David, king of Israel (Matt 1:1). Jesus was born King of the Jews. Nevertheless, Jesus was intent on showing His Jewish disciples that He was not simply their Lord and King, but Lord and King over all nations.

Throughout Matthew's Gospel we have seen Jesus' universal lordship. Consider some of the ways this has played out in these 28 chapters.

He has authority over nature and nations. Jesus calmed the sea with a rebuke (8:26), showing His mastery over nature. His authority over nations is one of the central themes of the Great Commission, since all peoples are to be His disciples.

He has authority over disease and demons. When Jesus speaks, the blind see, the lame walk, lepers are healed, and disease is gone (4:23-24). He speaks, and demons flee (8:28-34).

He has authority over sin and death. As the Son of God, Jesus has authority to forgive sin against God (9:1-7). He also has authority to overcome man's ultimate enemy, death, which is the payment for sin (28:1-10).

He has authority over our lives. Jesus' authority extends to every individual, which for us means dying to self (16:24-25). For the believer, there should be a glad submission to the lordship of Jesus. This means, in relation to the Great Commission in Matthew 28:18-20, that we must be open to whatever the Lord calls us to, including serving Him in another cultural context.

He has authority over every life. Jesus has authority over every life in this world (25:31-33), and this is why we seek to make disciples of all nations.

Obedience to the Great Commission isn't a man-made program, nor is it our own willpower that leads us to go. **Jesus' authority compels us to go**, for missions only makes sense if He has all authority in heaven and on earth. However, we don't go reluctantly, as if we're being forced to follow just any king. **His worth is the fuel of our mission.** In other words, we go because Jesus is worthy of the worship of every person on the planet. Our Savior deserves all praise (Rev 5:9-10), so we long to hear all people confess, "Jesus is Lord!" This also reminds us that **His worship is the goal of our mission.** Followers of Christ live for the day when every tribe and tongue and people and nation gather around our God to give Him the global glory that He is due (Rev 7:9-10).

While the Great Commission certainly compels us to go, even to difficult places, we're not left on our own in this mission. **Jesus' authority gives us confidence as we go.** Who are we to go to another people group, or even coworkers, and tell them that they are following false idols, and that if they don't turn to Jesus, they will die forever? The world views this as arrogant, and even as far as many people in the church are concerned, communicating this to people makes no sense. However, if Matthew's Gospel is true—that is, if Jesus died on the cross for the sins of the world, if He rose from the grave in victory over sin and death, and if there is no one like Him and He reigns as Lord over all—then telling a lost world about Jesus is the only thing that makes sense! What doesn't make sense is millions of Christians sitting back and saying nothing to the nations. Instead, we ought to go with confidence, knowing that the One who sent us is sovereign over all and worthy of worship from all.

One of the promises we have as we engage a lost world with the good news of Jesus Christ is that **this gospel will save.** This is true no matter where we are or how unlikely it may seem that someone will believe our message. I was recently in a Hindu home in the middle of an Indian slum with Hindu gods all over the walls. When I shared the good news of Christ, a Hindu woman whose family for generations had never even heard the gospel responded, "I believe in Jesus, and I want Him to save me." I was reminded that this gospel is powerful, and it will save. Do we believe that?

In addition to having confidence in the saving power of the gospel, we can have confidence on a larger scale concerning Christ's purposes for the church. **His mission will succeed** because His authority guarantees it. After Jesus spoke His final words to the disciples, He ascended to heaven (Acts 1:9) where He now sits at the right hand of the Father.

Now in His exalted position, Jesus empowers His people, directing, guiding, and providing them with everything they need to bring this mission to completion. Matthew 24:14 is a guarantee: "This good news of the kingdom will be proclaimed in all the world as a testimony to all nations. And then the end will come." We are on the front lines of a spiritual battle that is raging for the souls of men and women around the world, and the all-sovereign Son of God, our Savior, is in command of a commission that will be accomplished. This leads us to the next part of this passage.

We Will Obey the Command of Christ
MATTHEW 28:19

After telling us of His authority over heaven and earth, the next words out of Jesus' mouth are, "Go, therefore" (v. 19). It is as if He's saying, "In light of My authority, *go!*" Here is Jesus' full command in verses 19-20:

> *Go, therefore, and make disciples of all nations, baptizing them in the name of the Father and of the Son and of the Holy Spirit, teaching them to observe everything I have commanded you.*

This is not a comfortable call inviting most Christians to come, be baptized, and sit in one location. Yet, that is exactly what we are tempted to turn our mission into, and if we are not careful, this is what our Christianity will consist of. We may come to a worship service, participate in the life of the church, serve in the church, and give regularly, all the while neglecting to make disciples. The church is filled with people who have been Christians for 5, 10, 15, or even 50 years, who have never led someone outside of their family to be a reproducing disciple. We have missed our mission. In his penetrating book, *Born to Reproduce*, Dawson Trotman comments on our tendency in the church today:

> The curse of today is that we are too busy. I am not talking about being busy earning money to buy food. I am talking about being busy doing Christian things. We have spiritual activity with little productivity.

Trotman continues,

> The Gospel spread to the known world during the first century without radio, television or the printing press, because [the writings of the apostles] produced men who were

reproducing. But today we have a lot of pew-sitters—people think that if they are faithful in church attendance, put good-sized gifts into the offering plate and get people to come, they have done their part. . . . If I were a minister of a church and had deacons or elders to pass the plate and choir members to sing, I would say, "Thank God for your help. We need you. Praise the Lord for these extra things you do," but I would keep pressing home the big job—"Be fruitful and multiply." All these other things are incidental to the supreme task of winning a man or woman to Jesus Christ and then helping him or her to go on.

If Matthew 28:19 is not a comfortable call for most Christians, then what is it? **This is a costly command directing every Christian to go, baptize, and make disciples of all nations.** This has been the plan from the beginning. In Jesus' initial introduction to the disciples in this Gospel, He said, "Follow Me . . . and I will make you fish for people!" (Matt 4:19). From the very beginning, Jesus made clear that everyone who followed Him would fish for men. Consider how Matthew 28 serves as a fitting conclusion to this initial meeting between Jesus and His disciples in Matthew 4:

- Jesus' introduction in Matthew 4: Every follower of Jesus is a fisher of men.
- Jesus' conclusion in Matthew 28: Every disciple is a disciple-maker.

According to Jesus, from beginning to end, to *be* a disciple is to *make* disciples. Scripture knows nothing of disciples who aren't making disciples. Yet, if you were to ask Christians today what it means to make disciples, you'd likely get jumbled thoughts, ambiguous answers, and probably even some blank stares. Consequently, we urgently need biblical guidance on this foundational command.

There's one imperative verb in Matthew 28:19—"make disciples"—and it is surrounded by three participles: going, baptizing, and teaching. Based on this verse, we'll look at four non-negotiable facets of disciple making.

First, **we share the Word.** This is absolutely foundational to making disciples. **We speak about the gospel as we live according to the gospel.** The Spirit of God lives inside God's people so that they can bear witness to the gospel to the ends of the earth (Acts 1:8). The evangelistic strategy of the church is built upon every member of the church engaging the world with the gospel.

Yet making disciples doesn't end when people respond to the gospel. When people turn from their sin to Christ, we baptize them. This is another part of making disciples—**we show the Word**. Baptism is a part of what it means to make disciples because **baptism symbolizes identification with the person of Christ and inclusion in the body of Christ**. Every disciple of Jesus is baptized in the name of the Father and of the Son and of the Holy Spirit (v. 19). This is a command of the Lord Jesus Christ.

The number of people who say they are Christians today but have not been baptized is, quite frankly, shocking. If you are a follower of Christ and have not been baptized, you are living in direct disobedience to Christ. The New Testament knows nothing of unbaptized Christians. It's not that one has to be baptized in order to *become* a Christian, but once you are a Christian, your public declaration of faith in Christ *necessarily* involves baptism. To neglect baptism is to dishonor and disobey Christ. In fact, if you continue to be unrepentant in this area, refusing to identify with Christ in baptism, then there is serious reason to question whether or not you are a Christian at all.

Once someone is baptized, showing the word involves sharing life together as a member of the church. Disciple making is not simply what happens in a classroom for an hour or so each week; it's what happens when we walk through life together as a community of faith, modeling for one another how to follow Christ. We show one another how to pray, how to study God's Word, how to grow in Christ, and how to lead others to Christ. This is what Christ's body is to be about.

Third, as we make disciples, **we teach the Word**. Jesus speaks of "teaching them to observe everything I have commanded you" (v. 19). **We don't just receive the Word; we reproduce the Word.** God has certainly gifted some in the church to teach, especially elders (Titus 1:9; see also 1 Tim 3:2; Jas 3:1). However, every disciple of Jesus should saturate their words with God's Word. Our conversations ought to be filled with Scripture as we teach people all that Christ has taught us.

Fourth and finally, making disciples means that **we serve the world**. Jesus speaks of making disciples of "all nations," a phrase which in the original (*panta ta ethne*) refers not simply to nations or countries as we usually think of them, but rather to tribes, families, clans, and peoples, what we call "people groups" today. The Old Testament refers to such people groups: Amorites, Hittites, Perizzites, Canaanites, etc. Today there are more than 11,000 people groups spread throughout the world. These groups share similar language, heritage, and cultural characteristics. So **this is not just a general command to make disciples among as many people as possible.** Rather, **this is a specific command to make disciples among every people group in the world.** There are, as of this writing, more than 6,000 people groups who have still not been reached with the gospel. Therefore, obedience to the Great Commission necessarily involves intentionality in going after these 6,000 people groups.

In light of the massive needs and the commission Christ has given us, **may we make disciples and multiply churches** in our neighborhoods and among all peoples. We live in a world of sin, rebellion, suffering, and pain, a world where over three billion people live on less than $2 a day, and a billion of those people live in desperate poverty. Hundreds of millions are starving and dying of preventable diseases. Yet the spiritual condition of the world is even worse: billions of people across the world are engrossed in false religions, and approximately two billion of them have never even had a chance to hear the gospel. According to Scripture, they are all on a road that leads to an eternal hell. Yet as believers, we know that Jesus is Lord and that He has died on the cross for our sins and risen from the grave. The Spirit of God has opened our hearts to see and to believe. He has saved us to know God and to enjoy Him, and very soon we will be with Him forever in heaven. But while we're here, God has given us His Spirit for one purpose: We have been charged with reaching the world with the gospel.

We Will Depend On the Presence of Christ
MATTHEW 28:20

Finally, after seeing that we must believe in the authority of Christ and obey the command of Christ, we get the assurance in Matthew 28:20 that we can depend on the presence of Christ. The final words of this Gospel are comforting and encouraging, and they remind us of Matthew's description of Jesus in the first chapter: "See, the virgin will become pregnant and give birth to a son, and they will name Him Immanuel, which is translated 'God is with us'" (1:23). It is fitting, then, that Matthew would close His Gospel with Jesus' words, "And remember, I am with you always, to the end of the age" (28:20).

Be encouraged, follower of Christ, for **this mission is not based on who we are or what we can do**. This mission is assured based on Christ's presence through His Spirit. When I first came to the church I now pastor, I recall thinking that the church had such potential with all of its gifts and resources. But that's not a biblical mind-set. It doesn't matter how gifted a church is or how blessed it is materially, for the people of God can do nothing apart from power of the Holy Spirit (Acts 1:8). However, when the Spirit works among a people, that church can shake the nations for God's glory.

Rather than being based on what we can do, **this mission is based on who Jesus is and what He is able to do in and through our lives**. Christ is able to do "beyond all that we ask or think according to the power that works in us" (Eph 3:20). Oh, how we need to put aside small dreams and worldly ambitions. We need to give Christ a blank check with our lives and then see where He leads.

Together, let's experience the power of His presence with us. We want to be a part of something that is beyond us, something that requires supernatural strength. We don't want to be preoccupied with programs and practices that we can manage on our own. We should be desperate for the power of Jesus.

We know that obedience to the Great Commission will not be easy, and we know it will be costly. But we also know that it will be worth it. Jesus will return and His reward will be infinitely greater than any cost we have paid. So **together, let's hope in the promise of His return for us**. The kingdom of our Lord Jesus will one day be fully and finally established, and we will see His face (Rev 22:4). We are living—and longing— for that day. Amen! Come, Lord Jesus!

Reflect and Discuss

1. What is the church's mission?
2. How can the church do good things and yet miss the Great Commission?
3. Why is it crucial to recognize and believe in the authority of Christ as we seek to obey the Great Commission?
4. Explain the idea that the Great Commission is intended for all Christians.
5. How important is baptism to making disciples? Is it optional?

6. What is the result of aiming for converts but not following up with teaching Christ's commands? Describe the church's role in this process.

7. Explain the following statement: The Great Commission is not so much a call to "come and see" but rather to "go and tell."

8. On a day-to-day basis, what does it mean to depend on Jesus as you carry out the Great Commission?

9. What characteristics would you expect to find in a church being faithful to the Great Commission?

10. What might obedience to the Great Commission look like for a stay-at-home mom? How about a homebound member of your church? What about a student?

WORKS CITED

Adams, Jay E. *Marriage, Divorce, and Remarriage in the Bible*. Grand Rapids: Zondervan, 1980.

Anderson, Courtney. *To the Golden Shore: The Life of Adoniram Judson*. Grand Rapids: Zondervan, 1956.

Barclay, William. *The Gospel of Matthew: Chapters 11–28*. Vol. 2. Louisville: Westminster John Knox, 2001.

Bauer, Walter. *A Greek-English Lexicon of the New Testament and other Early Christian Literature*. Ed. and trans. William F. Arndt, F. Wilber Gingrich, and Frederick W. Danker. 3rd ed. Chicago: The University of Chicago, 2000. (BDAG)

Blomberg, Craig. *Matthew*. The New American Commentary, vol. 22. Nashville: Broadman, 1992.

———. *Neither Poverty Nor Riches: A Biblical Theology of Possessions*. Downers Grove: InterVarsity, 1999.

Boa, Kenneth D., and Robert M. Bowman Jr. *Faith Has Its Reasons: Integrative Approaches to Defending the Christian Faith*. Downers Grove: InterVarsity, 2005.

Boice, James Montgomery. *The Gospel of Matthew*. Vol. 1, *The King and His Kingdom (Matthew 1–17)*. Grand Rapids: Baker, 2001.

———. *The Gospel of Matthew*. Vol. 2, *The Triumph of the King (Matthew 18–28)*. Grand Rapids: Baker, 2001.

Bonar, Horatius. "I See the Crowd in Pilate's Hall." 1856. As cited in C. J. Mahaney, *Living the Cross Centered Life*. Colorado Springs: Multnomah Books, 2006, 87–88.

Bunyan, John. "Hell." In *New Cyclopedia of Prose Illustrations*, ed. Elon Foster. New York: T. Y. Crowell, 1877.

Carson, D. A. *God with Us: Themes from Matthew*. Eugene: Wipf & Stock, 2009.

———. "Matthew." In *The Expositor's Bible Commentary*, vol. 8, *Matthew, Mark, Luke*, ed. Frank E. Gaebelein. Grand Rapids: Zondervan, 1984.

————. *How Long, O Lord: Reflections on Suffering and Evil.* Grand Rapids: Baker Academic, 2006.

Dever, Mark. *9 Marks of a Healthy Church.* Wheaton: Crossway, 2004.

Duncan, J. Ligon. "The Ten Virgins." First Presbyterian Church, Jackson, MS. Accessed April 2, 2013, URL: http://www.fpcjackson .org/resources/sermons/matthew/matthew_vol_7-9/matt57a.htm.

Edwards, Jonathan. "Resolutions." In *The Works of Jonathan Edwards,* vol. 1. Carlisle: The Banner of Truth Trust, 1974.

Elliot, Elizabeth. *Shadow of the Almighty: The Life and Testament of Jim Elliot.* San Francisco: Harper & Brothers, 1958.

France, R. T. *The Gospel of Matthew.* New International Commentary on the New Testament. Grand Rapids: Eerdmans, 2007.

Ferguson, Sinclair. *A Heart for God.* Carlisle, PA: Banner of Truth, 1987.

Grudem, Wayne. *Systematic Theology.* Grand Rapids: Zondervan, 1994.

Gundry, Robert. *Matthew: A Commentary on His Handbook for a Mixed Church under Persecution.* Grand Rapids: Eerdmans, 1995.

Hendriksen, William. *Exposition of the Gospel According to Matthew.* Grand Rapids: Baker, 1973.

Keener, Craig S. *A Commentary on the Gospel of Matthew.* Grand Rapids: Eerdmans, 1999.

Keller, Tim. *The Reason for God: Belief in an Age of Skepticism.* New York: Penguin Group, 2008.

Ladd, George Eldon. *The Gospel of the Kingdom.* Grand Rapids: Eerdmans, 1959.

Laney, J. Carl. *A Guide to Church Discipline.* Minneapolis: Bethany House, 1985.

Lewis, C. S. *Mere Christianity.* New York: Simon & Schuster, 1980.

MacArthur, John. *1 Corinthians.* MacArthur New Testament Commentary Series. Chicago: Moody, 1984.

————. *Matthew 1–7.* The MacArthur New Testament Commentary Series. Chicago: Moody, 1987.

————. *Matthew 8–15.* The MacArthur New Testament Commentary Series. Chicago: Moody, 1987.

————. *Matthew 16–23.* The MacArthur New Testament Commentary Series. Chicago: Moody, 1987.

————. "Solving the Problem of Doubt," Sermon on Matthew 11:1-6, located at http://www.gty.org/resources/print/sermons/2285.

McGrath, Alister. "When Doubt Becomes Unbelief." *Tabletalk* 16, No. 1 (January 1992): 8–10.

Mahaney, C. J. *Living the Cross Centered Life.* Colorado Spring: Multnomah, 2006.

McKeever, Bill, and Eric Johnson. *Mormonism 101: Examining the Religion of the Latter-day Saints.* Grand Rapids: Baker, 2000.

Miller, Calvin. *The Book of Jesus: A Treasury of the Greatest Stories and Writings about Christ.* New York: Simon & Schuster, 1998.

Moore, Russell. *Tempted and Tried: Temptation and the Triumph of Christ.* Wheaton: Crossway, 2011.

Osborne, Grant R. *Matthew.* Zondervan Exegetical Commentary on the New Testament. Grand Rapids: Zondervan, 2010.

Osteen, Joel. *Becoming a Better You: 7 Keys to Improving Your Life Every Day.* New York: Free Press, 2007.

Packer, J. I. *Evangelism and the Sovereignty of God.* Downers Grove: InterVarsity, 2008.

———. "For Your Sakes He Became Poor," in *Come, Thou Long-Expected Jesus: Experiencing the Peace and Promise of Christmas,* ed. Nancy Guthrie. Wheaton: Crossway, 2008.

Pennington, Jonathan. *Heaven and Earth in the Gospel of Matthew.* Grand Rapids: Baker Academic, 2007.

Piper, John. "We Have Come to Worship Him" (Matt 2:1-12). The sermon can be found at www.desiringgod.org/resource-library/sermons/we-have-come-to-worship-him.

Quarles, Charles. *Sermon on the Mount: Restoring Christ's Message to the Modern Church.* NAC Studies in Bible and Theology. Nashville: B&H, 2011.

Ryle, J. C. *Expository Thoughts on the Gospels: St. Matthew.* New York: Robert Carter & Bros., 1870.

———. *Matthew.* The Crossway Classic Commentaries. Ed. Alister McGrath and J. I. Packer. Wheaton: Crossway, 1993.

———. *Principles for Churchmen: A Manual of Positive Statements on Doubtful or Disputed Points.* Ulan, 2012.

Schreiner, Thomas. *New Testament Theology: Magnifying God in Christ.* Grand Rapids: Baker Academic, 2008.

Spurgeon, Charles. "Psalm 69:14." Sermons 11.290.

Stott, John. *The Cross of Christ.* Downers Grove: InterVarsity, 1986.

———. *Sermon on the Mount* (Downers Grove, IL: IVP, 2000).

Taylor, Howard. *Hudson Taylor's Spiritual Secret.* Chicago: Moody, 2009.

Thomas, David. *The Gospel of Matthew.* 1873; repr., Grand Rapids: Kregel, 1979.

Thomas, W. Ian. *The Saving Life of Christ, and The Mystery of Godliness.* Grand Rapids: Zondervan, 1988.

Trotman, Dawson. *Born to Reproduce,* 4. Trotman's booklet can be found at http://www-rohan.sdsu.edu/~sdsunavs/resources/BornTo Reproduce.pdf.

Twelftree, G. H. "Sanhedrin," in *Dictionary of Jesus and the Gospels,* ed. Joel B. Green, Scot McKnight, and I. Howard Marshall. Downers Grove: InterVarsity, 1992.

SCRIPTURE INDEX